1997

MORAL DEVELOPMENT

A Compendium

Series Editor
BILL PUKA
Rensselaer Institute

A GARLAND SERIES

SERIES CONTENTS

VOLUME

1

DEFINING PERSPECTIVES IN MORAL DEVELOPMENT

Edited with introductions by
BILL PUKA

GARLAND PUBLISHING, Inc.
New York & London
1994

Library of Congress Cataloging-in-Publication Data

Moral development : a compendium / edited with introductions by Bill
Puka.
    p.   cm.
    Includes bibliographical references.
    Contents: v. 1. Defining perspectives in moral development — v.
2. Fundamental research in moral development — v. 3. Kohlberg's
original study of moral development — v. 4. The great justice
debate — v. 5. New research in moral development — v. 6. Caring
voices and women's moral frames — v. 7. Reaching out.
    ISBN 0–8153–1548–1 (v. 1 : alk. paper).
    1. Moral development.   I. Puka, Bill.
BF723.M54M66 1994
155.2'5—dc20   94–462
                                           CIP

Printed on acid-free, 250-year-life paper
Manufactured in the United States of America

CONTENTS

SERIES INTRODUCTION

Moral development is an interdisciplinary field that researches moral common sense and interpersonal know-how. It investigates how children evolve a sense of right and wrong, good and bad, and how adults hone their abilities to handle ethical issues in daily life. This includes resolving value conflicts, fermenting trusting, cooperative, and tolerant relationships, and setting ethical goals. It focuses most on how we think about these ethical issues (using our cognitive competences) and how we act as a result.

These seven volumes are designed to function as a standard, comprehensive sourcebook. They focus on central concerns and controversies in moral development, such as the relation between moral socialization and development, moral judgment and action, and the effects of culture, class, or gender on moral orientation. They also focus on central research programs in the field, such as the enduring Kohlberg research on moral stages, Gilligan research on ethical caring and women's development, and related prosocial research on altruism.

The studies contained here were compiled from the "wish lists" of researchers and educators in the field. These are the publications cited as most important (and, often, least available) for effective teaching and research training and for conveying the field to others. Unfortunately, the most crucial studies and essays in moral development are widely scattered across hard-to-find (sometimes out-of-print) volumes. Compiling them for a course is difficult and costly. This compendium eases these problems by gathering needed sources in one place, for a single charge. Regrettably, rising reprint fees frustrated plans to include *all* needed resources here, halving the original contents of these volumes and requiring torturous excising decisions. Even so, compared to other collections, this series approaches a true "handbook" of moral development, providing key sources on central issues rather than "further essays" on specialized topics.

A major aim of this series is to represent moral development accurately to related fields. Controversies in moral development have sparked lively interest in the disciplines of philosophy, education, sociology and anthropology, literary criticism, political science, gender and cultural studies, critical legal studies, criminology and corrections, and peace studies. Unfortunately, members of these fields were often introduced to moral development through the highly theoretical musings of Lawrence Kohlberg, Carol Gilligan, or Jean Piaget—or by highly theoretical commentaries on them. Jumping into the fray over gender or culture bias in stage theory, theorists in the humanities show virtually no familiarity with the empirical research that gave rise to it. Indeed, many commentators seem unaware that these controversies arise in a distinct research field and are context-dependent.

This compendium displays moral development as a social science, generating research findings in cognitive developmental, and social psychology. (Students are invited to recognize and approach the field as such.) Theory is heavily involved in this research—helping define the fundamental notions of "moral" and "development," for example. But even when philosophically or ethically cast, it remains psychological or social scientific theory. It utilizes but does not engage in moral philosophy per se. Otherwise, it is not moral development theory, but meta-theory. (Several extensively criticized Kohlberg articles on justice are meta-theory.) The confusion of these types and levels of theory has been a source of pervasive confusion in the field. The mistaken assessment of psychological theory by moral-philosophical standards has generated extremely damaging and misguided controversy in moral development. Other types of theory (moral, social, interpretive, anthropological) should be directed at moral development science, focusing on empirical research methods and their empirical interpretation. It should be theory of data, that is, not meta-theoretical reflection on the "amateur" philosophizing and hermeneutics interpolations of psychological researchers. (Likewise, social scientific research should not focus on the empirical generalizations of philosophers when trying to probe social reality or seek guidance in doing so from this theoretical discipline.) The bulk of entries in this compendium present the proper, empirically raw material for such "outside" theoretical enterprise.

To researchers, theorists, and students in related fields, this series extends an invitation to share our interest in the fascinating phenomena of moral development, and to share our findings thus far. Your help is welcomed also in refining our treacherously qualitative research methods and theories. In my dual disciplines of psychology and philosophy, I have found no more inspiring area of study. Alongside its somewhat dispassionate research orientation, this field carries on the ancient "cause" of its pre-scientific past. This is to show that human nature is naturally good—that the human psyche spontaneously unfolds in good will, cleaving toward fair-mindedness, compassion, and cooperative concern.

The first volume, *Defining Perspectives*, presents the major approaches to moral development and socialization in the words of chief proponents: Kohlberg, Bandura, Aronfreed, Mischel, Eysenck, and Perry. (Piaget is discussed in detail.) This first volume is required reading for those needing to orient to this field or regain orientation. It is crucial for clarifying the relations and differences between moral development and socialization that define research.

The second volume, *Fundamental Research*, compiles the classic research studies on moral levels and stages of development. These studies expose the crucial relation of role-taking and social perspective to moral judgment and of moral judgment to action. They also divine the important role of moral self-identity (viewing oneself as morally interested) in moral motivation.

The third volume contains *Kohlberg's Original Study*, his massive doctoral research project. The study, which has never before been published, sets the parameters for moral development research, theory, and controversy. (Major critical alternatives to Kohlberg's approach share far more in common with it than they diverge.) Here the reader sees "how it all started," glimpsing the sweep of Kohlberg's aspiration: to uncover the chief adaptation of humankind, the evolving systems of reasoning and meaning-making that, even in children, guide effective choice and action. Most major Kohlberg critiques fault features of this original study, especially in the all-male, all-white, all-American cast of his research sample. (Why look here for traits that characterize all humans in all cultures through all time?) It is worth checking these criticisms against the text, in context, as depictions of unpublished work often blur into hearsay. It is also worth viewing this study through the massive reanalysis of its data (Colby, Kohlberg, et al.) and the full mass of Kohlberg research that shaped stage theory. Both are liberally sampled in Volume Five.

The Great Justice Debate, the fourth volume, gathers the broad range of criticisms leveled at moral stage theory. It takes up the range of "bias charges" in developmental research—bias by gender, social class, culture, political ideology, and partisan intellectual persuasion. Chief among these reputed biases is the equation of moral competence and development with justice and rights. Here key features of compassion and benevolence seem overlooked or underrated. Here a seemingly male standard of ethical preference downplays women's sensibilities and skills. Responses to these charges appear here as well.

Volume Five, *New Research*, focuses on cross-cultural research in moral development. Studies in India, Turkey, Israel, Korea, Poland, and China are included. While interesting in itself, such research also supports the generalizability of moral stages, challenged above. Indeed, Volume Five attempts to reconceive or re-start the central research program of moral development from the inception of its matured research methods and statistically well-validated findings. From this point research is more data-based than theory-driven. It can address criticism with hard evidence. Regarding controversy in moral development, Volumes Four and Five go together as challenge and retort.

Volume Six, *Caring Voices*, is devoted to the popular "different voice" hypothesis. This hypothesis posits a distinct ethical orientation of caring relationship, naturally preferred by women, that complements justice. Compiled here is the main record of Gilligan's (and colleagues') research, including recent experiments with "narrative" research method. The significant critical literature on care is well-represented as well, with responses. While Gilligan's empirical research program is more formative than Kohlberg's, her interpretive observations have influenced several fields, especially in feminist studies. Few research sources have more common-sense significance and "consciousness-raising" potential. The student reader may find Gilligan's approach the most personally relevant and useful in moral development.

Reaching Out, the final volume, extends moral development concerns to "prosocial" research on altruism. Altruistic helping behavior bears close relation to caring and to certain ideals of liberal justice. This volume emphasizes the role of emotions in helping (and not helping), focusing on empathic distress, forgiveness, and guilt. It also looks at early friendship and family influences. Moral emotions are related to ethical virtues here, which are considered alongside the "vices" of apathy and learned helplessness. Leading researchers are included such as Hoffman, Eisenberg, Batson, and Staub.

INTRODUCTION

This volume provides readers with a clear and contrasting view of the major approaches to moral development. Traditionally, moral development has been studied through the twin perspectives of innatism and environmentalism. For innatists, our moral capacities are internally preprogrammed, unfolding over the life cycle in a natural process of growth. Environmentalists see moral psychology as shaped by social conventions and authority figures during our general enculturation. Just as we encounter these opposing perspectives in the ancient texts of Confucianism, we find them in modern disputes between Freudians and behaviorists.

The most plausible versions of each camp have long recognized the importance of both inherited and environmental factors in moral development. But the innovative Piagetian approach provided a third alternative by placing the interaction of these influences at the center of developmental process.

This volume showcases the best modern representatives of these opposing camps in research psychology. In his classic monograph "Stage and Sequence" Lawrence Kohlberg compares the modern alternatives of Freudian psychosexual development, social learning theory, and Piagetian cognitive development. While supporting the final approach, he emphasizes its inclusivity, citing Piagetian endorsements of and accommodations to major alternatives. (If Piaget's distinctive position was more easily excerpted from his writings, and more affordably reprinted, he would have spoken for himself in this volume.)

Of special interest in "Stage and Sequence" is Kohlberg's linking of modern moral development research to its theoretical past, and his depiction of cognitive-moral emotions, including love. Legion critics of Kohlberg's "rigid structuralism" in psychology and "rigid rationalism" in ethics typically miss this emotional component in cognition.

From an empirical research perspective, Freudianism does not update innatism well. However, important tenets of Freudian psychosexual development are preserved in social learning research. Here the determining cause of moral phenomena, observed in common by both camps, is merely shifted from the bio-psychological to the social side of the equation. In this first volume, prominent representatives of the environmentalist, social-learning camp (Bandura, Mischel, and Aronfreed) present findings and viewpoints. Contrasting these authors with Kohlberg-Piaget helps to clarify differences between socialization and self-constructive development, as well as differences in their yield. (Among these differences in yield, conventional value ideologies and attitudes versus systems of morally principled reasoning are the most glaring.) But similarities and complementarities may also be noted among these phenomena (see Gibbs, Volume Five).

To broaden perspective further, this volume also samples Eysenck's deeply innatist view, focusing on morality's biological basis. This perspective augers sociobiological accounts of moral development. In marked contrast, William Perry approaches moral development from its intellectually reflective heights. His initial research on how college students handle belief and value conflict spawned a movement in counseling psychology. It documented the reluctant sway of student allegiance between diametrically opposed theories and world views presented in class—spawning relativism and objectivism in turns. These processes bear analogy to how we approach moral conflict between social generations as between the generative phases of our life cycle. Perry's findings also worked an important influence on Gilligan's ethical caring, which emphasizes the need for tentativeness and shadedness in the most mature and competently deliberated moral judgments.

CHAPTER 6

Stage And Sequence:
The Cognitive-Developmental
Approach To Socialization

Lawrence Kohlberg

Harvard University

For a number of years, I have been engaged in research on moral and psycho-sexual development, guided not by a theory, but by an approach labeled "cognitive-developmental." The label "cognitive-developmental" refers to a set of assumptions and research strategies common to a variety of specific theories of social and cognitive development, including the theories of J. M. Baldwin (1906), J. Dewey (1930), G. H. Mead (1934), Piaget (1948), Loevinger (1966), and myself (Kohlberg, 1966b, 1968, 1969).

In this chapter, we shall attempt first to present and justify the general assumptions of the cognitive-developmental approach. Next we shall consider their application to the phenomena of moral socialization, contrasting our approach with social learning and psychoanalytic approaches. Finally, we shall consider processes of imitation and identification from our point of view, since these processes are held to be basic in cognitive-developmental theories as well as in social-learning and psychoanalytic theories of social development.

I. THEORIES OF COGNITIVE DEVELOPMENT
AND THE ORIGINS OF MENTAL STRUCTURE

Before considering the application of cognitive-developmental theories to socialization, we shall outline the basic characteristics of these theories in the cognitive area. Cognitive-developmental theories presuppose the assumptions listed in A. L. Baldwin's chapter on cognitive theory in this volume, but share a number of basic further assumptions as well. Baldwin defines as "cognitive"

Much of the author's research reported here has been supported by N.I.C.H.D. Grant HD 02469-01. The first half of the chapter is a revision of a paper prepared for the Social Science Research Council, Committee on Socialization and Social Structure, Conference on Moral Development, Arden House, November, 1963, supported by MH 4160 of N.I.M.H.

theories which postulate a representational or coding process intervening between stimulus and response. This representation is applicable to a variety of proximal stimuli and may elicit a variety of responses depending upon "noncognitive" motivational and situational factors. In Baldwin's version of cognitive theory, it is assumed that such representations are learned, but that such learning does not depend upon making an overt response to any of the stimulus elements in the environment being learned, nor does it depend upon any definite reinforcement for learning (though such reinforcement may be necessary for performance as opposed to learning). As Baldwin points out, his conception of cognitive theory embraces most theories giving attention to cognitive phenomena including mentalistic-associationistic theories of cognition like psychoanalysis as well as behavioristic-associationistic theories like S-R mediation theories. Drawing examples from this volume, Aronfreed's and Bandura's social-learning theories recognize cognitive principles of learning in Baldwin's sense, although Gewirtz's does not.

In contrast to associationistic theories of cognitive learning, cognitive-developmental theories make the following assumptions:

1. Basic development involves basic transformations of cognitive *structure* which cannot be defined or explained by the parameters of associationistic learning (contiguity, repetition, reinforcement, etc.), and which must be explained by parameters of organizational wholes or systems of internal relations.

2. Development of cognitive structure is the result of processes of *interaction* between the structure of the organism and the structure of the environment, rather than being the direct result of maturation or the direct result of learning (in the sense of a direct shaping of the organism's responses to accord with environmental structures).

3. Cognitive structures are always structures (schemata) of *action*. While cognitive activities move from the sensorimotor to the symbolic to verbal-propositional modes, the organization of these modes is always an organization of actions upon objects.

4. The direction of development of cognitive structure is toward greater *equilibrium* in this organism-environment interaction, i.e., of greater balance or *reciprocity* between the action of the organism upon the (perceived) object (or situation) and the action of the (perceived) object upon the organism. This balance in interaction, rather than a static correspondence of a concept to an object, represents "truth," "logic," "knowledge," or "adaptation" in their general forms. This balance is reflected in the underlying *stability* (conservation) of a cognitive act under apparent transformation, with development representing a widened system of transformations maintaining such *conservation*.

The assumptions just listed are assumptions which hold for cognitive development in general, i.e., for the development of ways of thinking about both physical and social objects. Their application to social development is made more concrete by the following additional assumptions about social-emotional

2

development, assumptions whose explanation is left to our section on moral development.

5. Affective development and functioning, and cognitive development and functioning are not distinct realms. "Affective" and "cognitive" development are *parallel;* they represent different perspectives and contexts in defining structural change.

6. There is a fundamental unity of personality organization and development termed the ego, or the self. While there are various strands of social development (psychosexual development, moral development, etc.), these strands are united by their common reference to a *single concept of self* in a *single social world.* Social development is, in essence, the restructuring of the (1) concept of self, (2) in its relationship to concepts of other people, (3) conceived as being in a common social world with social standards. In addition to the unity of level of social development due to general cognitive development (the *g* factor in mental maturity tests), there is a further unity of development due to a common factor of ego maturity.

7. All the basic processes involved in "physical" cognitions, and in stimulating developmental changes in these cognitions, are also basic to social development. In addition, however, social cognition always involves *role-taking,* i.e., awareness that the other is in some way like the self, and that the other knows or is responsive to the self in a system of complementary expectations. Accordingly developmental changes in the social self reflect parallel changes in conceptions of the social world.

8. The direction of social or ego development is also toward an equilibrium or *reciprocity* between the self's actions and those of others toward the self. In its generalized form this equilibrium is the end point or definer of morality, conceived as principles of justice, i.e., of reciprocity or equality. In its individualized form it defines relationships of "love," i.e., of mutuality and reciprocal intimacy. The social analogy to logical and physical conservations is the maintenance of an *ego-identity* throughout the transformations of various role relationships. (A concrete early developing example discussed later is the child's belief in his own unchangeable gender identity, which develops at the same age as physical conservations.)

The statement listed first presupposes a distinction between behavior changes or learning in general and *changes in mental structure.* Structure refers to the general characteristics of shape, pattern or organization of response rather than to the rate or intensity of response or its pairing with particular stimuli. Cognitive structure refers to rules for processing information or for connecting experienced events. Cognition (as most clearly reflected in thinking) means putting things together or relating events, and this relating is an active connecting process, not a passive connecting of events through external association and repetition. In part this means that connections are formed by selective and active processes of attention, information-gathering strategies, motivated thinking, etc. More basically, it means that the process of relating particular events depends upon

3

prior general modes of relating developed by the organism. The most general modes of relating are termed "categories of experience." These categories are modes of relating applicable to any experienced event, and include the relations of causality, substantiality, space, time, quantity and logic (the latter referring to relations of inclusion or implication between classes or propositions).

The awareness that the child's behavior has a cognitive structure or organizational pattern of its own which needs description independently of the degree of its correspondence to the adult culture is as old as Rousseau, but this awareness had only recently pervaded the actual study of cognitive development. Two examples of the revolution resulting from defining the structure of the child's mind in its own terms may be cited. The first is that of Piaget (1928), whose first psychological effort was to classify types of wrong answers on the Binet test. By moving beyond an analysis of intellectual development in terms of number of right answers to an analysis in terms of differences in structure, Piaget transformed the study of cognitive development. The second example comes from the study of children's language (Chomsky, 1968) based for a generation on counting frequency and correctness of nouns and verbs as defined by conventional adult grammar. In the last decade, psychologists have approached children's grammar with the methods of structural linguistics, as if the child's language were that of an exotic tribe with its own structure. While the implications of the Piagetian revolution in cognition and the Chomskian revolution in language are far from clear, they have made the conception of mental structure a reality accepted even by associationistic theories of cognition (cf. Berlyne, 1965), though not by most associationistic theories of social learning.

Our second statement suggested that cognitive-developmental theories are "interactional," i.e., they assume that basic mental structure is the product of the patterning of the interaction between the organism and the environment rather than directly reflecting either innate patterns in the organism or patterns of events (stimulus contingencies) in the environment. The distinction between theories stressing the innate and theories stressing the acquired has often been thought of as a contrast in quantitative emphasis on hereditary biological factors as opposed to environmental stimulation factors in causing individual differences. When the problem is posed in such a fashion, one can be led to nothing but a piously eclectic "interactionism" which asserts that all concrete behavior is quantitatively affected empirically by both hereditary and environmental factors. The theoretical issues are quite different, however. They are issues as to the location of the principles producing basic mental structure within or without the organism.

It is evident that general questions as to the origins and development of mental structure are not the same as questions as to the origins of individual differences in behavior. As an example, while the fact that one six-year-old child may pass all the six-year items on the Binet test and another fail them all might be attributed purely to hereditary differences in general intelligence, the patterns of behavior involved in the child's actual Binet performance (e.g., knowing the

4

word "envelope") may be purely culturally learned behavior. Because many American psychologists have been peculiarly concerned with individual differences rather than developmental universals, and because they have failed to understand the distinction between behavior differences in general and behavior structure, they have frequently misinterpreted European theories of development. As an example, some American writers have misinterpreted Piaget's stages as "maturational" and have thought that he claimed intelligence is unaffected by environment. Others (like J. McV. Hunt, 1961, 1963) have correctly interpreted Piaget's stages as being based on the assumption of organism-environment interactions, but take this assumption as indicating that individual differences in intellectual performance are less hereditary than was long believed. In fact, there is nothing in Piaget's theory which suggests that individual differences in speed of development through his stages are not primarily due to hereditary factors.

Distinctions between environmental, maturational and interactional theories of the origins of mental structure, then, are not distinctions based upon quantitative assumptions about the role of heredity in the formation of individual differences. In terms of quantitative role, maturational or nativistic theories, like those of Lorenz (1965), or Gesell (1954), recognize the importance of environmental stimulation in modifying genetically grounded behavior patterns. In a similar sense, associationistic-learning theorists like Pavlov (1928) or Hull (1943) recognize the quantitative role of hereditary traits of temperament and ability in causing individual differences in personality and in rate and type of learning. The difference between the two types of theories is not in the recognition of both innate and environmental causal factors in development but in which set of factors is seen as the source of basic patterning.

The contrast between the *modifying* and *structuring* roles awarded to experience becomes clear with regard to the issue of critical periods. Most research on the effects of experience upon development has postulated "critical periods" in which the individual is especially sensitive to environmental influence in a given domain. Yet this notion of extreme quantitative sensitivity depends upon a maturational or nativistic theory.

The existence of a fixed time period, during which a certain amount of stimulation is required to avoid irreversible developmental deficits, presupposes an innate process of growth with an inner time schedule and an inner pattern which can be arrested or distorted by deficits of stimulation.

In the nativistic view, stimulation may be needed to elicit, support, and maintain behavior patterns but the stimulation does not create these patterns, which are given by templates in the genotype. In fact, learning or environmental influence itself is seen as basically patterned by genetically determined structures. Learning occurs in certain interstices or open places in the genetic pattern, and the structuring of what is learned is given by these patterns (Lorenz, 1965). As an example, ethological "imprinting" or Freudian "libidinal fixation" represents a type of learning, a determination of response by environmental stimulation. However, the "learning" involved represents a specific sensitivity or open spot in a genetically patterned social-sexual response. As another example, an insect or bird may learn a specific "map" of the geography of its home place, but ethologists view this map as structured by an innate organization of space in general (Lorenz, 1965).

In dealing with developmental changes, nativistic theories such as Gesell's (1954) have stressed the notion of unfolding maturational stages. The patterning of these age-specific behavioral forms, their order and timing, is believed to be wired into the organism. The organism grows as a whole so that the effort to teach or force early maturation in one area will either be ineffective or will disrupt the child's total pattern and equilibrium of growth.

In contrast to nativistic theories, learning theories may allow for genetic factors in personality and in ease of learning of a complex response, but they assume that the basic structure of complex responses results from the structure of the child's environment. Both specific concepts and general cognitive structures, like the categories of space, time, and causality, are believed to be the reflections of structures existing outside the child, structurings given by the physical and social world.

Almost of necessity, the view that structure of the external world is the source of the child's cognitive structure has led to an account of the development of structure in associationistic terms. From John Locke to J. B. Watson and B. F. Skinner (Kessen, 1965), environmentalists have viewed the structure of behavior as the result of the association of discrete stimuli with one another, with responses of the child and with experiences of pleasure and pain.

We have contrasted the maturationist assumption that basic mental structure results from an innate patterning with the learning theory assumption that basic mental structure is the result of the patterning or association of events in the outside world. In contrast, the cognitive-developmental assumption is that basic mental structure is the result of an interaction between certain organismic structuring tendencies and the structure of the outside world, rather than reflecting either one directly.

This interaction leads to cognitive *stages* which represent the *transformations* of simple early cognitive structures as these are applied to (or assimilate) the external world, and as they are accommodated to or restructured by the external world in the course of being applied to it.

The core of the cognitive-developmental position, then, is the doctrine of cognitive stages. Cognitive stages have the following general characteristics (Piaget, 1960):

1. Stages imply distinct or *qualitative* differences in children's modes of thinking or of solving the same problem at different ages.

2. These different modes of thought form an *invariant sequence,* order, or succession in individual development. While cultural factors may speed up, slow down, or stop development, they do not change its sequence.

3. Each of these different and sequential modes of thought forms a *"structured whole."* A given stage-response on a task does not just represent a specific

response determined by knowledge and familiarity with that task or tasks similar to it. Rather it represents an underlying thought-organization, e.g., "the level of concrete operations," which determines responses to tasks which are not manifestly similar. According to Piaget, at the stage of concrete operations, the child has a general tendency to maintain that a physical object conserves its properties on various physical dimensions in spite of apparent perceptual changes. This tendency is structural, it is not a specific belief about a specific object. The implication is that both conservation and other aspects of logical operations should appear as a logically and empirically related cluster of responses in development.

4. Cognitive stages are *hierarchical integrations*. Stages form an order of increasingly differentiated and integrated structures to fulfill a common function. The general adaptational functions of cognitive structures are always the same (for Piaget the maintenance of an equilibrium between the organism and the environment, defined as a balance of assimilation and accommodation). Accordingly higher stages displace (or rather reintegrate) the structures found at lower stages. As an example, formal operational thought includes all the structural features of concrete operational thought but at a new level of organization. Concrete operational thought or even sensorimotor thought does not disappear when formal thought arises, but continues to be used in concrete situations where it is adequate or when efforts at solution by formal thought have failed. However, there is a hierarchical preference within the individual, i.e., a disposition to prefer a solution of a problem at the highest level available to him. It is this disposition which partially accounts for the consistency postulated as our third criterion. "Hierarchical" and structural cognitive stages may be contrasted with "embryological," motivational, or content stages (Loevinger, 1966). The latter represent new interests or functions rather than new structures for old functions, e.g., anal interests are not transformations of oral interests, they are new interests. While to some extent higher psychosexual stages are believed to typically include and dominate lower stages (e.g., genital interests dominate or include pregenital interests), this integration is not a necessary feature of the higher stage (e.g., lower stage interests may be totally repressed or be in conflict with higher stage interests).

The question of whether cognitive stages "exist" in the sense just defined is an empirically testable question. It has been held by B. Kaplan (1966) and others that stages are theoretical constructions, and that their theoretical value holds independently of whether or not they define empirical sequences in ontogeny. One cannot hold this to be true for embryological stages because there is no clear logical reason why an "anal" content is higher than an oral content. In the case of structural stages, however, their conceptual definition is based on a hierarchy of differentiation and integration. Every theoretical set of structural stages is defined in such a way that a higher stage is more differentiated and integrated than a lower stage. In this sense, a set of structural stages forms a valid hierarchy regardless of whether or not they define an ontogenetic sequence.

In spite of this fact, it is extremely important to test whether a set of

7

theoretical stages does meet the empirical criteria just listed. If a logical developmental hierarchy of levels did not define an empirical sequence, the hierarchy would neither tell us much about the process of development nor justify our notion that the sequence is interactional in nature. If an empirical sequence were not found, one would argue that the "stages" simply constituted alternative types of organization of varying complexity, each of which might develop independently of the other. In such a case, the "stages" could represent alternative expressions of maturation or they could equally well represent alternative cultures to which the child is exposed. It would hardly be surprising to find that adult physical concepts are more complex, more differentiated and integrated in educated Western culture than in a jungle tribe. The fact that the Western and tribal patterns can be ordered at different levels of structural organization, however, would tell us little about ontogenesis in either culture, and would leave open the possibility that it was simply a process of learning cultural content.

In contrast, if structural stages do define general ontogenetic sequences, then an interactional type of theory of developmental process must be used to explain ontogeny. If the child goes through qualitatively different stages of thought, his basic modes of organizing experience cannot be the direct result of adult teaching, or they would be copies of adult thought from the start. If the child's cognitive responses differed from the adult's only in revealing less information and less complication of structure, it would be possible to view them as incomplete learnings of the external structure of the world, whether that structure is defined in terms of the adult culture or in terms of the laws of the physical world. If the child's responses indicate a different structure or organization than the adult's, rather than a less complete one, and if this structure is similar in all children, it is extremely difficult to view the child's mental structure as a direct learning of the external structure. Furthermore, if the adult's mental structure depends upon sequential transformations of the child's mental structure, it too cannot directly reflect the current structure of the outer cultural or physical world.

If stages cannot be accounted for by direct learning of the structure of the outer world, neither can they be explained as the result of innate patterning. If children have their own logic, adult logic or mental structure cannot be derived from innate neurological patterning because such patterning should hold also in childhood. It is hardly plausible to view a whole succession of logics as an evolutionary and functional program of innate wiring.

It has just been claimed that it is implausible to view a succession of cognitive stages as innate. This claim is based on an epistemological assumption, the assumption that there is a reality to which psychology may and must refer, i.e., that cognition or knowing must be studied in relation to an object known. The claim does not hold for postural or other stages which are not directly defined by reference to an outer reality. The invariant sequences found in motor development (Shirley, 1933) may well be directly wired into the nervous system. The fact that the postural-motor development of chimpanzees and man proceed through the same sequence suggests such a maturational base (Riesen and Kinder, 1952). The existence of invariant sequence in cognition is quite a different matter, however, since cognitions are defined by reference to a world. One cannot speak of the development of a child's conception of an animal without assuming that the child has had experiences with animals. Things become somewhat more complicated when we are dealing with the development of categories, i.e., the most general modes of relating objects such as causality, substance, space, time, quantity, and logic. These categories differ from more specific concepts, e.g., the concept of "animal," in that they are not defined by specific objects to which they refer but by modes of relating any object to any other object. Every experienced event is located in space and time, implies or causes other events, etc. Because these categories or structures are independent of specific experiences with specific objects, it has been plausible for philosophers like Kant to assume that they are innate molds into which specific experiences are fitted. If structures or categories like space and time are Kantian innate forms, it is difficult to understand how these structures could undergo transformation in development, however.

The interactional account assumes that structural change in these categories depends upon experience, then. The effects of experience, however, are not conceived of as learning in the ordinary sense in which learning implies training by pairing of specific objects and specific responses, by instruction, by modeling, or by specific practice of responses. Indeed, the effects of training are determined by the child's cognitive categories rather than the reverse. If two events which follow one another in time are cognitively connected in the child's mind, it implies that he relates them by means of a category such as causality, e.g., he perceives his operant behavior as causing the reinforcer to occur. A program of reinforcement, then, cannot directly change the child's causal structures since it is assimilated to it.

An understanding of the effect of experience upon cognitive stages presupposes three types of conceptual analysis customarily omitted in discussions of learning.

In the first place, it depends on analysis of universal structural features of the environment. While depending on structural and functional invariants of the nervous system, cognitive stages also depend upon universal structures of experience for their shape. Stages of physical concepts depend upon a universal structure of experience in the physical world, a structure which underlies the diversity of physical arrangements in which men live and which underlies the diversities of formal physical theories held in various cultures at various periods.

In the second place, understanding cognitive stages depends upon a logical analysis of orderings inherent in given concepts. The invariance of sequence in the development of a concept or category is not dependent upon a prepatterned unfolding of neural patterns; it must depend upon a logical analysis of the concept itself. As an example, Piaget (1947) postulates a sequence of spaces or geometries moving from the topological to the projective to the Euclidean. This sequence is plausible in terms of a logical analysis of the mathematical structures involved.

In the third place, an understanding of sequential stages depends upon analysis of the relation of the structure of a specific experience of the child to the behavior structure. Piaget (1964) has termed such an analysis an "equilibration" rather than a "learning" analysis. Such an analysis employs such notions as "optimal match," "cognitive conflict," "assimilation," and "accommodation." Whatever terms are used, such analyses focus upon discrepancies between the child's action system or expectancies and the experienced events, and hypothesize some moderate or optimal degree of discrepancy as constituting the most effective experience for structural change in the organism.

In summary, an interactional conception of stages differs from a maturational one in that it assumes that experience is necessary for the stages to take the shape they do as well as assuming that generally more or richer stimulation will lead to faster advances through the series involved. It proposes that an understanding of the role of experience requires: (1) analyses of universal features of experienced objects (physical or social), (2) analysis of logical sequences of differentiation and integration in concepts of such objects, and (3) analysis of structural relations between experience-inputs and the relevant behavior organizations. While these three modes of analysis are foreign to the habits of associationistic-learning theorists, they are not totally incompatible in principle with them. While associationistic concepts are clumsy to apply to universal objects of experience or to the logical structures of concepts and to the problem of match, it can be done, as Berlyne (1961, 1965) has demonstrated. As yet, such associationistic analyses have not led to the formulation of new hypotheses going beyond translations of cognitive-developmental concepts into a different language.

The preceding presentation of the cognitive-developmental approach has been rather abstract. Accordingly it may be useful to present an empirical example of a cognitive-stage sequence and elaborate why it requires an interactional theory of process for its explanation. The dream concept, studied by Piaget (1928), Pinard and Laurendeau (1964), and myself (Kohlberg, 1966a) presents a simple example. The dream is a good example of an object or experience with which the child is familiar from an early age, but which is restructured in markedly different ways in later development. One of the general categories of experience is that of substantiality or reality. Any experience must be defined as either subjective or objective. As the child's structuring of this category develops, his experience of the dream changes. According to Piaget, the young child thinks of the dream as a set of real events, rather than as a mental imagining. This represents the young child's "realism," his failure to differentiate the subjective appearance from objective reality components of his experience.

Table 6.1 indicates the actual steps of development which are found in children's beliefs about dreams. The first step (achieved by about 4 years, 10

TABLE 6.1

SEQUENCE IN DEVELOPMENT OF DREAM CONCEPT IN AMERICAN AND ATAYAL CHILDREN

Step	Scale Pattern Types						
	0	1	2	3	4	5	6
1. *Not Real*—Recognizes that objects or actions in the dream are not real or are not really there in the room.	–	+	+	+	+	+	+
2. *Invisible* — Recognizes that other people cannot see his dream.	–	–	+	+	+	+	+
3. *Internal Origin* —Recognizes that the dream *comes from* inside him.	–	–	–	+	+	+	+
4. *Internal Location* —Recognizes that the dream *goes on* inside him.	–	–	–	–	+	+	+
5. *Immaterial* — Recognizes that the dream is not a material substance but is a thought.	–	–	–	–	–	+	+
6. *Self-caused* —Recognizes that dreams are not caused by God or other agencies but are caused by the self's thought processes.	–	–	–	–	–	–	+
Median age of American children in given pattern or stage (Range=4 to 8)	4,6	4,10	5,0	5,4	6,4	6,5	7,10
Median age of Atayal of given pattern. (Range=7 to 18)	8	8	10	16	12	11	

No. of American children fitting scale types=72; not fitting=18.

No. of Atayal children fitting scale types=12; not fitting=3.

months by American middle-class children) is the recognition that dreams are not real events; the next step (achieved soon thereafter), that dreams cannot be seen by others. By age six, children are clearly aware that dreams take place inside them and by seven, they are clearly aware that dreams are thoughts caused by themselves.

The concept of stages implies an invariant order or sequence of development. Cultural and environmental factors or innate capabilities may make one child or group of children reach a given step of development at a much earlier point of time than another child. All children, however, should still go through the same order of steps, regardless of environmental teaching or lack of teaching.

Table 6.1 shows a series of patterns of pluses or minuses called Guttman scale types, suggesting that the steps we have mentioned form an invariant order or sequence in development. If there is an invariant order in development, then children who have passed a more difficult step in the sequence, indicated by a plus, should also have passed all the easier steps in the sequence and get pluses on all the easier items. This means that all children should fit one of the patterns on Table 6.1. For instance, all children who pass or get a plus on Step 3, recognizing the dream's internal origin, should also pass Step 2 and Step 1. The fact

11

that only 18 out of 90 children do not fit one of these patterns is evidence for the existence of invariant sequence in the development of the dream concept. (This is more precisely indicated by a coefficient of reproducibility of .96 and an index of consistency of .83, calculated following Green [1956].)

The importance of this issue of sequence becomes apparent when we ask, "How does the child move from a view of dreams as real to a view of dreams as subjective or mental?" The simplest answer to this question is that the older child has learned the cultural definition of words like "dream" and "real." The child is frequently told by parents that his dreams are not real, that he shouldn't be upset by them, that dreams are in your mind, etc. In the learning view, this verbal teaching eventually leads the child from ignorance to knowledge of the culture's definition of the dream. It is a little hard for this verbal-learning view to account for invariant sequence in the development of the dream concept since it seems unlikely that children are taught Step 3 later than Step 2 or Step 1.

The issue of sequence becomes more critical when sequence can be examined in cultures with different adult cognitive beliefs than our own (Kohlberg, 1966a). The Atayal, a Malaysian aboriginal group on Formosa, believe in the reality of dreams. Most adult Atayal interviewed on the dream equated the soul, the dream, and ghosts. Dreams, like ghosts, are neither thoughts nor things; dreams are caused by ghosts and during the dream the soul leaves the body and experiences things in far places.

Interviews of Atayal boys and young men of various ages indicated a very interesting pattern of age development. The youngest Atayal boys were much like the youngest American boys in their responses. Up until the age of eleven, the Atayal boys seemed to develop toward a subjective conception of the dream through much the same steps as American children, though more slowly. As the table shows, the Atayal boys' answers fell into the same sequential scale pattern as the American boys. This suggests that the Atayal children tend to develop naturally toward a subjective concept of the dream up to age 11, even though their elders do not believe dreams are subjective and hence are giving them no teaching to this effect. Both the youngest child's conception of the dream as real and the school age child's view of the dream as subjective are their own; they are products of the general state of the child's cognitive development, rather than the learning of adult teachings (though the adolescent's later "regression" to concepts like those held by the younger children does represent such direct cultural learning).

The apparent invariant universal sequence in the development of the dream concept in the absence of adult cultural support cannot be interpreted as being the direct result of maturational unfolding, since the culture can "reverse" it by specific training, a reversal presumably very difficult to teach for maturational postural-motor sequences. A maturational interpretation is also contradicted by the fact that the Atayal children go through the same sequence more slowly than do their Taiwanese and American age-mates, presumably because the Atayal exist in a somewhat cognitively impoverished general culture, i.e., they have less *general* experience. In this regard the Atayal children are like culturally deprived American slum Negro children who also appear to go through the dream sequence more slowly than middle-class Negro controls, even when the two groups are matched on psychometric intelligence (Kohn, 1969).

The culturally universal invariants of sequence found in the dream concept can be adequately understood through a logical analysis of the stages themselves. The steps represent progressive differentiations of the subjective and objective which logically could not have a different order. The first step involves a differentiation of the *unreality* of the psychic event or dream image. The next step the differentiation of the *internality* of the psychic event from the externality of the physical event. A still later step is the differentiation of the *immateriality* of the psychic event from the materiality of other physical events. This sequence corresponds to the logical tree in Figure 6.1.

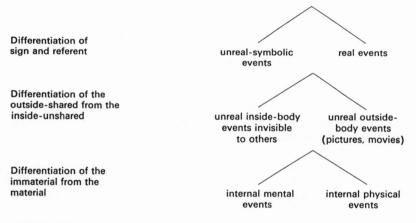

Differentiation of
sign and referent

unreal-symbolic events   real events

Differentiation of the
outside-shared from the
inside-unshared

unreal inside-body events invisible to others   unreal outside-body events (pictures, movies)

Differentiation of the
immaterial from the
material

internal mental events   internal physical events

FIGURE 6.1.

It is apparent that the differentiation of the immaterial from the material presupposes the inside-outside distinction since all immaterial events are inside the body (but not vice versa). It is also apparent that internality (location of the dream experience inside the body) presupposes unreality (recognition that the dream is not a real object) since a real object could hardly be in the body. The observed sequence, then, is one which corresponds to an inner logic of the concept of reality itself.

It is apparent that dreams are universal features of the child's experience. It is also apparent that a considerable degree of conflict between the dream experience and the waking experience of reality is a universal feature of experience. This experienced conflict or disequilibrium is presumably the "motor" for movement through the sequence in the absence of adult teaching, though the

13

discrepancies and matches in experience in this area have not been clearly specified.

The data on Atayal dream "regression" introduce a useful additional clarification of the nature of the cognitive-developmental approach. The approach is not a theory about the process by which *all* behavior change occurs, as "learning theories" are. It is rather a program of analysis. Some behavior changes are "structural" and "directed" as evidenced by proceeding through sequential stages while other behavior changes are not. This is the first question for empirical investigation since it determines any further theorizing about processes of development of the phenomena. Behavior changes which are universal, progressive, and irreversible require a different analysis than do reversible situation-specific learnings. While a cognitive-developmental approach may attempt to account for reversible situational learning (as we do in discussing imitative learning), it may also be satisfied with associationistic accounts of situational learning. As an example Turiel's (1969) cognitive-developmental interpretation accounts for Atayal children's "regressive" learning of the adult culture's ideology as a reversible content-learning fitting associationistic notions of social training, modeling and reinforcement; a learning that is superimposed upon the structural development of subjective-objective differentiation. In Turiel's view, only this latter type of change requires an interactional equilibration theory of process.

The Atayal example, however, also suggests that a third "regressive" type of behavior change may require elaboration by cognitive-developmental theory. Turiel assumes that the Atayal's dream regression is not a true regression in structure, but is a content learning superimposed on a mature cognitive structure and hence does not require special theoretical principles for its explanation. While the Atayal example is an extremely ambiguous case of regression, it is obvious that true regression does occur. As is described elsewhere (Kohlberg, 1969), Piaget's cognitive tasks are passed at markedly lower levels by schizophrenic and brain-damaged subjects than by mental age normal controls. While longitudinal studies have not been carried out, we can assume that where brain damage or the onset of schizophrenia occurred in late childhood, actual regression (rather than failure of development) has occurred. It is obvious that processes accounting for such regressive change are distinct from those producing either progressive sequential change or those producing reversible specific learnings. We may simply decide to exclude such regressive processes from our analysis on the grounds that they are outside the psychological system which assumes an intact nervous system and are not required to account for the effects of a blow on the head. Or we may decide that a developmental theory must include a systematic analysis of regression, along the lines outlined by Kramer (1968) and by Langer (1967).

The need to include an account of regression in a cognitive-developmental theory is suggested by some additional data from the Atayal study. The Atayal's learning of the adult dream ideology did not appear to be a smooth and painless superimposition of social content on an underlying cognitive structure. Rather

14

it appeared to engender complications and conflict in the adolescents' cognitive responses. Atayal children acquired the conservation of mass of a ball of clay at the usual age (7-8). Nevertheless, at age 11-15, the age of dream "regression," they partially "lost" conservation. The loss did not seem to be a genuine regression, but an uncertainty about trusting their own judgment, i.e., there was an increase in "don't know" responses. Apparently, adolescent confrontation with adult magical beliefs led them to be uncertain of other naturally developing physical beliefs, even when the latter were not in direct conflict with the adult ideology. The findings on the Atayal, then, seem loosely compatible with experimental findings by Langer (1967) suggesting that some forms of cognitive conflict lead to progressive change while others lead to regressive change. The eventual goal of a cognitive-developmental theory, then, is a specification of the types of discrepancies in experience which lead to forward movement, to backward movement, and to "fixation" or to lack of movement.

II. THE PROBLEM OF STRUCTURE IN SOCIALIZATION—THE FAILURE OF NATURALISTIC STUDIES

Before elaborating on the application of the cognitive-developmental approach just outlined to the socialization field, we need to briefly consider the more popular alternatives, the psychosexual-maturational and associationistic-learning approaches to socialization.

For the past generation, socialization research has consisted primarily of naturalistic cross-sectional studies correlating individual and cultural differences in parental practices with differences in children's motivational behavior. The theoretical framework guiding most of this research has represented varying balances of reinforcement learning theory (primarily of a Hullian variety), Freudian psychosexual theory, and anthropological culturology. A clear statement of the theoretical framework, with special focus on the psychosexual-maturational, is provided in D. R. Miller's chapter in this volume; an earlier statement is provided by Child (1954).

In the last few years, widespread dissatisfaction with the approach has been expressed by many researchers, including many of those most active in its development. This dissatisfaction has arisen because the correlations found in the studies have been low in magnitude and inconsistently replicated from one study to the next. As a result, neither clear, practical, nor theoretical conclusions can be drawn from the findings. In this section, we shall briefly document the problematic nature of the findings in one sample area, moral development. We shall then go on to consider the reasons for these difficulties, arguing that while part of the difficulties have arisen because of specific defects of theory and of measurement methodology, these defects are incidental to an unfeasible definition of the whole problem of socialization research. In particular we shall argue that studies correlating individual differences in child-rearing practices with individual dif-

15

ferences in cross-sectional traits cannot in themselves help answer the problems of the development of universal personality structures to which such theories as psychoanalysis are basically addressed. Our critique, then, is similar to that advanced in the previous section in which we noted confusions introduced by American misinterpretation of Piaget's theory of the development of cognitive structure as a theory about the quantitative influence of various factors upon individual differences in cognitive traits.

My own pessimism about the naturalistic studies of socialization came as the result of engaging in comprehensive reviews of the socialization of moral Kohlberg, 1963a) and psychosexual (Kohlberg, 1966b) behaviors.

With regard to morality, the hypothetical personality structure focused upon has usually been termed "conscience" or "superego." This "structure" has been studied as behavior through measures of "resistance to temptation" (failure to deviate from cultural standards under conditions of low surveillance) and as affect through measures of guilt (self-critical or self-primitive symbolic response after deviation from such cultural standards). Conscience or superego as studied has been loosely similar, then, to common-sense concepts of moral character (conceived as a set of virtues like honesty, service and self-control) such as were used by Hartshorne and May (1928-30) and the socialization studies have often employed "moral character" measures as measures of "conscience."

The socialization studies, then, have attempted to relate childhood and adolescent measures of individual differences in "conscience strength" to:

1. Early experiences of restraint or gratification of oral, anal and sexual drives;
2. Amount and method of moral discipline;
3. Parent attitudes and power structures relevant to various theories of identification.

In general, no correlations have been found between parental modes of handling infantile drives and later moral behaviors or attitudes.

With regard to reward, no relations have been found between amount of reward and moral variables in twenty different studies of moral socialization. With regard to physical punishment, two studies find a positive correlation between *high* physical punishment and *high* moral resistance to temptation. Two studies find *no* correlation between physical punishment and resistance to temp‑ tation. Two studies find *high* punishment correlated with *high* delinquency, i.e., with *low* resistance to temptation. Three studies find *high* punishment correlated with *low* projective guilt (low morality). Three studies find *no* correlation between punishment and guilt. One is tempted to interpret these findings as representing a pattern of correlations randomly distributed around a base of zero.

With regard to psychological punishment, findings are more consistent. While only one of six studies found any relation between psychological discipline and moral behavior (resistance to temptation), a majority of studies (eight out of twelve) found a relation between psychological punishment and "guilt," usually defined as making confessional and self-critical responses. In most of these studies,

16

"psychological discipline" has included both parental "love-withdrawal" and parental "induction" in Aronfreed's (1961) sense of verbal elaboration of the bad nature and consequences of the act for other people and for the self. When "induction" is distinguished from "love-withdrawal," it is found to correlate with both verbal "guilt" and internalized moral judgment in preadolescents (Aronfreed, 1961 ; Hoffman & Saltzstein, 1967), while "love-withdrawal" is not. Thus it appears that the findings on "love-withdrawal" are probably an artifact of combining love-withdrawal with "induction," which is why the relations are found in some studies but not others. Induction, however, is not punishment in the ordinary sense of the term, since it is difficult to view it, as one can love-withdrawal, as the infliction of psychological pain on the child. Rather it appears to be a cognitive stimulation of a moral awareness of the consequences of the child's action for other people. That this is the case is suggested by the fact that induction is also related to internalized moral judgment, which in turn is related to age and intelligence.

In summary, neither early parental handling of basic drives nor amount of various types of discipline have been found to directly correlate with moral attitudes or behavior in the studies surveyed.

With regard to parent attitudes, some consistent findings appear but their theoretical interpretation is unclear. In particular they give no clear support for the notion that early identifications are central to a moral orientation. Investigators concerned with identification have focused especially upon dimensions of parental power and nurturance. With regard to power, no clear relation with moral variables has been found. As an example, three studies report a positive correlation between paternal power and the boy's conscience, three report a negative correlation, and three report no correlation. With regard to affection, the findings are more consistent. Eight studies report a positive correlation of maternal warmth and conscience, one reports a negative correlation (among girls only), and four report no correlation. These findings, while weak, are consistent with a "developmental-identification" theory of conscience. However, a detailed examination of these findings does not support such an interpretation (Kohlberg, 1963a, 1964 ; Aronfreed, 1969). The common notions that if children like their parents, they will be accepting of their admonitions and that "bad children come from bad homes" are adequate to account for these findings. In other words, both the findings on inductive discipline and the findings on parental warmth suggest that children living in a positive social climate will be more willing to learn, and more accepting of, social norms than children living in a hostile or frightening climate. The finding does not seem to be specific to a moral structure but is a general tendency in the social attitude field (W. Becker, 1964). The same correlations with parental warmth and acceptance are found for the learning of achievement standards, for instance. In general, the clearer and the more consistent the findings in the moral area, the more obviously they fit a common-sense interpretation. As an example, perhaps the clearest set of findings in the family and personality literature is that delinquents come from bad homes compared to social-class con-

17

trols. The badness of these homes is nonspecific, and interpretation in terms of single theoretically meaningful variables used to define these homes as bad (e.g., low warmth, use of physical punishment, frequency of divorce) fails to hold up because the interpretation or variable does not explain much variance in the normal population.

Furthermore, the more clear findings are generally ones relating current parent attitudes to current child attitudes, rather than relating early childhood experience to later personality structure. Correlations such as those mentioned on warmth and inductive discipline are clearest when they are taken as between current parent attitudes and adolescent or preadolescent attitudes. Positive relations between parental warmth and moral attitudes have not been found at the preschool-kindergarten level (Sears, Rau & Alpert, 1965; Burton, Maccoby & Allinsmith, 1961) nor does kindergarten parental warmth predict to preadolescent moral attitudes.

Our survey indicates that socialization studies of morality have yielded few empirically powerful predictors of moral behavior. Where powerful predictors have been found (as in the Glueck studies [Glueck & Glueck, 1950] of delinquency), these predictors shed little light on any theory of socialization process. One line of reasoning as to why the studies of socialization have failed is embodied in the writings of social learning revisionists, such as Aronfreed, Bandura, and Gewirtz in this volume, who once engaged in child-rearing studies of the type described. In their view, this failure is partly methodological and partly theoretical. On the methodological side, the assessment of behavior by verbal interview and test methods and the use of a correlational methodology cannot be expected to lead to the firm conclusions found through experimental manipulations of social behavior. On the theoretical side, guidance of naturalistic studies by Freudian (and Hullian) hypothetical constructs concerning internal states (e.g., "identification," "guilt") with vague surplus meaning, has led to the inability of researchers to agree on appropriate measures of these states, or to derive unambiguous predictions from the theories involved.

The cogency of these critiques is indicated by the quite powerful results obtained in their experimental studies of socialization, reported in the chapters by Aronfreed, Bandura, and Gewirtz. As an example, Aronfreed is able to show that all children learn to at least minimally "resist the temptation" to take an attractive toy because of experimental punishment (disapproval and candy withdrawal) but that degree of resistance is regularly related to the timing of punishment. These extremely clear experimental results are not supported by the naturalistic studies, which do not show amount of punishment or timing of punishment (Burton et al., 1961) related to resistance to temptation. From the perspective of the experimenter, one can cogently argue "so much the worse" for the naturalistic studies. Findings based on a clear methodology are not invalidated by lack of support from a muddy methodology. More basically, however, the theory behind the social-learning experiments does not imply any predictions as to the effects of early parental reinforcement upon later social

18

behavior. Reinforcement-learning theories are not theories of structural change, i.e., they do not assert that childhood learnings are irreversible or that they should determine later behavior in different situations. It is part of the routine strategy of many social-learning experiments to demonstrate reversibility of the learned performance, i.e., to show that the learned behavior extinguishes under nonreinforcement. Social-learning theories do not claim extensive transfer of learning, i.e., they do not claim that reinforcement learning creates generalized traits of personality manifested in many situations. The experimental studies of socialization are, in effect, cogent demonstrations of the irrelevance of early home reinforcement parameters for later behavior. Insofar as Aronfreed demonstrates "resistance to temptation" behavior is largely determined by the experimental manipulation in a given situation and not by individual differences in traits of conscience, he demonstrates the irrelevance of early childhood learnings to the behaviors in question. It can be argued, then, that the failure of social-learning theory to receive support from naturalistic as well as experimental studies is not only due to the measurement problems and the absence of controls in the naturalistic studies but to the fact that they were misconceived as applications of the theories of learning used in them. An appropriate naturalistic study of social learning would not relate individual differences in parental practices of a global nature to individual differences in later global personality traits. Instead, it would relate trial-by-trial changes in children's situational behavior to the trial-by-trial training inputs of the parents.

Our discussion of the social-learning critique of the naturalistic studies has emphasized that the problems to which the naturalistic studies were addressed are not those to which social-learning theories are addressed. The original assumptions of the naturalistic studies were those shared by psychoanalytic and neo-psychoanalytic theories of personality development, i.e., theories which assumed the existence of relatively irreversible structural changes in generalized personality organization. The problems addressed by the studies were those of the ways in which early experiences formed fixed personality structures, and have used the term "socialization" to refer to the establishment of such enduring personality structures as were compatible with the demands of the child's culture.

The studies, then, assumed that early childhood represented a "critical period," i.e., a period of age-specific irreversible changes in personality. They have also assumed that the social processes and influences (primarily parental) forming personality in this period were different than the general processes of reversible social learning or social influence found in adult behavior. This assumption is most clear in the psychoanalytic theory, which assumes that structural change seldom occurs in adulthood, and that such structural change as does occur in adulthood rests on transference of infantile attitudes. These notions of childhood as a critical period have derived primarily from psychoanalytic conceptions of maturational sequences of basic drives. While psychoanalysis has stressed maturational content rather than cognitive structure, and has conceived of sequences as maturational rather than interactional, it agrees with the cognitive-developmental approach in analyzing behavior change as a process of development, i.e., as a directed process of structural change exemplified in culturally universal sequential stages. Because it is maturational, psychoanalytic theory is even more clear than cognitive-developmental theory in distinguishing between the causes of forward movement (which is maturational) and the causes of fixation or of backward movement (which represent environmentally induced strains or frustrations).

It is evident that insofar as the naturalistic studies were based on psychosexual theory, these studies should have started by empirically establishing the natural age-developmental trends postulated by psychosexual theory, since psychosexual theory describes socialization in terms of fixations, regressions, or inhibitions in such developmental trends. Almost none of the myriad studies of socialization have actually attempted to do this. Instead most have "bootstrapped" this essential first phase of the task. Insofar as they have been psychoanalytically oriented, they have (1) theoretically assumed (rather than observed) psychosexual stages, (2) theoretically assumed that some behavior measure was in fact a valid measure of some aspect of psychosexual development, and have then gone on to (3) hypothesize some relation of a child-rearing practice to individual differences in the behavior measure at a given age. The "bootstrapping" strategy has assumed that if the predicted correlation between child-rearing practices and the variable was found, that this would confirm (1) the postulated psychosexual sequences, (2) the validity of the measures employed, and (3) the postulated relation between the child-rearing practice and fixation of the psychosexual sequences. Obviously this research strategy is unworkable as the results of the studies have demonstrated.

From one point of view the strategy might be considered one in which psychosexual stages are considered postulates useful in discovering some reliable and powerful relations between early experience and later personality. From another perspective, the strategy might be conceived as one of testing the validity of psychosexual theory. From either point of view, the strategy has failed. With regard to the first point of view, very few reliable and powerful empirical correlations have been obtained which would aid in predicting the behavior of any individual or group of children. From the second point of view, the bootstrapping approach cannot be said to be testing psychoanalytic theory. If it had worked, it might have provided some support for the theory, but its failure is not evidence against the theory which cannot be said to be "tested" by such studies.

The objection to the bootstrapping approach is not so much that it was methodologically inappropriate to the difficult problem of socialization as that it was based on a misconception of psychoanalytic theory. We noted that Piaget's (1964) theory of the *development* of cognitive structures found in every human has been frequently misinterpreted by Americans as a theory of the origins of individual differences in intellectual abilities or traits, leading some Americans to view his interactionism as genetic maturationism and others to view his interactionism as a doctrine of the environmental determination of IQ difference. We have noted that theories of reinforcement learning have also sometimes been misinterpreted as theories designed to account for stable individual differences in personality traits, whereas these theories do not postulate personality traits in the first place. Learning theories are statements of laws or functional relations holding for all men, not theories designed to make statements about individual differences. It is an equally American misinterpretation to view psychoanalytic theory as directly relevant to an understanding of individual differences in personality traits. In part, psychoanalytic theory is a theory of laws of mental functioning in all humans. In part, it is a theory of a development and maturation. In part, it is a theory of psychopathology. It has never claimed, however, to be a theory designed to predict adult individual differences or traits from specific childhood experiences; a task Freud (1938) claimed was impossible.

While Freud had special reasons for viewing the problem of the prediction of individual differences as unresolvable, a little thought leads to the recognition that there is no general theoretical question as to the origin of individual differences nor any conceivable general answer to such a question. While American researchers will always be obsessed with the problem of the prediction of individual differences, this problem is no more likely to lead to conceptual advance in social science than is meteorological prediction likely to lead to general advance in physical science. This contention may perhaps be clarified by pointing to certain extreme examples of "meteorological" studies of child-rearing antecedents of student activism. Of what theoretical significance could it be to examine the child-rearing antecedents to participation in a transitory social movement in the United States? It certainly can contribute nothing to the understanding of personality development or socialization defined outside of the culture of the American college of the 1960's. It is of equally little sociological or practical significance. One might be practically interested in the current values and personality integration of student activists, but hardly in the childhood correlates of activism. If this criticism is accepted, one must ask whether a study of the child-rearing correlates of variations in American middle-class five-year-old boys' performance on some cheating tasks in the year 1965 is likely to be of conceptual interest, since the correlations are unlikely to hold true in another society, in another moral task, at another year or in another historical period, as the lack of replicability of the conscience studies suggests.

We have stated that the conceptually interesting problems of socialization are not the problems of accounting for the natural correlates of individual differences in behavior traits. Indeed, some understanding of the inconsistencies of the naturalistic studies arises when it is recognized that socialization seldom gives rise to traits as usually conceived. With regard to "resistance to temptation" or "moral internalization" no findings have been reported suggesting fundamental revisions of Hartshorne and May's (1928-30) conclusions as to the situational specificity and longitudinal instability of moral character, as is discussed in detail elsewhere (Kohlberg, 1964; Sears et al., 1965; Grim, Kohlberg & White, 1968).

21

Correlations between tests of resistance to temptation are low, and test-retest stability of these measures is low (correlations between cheating tests typically range between 0 and 40, six-month test-retest coefficients range between 30 and 60).

An example of the failure of resistance to temptation tests to represent conscience structure comes from a study by Lehrer (1967). Lehrer made use of Grinder's (1964) ray gun test of resistance to temptation. Grinder reports that a large majority (about 80 per cent) of sixth-grade children cheat for a prize badge on this test. Lehrer decided to improve the circuitry and the instructions involved in the test to control for certain minor factors that might discourage cheating. Rather than making cheating more likely, her improvements led to less than 25 per cent of the sixth-graders cheating. Probably the increased size and computer-like appearance of the gun led the children to believe it had score-keeping powers. Obviously the behavior of the 55 per cent of children who cheat on one machine but not the other is not determined by features of conscience strength.

Long ago MacKinnon (1938) suggested that conscience or superego was only one factor in actual moral behavior, such as the decision to cheat. A clearer index of conscience would be provided by assessments of guilt, a more stable or general tendency. While guilt was the moral force in personality, actual moral decisions depended on the interaction between guilt and other factors in the personality and in the situation. This plausible view led socialization analysts to proliferate projective measures of guilt and to relate them to child-rearing practices. There has been little agreement on what constitutes guilt in projective responses to transgression stories, however. The chief disagreement has been between those who view guilt as a conscious cognitive moral judgment (i.e., statements that an actor feels bad and blames himself after transgressions) and those who view it as unconscious anxiety and self-punitive tendencies (projections of harm, punishment, catastrophe and self-injury after transgression). Needless to say, the two are empirically unrelated. Furthermore, when the latter conception of guilt is employed, varying indices of guilt do not correlate well with one another and little story-to-story generality or test-retest stability of guilt is found (studies reviewed in Kohlberg, 1963a). Not surprisingly, then, little consistency from study to study has been found as to child-rearing antecedents of guilt (studies reviewed in Kohlberg, 1963a).

Consistencies between studies of child-rearing antecedents of conscience presuppose that the measures of conscience in one situation relate to measures in another, and that measures of conscience at one age correlate with measures at another. While no longitudinal studies of child-rearing correlates of conscience have been carried out, a study of aggression has (Sears, 1961). Sears found that child-rearing correlates of aggression in children age 5 failed to correlate with aggression to these same children at age 12. This is hardly surprising in light of the fact that measures of aggression at age 5 failed to predict aggression at age 12. Given a similar longitudinal instability in "conscience strength," the lack of consistency in findings on its child-rearing correlates is not surprising.

III. AN EXAMPLE OF SOCIAL DEVELOPMENT DEFINED IN COGNITIVE-STRUCTURAL TERMS— MORAL STAGES

At first, the disappointing results summarized in the previous section suggest that all social behavior is reversible situation-specific behavior to be studied by such methods and concepts as those used by social-learning theorists. However, we shall now try to show that there are stages or directed structural age-changes in the area of social-personality development just as there are in the cognitive area. In Section V we shall go on to argue that these structural changes are not explainable in terms of the methods and concepts of social learning. In this section, we shall attempt to show that these structural-developmental changes can provide definitions of individual differences free of the problems which have confounded the naturalistic socialization studies in the sense that they generate situationally general and longitudinally stable measures which relate meaningfully to social-environmental inputs. Our argument will be based on findings in a specific area, morality. However, we shall argue that success in this area is only a special case of the potential success arising from definitions of social development in cognitive-structural terms.

In spite of its obviousness, our focus upon situational generality and longitudinal predictability as a prerequisite for the meaningful study of socialization deserves some elaboration. The bulk of thinking about socialization is thinking about personality and culture, conceived as patterns or structures abstractable from the raw data of the myriad social behaviors in which individuals engage. The legitimate abstraction of a concept of personality from such raw data depends on the ability to predict behavior from one situation or time period to the next from the personality concept in question, i.e.; it depends upon the demonstration of its situational generality and longitudinal continuity.

In the previous section we pointed out that the ordinary personality "traits" focused upon in naturalistic studies of socialization are not stable in development. The ordering of individuals on motivated traits like dependency, aggression, affiliation, anxiety, need-achievement, and conscience-strength either predicts very little or not at all to later ordering on these same traits, if the two orderings are separated by many years (Kagan & Moss, 1962; MacFarlane, Allen & Honzik, 1954; Sears, 1961; Emmerich, 1964). The personality traits outside the cognitive domain which have proved most stable are those of little interest to socialization theory, e.g., traits of temperament like introversion-extroversion and activity-passivity (Kagan & Moss, 1962; Emmerich, 1964). These traits are uninteresting to socialization theory because their stable components seem to be largely innate (Gottesman, 1963) rather than to be the products of socialization, because they are traits of style rather than content of social action, and because they do not predict the general adjustment of the individual to his culture (La Crosse & Kohlberg, 1969).

The study of socialization in terms of personality formation under the assumption of trait stability, then, is unjustified. Most theories of personality formation do not assume trait stability, however. They assume rather that personality undergoes radical transformations in development but that there is continuity in the individual's development through these transformations. In other words, they conceptualize personality development as an orderly sequence of change, with the individual's location at a later point in the sequence being related to location at an earlier point in the sequence. In the words of John Dewey (1930), "Psychology is concerned with life-careers, with behavior as it is characterized by changes taking place in an activity that is serial and continuous, in reference to changes in an environment which is continuous while changing in detail."

While Dewey assumed that behavior is determined by the current ongoing situation in which the person is engaged, the situation is as that person defines it. This definition, in turn, is a result of sensitivities developing out of earlier situations, e.g., "One and the same environmental change becomes a thousand different actual stimuli under different conditions of ongoing or serial behavior" (Dewey, 1930).

In this view, early experience determines the choice of one or another path or sequence of development. It does not lead to the stamping in or fixation of traits carried from situation to situation throughout life. As stated by John Anderson (1957), "The young organism is fluid, subsequent development can go in any one of many directions. But once a choice is made and direction is set, cumulative and irreversible changes take place."

While continuity in personality development may be defined in terms of a number of alternative sequences available to different individuals in different social settings, most developmental theories of personality have employed some notion of a single, universal sequence of personality stages (S. Freud, 1938; Gesell, 1954; Erikson, 1950; Piaget, 1928). Such stage theories view the child's social behavior as reflections of age-typical world views and coping mechanisms rather than as reflections of fixed character traits. As the child moves from stage to stage, developmental theorists expect his behavior to change radically but to be predictable in terms of knowledge of his prior location in the stage sequence and of the intervening experiences stimulating or retarding movement to the next stage.

If continuity in personality development is to be found, then, stage theories hold that personality must be defined in terms of location in regular sequences of age development. The first and grossest implication of this view is that personality description must be phrased in age-developmental terms. In most studies of socialization, concepts of age-development have been theoretically assumed and empirically ignored. We have noted this in psychoanalytically oriented studies which continue to define individual differences with "superego strength" measures theoretically assumed to be related to psychosexual age-development in spite of the fact that these measures do not relate empirically to age-development. It is also true in more learning-theory oriented studies of socialization, which define socialization as *learned conformity* to the standards of the group, and ignore the relations of such conformity to age-development. Usually these studies assume that social age-development generally coincides with "socialization."

In Child's (1954) definition socialization is "the process by which an individual, born with behavior potentialities of an enormously wide range, is led to develop actual behavior confined within the narrower range of what is customary for him according to the standards of his group." The socialization conception of moral development is implied in its definition in terms of strength of resistance to temptation and strength of guilt. "Resistance to temptation" means amount of conformity to cultural moral rules, "guilt" means degree of conformity to these rules after deviation in the form of culturally expected forms of reparation for deviance. In the psychosexual field, socialization has been defined as increased conformity of attitudes to cultural norms for masculine or feminine roles, usually as measured by M-F tests.

While it has seemed plausible to equate "moral development" or "psychosexual development" with degree of conformity to the culture, it turns out that conformity does not in fact define trends of age-development. In the area of morality, the dimension of increased "resistance to temptation" as experimentally measured (honesty in old-fashioned terms) does not seem to define a trend of age-development at all. Sears et al. (1965) did not find an increase in experimental honesty from age 4 to 6 ; Grinder (1964) did not find an increase from 7 to 11; and Hartshorne and May (1928-30) did not find an increase from 11 to 14. In the psychosexual area, "internalization" or "identification," i.e., sex-typed preference and choice, does not increase regularly or clearly with age after 7 (Kohlberg, 1966b). The lack of longitudinal stability in measures of "conscience strength," then, becomes more intelligible when it is recognized that the child's moral maturity, in an age-developmental sense, does not predict to his performance on these measures. In some sense, we know that the average adult is morally different from the average four-year-old. Measures which fail to capture this difference must completely fail to capture whatever continuities exist in development.

The fact that degree of conformity measures fail to capture age-development is only a special case of the fact that polar traits in the personality area are seldom either age-developmental or longitudinally stable. By polar traits are meant traits defined by a quantitative ordering of individuals on a single dimension (such as aggression, dependency, etc., e.g., Loevinger, 1966). Most developmental theories of personality assume that such "traits" are differential balancings of conflicting forces and that these balancings differ at different points in the life cycle as new developmental tasks are focused upon. Developmental theories assume that a certain minimal level of certain polar traits must be present for solution of a developmental task, but further increase on the variable is no sign of increased maturity. As an example, achieving a certain level of conformity may become a "milestone" representing the formation of conscience in various theories. Further development, however, may lead to a relaxation of conformity with assurance

25

that impulse control has been achieved, or it may lead to an apparent non-conformity as autonomous and individual principles of values are developed. As an example, guilt has typically been measured by number and intensity of self-blaming and reparative reactions to stories about deviation from conventional norms for children (e.g., opening some boxes hidden by one's mother, cheating in a race, etc.). Age-developmental studies indicate that almost no direct or conscious guilt is expressed to such stories of conventional deviation by children under eight, that the majority of children age 11-12 express some guilt, and that there is no age increase in amount or intensity of guilt after this age (evidence reviewed in Kohlberg, 1969). Ratings of intensity of guilt, then, may group at the low to moderate end both the immature who have not achieved a minimal level of conformity and the mature who have transcended such conformity and have a humorously detached sense that they do not have to show what good boys they are in obeying mother in such stories. If one were interested in using projective "guilt" as an index of moral maturity, one would simply note the qualitative presence of conventional guilt reactions to some transgression story as an indication of having passed one of a number of milestones in moral development, rather than constructing a polar trait of guilt intensity.

While the study of age-development can go a certain distance using moderate levels of polar traits as milestones, the developmentalist holds that satisfactory definition or measurement of age-development requires definition of changes in the shape, pattern, or organization of responses. The developmentalist holds that a closer look at changes over time indicates regularities representing basic changes in the shape of responses rather than changes in their strength. This is, of course, the implication of an account of development in terms of stages. Stage notions are essentially ideal-typological constructs designed to represent different psychological organizations at varying points in development. The stage doctrine hypothesizes that these qualitatively different types of organization are sequential, and hence that the individual's developmental status is predictable or cumulative in the sense of continuity of position on an ordinal scale.

In what has been said so far, there is little divergence between the views of psychoanalytic, neo-psychoanalytic and cognitive-developmental approaches to personality. The cognitive-developmental approach diverges from the others, however, in stressing that directed sequences of changes in behavior organization or shape always have a strong cognitive component. On the logical side, our approach claims that social development is cognitively based because any description of shape or pattern of a structure of social responses necessarily entails some cognitive dimensions. Description of the organization of the child's social responses entails a description of the way in which he perceives, or conceives, the social world and the way in which he conceives himself. Even "depth" psychologies recognize that there are no affects divorced from cognitive structure. While social psychology for a long time attempted to measure attitudes as pure intensities, the birth of a theoretical social psychology of attitudes (e.g., various cognitive balance theories) has come from the recognition that the affect component of attitudes is largely shaped and changed by the cognitive organization of these attitudes.

On the empirical side the cognitive-developmental approach derives from the fact that most marked and clear changes in the psychological development of the child are cognitive, in the mental-age or IQ sense. The influence of intelligence on children's social attitudes and behavior is such that it has a greater number of social-behavior correlates than any other observed aspect of personality (Cattell, 1957). In terms of prediction Anderson (1960) summarizes his longitudinal study of adjustment as follows:

> We were surprised at the emergence of the intelligence factor in a variety of our instruments (family attitudes, responsibility and maturity, adjustment) in spite of our attempts to minimize intelligence in selecting our personality measures. Next we were surprised that for prediction over a long time, the intelligence quotient seems to carry a heavy predictive load in most of our measures of outcomes. It should be noted that in a number of studies, adjustment at both the child and the adult level, whenever intelligence is included, emerges as a more significant factor than personality measures.

It is apparent that the power of IQ to predict social behavior and adjustment springs from numerous sources, including the social and school success experiences associated with brightness. However, a large part of the predictive power of IQ derives from the fact that more rapid cognitive development is associated with more rapid social development. This interpretation of IQ effects has been thoroughly documented in the area of sex-role attitudes. An example of this fact comes from a semilongitudinal study of the sex-role attitudes of bright and average boys and girls (Kohlberg & Zigler, 1967). In the first place, this study indicated significant IQ effects in performance on seven tests of sex-role attitudes (some experimental-behavioral, some verbal, some projective doll-play). In the second place, the study indicated that while there were marked and similar developmental trends for both bright and average children, these trends were largely determined by mental as opposed to chronological age. Parallel curves of age-development were obtained for both groups with the curves being about two years advanced for the bright children (who were about two years advanced in mental age). As an example, bright boys would shift from a preference for adult females to a preference for adult males on experimental and doll-play tests at about age 4 whereas the average boys would make the shift about age 6. The same findings held in a study of retarded and average lower-class Negro boys, half father-absent, half father-present (unpublished study by C. Smith, summarized in Kohlberg, 1966b). The average boys made the shift to the male at age 5-6, the retarded boys at age 7-8. Clearly, then, sex-role age-developmental trends are mediated by cognitive development.

Turning to morality, "resistance to temptation" has a moderate but clearly documented correlation with IQ.[1] These findings are not too helpful, however, since resistance to temptation does not define any dimension of age-development of morality. We shall now attempt to show that more "cognitive" dimensions of moral judgment do define moral age-development, and that once moral judgment development is understood, the development of moral action and moral affect becomes much more intelligible and predictable. The assertion that moral judgment undergoes regular age-development and that this development is in some sense cognitive has seldom been questioned since the work of Hartshorne and May (1928-30) and Piaget (1948). However, extreme proponents of the cultural relativism of values must logically question both these contentions, as Bronfenbrenner (1962) has recently done. Bronfenbrenner has claimed that class, sex, and culture are more important determinants of Piaget-type moral judgment than is age-development. Examination of this claim may usefully clarify the sense in which moral judgment is said to have a cognitive-developmental component. One sense of the assertion that moral judgment development is cognitive is that it involves an increase in the child's knowledge of the content of conventional standards and values of his group. This is indeed the nature of moral judgment as measured by conventional "moral knowledge" tests like those of Hartshorne and May (1928-30). In this sense, it is plausible to assert that insofar as the content of standards and value labels differs by class, sex, and culture, so will the development of moral judgment. In another sense, however, moral judgments change in cognitive form with development. As an example, it is generally recognized that conceptions and sentiments of justice ("giving each his due") are based on conceptions of reciprocity and of equality. Reciprocity and equality are, however, cognitive as well as moral forms. Piaget (1947) has done a number of studies suggesting that the awareness of logical reciprocity (e.g., recognition that I am my brother's brother) develops with the formation of concrete operations at age 6-7. Our studies (Kohlberg, 1969) indicate that use of reciprocity as a moral reason first appears at the same age.

Another example of cognitive form in moral judgment is the consideration of intentions as opposed to physical consequences in judging the badness of action. According to Piaget (1948), the development of moral intentionality corresponds to the more general cognitive differentiation of objective and subjective, physical and mental, discussed in Section I. Accordingly, it is not surprising to find that in every culture, in every social class, in every sex group, and in every subculture studied (Switzerland, United States, Belgium, Chinese, Malaysian-aboriginal, Mexican, Israel, Hopi, Zuni, Sioux, Papago) age trends toward increased intentionality are found. It is also not surprising to find this trend is always correlated with intelligence or mental development in all groups where intelligence measures have been available. Finally, it is not surprising to find that such cultural or subcultural differences as exist are explainable as due

---

[1] All findings on moral development discussed are documented and referenced in Kohlberg, 1969; some are to be found in Kohlberg, 1963a, 1964; so they will not be referenced in this chapter.

to the amount of social and cognitive stimulation provided by the culture in question.

As an example, in all nations studied, there are social-class differences in the direction of earlier intentionality for the middle class. These are not class differences in values, but class differences in the cognitive and social stimulation of development. In each class, the older and more intelligent children are more intentional. If the "retardation" of the lower-class child were to be explained as due to a different adult subcultural value system, the older and brighter lower-class children would have to be more "retarded" than the younger and duller lower-class children, since they should have learned the lower-class value system better. Intentionality, then, is an example of a culturally universal developmental trend, which is universal and regular in its development because it has a "cognitive form" base in the differentiation of the physical and the mental.

In contrast, however, a number of the dimensions of moral judgment studied by Piaget are really matters of content rather than cognitive form. An example is the dimension of responsiveness to peer, as opposed to adult, expectations. While Piaget (1948) hypothesizes this dimension as part of his autonomous stage, his rationale for deriving this from a consideration of cognitive form is vague and unconvincing. There is nothing more cognitively mature to preferring a peer than an adult. It is not surprising to find, then, that this dimension does not vary regularly with chronological and mental age, that what age trends exist are absent in some national groups (e.g., the Swiss), and that in general this dimension is sensitive to a wide variety of cultural and subcultural influences which cannot be analyzed in rate of development terms.

In summary, then, universal and regular age trends of development may be found in moral judgment, and these have a formal-cognitive base. Many aspects of moral judgment do not have such a cognitive base, but these aspects do not define universal and regular trends of moral development.

Using the Piaget (1948) material, we have indicated that there are "natural" culturally universal trends of age-development in moral judgment with a cognitive-formal base. Age trends, however, are not in themselves sufficient to define stages with the properties discussed in our first section. While Piaget attempted to define two stages of moral judgment (the heteronomous and the autonomous), extensive empirical study and logical analysis indicate that his moral stages have not met the criteria of stage he proposes (summarized in our first section), as his cognitive stages do.

Taking cognizance of Piaget's notions as well as those of others such as Hobhouse (1906), J. M. Baldwin (1906), Peck and Havighurst (1960), and McDougall (1908), I have attempted to define stages of moral judgment which would meet these criteria. A summary characterization of the stages is presented in Table 6.2. The relations of the stages to those of other writers is indicated by Table 6.3.

The stages were defined in terms of free responses to ten hypothetical moral dilemmas, one of which is presented subsequently in Table 6.5. Stage definition

29

TABLE 6.2

CLASSIFICATION OF MORAL JUDGMENT INTO LEVELS AND STAGES OF DEVELOPMENT

Levels	Basis of Moral Judgment	Stages of Development
I	Moral value resides in external, quasi-physical happenings, in bad acts, or in quasi-physical needs rather than in persons and standards.	Stage 1: Obedience and punishment orientation. Egocentric deference to superior power or prestige, or a trouble-avoiding set. Objective responsibility.
		Stage 2: Naively egoistic orientation. Right action is that instrumentally satisfying the self's needs and occasionally others'. Awareness of relativism of value to each actor's needs and perspective. Naive egalitarianism and orientation to exchange and reciprocity.
II	Moral value resides in performing good or right roles, in maintaining the conventional order and the expectancies of others.	Stage 3: Good-boy orientation. Orientation to approval and to pleasing and helping others. Conformity to stereotypical images of majority or natural role behavior, and judgment by intentions.
		Stage 4: Authority and social-order maintaining orientation. Orientation to "doing duty" and to showing respect for authority and maintaining the given social order for its own sake. Regard for earned expectations of others.
III	Moral value resides in conformity by the self to shared or shareable standards, rights, or duties.	Stage 5: Contractual legalistic orientation. Recognition of an arbitrary element or starting point in rules or expectations for the sake of agreement. Duty defined in terms of contract, general avoidance of violation of the will or rights of others, and majority will and welfare.
		Stage 6: Conscience or principle orientation. Orientation not only to actually ordained social rules but to principles of choice involving appeal to logical universality and consistency. Orientation to conscience as a directing agent and to mutual respect and trust.

Source: Kohlberg, 1967, p. 171.

is based on a subsumption of a moral judgment under one of twenty-five aspects of moral judgment listed in Table 6.4.

These aspects represent basic moral concepts believed to be present in any society. As an example, "10, punishment" is a culturally universal concept entering into moral judgment as is "19, rights of property" or "23, contract." Each of these concepts is differently defined and used at each of the six stages. Definition or usage of concepts at each stage can logically be claimed to represent a differentiation and integration of the concept as it is used at the preceding

30

TABLE 6.3

Author	Amoral	1. Fearful-Dependent	2. Opportunistic	3. Conforming to Persons	4. Conforming to Rule	5,6. Principled-Autonomous
			Moral Stages			
McDougall (1908)	1. instinctive		2. reward and punishment	3. anticipation of praise and blame		4. regulation by an internal ideal
J. M. Baldwin (1906)		1. adualistic	2. intellectual		3. ideal	
L. Hobhouse (1906)	1. instinctive	2. obligation as magical taboo		3. obligation as ideals of personal virtue	4. obligation as rules of society	5. rational ethical principles
Piaget (1948)	1. premoral	2. heteronomous obedience to adult authority	3. autonomous reciprocity and equality oriented			4. autonomous—ideal reciprocity and equality
Peck and Havighurst (1960)	1. amoral		2. expedient	3. conforming	4. irrational—conscientious	5. rational—altruistic
Kohlberg (1958)		1. obedience & punishment oriented	2. instrumental egoism and exchange	3. good-boy approval oriented	4. authority, rule and social order oriented	5. social contract legalist orientation 6. moral principle orientation
			Ego or Character Types			
Fromm (1955) Riesman (1950)		1. receptive, tradition-directed	2. exploitative, anomic	3. marketing, other-directed	4. hoarding, inner-directed	5. productive, autonomous
C. Sullivan, Grant and Grant (1957)		I_2 passive-demanding	I_3 conformist (exploitative)	I_3 conformist (cooperative)	I_4 authoritarian-guilty	I_6 self-consistent I_7 integrative
Harvey, Hunt & Shroeder (1961)		1. absolutistic-evaluative	2. self-differentiating	3. empathic		4. integrated—independent
Loevinger (1966)	1. presocial	2. impulse-ridden, fearful	3. expedient	4. conformist	5. conscientious	6. autonomous 7. integrated

stage. An example of the six stages of definition of one aspect of moral judgment is presented in Table 6.5. This table indicates how the aspect of intentionality studied by Piaget (1948) has been defined in terms of each of the six qualitative

TABLE 6.4

CODED ASPECTS OF DEVELOPING MORAL JUDGMENT

Code	Description	Aspects
I. Value	Locus of value —modes of attributing (moral) value to acts, persons, or events. Modes of assessing value consequences in a situation.	1. Considering motives in judging action. 2. Considering consequences in judging action. 3. Subjectivity vs. objectivity of values assessed. 4. Relation of obligation to wish. 5. Identification with actor or victims in judging the action. 6. Status of actor and victim as changing the moral worth of actions.
II. Choice	Mechanisms of resolving or denying awareness of conflicts.	7. Limiting actor's responsibility for consequences by shifting responsibility onto others. 8. Reliance on discussion and compromise, mainly unrealistically. 9. Distorting situation so that conforming behavior is seen as always maximizing the interests of the actor or of others involved.
III. Sanctions and Motives	The dominant motives and sanctions for moral or deviant action.	10. Punishment or negative reactions. 11. Disruption of an interpersonal relationship. 12. A concern by actor for welfare, for positive state of the other. 13. Self-condemnation.
IV. Rules	The ways in which rules are conceptualized, applied, and generalized. The basis of the validity of a rule.	14. Definition of an act as deviant. (Definition of moral rules and norms.) 15. Generality and consistency of rules. 16. Waiving rules for personal relations (particularism).
V. Rights and Authority	Basis and limits of control over persons and property.	17. Non-motivational attributes ascribed to authority (knowledge, etc.). (Motivational attributes considered under III above.) 18. Extent or scope of authority's rights. Rights of liberty. 19. Rights of possession or property.

32

Code	Description	Aspects
VI. Positive Justice	Reciprocity and equality.	20. Exchange and reciprocity as a motive for role conformity. 21. Reciprocity as a motive to deviate (e.g., revenge). 22. Distributive justice. Equality and impartiality. 23. Concepts of maintaining partner's expectations as a motive for conformity. Contract and trust.
VII. Punitive Justice	Standards and functions of punishment.	24. Punitive tendencies or expectations. (a) Notions of equating punishment and crime. 25. Functions or purpose of punishment.

Source: Kohlberg, 1967, pp. 172-173.

stages. To document the way in which form of moral judgment is distinct from action content, Table 6.5 presents standardized arguments (Rest, 1968) at each stage of intentionality both for and against stealing the drug in the dilemma involved. Table 6.5 also indicates the sense in which each stage of orientation to intentions entails a differentiation not made at the preceding stage.

TABLE 6.5

SIX STAGES OF ORIENTATION TO INTENTIONS AND CONSEQUENCES (ASPECTS 1 AND 2) IN RESPONSE TO A MORAL DILEMMA

In Europe, a woman was near death from cancer. One drug might save her, a form of radium that a druggist in the same town had recently discovered. The druggist was charging $2,000, ten times what the drug cost him to make. The sick woman's husband, Heinz, went to everyone he knew to borrow the money, but he could only get together about half of what it cost. He told the druggist that his wife was dying and asked him to sell it cheaper or let him pay later. But the druggist said, "No." The husband got desperate and broke into the man's store to steal the drug for his wife. Should the husband have done that? Why?

Stage 1. Motives and need-consequences of act are ignored in judging badness because of focus upon irrelevant physical form of the act (e.g., size of the lie), or of the consequences of the act (e.g., amount of physical damage).

 Pro —He should steal the drug. It isn't really bad to take it. It isn't like he didn't ask to pay for it first. The drug he'd take is only worth $200, he's not really taking a $2,000 drug.

 Con —He shouldn't steal the drug, it's a big crime. He didn't get permission, he used force and broke and entered. He did a lot of damage, stealing a very expensive drug and breaking up the store, too.

Stage 2. Judgment ignores label or physical consequences of the act because of the instrumental value of the act in serving a need, or because the act doesn't do harm in terms of the need of another. (Differentiates the human need-value of the act from its physical form or consequences.)

 Pro —It's all right to steal the drug because she needs it and he wants her to live. It isn't that he wants to steal, but it's the way he has to use to get the drug to save her.

 Con —He shouldn't steal it. The druggist isn't wrong or bad, he just wants to make a profit. That's what you're in business for, to make money.

33

TABLE 6.5 (continued)

Stage 3. Action evaluated according to the type of motive or person likely to perform the act. An act is not bad if it is an expression of a "nice" or altruistic motive or person and it is not good if it is the expression of a "mean" or selfish motive or person. Circumstances may excuse or justify deviant action. (Differentiates good motives to which an act is instrumental from human but selfish need to which it is instrumental.)

Pro —He should steal the drug. He was only doing something that was natural for a good husband to do. You can't blame him for doing something out of love for his wife, you'd blame him if he didn't love his wife enough to save her.

Con —He shouldn't steal. If his wife dies, he can't be blamed. It isn't because he's heartless or that he doesn't love her enough to do everything that he legally can. The druggist is the selfish or heartless one.

Stage 4. An act is always or categorically wrong, regardless of motives or circumstances, if it violates a rule and does foreseeable harm to others. (Differentiates action out of a sense of obligation to rule from action for generally "nice" or natural motives.)

Pro —You should steal it. If you did nothing you'd be letting your wife die, it's your responsibility if she dies. You have to take it with the idea of paying the druggist.

Con —It is a natural thing for Heinz to want to save his wife but it's still always wrong to steal. He still knows he's stealing and taking a valuable drug from the man who made it.

Stage 5. A formal statement that though circumstances or motive modify disapproval, as a general rule the means do not justify the ends. While circumstances justify deviant acts to some extent they do not make it right or lead to suspension of moral categories. (Differentiates moral blame because of the intent behind breaking the rule from the legal or principled necessity not to make exceptions to rules.)

Pro —The law wasn't set up for these circumstances. Taking the drug in this situation isn't really right, but it's justified to do it.

Con —You can't completely blame someone for stealing but extreme circumstances don't really justify taking the law in your own hands. You can't have everyone stealing whenever they get desperate. The end may be good, but the ends don't justify the means.

Stage 6. Good motives don't make an act right (or not wrong); but if an act follows from a decision to follow general self-chosen principles, it can't be wrong. It may be actually right to deviate from the rules, but only under circumstances forcing a choice between deviation from the rules and concrete violation of a moral principle. (Differentiates good motives of following a moral principle from natural motives as following a rule. Recognizes that moral principles don't allow exceptions any more than do legal rules.)

Pro —This is a situation which forces him to choose between stealing and letting his wife die. In a situation where the choice must be made, it is morally right to steal. He has to act in terms of the principle of preserving and respecting life.

Con —Heinz is faced with the decision of whether to consider the other people who need the drug just as badly as his wife. Heinz ought to act not according to his particular feelings toward his wife, but considering the value of all the lives involved.

Source: Rest, 1968.

While it is not surprising to consider concepts of intentionality developing along cognitive-formal dimensions, it may surprise the reader to find that motives for moral action (Aspects 10 and 13 of Table 6.4) also have a cognitive-formal element. Table 6.6 presents the definition of moral motives characteristic of each stage, in a form similar to that of Table 6.5. It should be recalled that we are still dealing with concepts, here concepts of motives manifestly relevant to the concepts of intentions involved in the previous table. As Table 6.6 indicates, each stage involves a differentiation not present at the preceding stage.

The definition of the stages is not dependent on responses to a particular set of materials, however, but is based on a system for scoring any moral judgment

TABLE 6.6

MOTIVES FOR ENGAGING IN MORAL ACTION
(ASPECTS 10 AND 13)

Stage 1. Action is motivated by avoidance of punishment and "conscience" is irrational fear of punishment.

  Pro —If you let your wife die, you will get in trouble. You'll be blamed for not spending the money to save her and there'll be an investigation of you and the druggist for your wife's death.

  Con —You shouldn't steal the drug because you'll be caught and sent to jail if you do. If you do get away, your conscience would bother you thinking how the police would catch up with you at any minute.

Stage 2. Action motivated by desire for reward or benefit. Possible guilt reactions are ignored and punishment viewed in a pragmatic manner. (Differentiates own fear, pleasure, or pain from punishment-consequences.)

  Pro —If you do happen to get caught you could give the drug back and you wouldn't get much of a sentence. It wouldn't bother you much to serve a little jail term, if you have your wife when you get out.

  Con —He may not get much of a jail term if he steals the drug, but his wife will probably die before he gets out so it won't do him much good. If his wife dies, he shouldn't blame himself, it wasn't his fault she has cancer.

Stage 3. Action motivated by anticipation of disapproval of others, actual or imagined-hypothetical (e.g., guilt). (Differentiation of disapproval from punishment, fear, and pain.)

  Pro —No one will think you're bad if you steal the drug but your family will think you're an inhuman husband if you don't. If you let your wife die, you'll never be able to look anybody in the face again.

  Con —It isn't just the druggist who will think you're a criminal, everyone else will too. After you steal it, you'll feel bad thinking how you've brought dishonor on your family and yourself; you won't be able to face anyone again.

Stage 4. Action motivated by anticipation of dishonor, i.e., institutionalized blame for failure of duty, and by guilt over concrete harm done to others. (Differentiates formal dishonor from informal disapproval. Differentiates guilt for bad consequences from disapproval.)

  Pro —If you have any sense of honor, you won't let your wife die because you're afraid to do the only thing that will save her. You'll always feel guilty that you caused her death if you don't do your duty to her.

  Con —You're desperate and you may not know you're doing wrong when you steal the drug. But you'll know you did wrong after you're punished and sent to jail. You'll always feel guilty for your dishonesty and lawbreaking.

35

TABLE 6.6 (continued)

Stage 5. Concern about maintaining respect of equals and of the community (assuming their respect is based on reason rather than emotions). Concern about own self-respect, i.e., to avoid judging self as irrational, inconsistent, nonpurposive. (Discriminates between institutionalized blame and community disrespect or self-disrespect.)

> Pro —You'd lose other people's respect, not gain it, if you don't steal. If you let your wife die, it would be out of fear, not out of reasoning it out. So you'd just lose self-respect and probably the respect of others too.

> Con —You would lose your standing and respect in the community and violate the law. You'd lose respect for yourself if you're carried away by emotion and forget the long-range point of view.

Stage 6. Concern about self-condemnation for violating one's own principles. (Differentiates between community respect and self-respect. Differentiates between self-respect for general achieving rationality and self-respect for maintaining moral principles.)

> Pro —If you don't steal the drug and let your wife die, you'd always condemn yourself for it afterward. You wouldn't be blamed and you would have lived up to the outside rule of the law but you wouldn't have lived up to your own standards of conscience.

> Con —If you stole the drug, you wouldn't be blamed by other people but you'd condemn yourself because you wouldn't have lived up to your own conscience and standards of honesty.

Source: Rest, 1968.

unit or sentence in any context. As an example, Table 6.7 indicates some statements by Adolf Eichmann which were scored by stage and aspect with good interjudge agreement, using general definitions of each stage at each aspect, such as those provided by Tables 6.4 and 6.5 for two aspects.

While the evidence is far from complete, all the evidence to date suggests that the stages do meet the criteria of stages proposed in our first section. This evidence comes from studies conducted in Taiwan, Great Britain, Mexico, Turkey and the United States. In addition to middle- and lower-class urban boys, the studies have included preliterate or semi-literate villagers in Turkey, Mexico (a Mayan group) and Taiwan (an Atayal group).

Figures 6.2 and 6.3 suggest the cultural universality of the sequence of stages which we have found. Figure 6.2 presents the age trends for middle-class urban boys in the U.S., Taiwan and Mexico. At age 10 in each country, the order of use of each stage is the same as the order of its difficulty or maturity. In the U.S., by age 16 the order is the reverse, from the highest to the lowest, except that Stage 6 is still little used. At age 13, Stage 3, the good-boy middle stage is most used. The results in Mexico and Taiwan are the same, except that development is a little slower. The most conspicuous feature is that Stage 5 thinking is much more salient in the U.S. than it is in Mexico or Taiwan at age 16. Nevertheless, it is present in the other countries, so we know that it is not purely an American democratic construct. The second figure (6.3) indicates results from two isolated villages, one in Yucatan, one in Turkey. The similarity of pattern in the two villages is striking. While conventional moral thought (Stages 3 and 4) increases

36

TABLE 6.7

SCORING OF MORAL JUDGMENTS OF EICHMANN FOR DEVELOPMENTAL STAGE

Moral Judgments	Score *
In actual fact, I was merely a little cog in the machinery that carried out the directives of the German Reich.	1/7
I am neither a murderer nor a mass-murderer.	
I am a man of average character, with good qualities and many faults.	3/1
Yet what is there to "admit"?	
I carried out my orders.	
It would be as pointless to blame me for the whole final solution of the Jewish problem as to blame the official in charge of the railroads over which the Jewish transports traveled.	1/7
Where would we have been if everyone had thought things out in those days?	
You can do that today in the "new" German army.	
But with us an order was an order.	1/15
If I had sabotaged the order of the one-time Fuhrer of the German Reich, Adolf Hitler, I would have been not only a scoundrel but a despicable pig like those who broke their military oath to join the ranks of the anti-Hitler criminals in the conspiracy of July 20, 1944.	1/1
I would like to stress again, however, that my department never gave a single annihilation order.	
We were responsible only for deportation.	2/7
My interest was only in the number of transport trains I had to provide.	
Whether they were bank directors or mental cases, the people who were loaded on these trains meant nothing to me.	2/3
It was really none of my business.	2/7
But to sum it all up, I must say that I regret nothing.	
Adolf Hitler may have been wrong all down the line, but one thing is beyond dispute: the man was able to work his way up from lance corporal in the German army to Fuhrer of a people of almost eighty million.	1/6
I never met him personally, but his success alone proves to me that I should subordinate myself to this man.	
He was somehow so supremely capable that the people recognized him.	
And so with that justification I recognized him joyfully, and I still defend him.	1/17
I must say truthfully, that if we had killed all the ten million Jews that Himmler's statisticians originally listed in 1933, I would say, "Good, we have destroyed an enemy."	2/21
But here I do not mean wiping them out entirely.	
That would not be proper —and we carried on a proper war.	1/1

* The first code number in this column refers to Stages 1-6 (see Table 6.2); the second number refers to the aspect of morality involved (see Table 6.4).
Source: Kohlberg, 1967, p. 177.

steadily from age 10 to 16, at 16 it still has not achieved a clear ascendency over premoral thought (Stages 1 and 2). Stages 5 and 6 are totally absent in this group. Trends for lower-class urban groups are intermediate in rate of development between those for the middle-class and the village boys.

While the age trends of Figures 6.2 and 6.3 indicate that some modes of thought are generally more difficult or advanced than other modes of thought, they do not demonstrate that attainment of each mode of thought is prerequisite to the attainment of the next higher in a hypothetical sequence.

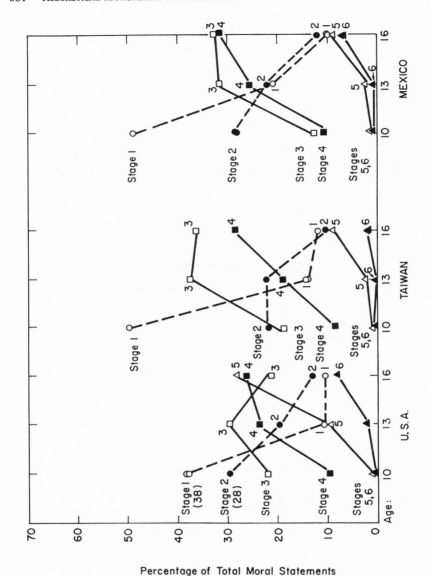

FIGURE 6.2. Age trends in moral judgment in middle class urban boys in three nations.

Percentage of Total Moral Statements

The importance of the sequentiality issue may be brought out from two points of view. With regard to the definition of moral development, it is not at all clear that Stages 5 and 6 should be used to define developmental end points in morality. Figure 6.2 indicates that Stage 4 is the dominant stage of most adults.

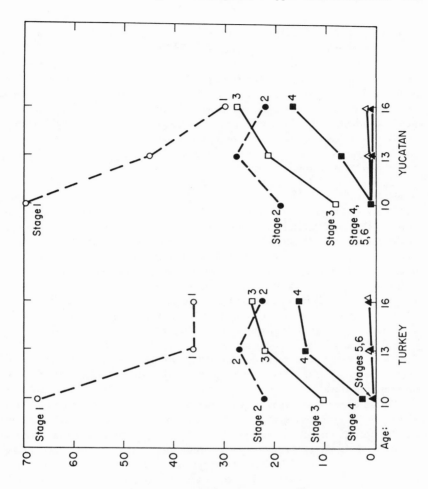

Percentage of Total Moral Statements

FIGURE 6.3. Age trends in moral judgment in isolated village boys in two nations.

It is possible to view Stages 4, 5, and 6 as alternative types of mature response rather than as a sequence. Indeed, this is the view of some writers who view conventional-authoritarian (Stage 4) adult character types as opposed to humanistic (Stages 5 and 6) character types as representing alternative channels of personality crystallization. If Stages 5 and 6 persons can be shown to have gone through Stage 4 while Stage 4 persons have not gone through Stages 5 and 6, it can be argued that the stage hierarchy constitutes more than a value judgment by the investigator.

Our age trends indicate that large groups of moral concepts and ways of

39

thought only attain meaning at successively advanced ages and require the extensive background of social experience and cognitive growth represented by the age factor. From usual views of the moralization process, these age changes in modes of moral thought would simply be interpreted as successive acquisitions or internalizations of cultural moral concepts. Our six types of thought would represent six patterns of verbal morality in the adult culture which are successively absorbed as the child grows more verbally sophisticated. The age order involved might simply represent the order in which the culture presented the various concepts involved, or might simply reflect that greater mental age is required to learn the higher type of concept.

In contrast, we have advocated the developmental interpretation that these types of thought represent structures emerging from the interaction of the child with his social environment, rather than directly reflecting external structures given by the child's culture. Awareness of the basic prohibitions and commands of the culture, as well as some behavioral "internalization" of them, exists from the first of our stages and does not define their succession. Movement from stage to stage represents rather the way in which these prohibitions, as well as much wider aspects of the social structure, are taken up into the child's organization of a moral order. This order may be based upon power and external compulsion (Stage 1), upon a system of exchanges and need satisfactions (Stage 2), upon the maintenance of legitimate expectations (Stages 3 and 4), or upon ideals or general logical principles of social organization (Stages 5 and 6). While these successive bases of a moral order do spring from the child's awareness of the external social world, they also represent active processes of organizing or ordering this world.

Because the higher types of moral thought integrate and replace, rather than add to the lower modes of thought, the Guttman (1954) scaling technique used for the dream concept in our first section is not appropriate for our material, based on the usage of the stages in free responses. It does become appropriate, however, if we measure children's comprehension of each stage instead of their use of it. Rest (1968) has asked S's to recapitulate in different words statements at each stage of the sort presented in Tables 6.5 and 6.6. In general, subjects can correctly recapitulate statements at all stages below or at their own level, correctly recapitulate some, but not all statements at one stage above their own, and fail to correctly recapitulate statements two or more stages above their own (Rest, 1968; Rest, Turiel & Kohlberg, 1969). Even where this is not the case, e.g., where an S can recapitulate a statement two stages above his own, his comprehension still fits a Guttman scale pattern, i.e., he will comprehend all the statements below the plus-two statement including the statement one above his own.

While the pattern of actual usage of stages does not fit a cumulative model, it does fit a non-cumulative model of sequence. The profile of usage of other stages in relation to the child's modal stage is presented in Figure 6.4. This figure indicates that on the average, 50 per cent of a child's moral judgments fit a

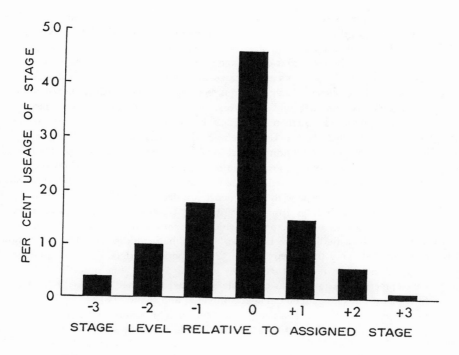

FIGURE 6.4. Profile of stage usage.

single stage. The remainder are distributed around this mode in decreasing fashion as one moves successively farther on the ordinal scale from the modal stage. An individual's response profile, then, typically represents a pattern composed of the dominant stage he is in, a stage he is leaving but still uses somewhat and a stage he is moving into but which has not yet "crystallized."

The pattern of usage of different stages becomes intelligible when it is recalled that, in a certain sense, all the lower stages are available or at least comprehensible to the S. The pattern of usage, then, is dictated by a hierarchical preference for the highest stage a subject can produce. While S's have difficulty comprehending stages above their own, and do not have difficulty with stages below their own, they prefer higher stages to the lower stages. If they can comprehend a statement two stages above their own, they prefer it to a statement one above. If they comprehend statements one stage but not two above their own, they prefer them to statements either two above or one below their own. If hypothetical statements at their own stage are presented to S's, and they have not yet produced statements of their own, the S's tend to prefer the one above to their own level statement.

It appears, then, that patterns of actual usage of stages are dictated by two opposed sequential orders, one of preference and one of ease, with an individual

41

modal stage representing the most preferred stage which he can readily use. It is apparent, then, that the moral stages empirically meet the criterion of sequence and of hierarchical integration discussed in our first section, and that they logically meet it in the sense that each stage represents a logical differentiation and integration of prior concepts as indicated in Tables 6.5 and 6.6. In some sense, then, one can discuss the stages as representing a hierarchical sequence quite independent of the fact that they correspond to trends of age-development. Table 6.7 presented statements by Adolf Eichmann, a Nazi leader, which are largely Stage 1 and Stage 2. It can be argued that German adolescents grew up into a Stage 1 and 2 Nazi adult moral ideology in the same sense that it can be argued that Atayal children grow up into a Stage 1 or 2 conception of the dream. In such a case, we would hardly argue that the actual sequence of age-development would fully correspond to the sequence just described.

Preliminary findings from a longitudinal study of American boys speak directly to the issue of the extent to which ontogeny actually follows the logical sequence. These findings are based on 50 boys, half middle class, half working class, studied every three years over a 12-year period. Originally ranging in age from 10 to 16, on terminal study they were 22 to 28. While only the data on development after age 16 has been fully analyzed (Kramer, 1968), the findings fit a picture of ontogenetic change as directed and sequential, or stepwise. The one exception is that at one age period (end of high school to mid-college) 20 per cent of the middle-class boys "regress," or drop in total score. They come up again after college so that none of them are below their high-school level in the late twenties and almost all are above that level. No such temporary "regression" occurs in the non-college or lower-class population. The only cases of "regression" found in the lower-class sample were among six delinquents followed longitudinally. For three of these, reform school and jail had an actual "regressive" effect on morality.

The findings on regression are cited to clarify the meaning of sequence in the study of ontogeny suggested in connection with the Atayal dream concept. The claim of the theory is that the "normal" course of social experience leads to progression through the sequence. Special forms of experience, like jail, may have a "regressive" effect. If one finds "regression" because of college experience, one must analyze the college experience in terms different from those appropriate for earlier or later sequential movement, as Kramer (1968) has done using "cognitive conflict" concepts.

In addition to sequence, stages must meet the criterion of consistency implied by the notion of a "structured whole." On the logical side, consistency is found in the fact that twenty-five distinct aspects of moral judgment may be logically defined from the core concepts of the six stages. On the empirical side, both consistency across aspects and consistency across verbal situations are to be found. Such consistency is indicated, first, by the fact that an average of 50 per cent of a subject's moral judgments fit a single stage. Second, such consistency is indicated by fairly high correlations in moral levels from one story to another. The highest

42

such correlation is .75, the lowest .31, the median .51. Third, it is indicated by the fact that these correlations between situations are not specific, i.e., there is a general moral level factor. A general first moral level factor accounts for most of covariations from situation to situation (Kohlberg, 1958, 1969).

While the stage conception implies that stages constitute "structured wholes," the stage notion also suggests that (1) age should lead to increasing consolidation or equilibrium in a given stage, and (2) that higher stages eventually represent better or more equilibrated structures than lower stages (Turiel, 1969). As children move into adulthood, then, those who remain primarily at Stages 1 and 2 crystallize into purer types, an extreme being some delinquents with an explicit Stage 2 con-man ideology. Subjects moving into the higher stages (4, 5 and 6) stabilize more slowly than the lower stage subjects, but by the middle twenties have become the purest types of all (Turiel, 1969; Kramer, 1968).

We have reported a variety of evidence suggesting that moral stages fit all the criteria of stages in the social domain. Our earlier discussion claimed that if this were the case, we should be able to solve the problem of longitudinal predictability which has frustrated so much of socialization research. Preliminary longitudinal findings indicate that this is the case. The correlation between moral maturity scores at age 16 and in the mid-twenties was .78 ($n = 24$).[2] While only a very small sample ($n = 8$) of middle-class 13-year-olds have reached the mid-twenties, the correlation between moral maturity at age 13 and in the mid-twenties was equally high (r between age 13 and age 24 $= .92$; r between age 16 and age 24 $= .88$). It is clear, then, that a study of environmental determinants of moral level at 13 can have long-range meaning. The degree of predictability achieved suggests the potential fruitfulness of defining social behavior in terms of developmental sequence instead of in terms of traits for socialization research.

IV. RELATIONS BETWEEN COGNITION, AFFECT AND CONDUCT IN SOCIAL DEVELOPMENT

We have seen that moral judgment stages provide a definition of continuity through transformations of development necessary before the naturalistic study of socialization can begin. We shall now consider how these "cognitively" defined stages of judgment illuminate "non-cognitive" moral development in the spheres of affect and of action. This sentence is, however, a misstatement of both Piaget's and our position, which is not the position that cognition determines affect and behavior, but that the *development* of cognition and the development of affect have a common structural base. Rather than saying, as we did earlier, that "regular age-developmental trends in moral judgment have a formal-cognitive

---

[2] Because of shakeup and "regression" in college, the correlations between moral maturity at age 16 and in college were much lower ($r = .24$). As previously noted the regressors all "straightened out" by the mid-twenties (Kramer, 1968).

base," we should have said that "age-developmental trends in moral judgment have a formal-structural base parallel to the structural base of cognitive development." While the notion of cognitive-affective parallelism is not abstruse, it has been difficult for American psychologists to grasp. The doctrine has, however, entered the American research literature as it has been independently elaborated by Werner (1948) and his followers (Witkin, 1969). A structural dimension of development, such as "differentiation," is considered to characterize all aspects of the personality—the social emotional, the perceptual, and the intellective. As measured by age-developmental perceptual tasks, "differentiation" is quite highly correlated with standard psychometric intelligence measures as well as with a variety of social attitudes and traits. Harvey et al. (1961) also elaborated a "structural parallelism" view of personality development in terms of increased structural differentiation and integration of conceptions of self and others, implying both cognitive and attitudinal correlates.

In Piaget's (1952a) view, both types of thought and types of valuing or of feeling are schemata which develop a set of general structural characteristics which represent successive forms of psychological equilibrium. The equilibrium of affective and interpersonal schemata involves many of the same basic structural features as the equilibrium of cognitive schemata. It is generally believed that justice (portrayed as balancing the scales) is a form of equilibrium between conflicting interpersonal claims, so Piaget (1948) holds that "In contrast to a given rule imposed upon the child from outside, the rule of justice is an imminent condition of social relationships or a law governing their equilibrium." In Piaget's view logic is also not a learned cultural rule imposed from the outside, but a law governing the equilibrium between ideas rather than between persons. Both violation of logic and violation of justice may arouse strong affects. The strong affective component of the sense of justice is not inconsistent with its structural base. As was already stated, the structure of reciprocity is both a cognitive structure and a structural component of the sense of justice.

What is being asserted, then, is not that moral judgment stages are cognitive but that the existence of moral stages implies that moral development has a basic structural component. While motives and affects are involved in moral development, the development of these motives and affects is largely mediated by changes in thought patterns.

Among the implications of this statement are the following:

1. There should be an empirical correlation between moral judgment maturity and non-moral aspects of cognitive development.

2. Moral judgment stages or sequences are to be described in cognitive-structural terms even in regard to "affective" aspects of moral judgment, like guilt, empathy, etc.

3. There should be an empirical correlation between maturity on "affective" and cognitive aspects of morality, even if affective maturity is assessed by projective test or interview methods not explicitly focused on moral judgment.

4. The way in which moral judgment influences action should also be characterizable in cognitive-structural terms.

44

5. The socioenvironmental influences favorable to moral judgment development should be influences characterizable in cognitive-structural terms, for example, in terms of role-taking opportunities.

With regard to the first point, correlations between group IQ tests and moral judgment level at age 12 range from .30 to .50 in various studies. These correlations indicate that moral maturity has a cognitive base but is not simply general verbal intelligence applied to moral problems. This fact is indicated by the existence of a general moral level factor found among our situations after correlations due to intelligence are controlled for. The relation of moral judgment to intellective development is suggested by the fact that our stage definitions assume that Piagetian concrete operations are necessary for conventional (Stage 3 and 4) morality and that formal operations are necessary for principled (Stage 5 and 6) morality. Some crude and preliminary evidence that this is the case comes from a finding that moral judgment maturity and a crude test of formal operations correlated .44 with tested verbal intelligence. The Piagetian rationale just advanced, as well as other considerations, suggests that cognitive maturity is a necessary, but not a sufficient, condition for moral judgment maturity. While formal operations may be necessary for principled morality, one may be a theoretical physicist and yet not make moral judgments at the principled level. In fact, a curvilinear relation between IQ and moral maturity is found. In the below-average range, a linear correlation ($r = .53$) is found between IQ and moral maturity, whereas no relationship ($r = .16$) is found between the two measures in the above-average group. In other words, children below average in IQ are almost all below average in moral maturity. Children above average in IQ are equally likely to be low or high in moral maturity. The theories just proposed suggest not only a nonlinear relation between IQ and moral maturity but a decline in the correlation between the two with age. Moral judgment continues to develop until age 25 (Kramer, 1968), although only for half the middle-class population, whereas general intellectual maturity does not. While bright children attain formal operations earlier than duller children, most of the dull children eventually attain them. The duller children, then, tend to develop more slowly in moral judgment but may develop longer. IQ is then a better indicator of early rate of development than it is of terminal status, which is more determined by social experience.

The second point (that affective aspects of moral development are to be described in cognitive-structural terms) was partially documented by our indicating how our stages defined moral affects in Table 6.6 just as they defined "cognitive" dimensions like intentionality in Table 6.5. Table 6.6 indicates that each "higher" affect involves a cognitive differentiation not made by the next "lower" affect.

Table 6.6 assigns guilt over deviation from conventional rules leading to injury to others to Stage 4 (guilt over violation of internal principles was assigned to Stage 6). Stage 4 guilt implies differentiating concern about one's responsibility according to rules from Stage 3, "shame" or concern about the diffuse disapproval of others. Stage 3 concern about disapproval is, in turn, a differentiation of Stage

45

1 and 2 concerns about overt reward and punishment characteristic of lower stages.

In a certain sense, the cognitive-structural component of guilt would be obvious if it had not been ignored in psychoanalytic theory. Guilt in its most precise sense is moral self-judgment, and it presupposes the formation of internal or mature standards of moral judgment. Psychoanalysts have assumed the early formation of internalized guilt, of self-punishment and self-criticism tendencies, and have generally assumed that this formation occurs in the early latency period, ages 5 to 7, as a reaction to the Oedipus complex. In fact, however, researchers who have used story completion tests of guilt reactions do not find open self-criticism and self-punishment tendencies appearing in response to transgression stories until preadolescence or late childhood. When asked, children under seven almost never say a deviant child who escaped punishment would feel bad. While young children do not show conscious guilt, they do project unrealistic punishment into incomplete stories of transgression. Psychoanalytically oriented researchers have assumed such punishment concerns reflect the child's unconscious guilt, projected out into the world because it is unconscious. In fact, no satisfactory evidence has been accumulated for thinking this is true, since punishment concerns do not correlate positively with other behaviors which might represent moral internalization. Both the punishment concerns of Stage 1 and the guilt of Stage 4 or Stage 6 represent anxiety about deviating from the rules, structured in different ways. In some sense, the feeling in the pit of one's stomach is the same whether it is dread of external events or dread of one's own self-judgment. The difference between the two is that in one case the bad feeling is interpreted by the child as fear of external sanctioning forces while in the other case, it is interpreted by the child as produced by the self's own moral judgments. When the child reaches adolescence, he tends to reject fear as a basis for conformity. If he is a member of a delinquent gang he will deny the anxiety in the pit of his stomach because it is chicken to fear the cops. If he has developed more mature modes of moral judgment, he will link the same dread in the pit of his stomach to his own self-judgments and say, "I could never do that, I'd hate myself if I did." The difference between the two is a cognitive-structural difference, not a difference in intensity or type of affect. The difference is a real one, however, since intense fear of punishment does not predict to resistance to temptation, whereas self-critical guilt does.

We have already noted that projective-test studies indicate that self-critical guilt appears at about the same age as conventional moral judgment. The coincidence in the age of appearance of projective guilt and of "mature" or conventional moral judgment suggests that the two should be correlated among individual children of a given age. (As stated, this was the third implication of the structural parallelism interpretation of our stages.) The clearest findings of correlation are those reported by Ruma and Mosher (1967). Ruma and Mosher decided they could avoid the many problems of measuring imaginary guilt by assessing guilt about real behavior through use of a population of thirty-six delinquent boys. Measures of guilt were based on responses to a set of interview questions as to how the boy felt during and after his delinquent acts (assault or theft). The primary measure was the sum of weighted scores for responses expressing negative self-judgment and remorse (2) as opposed to responses expressing concern about punishment (1) or lack of concern (0). The correlation between this measure and a moral maturity score based on stage-weighted ratings of response to each of six of our conflict situations was .47 ($p < .01$). This correlation was independent of age, IQ, or social-class effects. They also found a correlation of .31 ($p < .05$) between the life-situation guilt measure and the Mosher guilt scale, "...a sentence completion measure of guilt using referents suggested by the psychoanalytic conception of guilt" (Ruma & Mosher, 1967). The correlation of moral judgment maturity and the Mosher guilt scale was .55. Maturity of moral judgment ideology, then, related somewhat better to two measures of guilt—one real-life, one projective—than they do to each other.

With regard to moral emotion, then, our point of view is that the "cognitive" definition of the moral situation directly determines the moral emotion which the situation arouses. This point of view has been generally held by the "symbolic interactionist" school of social psychology, which has stressed that socially communicated symbolic definitions determine the actual felt attitudes and emotions experienced by the individual in given situations. The empirical findings supporting this general point of view are cumulative and striking, and constitute much of the core content of many social-psychology textbooks. One striking line of evidence is that on the effects of drugs on behavior. Naturalistic studies by sociologists clearly suggest that pleasurable marijuana experiences and marijuana "addiction" are contingent on learning the "appropriate" symbolic definitions of the experience (H. Becker, 1963). Experimental studies indicate that while autonomic stimulants elicit generalized arousal, whether such arousal is experienced as anger, elation, or some other emotion is contingent on the social definition of the situation attendant on administration of the drugs (Schachter, 1964).

In our view, the basic way in which "affect" is socialized is not so much by punishment and reward as it is by communication of definitions of situations which elicit socially appropriate affect. In addition, our approach points to certain fundamental and "natural" cognitive bases of moral emotion, and views cultural definitions as representing only certain selective emphases and elaborations of these bases. The utilitarians were almost certainly correct in emphasizing that the central basis of moral emotion is the apprehension of the results of human action for the pain and harm (or joy and welfare) to human (or quasi-human) beings. Our studies of moral judgment in a variety of Western and non-Western cultures indicates that the overwhelming focus of moral choice and feeling is such personal welfare consequences. The child's whole social life is based on "empathy," i.e., on the awareness of other selves with thoughts and feelings like the self. The analyses of the development of the self by Baldwin (1906) and G. H. Mead (1934) have clearly indicated that the self-concept is largely a concept of a shared self, of a self like other selves. The child cannot have a self-conscious self without having concepts of other selves. Perceived harm to others is as immediately, if not as intensely, apprehended as is harm to the self. Empathy does not have to be taught to the child or conditioned; it is a primary phenomenon. What development and socialization achieve is the organization of empathic phenomena into consistent sympathetic and moral concerns, not the creation of empathy as such.

Our view of the way in which moral values influence action is generally similar. We noted in our second section that socialization studies of "resistance to temptation" had provided few solid findings because "resistance to temptation" is largely situation-specific, as Hartshorne and May (1928-30) demonstrated. While low correlations between cheating in one situation and cheating in another are to be found, these correlations are not due to internalized moral values or standards in the usual sense. These correlations are largely due to nonmoral "ego strength" factors of IQ and attention, and the correlations between cheating tests disappear when these ego factors are controlled (Grim et al., 1968). Attention, measured as standard deviation of reaction time, has been found to correlate in the 50's and 60's with scores on cheating tests. Moral "values" or attitudes conceived as affective quanta in the usual social attitude sense do not predict directly to behavior in conflict situations. Half a dozen studies show no positive correlation between high school or college students' verbal expression of the value of honesty or the badness of cheating, and actual honesty in experimental situations. Undoubtedly part of this failure of correlation is due to "deceptive" self-report tendencies. The same desire leading to a desire to cheat to get a good score leads to an over-espousal of conventional moral values. However, the problem is deeper than this, since affect-intensity projective measures of guilt fail to predict resistance to temptation unless they include the cognitive-structural self-critical components already discussed. The real problem is that general intensity measures of espousal of moral attitudes have little relation to the forces determining behavior in concrete conflict situations.

When cognitive and developmental measures of moral judgments and attitudes are used, better results are obtained. While Hartshorne and May (1928-30) found only low correlations between these tests of conventional moral knowledge ($r = .30$) and experimental measures of honesty, the correlations were at least positive and significant. When my transcultural measure of moral maturity is employed, better results are obtained. In one study, correlations of moral judgment maturity with teachers' ratings of moral conscientiousness were .46, and with teacher ratings of fair-mindedness with peers were .54. In another study the correlation of moral maturity with peer ratings of moral character was .58. These correlations are not too clear in meaning since moral judgment is a clear age-developmental variable, whereas ratings of moral character are not. Clearer relations of judgment and action come if particular stages of moral judgment are related to theoretically meaningful types of moral decisions.

As an example, in the ordinary experimental cheating situations, the critical issue is whether to follow the norm when the conventional expectations of the adult and the group about not cheating are not upheld. The experimenter explicitly leaves the child unsupervised in a situation where supervision is expected. Not only does the experimenter indicate he does not care whether cheating goes on, he almost suggests its possibility (since he needs cheaters for his study). While the conventional child thinks "cheating is bad" and cares about supporting the authority's expectations, he has no real reason not to cheat if he is tempted, if the authorities don't care and if others are doing it. In contrast, a principled (Stage 5 or 6) subject defines the issue as one involving maintaining an implicit contract with the adult and reflects that the general inequality or taking advantage implied by cheating is still true regardless of the ambiguity of social expectations in the situation. As a result, it is not surprising to find that principled subjects are considerably less likely to cheat than conventional or premoral subjects. In a college group only 11 per cent of the principled students cheated as compared to 42 per cent of the conventional subjects. In a sixth grade group, only 20 per cent of the principled children cheated as compared to 67 per cent of the conventional children and 83 per cent of the premoral children.

In the studies mentioned, the critical break was between the principled and the conventional subjects. Another break occurs where the subject is faced with disobeying the rules formulated by an authority figure who is seen as violating the rights of another individual. An example is the Milgram (1963) obedience situation. In this situation the experimenter orders the subject to give an increasingly severe electric shock to a stooge "learner" who has agreed to participate in a nonsense-syllable learning experiment. In this study, only the Stage 6 subjects would be expected to question the authority's moral right to ask them to inflict pain on another. Stage 5, "social contract" subjects, would tend to feel the victim's voluntary participation with foreknowledge released them from responsibility to him while their agreement to participate committed them to comply. As expected, 75 per cent of a small group (6) of Stage 6 subjects quit as compared to only 13 per cent of the remaining 24 subjects at lower moral stages. Some replication of this result comes from preliminary findings of a study of the Berkeley students who did and did not participate in the original free speech sit-in. As expected, 80 per cent of the Stage 6 subjects sat in, as compared to 10 per cent of the conventional and 50 per cent of the Stage 5 subjects. A similar majority of the Stage 2 subjects also sat in, for different though predictable reasons (Haan, Smith & Block, 1969).

The studies just cited help to clarify the relative role of cognitive definitions and of affect-intensity in determining moral choice. We have seen that cognitive definitions determined cheating behavior whereas attitude-strength measures did not. In the Milgram (1963) situation, Stage 6 cognitive definitions determined choice but a projective measure of sympathy did not. High-empathy subjects were no more likely to quit than low-empathy subjects. In the Berkeley situation, Stage 6 subjects also chose to disobey authorities in the name of individual rights, but without concern for individual rights involving empathy for a concrete victim, supporting the interpretation that the Stage 6 decision to resist was not based on a quantitative affective base. Some tentative findings suggest that amount of empathy was influential in the conventional level subjects' decisions, though not in the principled's subjects' decision. Indeed the Stage 5 subjects were the most prone to say they wanted to quit but did not, i.e., they were restrained by contractual principles in spite of their empathic feelings. This interpretation of the affective and situational influence in the Milgram moral decision is similar to that just advanced for the cheating decision. When affectively or situationally strongly tempted, conventional subjects will cheat. Similarly, when empathy leads to strong "temptation" to violate the rules and authority of the experimenter, conventional subjects will quit (or when fear of the authority leads to strong temptation to violate conventional rules against hurting others, conventional subjects will comply).

The interpretation just advanced suggests that quantitative affective-situational forces are less determining of moral decisions at the principled than at the conventional level. This interpretation coincides with another cognitive-developmental interpretation as to the relation of moral judgment to moral action. It was noted that the "cognitive" traits of IQ and attention correlated with measures of honesty, even though honesty is not directly an age-developmental or a cognitive-developmental trait. Drawing upon Williams James' (1890) doctrine of the will as attention, our interpretation holds that IQ, and especially attention, enter into moral decisions as non-moral tendencies of "strength of will" or "ego strength" (Grim et al., 1968). In part, the moral neutrality of "ego strength" is indicated by the fact that attentive children simply are not tempted and hence need make no moral decision to resist temptation. Attentive children are not only more likely to resist temptation, but attentive non-cheaters are more likely to say that they did not think of cheating after temptation than are inattentive non-cheaters (Krebs, 1967). In part the moral neutrality of "ego strength" or "will" is also indicated by the fact that while "strong-willed" conventional subjects cheat less, "strong-willed" premoral subjects cheat more (Krebs, 1967). Among conventional Stage 4 children, only 33 per cent of the "strong-willed" (high IQ, high attention) cheated as compared to 100 per cent of the "weak-willed" (low IQ, low attention). In contrast among the Stage 2 "instrumental egoists," 87 per cent of the "strong-willed" children cheated whereas only 33 per cent of the "weak-willed" children cheated. Presumably the weak-willed Stage 2 children were tempted (distracted and suggested) into violating their amoral "principles." At the principled level, however, resistance to temptation is less contingent on "strength of will," and hence is also less contingent on situational-affective forces of a sort irrelevant to their moral principles. All of the children at the principled stage were low on attention, yet only 20 per cent cheated.

In summary, then, while moral judgment maturity is only one of many predictors of action in moral conflict situations, it can be a quite powerful and meaningful predictor of action where it gives rise to distinctive ways of defining concrete situational rights and duties in socially ambiguous situations. The causal role of moral judgment appears to be due to its contribution to a "cognitive" definition of the situation rather than because strong attitudinal or affective expressions of moral values activate behavior. To a certain extent, it is no more surprising to find that cognitive moral principles determine choice of conflicting social actions than it is to find that cognitive scientific principles determine choice of conflicting actions on physical objects. Moral principles are essentially believed by their holders to define social "laws" or realities just as physical principles are felt to define physical laws or realities. This is true less in the abstract than in the concrete definition of the situation. While the "value of trust and contract" sounds like an empty abstraction, the principled subject's awareness that the experimenter in the cheating situation trusts him is concrete and real and is an awareness missing at lower stages.

In terms of implication for research strategy, the findings suggest that situational action is not usually a direct mirror of structural-developmental change. Once structural-developmental change has been assessed by more cognitive methods, however, it is possible to define structural-developmental changes in situational behavior, e.g., consistent non-cheating becomes a "milestone" behavior for Stage 5. Whether the milestones are reached first in action (consistent non-cheating) or in judgment (Stage 5) is an open empirical question.

V. CONCEPTUALIZING SOCIAL ENVIRONMENT IN TERMS OF ROLE-TAKING OPPORTUNITIES AND STRUCTURAL MATCH

We stated in Section I that an understanding of hierarchical interactional stages depends upon analyses of (1) universal structural features of the environment, (2) the order of differentiations inherent in given concepts, and (3) relations between the structure of specific experiences and the child's behavior structures, defined in terms of conflict and match. The universal structural features of the environment relevant to moral stages are partly those of the general physical environment since moral stages presuppose cognitive stages. At the first moral stage, the regularities of the physical and the social environment are confused and the basis of conformity to social laws is not much different than the basis of conformity to physical laws. More fundamentally, however, there are universal structures of the social environment which are basic to moral development. All societies have many of the same basic institutions, institutions of family, economy, social stratification, law, and government. In spite of great diversity in the detailed definition of these institutions, they have certain transcultural functional meanings. As an example, while the detailed prescriptions of law vary from nation to nation, the form of "law" and the functional value of its importance and regular maintenance are much the same in all nations with formal law.

In addition to common institutions, however, all societies are alike in the sheer fact of having institutions, i.e., in having systems of defined complementary role expectations. In cognitive-developmental or "symbolic-interactional" theories of society, the primary meaning of the word "social" is the distinctively human structuring of action and thought by role-taking, by the tendency to react to the other as someone like the self and by the tendency to react to the self's behavior in the role of the other (Mead, 1934; Baldwin, 1906; J. Piaget, 1948). There are two subsidiary meanings of "social," the first that of affectional attachment, the second that of imitation. Both human love and human identification, however, presuppose the more general sociality of symbolic communication and role-taking. Before one can love the other or can model his attitudes, one must take his role through communicative processes (Mead, 1934; Kohlberg, 1966b). The structure of society and morality is a structure of interaction between the self and other selves who are like the self, but who are not the self. The area of the conflicting claims of selves is the area of morality, or of moral conflict, and the modes of role-taking in such conflict situations represent the varying structures of moral judgment and choice defining our various stages. Role-taking itself represents a process extending beyond the sphere of morality or of conflicting claims. Moral role-taking itself may have many affective flavors, as our discussion of attitudes of empathy, guilt, disapproval, and respect suggested. Basically, however, all these forms imply a common structure of equality and reciprocity between selves with expectations about one another. Our moral stages represent successive forms of reciprocity, each more differentiated and universalized than the preceding form.

We have discussed the logical ordering of the stages in terms of the differentiation of twenty-five specific moral categories or aspects. However, we take as primary the categories of reciprocity and equality, e.g., the categories of justice, as these are used to define social expectations and rules. The most primitive form of reciprocity is that based on power and punishment, i.e., the reciprocity of obedience and freedom from punishment. Next (Stage 2) comes literal exchange. Then comes a recognition (Stage 3) that familial and other positive social relations are systems of reciprocity based upon gratitude and the reciprocal maintenance of expectations by two social partners. At Stage 4, this develops into a notion of social order in which expectations are earned by work and conformity, and in which one must keep one's word and one's bargain. At Stage 5, the notion of social order becomes a notion of flexible social contract or agreement between free and equal individuals, still a form of reciprocity (and equality). At Stage 6, moral principles are formulated as universal principles of reciprocal role-taking, e.g., the Golden Rule or the categorical imperative "So act as you would act after considering how everyone should act if they were in the situation." In other words, at the conventional level, the social order is felt to embody the structures of reciprocity defining "justice," whereas at the principled level the social order is derived from principles of justice which it serves. Principles of justice or moral principles are themselves essentially principles of role-taking, i.e., they essentially state "act so as to take account of everyone's perspective on the moral conflict situation" (Mead, 1934). At the principled level, then, obligation is to the principles of justice lying behind the social order rather than to the order itself, and these principles are principles of universalized reciprocity or role-taking.

If moral development is fundamentally a process of the restructuring of modes of role-taking, then the fundamental social inputs stimulating moral development may be termed "role-taking opportunities." The first prerequisite for role-taking is participation in a group or institution. Participation is partially a matter of sheer amount of interaction and communication in the group, since communication presupposes role-taking. In addition, the centrality of the individual in the communication and decision-making structure of the group enhances role-taking opportunities. The more the individual is responsible for the decision of the group, and for his own actions in their consequences for the group, the more must he take the roles of others in it. It has sometimes been held that the subordinate takes the role of the superior more than vice versa (Brim, 1958). If true, this is true only at the level of the dyad. The group leader must role-take all the subordinate's roles and be aware of their relations to one another, while the subordinate is only required to take the role of the leader. It is likely that leadership positions require not only more complex or organized role-taking but more affectively neutral objective and "rules and justice" forms of role-taking, since the leader must mediate conflicts within the group, as Parsons and Bales (1955) have claimed is the case for the "father" or "instrumental leader" role. While leadership roles might be expected to require more role-taking than follower roles, it is also likely that "democratic leadership" requires more role-taking than "autocratic leadership" on the part of both leader and follower, since the group leader must be more sensitive to the members' attitudes, and the members will engage in more communication with the leader and have more responsibility for the group decision, as Lippett and White's (1943) studies suggest.

For the developing child, there is presumably a rough sequence of groups or institutions in which he participates. The first, the family, has received the most attention in socialization theories. From our point of view, however, (1) family participation is not unique or critically necessary for moral development, and (2) the dimensions on which it stimulates moral development are primarily general dimensions by which other primary groups stimulate moral development., i.e., the dimensions of creation of role-taking opportunities. With regard to the first point, there is no evidence that the family is a uniquely necessary setting for normal moral development. An ordinary orphanage is a poor setting in terms of role-taking opportunities so it is not surprising to find institutionalized retardates more retarded in moral judgment development than control retardates living with their families. On the same Piaget (1948) measures on which institutionalized children are more backward than children in families, however, kibbutz children are equal to city children living in families. In general kibbutz children are "normal" in moral development in spite of marked reduction in amount of interaction with their parents. In Section II, we pointed out that bad families contribute heavily to delinquency, and it may be noted that delinquency is associated with a low level of moral judgment development. The fact that bad families lead to moral arrest and moral pathology does not imply, however, that a good family is necessary for moral development. While parental rejection and use of physical punishment are both negatively correlated with moral internalization and moral stage-development measures, this again is indicative of the negative rather than the positive influence of the family. Extremely high warmth and complete absence of punishment do not seem to be particularly facilitating of moral development. With regard to the second point, the positive dimensions of family interaction contributing to moral development seem understandable in terms of role-taking opportunities. Hostility and punishment obviously do not facilitate the child's taking of his parents' role. Peck and Havighurst (1960) report that ratings of maturity of moral character are related to ratings of common participation in the family, to confidence sharing, to sharing in family decisions, and to awarding responsibility to the child, a cluster well summarized under the rubric of "role-taking opportunities." As cited earlier, Hoffman and Saltzstein (1967) found "inductive discipline" associated with moral internalization. Inductive discipline, i.e., pointing out to the child the consequences of his action to others and his own responsibility for it, would seem to represent a form of creating moral role-taking opportunities.

With regard to my own measure of moral maturity, a study by Holstein (1968) indicates that parental provision of role-taking opportunities in moral discussion is a powerful predictor of moral judgment at age 13. Holstein taped discussions over revealed differences in moral opinions on hypothetical situations between mother, father and child for 52 suburban middle-class families. Parents who encouraged their child to participate in the discussion (i.e., who were rated as "taking the child's opinion seriously and discussing it") tended to have relatively mature or conventional-level (Stage 3 or 4) children. Seventy per cent of the encouraging parents had conventional children, while only 40 per cent of the non-encouraging parents had conventional children. Amount of paternal and maternal interaction with the child (play, discussion, affection) was also related to the child's moral level.

The second group in which the child participates is the peer group. While psychoanalysts have taken the family as a critical and unique source of moral role-taking (e.g., identification), Piaget (1948) has viewed the peer group as a unique source of role-taking opportunities for the child. According to Piaget, the child's unilateral respect for his parents, and his egocentric confusion of his own perspective with that of his parents, prevents him from engaging in the role-taking based on mutual respect necessary for moral development. While the empirical findings support the notion that peer-group participation is correlated with moral development, it does not suggest that such participation plays a critical or unique role for moral development. Peer-group isolates matched for social class and IQ with children highly chosen by their classmates tend to be quite markedly slower in moral development than the leaders. This slowness, however, is not particularly manifested as an arrest at Stage 1, more or less equivalent to Piaget's heteronomous stage. In particular, peer-group participation is not especially facilitative of development on the moral dimensions focused upon by Piaget, as opposed to other dimensions of moral development. Indeed no differences have been found on measures of intentionality between sociometric stars and isolates, or between kibbutz (peer-group centered) and city children. In summary, then, while peer-group participation appears to be stimulating of moral development, its influence seems better conceptualized in terms of providing general role-taking opportunities rather than as having very specific and unique forms of influence.

A third type of participation presumed important for moral development is that of participation in the secondary institutions of law, government and, perhaps, of work. One index of differential opportunities for participation in the social structures of government and of work or economy is that of socioeconomic status. It is abundantly clear that the lower class cannot and does not feel as much sense of power in, and responsibility for, the institutions of government and economy as does the middle class. This, in turn, tends to generate less of a disposition to view these institutions from a generalized, flexible and organized perspective based on various roles as vantage points. The law and the government are perceived quite differently by the child if he feels a sense of potential participation in the social order than if he does not. The effect of such a sense of participation upon development of moral judgments related to the law is suggested by the following responses of sixteen-year-olds to the question, "Should someone obey a law if he doesn't think it is a good law?" A lower-class boy replies, "Yes, a law is a law and you can't do nothing about it. You have to obey it, you should. That's what it's there for." (For him the law is simply a constraining thing that is there. The very fact that he has no hand in it, that "you can't do nothing about it," means that it should be obeyed—Stage 1.)

An upper middle-class boy of the same IQ replies, "The law's the law but I think people themselves can tell what's right or wrong. I suppose the laws are made by many different groups of people with different ideas. But if you don't believe in a law, you should try to get it changed, you shouldn't disobey it." (Here the laws are seen as the product of various legitimate ideological and interest groups varying in their beliefs as to the best decision in policy matters. The role of law-obeyer is seen from the perspective of the democratic policy-maker—Stage 5.)

Studies of moral judgment development in Taiwan, Mexico, the United States (where class groups were matched on IQ), and Turkey indicate that middle-class and lower-class urban males go through the same stages and that the lower class is more retarded in development than the middle class. Retardation is more marked when the lower class is more impoverished (Mexico, Turkey) than where it is more stable economically (United States, Taiwan). Development of Negro slum groups is more like that found in Mexico than that found in the stable upper lower-class American group.

To some extent, differences between peasant village and urban groups may also be viewed as representing differential opportunities for role-taking and participation in secondary institutions. The Mexican, Turkish, and Taiwanese villager grows up with a sense of participation in the village, but little in the more remote political, economic, and legal system. To a considerable extent, age progressions of development are similar to those of the lower-class urban males except for a total, rather than relative, failure to attain the more generalized stages of moral principle, and except for less tendency toward adult fixation at a morally alienated (Stage 2) level.

These findings contrast with many sociological notions as to how group memberships determine moral development. It is often thought that the child gets some of his basic moral values from his family, some from the peer group, and others from his social-class group, and that these basic values tend to conflict with one another. Instead of participation in various groups causing conflicting developmental trends in morality, it appears that participation in various groups converges in stimulating the development of basic moral values, which are not transmitted by one particular group as opposed to another. The child lives in a total social world in which perceptions of the law, of the peer group, and of parental teachings all influence one another. While various people and groups make conflicting *immediate demands* upon the child, they do not seem to present the child with basically conflicting or different stimulation for *general moral* development.

The examples of role-taking opportunities just elaborated are essentially specifications of the general belief that the more the social stimulation, the faster the rate of moral development. These theories do not account for specific transitions from stage to stage or to eventual fixation at a particular stage. Such explanation requires theories of structural conflict and structural match, extensively elaborated in the moral domain by Turiel (1969). The problem posed by stage theory is that the stimulus inputs received by the child are usually either assimilated to his own level or are not perceived as stimuli at all. As an example, a Stage 2 delinquent is offered "role-taking opportunities" by an understanding psychotherapist, but these opportunities are perceived as opportunities to "con a sucker" and do not stimulate development beyond Stage 2. In the Rest studies (Rest, 1968; Rest et al., 1969), it was found that there was a strong tendency to assimilate higher level moral judgments to the subject's own level or one below it. The problem of moral change would appear to be one of presenting stimuli which are both sufficiently incongruous as to stimulate conflict in the child's existing stage schemata and sufficiently congruous as to be assimilable with some accommodative effort.

With regard to the assimilation of moral judgments made by others, the "match" notions just presented suggest that there would be maximal assimilation of moral judgments one level above the subject's own. The rationale for this was made clear in the discussion of the Rest studies of the hierarchy of comprehension and preference for the six stages (see p. 379 ff.). To test this "match" hypothesis, Turiel (1966) divided sixth-grade children (themselves equally divided by pretests among Stages 2, 3 and 4) randomly to one of three treatment groups. The treatments consisted of exposure to advice by an adult E on two hypothetical moral conflict situations. The first treatment group received advice one stage above their own, the second two stages above their own and the third one stage below their own. The children were post-tested one month later on both the pretest and the treatment situations. Turiel found a significant increase in usage of thinking one stage above in the plus-one treatment group. He found no significant increase in usage of thinking two stages above in the plus-two treatment group. He found an increase in usage of thinking one stage below in the minus-one group, but this increase was significantly less than the increase of plus-one thinking in the plus-one treatment group.

Turiel's laboratory study has received naturalistic validation from Blatt's (1969) program of classroom discussions of moral dilemmas held once a week for three months at the sixth-grade level. Blatt's procedure was to elucidate the arguments of the Stage 3 children as against the Stage 2 children on hypothetical moral conflicts, then to pit the Stage 3's against the Stage 4's, and finally to himself present Stage 5 arguments. The effect of this procedure was to raise 45 per cent of the children up one stage (as compared to 8 per cent in a control group), and 10 per cent up two stages. A majority of the Stage 2 subjects moved to Stage 3, a majority of the Stage 3 subjects to Stage 4. There was very little movement from Stage 4 to the Stage 5 level presented by the teacher.

One reason the Blatt study induced more change than the Turiel study was because the discussions were carried on over a greater time period. The Blatt procedure also differed in inducing greater conflict through disagreement. Presumably a sense of contradiction and discrepancy at one's own stage is necessary for reorganization at the next stage. A series of studies by Turiel (1969) are systematically exploring the role of such cognitive-conflict parameters in moral judgment change.

Findings on "match" in parent influences on moral development are still ambiguous. No relationship has been found between the moral level of fathers and of their children (Kramer, 1968; Holstein, 1968). A clear relationship between mother's level and the level of her child (of either sex) has been found by Holstein. While 50 per cent of 41 mothers at a conventional level had premoral (Stage 1 or 2) children, none of 12 principled mothers had children at this low level. From a direct transmission or social learning point of view, there is no reason why conventional mothers should be less effective in transmitting (their own) conventional moral ideology to their children than principled mothers. The one-above hypothesis also does not account for the superiority of principled mothers in stimulating movement from the premoral to the conventional level. It may be that it is the match of the principled mothers' action, not their judgment, which is crucial to this effect.

The problem of "match" is not only a problem of the assimilation of moral statements by others but a problem of the assimilation of their actions. With regard to actions, the slum child may well interpret the behavior of policemen, teachers, and gang buddies as being based on his own Stage 2 individual behavior and exchange conceptions. It may be that if the boy also has a bad family, in the Gluecks' (Glueck & Glueck, 1950) sense, there is no model of altruistic Stage 3 action to generate either conflict in his Stage 2 schema or any Stage 3 moral material to be assimilated. The problem of match is also a problem of assimilation of the child's own behavior to his moral ideology. Freedman (1965) has stressed the accommodation of moral attitudes to actual behavior in the service of reduction of cognitive dissonance, where moral attitudes are defined in the "non-predictive" sense discussed earlier. Our developmental conception is one in which cognitive balance is not so simple and in which cognitive dissonance can lead to reorganization upward or downward. However, no work has yet been done on moral behavior—moral ideology relations—from this perspective.

In summary, then, a theory of "match" in morality should account for the effect of inputs of moral judgment and moral action at particular stages. In its broadest sense the match problem is the problem of the fit of the individual's ideology to his world. Stage 2 "fits" a slum or jail world, Stage 4 fits the traditional army world, Stage 5 fits the academic and bureaucratic worlds. In this regard, the changes of "world" characterizing adult socialization may require the same types of theoretical analysis as those of childhood.

VI. EXPERIMENTAL STUDIES OF SOCIAL LEARNING AND STRUCTURAL-DEVELOPMENTAL CHANGE

In Section II, we suggested that the major rationale for conducting naturalistic studies of socialization rested on the assumption that personality development involved structural change and that the effects of early experience upon behavior are relatively permanent, irreversible and different in kind than are the effects of experience upon behavior change in adulthood. We noted that theories of socialization based on general learning theories typically do not make such assumptions about structural change. It is not surprising, then, to find that socialization theorists oriented to general principles of learning have turned away from naturalistic studies to studies involving the experimental modification of situational behavior. It is also not surprising to find that these studies have shown social-learning principles to be powerful predictors of behavior, while the naturalistic studies have not. The discrepancy between the degree of support for social-learning theory coming from experimental and from naturalistic findings may be explained on two grounds. The first is that the long-run effects of natural socialization inputs upon structural change require different principles of explanation than are applicable to short-run situational change. The second is that there is no such thing as long-run structural change, and the short-run situational changes explained by social-learning theories cancel each other out so as not to yield long-range predictions at the trans-situational and longitudinal level explored by the naturalistic studies of personality. Because the methodological ambiguities of the naturalistic studies are great, most social-learning theorists have not taken a clear position on this issue, but have tended to dismiss the findings of the naturalistic studies as too weak methodologically to require detailed explanation.

With regard to the actual experimental studies, some seem designed with the assumption that there is no such thing as structural change in development. Others seem to be asserting that some behavior changes have more "structural" properties than other behavior changes, but that these changes, too, are explicable by the general principles of learning. As discussed earlier, the empirically minimal properties of structural change are a considerable degree of stability or irreversibility of the change (e.g., resistance to extinction or counter-conditioning) and a considerable degree of generalization of the change to situations not manifestly similar to the situations in which change was initially induced.

The simplest type of study based on the first assumption is one showing that conditioning can change or mimic behavior having a label the same as that employed in a structural theory. An example is Azrin and Lindsley's (1956) study of the "learning of cooperation." Cooperation is thought of by Piaget and others as a natural and relatively irreversible developmental trend resulting from the child's differentiation of his own "egocentric" perspective from that of others. Parten and Newhall (1943) provide considerable support for this "structural" view of cooperation since they find regular relationships of naturalistically observed cooperation to chronological and mental age, and considerable day-by-day or situational stability to the child's level of cooperation. Azrin and Lindsley conducted a training study inducing "cooperation," apparently to demonstrate that cooperation was a product of operant learning. Their operational definition of cooperation was the matching of one child's placement of a stylus to the other's placement, such matching being a contingency for receiving a candy. Needless to say, the children's rate of stylus matching increased after reinforcement and extinguished after non-reinforcement. The reversibility of the learning of the response, then, indicated that no structural change was induced. No transfer of training was tested, nor was there any definition of what the term "cooperation" might mean in terms of some generalization dimension. ("Sharing" of the reinforcer was not even involved as a learning dimension in the study, from the outset the children shared.) The study, then, leads only to the conclusion that children will adjust the placement of a stylus in such a way as to receive a reinforcer, but this finding does not appear to have any theoretical significance for the problem of structural change in development.[3]

A second type of social-learning approach to developmental structure is

---

[3] The positive side of these studies emerges where the behavior studied is of obvious practical significance. Thus Baer and his coworkers (Baer, Peterson & Sherman, 1967) demonstrate that specific problem behaviors of preschool children are amenable to replacement with more positive behavior by operant techniques. In light of the tendencies of teachers to inappropriately define annoying behavior as representing pathological personality structures and to respond accordingly, these studies have obvious usefulness. However, except in their impact upon the evaluation of the child by others, the Baer manipulations are presumably as structurally irrelevant to the child's personality development as are the Azrin and Lindsley (1956) induction of changed stylus behaviors in their children.

exemplified by Bandura and MacDonald's (1963) experimental induction of changes in Piagetian moral judgment. It is not quite clear whether the intent of the study was to explain structural change in social-learning terms or to demonstrate that Piaget's (1948) behavior definitions did not have any structural component.

The first intent would imply that Piaget had correctly identified a response with some structural properties but had employed a faulty "maturational" theory to explain its development, which could be better explained by social-learning processes. The second intent would imply that Piaget had incorrectly attributed structural properties to his moral stage measures, either because his methods were poor or because moral judgment responses have no structural properties. Piaget (1948) himself believed that his moral judgment stages are structural in the sense that (1) they represent "structural wholes," i.e., a constellation of traits indicative of global heteronomous or autonomous attitudes toward rules, and (2) that they constitute a relatively irreversible sequence. According to Piaget, one index of the child's stage location is that of his judgment in terms of intentions or consequence when the two conflict, e.g., judging it is worse to break ten cups while washing the dishes than one cup while stealing candy. Bandura and MacDonald (1963) tested second grade children on a series of these items and found some were "at the autonomous stage" (judged in terms of intentions) while some were "at the heteronomous stage." Children at each stage were then exposed to reinforced models emitting the opposite type of judgment. Bandura and MacDonald found substantial learning of the opposite type response. Not only was a "higher stage" readily learned, but it generalized to some new items. Learning was about equal whether it was "progressive" or "regressive." The apparent conclusion to be drawn from the study is that intentionality is learned by ordinary reversible social-learning mechanisms, and that the age trends in intentionality found by Piaget correspond to a learning of the adult cultural norms.

The findings from a number of other studies warn us against accepting these conclusions at face value. Some of these findings come from experimental studies of the training of conservation (reviewed in Sigel & Hooper, 1968; Kohlberg, 1968). Almost all of these studies have given great attention to the issue of whether the behavior changes induced by training are "structural" or not. "Structural change" has been assessed by:

1. the degree of generality or transfer of conservation (e.g., conservation of liquid to conservation of solids to conservation of number);
2. the degree of irreversibility of conservation in the face of training or trick demonstrations designed to induce non-conservation.

While the findings are somewhat conflicting, the following conclusions emerge (Kohlberg, 1968):

1. "Naturally" developed concepts of conservation are quite generalized (i.e., there is a general "conservation factor" in conservation tests).
2. Naturally developed concepts of conservation are quite irreversible.

3. Conservation is difficult to teach by ordinary learning methods to children at an appropriate readiness "age" and almost impossible at younger ages.
4. When taught by some methods, conservation shows some generality and irreversibility. In this it deviates from the specificity and extinguishability of most social-learning study changes. At the same time, however, taught conservation is far less generalized and irreversible than natural conservation.

In light of these findings, the ready reversibility of moral judgment responses in the Bandura and MacDonald (1963) study is suspicious. How are the discrepancies between the ease of learning or unlearning of Piaget's (1948) moral judgment and the difficulty of learning Piaget's (1947) conservation to be accounted for? One answer would be that cognitive tasks (e.g., conservation) do involve structural development but that social or moral tasks do not, but simply involve the learning of cultural values. A second answer would be that morality is an area of structural development, but that Piaget's concepts and methods for defining structure are not as adequate in the moral field as are his concepts and methods in the area of logical operations.

A number of facts point to the validity of the second rather than the first conclusion.[4] Our review of the findings with our own moral stages indicated that they did have structural properties. Our review also indicated that the studies of Turiel (1966) and of Rest et al. (1969) yielded quite different results than those of the Bandura and MacDonald study. "Social learning" of the stage above the child's own was much greater than learning of the stage below the child's own. The discrepancy, however, was one of preference and assimilation not of cognitive learning, since children recalled the one-below arguments better than the one-above arguments.

The Turiel studies (1966, 1969), then, suggest that moral judgment is an area of structural development, but that Piaget's concepts and methods are not good measures of structure in this area. The Kohlberg (1969) assessment method involved classifying open-ended responses into one of six stage categories, whereas Piaget's (1948) assessment involved asking children to choose between two prepackaged alternatives, e.g., "Was John who broke one cup or Charles who broke ten cups worse?" This facilitates children's social learning of the content of the "right answer" without necessarily implying development of awareness of the structure underlying the right answer. Furthermore the Piaget stories do not reveal awareness or unawareness of intentions in moral judgment, but simply how much these are weighted against consequences. Age-developmental studies indicate an awareness of the modifying role of intention among almost all children of the age of the Bandura and MacDonald subjects. Some limitation of the role of intention, as opposed to consequence, is involved even in

---

[4] The points made here are elaborated and documented in the discussions of replications of the Bandura and MacDonald (1963) study made by Crowley (1968) and Cowen, Langer, Heavenrich and Nathanson (1968).

judgment of adults, who consider it worse to kill someone in a car accident by negligence than to purposefully and malevolently insult someone. Accordingly, the shifts in the Bandura and MacDonald study do not represent an actual learning or "unlearning" of a basic concept of intentions, but a learning to weigh them more or less heavily as opposed to consequence. Piaget asserts that awareness of intention is "structural" in the sense that it represents advance on one of eleven dimensions defining the autonomous stage of moral judgment. However, empirical studies reviewed elsewhere (Kohlberg, 1963a, 1969) indicate that children of a given age who are mature on Piaget's tests of intentionality are not more mature on the other Piaget dimensions of the morally autonomous stage, i.e., there is no general Piaget moral stage factor (while there is a general moral stage factor in the various Kohlberg situations and dimensions).

In summary, then, Piaget's definitions of moral judgment responses do not meet the naturalistic criteria of structural stages and hence social-learning manipulations of these responses do not indicate that moral judgment is not structural nor do they indicate that social-learning operations can account for structural development. A hypothetical comparison may clarify the basic point. Bandura and MacDonald's (1963) intent was analogous to operant manipulations of a behavior, such as guilt-strength, which is considered structural in psychoanalytic theory. The theoretical futility of such efforts is self-evident, since the psychoanalyst always says the behavior changed is not structural, and is not what they would term "real guilt," regardless of the outcome of the study. In the moral judgment case, however, the issue of the structural nature of the variable is an empirically definable matter, not an issue of what Piaget's theory might be assumed to say, and this line of experimentation can eventually lead to some conclusions.

Our comparison of the Turiel and the Bandura and MacDonald studies indicates, then, that prior naturalistic study of structural aspects of development is required before experimental manipulations can lead to conclusions about structural development. The contrast between the intent of the Bandura and MacDonald study and that of the experimental studies of conservation is enlightening. The conservation studies assume the existence of structural development and manipulate inputs in order to accelerate such development. The purpose of such studies is to allow us to conceptualize the conditions for cognitive structural change, not to reduce explanations of structural change to explanations developed for other purposes. It is hard to believe that experimental studies of socialization will not take on the same intent soon.

The Bandura and MacDonald (1963) study suggests an additional positive goal for studies manipulating developmental responses besides the goal of accelerating development common to the conservation studies. While Piaget's measures of intentionality are not direct assessments of "structural" stages, they do reflect some natural or cross-culturally universal trends of development. Age trends toward intentionality have been found in every literate culture studied (Switzerland, Belgium, Britain, Israel, United States, Taiwan) as well as in all but one preliterate or semi-literate culture studied (Atayal, Hopi, Zuni, Papago, Mayan, Sioux) (Kohlberg, 1969). Accordingly, the social learning processes exemplified by the Bandura and MacDonald "backward" manipulations are not only distinguishable from the processes naturally leading to the development of intentionality, but they are in partial conflict with them. The same statement may be made about the Turiel (1966) study which did induce some learning in the one-below condition. This type of learning may not be unusual in actual social life. An extreme natural example offered earlier was the Atayal adolescent's social learning of "regressive" dream beliefs. Perhaps another, more artificial, example is provided by the Milgram (1963) obedience study in which the subjects may "learn" from an authority that it is right to shock people in certain situations.

In our discussion of the Atayal dream concept, we suggested that the "social learning" of such regressive beliefs was not smoothly superimposed upon the child's previous cognitive structure, but engendered conflict and doubt in the child or to his other "natural" beliefs. A study by Cowen et al. (1968) suggests that the regressive learning in the Bandura and MacDonald study involved some such conflict and that this learning had somewhat different properties than progressive learning. In one part of their study, Cowen et al. replicated the Bandura and MacDonald findings. Their study also involved a more extensive test of the generality and stability of the learning involved. Such tests indicated that the downward learning was less stable over time than the upward learning as expressed in the decline of use of the model's downward moral reasons (consequences) in a two-week delayed post-test for the regressive group, in contrast to no such decline in retention of the model's reasons in the upward-learning group. This discrepancy between upward and downward reasoning was especially marked for new, as opposed to retest, items. In addition, the authors note that for both learning groups almost all learning took place in the first two trials, that learning seldom went above the 60 per cent criterion, and that the children seemed extremely confused and uncertain as to their reasons after the learning trials. Rather than smooth change following the general laws of learning, the children seemed to have been confronted with the fact that a social authority contradicted their own notions. Their long-range response to this contradiction varied according to whether the authority espoused a view above or below the child's own. In summary, then, the study of the effects of social influence upon responses at various developmental levels may contribute an understanding to that vast border line of socialization in which both cultural learning processes and cognitive-structural processes influence one another.

VII. SOCIAL-LEARNING STUDIES AND THE CONCEPT OF INTERNALIZATION

The social-learning studies considered so far have been primarily efforts to deny, rather than to explain, structural-developmental change. The work of Aronfreed and others, however, represents a positive effort to explain structural-developmental change within the general principles of associationistic theories of social learning. As Aronfreed's discussion in this volume suggests, structural-developmental change is usually defined by social-learning theorists as "internalization." According to Aronfreed,

> The young child's behavior is initially highly dependent on its experience of external events which are transmitted through the presence and activity of its socializing agents. But its behavior gradually comes to be governed, to a considerable extent, by internal monitors which appear to carry many of the functions of the external controls originally required to establish the behavior (Aronfreed, 1969, p. 263).

The concept of internalization is an attractive one since it seems to define basic structural-developmental changes in a way amenable to experimental investigation. As an example, Aronfreed finds that mild experimental punishment will lead children to resist touching attractive toys even in the absence of an adult monitor, and that this punishment is more effective if it is closely timed to follow onset of the touching act. Aronfreed interprets this effect as the result of classical conditioning of anxiety directly to internal proprioceptive cues of incipient action (as opposed to the conditioning of anxiety to external cues of punishment). Such an experimental induction of internalization seems analogous to the basic processes of natural socialization designed to produce reliable conformity in the absence of sanctions. It also seems analogous to the natural developmental trend in children toward increased self-government, self-control or ego strength. When the analogy to self-control is considered carefully, however, it becomes clear that the child conditioned to feel anxiety over kinesthetic cues of incipient action has no more made a gain in self-control than has the dog conditioned in a similar fashion or the child whose conditioned anxiety represents a phobia. Self-control implies control and inhibition of action by an organized self or ego with cognitive representations of itself and the world, and with an intelligent flexibility as to the cues and conditions of inhibition or release of action. Insofar as inhibition of action is determined rigidly by the paradigms of classical conditioning, it indicates the absence of self-control in the usual sense.

If internalization as experimentally studied has not represented the formation of new structural mechanisms of self-control, neither has it represented structural-developmental change itself. As Aronfreed notes, there is little evidence that experimental inductions of resistance to temptation have the situationally general and irreversible character of structural-developmental change. The sheer fact that a child will follow instructions without someone in the room is itself no evidence that something more than reversible situational learning has been induced. It is clear, then, that experimental inductions of "internalization" cannot be considered to represent the induction of structural-developmental change in the absence of direct evidence of situational generality and irreversibility of such learning.

We have claimed that the experimental studies of internalization have not actually studied either the acquisition of new mechanisms of self-control or the formation of irreversible trans-situational learning, and hence do not really shed light on any process of "internalization" distinct from the general processes of reversible situation-specific learning. In this regard, they are no different than the naturalistic studies of internalization discussed earlier. The experimental studies have operationally defined internalization as degree of conformity to the experimenter's instructional or modeling behavior. As indicated earlier, naturalistic studies of moral internalization have also defined it in conformity terms, i.e., as behavioral, affective, or cognitive conformity to the moral standards of the child's culture. As another example, sex-role "internalization" has been studied in terms of "masculinity-femininity," or "sex-role identification," i.e., in terms of tests of conformity to statistically modal responses of males as opposed to females in the child's culture (studies and measures reviewed in Kohlberg, 1966b).

In our earlier discussion, we noted that these naturalistic measures of moral internalization did not seem to represent measures of structural change any more than did the measures used in experimental studies of internalization like Aronfreed's. The naturalistic measures also appeared to be situation specific and longitudinally unstable (i.e., reversible). The same is more or less true of measures of "sex-role internalization" (evidence reviewed in Kohlberg, 1966b). In essence, we argued that conformity definitions of response were inadequate to define structural change in development because they ignored sequential changes in the shape or patterning of responses.

We must ask, then, in what sense the internalization concept is useful in the definition of structural-developmental change. It is evident that natural moral development is grossly defined by a trend toward an increasingly internal orientation to norms. Our moral stages, as defined by the aspect of sanctions in Table 6.6, clearly represent increasing interiorized orientations to moral norms moving from a concern for sanctions to a concern for praise and blame to a concern for internal principles. This stage conception of internalization is similar to that stated by McDougall (1908) in the first textbook of social psychology:

> The fundamental problem of social psychology is the moralization of the individual into the society into which he is born as an amoral and egoistic infant. There are successive stages, each of which must be traversed by every individual before he can attain the next higher: (1) the stage in which the operation of the instinctive impulses is modified by the influence of rewards and punishments, (2) the stage in which conduct is controlled in the main by anticipation of social praise and blame, (3) the highest stage in which conduct is regulated by an ideal that enables a man to act in the way that seems to him right regardless of the praise or blame of his immediate social environment.

There are certain fundamental differences in this stage concept of moral internalization and the conformity concept, however. In the first place while "internality" is an essential component of McDougall's idea of mature morality, this internality is not defined relative to degree of conformity to a cultural standard, as in a resistance-to-temptation study. Rather it is defined in terms of an "ideal enabling a man to act in a way that seems to him right regardless of praise or blame." This ideal hardly needs to be an internalized cultural standard. When Luther said, "Here I stand, I can do no other," he represented McDougall's highest stage but he was not conforming to an internalized cultural standard of any recognizable sort, since the ideal was self-formulated. In practice, then, the developmentalist is arguing that we can tell whether the norm an individual is following is "moral" or "internal" by looking at the way in which the individual formulates the norm, i.e., its form, and without reference to a specific external cultural standard. A cultural norm, common especially in the lower class, is "stay out of trouble." It is clear that such a norm cannot be held as a moral ideal by an individual regardless of the processes of "norm-internalization" to which the individual is exposed. Our own position is that the only fully internal norm is a moral principle, and that a moral principle (our Stage 6) is definable according to a set of formal attributes which are culturally universal.

The first point brought out by the stage conception, then, is that internality is merely part of the conception of a moral orientation rather than being a general socialization dimension definable without reference to the concept of a moral orientation. The distinction between moral principles and other cultural standards is just that one is not expected to have as fully an internalized orientation to other cultural standards. Moral principles are categorical imperatives, all other standards are hypothetical imperatives contingent on the individual's aims in the situation. The young child may first require admonition and punishment to brush his teeth and eventually brush his teeth without sanctions. In the adult, such an "internalized" orientation of the norm of toothbrushing is quite different from an internalized orientation to a moral norm. If the adult forgets his toothbrush when travelling, he feels no obligation to brush his teeth nor any guilt for failing to do so. He will justify his toothbrushing instrumentally and selfishly (it prevents cavities and keeps his teeth clean) rather than because of respect for the rule or principle of toothbrushing. In sum, then, moral internalization in the sense of development of moral principles cannot be equated with some general dimension of social-norm learning.

The meaning of internalization in the moral domain also makes clear a second point implied by the stage position, which is that internalization must imply cognitive as well as affective correlates. The man in the street knows that a dog or an infant can be trained to refrain from eating meat powder when hungry even in the absence of surveillance by the socializing agent but refuses to consider such conformity "moral." Likewise, the dog's deviance is not considered immoral nor does it arouse moral indignation, because the dog is not considered moral. The dog is neither moral nor immoral "because he doesn't know right from wrong." When the dog has "internalized" the rule to refrain from eating meat powder, it is not because he is "acting in terms of an ideal that seems to him right regardless of praise or blame," but because he has not correctly discriminated the occasions where punishment is likely from those where it is not. The animal or infant has no concept of a rule which is guiding his behavior but instead is responding to cues in the physical or social situation to which he has been aversively conditioned. Children acquire conceptions of rules by age 5-6, but it is not until adolescence that children cognitively formulate moral principles in McDougall's sense of ideals guiding the self's behavior regardless of external social or authoritative support.

In summary, then, there is a sense in which socialization agents hold as their goal the development of internalized moral standards in the young and there is also a sense in which the development of internalized moral standards is a "natural" trend regardless of the specific expectations and practices of socialization agents. Neither the expectations of socialization agents nor the natural trends of development are well defined by a conformity conception of internalization, however. This is apparent in the case of Western adults who do not define moral internalization as behavioral conformity to the cultural code, but rather as the development of a morality of principle which is above actual conformity to cultural expectations. The existence of such parental expectations for socialization "above the culture" must in turn arise from parental recognition of partly natural or autonomous developmental trends in the formation of an internal morality.

Socialization analyses have tended to take an ethnographic description of the content of adult cultural expectations as defining the end point and direction of the socialization process, apart from natural age trends. It is obvious that there is some gross match between trends of age-development and adult expectations in any culture, or the culture would hardly be transmitted. This gross correspondence, however, may as much represent the shaping of adult expectations by developmental realities as the shaping of developmental progressions by adult expectations. There is, we believe, common meaning to the image of maturity guiding socialization in any culture, an image largely reflecting universal and natural trends of social development. In our contemporary culture this core of common meaning is generally called "ego maturity" or "ego strength." There are a large number of competencies expected of adults in our culture which psychologists include in this rubric. The most general of these capacities are those for love, work, and morality. There can be little question that middle-class American socialization expectations are more centrally oriented to the development of such basic capacities than they are to the teaching of detailed conformity to the set of specific and culturally arbitrary definitions of behavior in specific roles defined by the ethnographer or the sociologist. It seems likely that there are culturally universal or near-universal values suggested by the words "love," "work," and "morality," and that these values recognize natural developmental trends and progressions. The development of moral capacities (as well as capacities to work and to love) involves an orientation to internal norms, but this development cannot be defined as a direct internalization of external cultural norms.

If the student of socialization ignores these maturity components of social development in favor of simpler conformity or internalization concepts he will not only fail to describe "natural development" correctly but he will fail to describe the aims and expectations of socialization agents correctly. As a result he will fail to understand the socialization process insofar as this process is essentially a matching (or mismatching) of the developmental expectations of the parent and the developing capacities of the child.

VIII. IMITATION AS A FUNDAMENTAL PROCESS IN SOCIAL DEVELOPMENT: BALDWIN'S THEORY

In the preceding sections, we have argued that the enduring products of socialization must be conceived of in terms of cognitive-structural changes with "natural" courses or sequences of development rather than in terms of the learning of culture patterns. These changes are results of the general processes of cognitive development as these restructure conceptions of the social self, the social world, and the relations between the two. While cognitive, these processes responsible for social development are theoretically different from those responsible for development of physical concepts because they require role-taking. Since persons and institutions are "known" through role-taking, social-structural influences on cognitive-structural aspects of social development may be best conceived in terms of variations in the amount, kind and structure of role-taking opportunities.

In order to tie our conceptions of role-taking to notions of socialization "processes" (of motivation and learning), we shall now elaborate a cognitive-developmental account of processes of imitation and identification. As we indicated earlier, role-taking is a broader term than imitation, but in our opinion all role-taking has imitative components or roots. At the adult level, however, we do not overtly imitate, we "role-take."

In our earlier discussion of the Bandura and MacDonald (1963) study of modeling of moral judgment, we indicated some of the ways in which imitation did not help explain structural development. Is there a sense in which it does? J. M. Baldwin (1906) and Piaget (1951) have postulated that imitation is a natural and active tendency in the human infant, and that this tendency is necessary to account for the infant's cognitive and social development.

One sense in which Baldwin and Piaget have claimed that imitation was an explanatory principle of development is the sense in which they equate imitation with a basic functional tendency they call "accommodation." As stated by Baldwin, "Reaction of the imitative type is the original form of mental accommodation to the environment" (1906, p. 528). We will not elaborate this difficult conception here beyond suggesting some of its intuitive rationale. It is clear that imitation involves a cognitive copying process. There is a sense in which any cognition is a copy of a part of the environment, since an image or symbol has a relation of "likeness to" an environmental object or structure. In Baldwin's and Piaget's view, representation or imagery then implies a distinctive active copying tendency, since they believe all images and representations are forms of action, not passive redintegration of sensations (as introspective associationism and psychoanalysis claimed).

Whatever one's views as to the role of imitation in the development of cognitive representation, there can be little question that imitation is an extremely basic mechanism in the formation of social knowledge. Struck by such phenomena as sociodramatic play, there is hardly a writer concerned with the problem of how the child comes to know his society who has not been struck by the place of the child's imitative or role-taking tendencies in the growth of such knowledge.

Baldwin's view that the child's knowledge of society develops at first through imitation seems to be saying little more than the social-learning truism that the child's knowledge of society grows through the observational learning of the behavior of others (learning, which translated into performance, is termed "imitation"). The more distinctive feature of Baldwin's view is that such imitation provides the structure of the child's social relationships, i.e., of his self as it relates to other selves. In the social-learning view of imitation, it is a matter of little moment whether a response is learned by imitation or by reinforced trial and error since it functions in the same way once learned. In contrast, Baldwin argues that imitation is important because it determines the structure of the child's self-concept, and of his concepts of others, a structure, in turn, determining the use of the behavior pattern learned through imitation.

According to Baldwin,

> the growth of the individual's self-thought, upon which his social development depends, is secured all the way through by a twofold exercise of the imitative function. He reaches his subjective understanding of the social copy by imitation, and then he confirms his interpretations by another imitative act by which he ejectively leads his self-thought into the persons of others (1906, p. 527).

Baldwin's central claim (made also by Mead [1934]) is that the child's self-concept and his concept of other selves necessarily grow in one-to-one correspondence. The child cannot observationally learn the behavior pattern of another without putting it in the manifold of possible ways of acting open to the self. Once it becomes something the self might do, when others do it, they, too, are ascribed the subjective attitudes connected with the self's performance of the act.

As stated by Baldwin,

> What the person thinks as himself is a pole or terminus and the other pole is the thought he has of the other person, the "alter." What he calls himself now is in large measure an incorporation of elements that at another period he called another. Last year I thought of my friend, W., as someone with skill on a bicycle. This year I have learned to ride and have imitatively taken the elements formerly recognized in W's personality over to myself. All the things I hope to learn to become are, now, before I acquire them, possible elements of my thought of others.
>
> But we should note that when I think of the other, I must construe

him as a person in terms of what I think of myself, the only person whom I know in the intimate way called "subjective." My thought of my friend is not exhausted by the movements of bicycling, nor by any collection of such acts. Back of it all there is the attribution of the very fact of subjectivity which I have myself. I constantly enrich the actions which were at first his alone, and then became mine by imitation of him, with the meaning, the subjective value, my appropriation of them has enabled me to make (1906, pp. 13-18).

According to Baldwin, then, there are two intertwined mechanisms of society, of sharing. The first is imitation of the other, the second is "ejection," i.e., empathy or "projection" of one's own subjective feelings into the other. Imitation of the other not only leads to a changed self-concept (e.g., a self who rides the bicycle), but it leads to a changed concept of the other because the activity (bicycle-riding) has a new meaning after it is done by the self, and this meaning is read back as part of the other.

The basic starting point of any analysis of the growth of social knowledge, then, must be the fact that all social knowledge implies an act of sharing, of taking the viewpoint of another self or group of selves. This fact is paralleled on the active side by the fact that all social bonds, ties, or relationships involve components of sharing. The word "social" essentially means "shared." The motivational problem usually proposed to socialization theory is the question of why the "selfish" or impulsive infant develops into a social being, i.e., one who wants to share activities with others, to share goods with others, to be a member of a common group, to maintain shared norms, and to pursue shared goals. The answer of developmental theory is that the self is itself born out of the social or sharing process, and therefore, motives for self-realization or self-enhancement are not basically "selfish" in the perjorative sense, but require sharing. Developmental theory, then, presents a radically different picture of the birth of social motives than do all other theories. Other theories have assumed that social motives are either instinctive or result from the association of socializing agents and their behavior with gratification and anxiety to the child. In contrast, developmental theories assume a primary motivation for competence and self-actualization which is organized through an ego or self whose structure is social or shared.

Two basic psychological mechanisms of sharing have been proposed by developmental theory, "role-taking" and imitation. Baldwin (1906) and Mead (1934) engaged in extensive written debate as to the relative priority of the two mechanisms in social development. Baldwin viewed similarity of self and other as directly striven for through imitation, whereas Mead viewed it as the indirect result of role-taking involved in communicative acts. The child's attitude, he thought, became like that of the other because both respond alike to a common symbol or gesture. Because the child has responded in the past to the other's gesture, when he makes the gesture himself, he calls out in himself implicitly the response he calls out in the other. Mead further points out that much sociality, much mutual role-taking, occurs through cooperative interaction in which each individual's role is different, in which roles are complementary rather than similar. Nevertheless, the study of infancy indicates that similarity to others is directly striven for, and that such striving or imitation precedes, rather than follows, the development of linguistic communication. Accordingly, it seems to us that Mead's conceptions must be embedded in a broader developmental account of the self which includes early imitative behavior and the matrix of infant cognitive development out of which the self emerges.

Like Mead, Baldwin was struck by the fact that the younger child's social interaction is structured in terms of dyadic complementary roles, and that young children tend to play out both sides of these complementary roles as a mechanism of self-development. As stated by Mead,

> The child plays that he is offering himself something, and he buys it; he gives himself a letter and takes it away; he addresses himself as a parent, as a teacher; he arrests himself as a policeman. He has a set of stimuli which call out in himself the sort of response they call out in others. A certain organized structure arises in him and in his other which replies to it, and these carry on the conversation of gestures between themselves (1934, pp. 150-151).

According to Baldwin also, the basic unit of the self is a bipolar self-other relationship, with a resulting tendency to play out the role of the other, i.e., the child either has an "imitative" or an "ejective" attitude toward another person. When the child is imitating or learning from the other, his attitude is one of "accommodation," i.e., his behavior is being structured by the structure of the behavior of the other. It is a matter of little import whether the child's action is structured by the other in the form of spontaneous imitation or in the form of instruction or command. A modeling is taken as an implicit command, and an explicit command can always be modeled (i.e., "Do it this way," accompanied by a demonstration). In either case, the structure of the activity belongs to both parties, but it is being passed on from the active to the passive one. The central focus is upon a novel structure which the active agent has which the passive agent does not.

In contrast, the active or assimilative self is one which knows what it is doing, and which ejects its own past attitudes into the other. Whether the child is active or passive, there is a focus upon an activity of one person with an attitude of accommodation to it in the other. The attitude of the child practicing something he has already learned through imitation or compliance, then, is always different than the attitude he held in the process of learning it. In learning an activity associated with the superior power or competence of the adult, the child's attitude is accommodatory and, in that sense, inconsistent with the prestigeful activity being learned. Accordingly, the child tends to turn around and practice the activity on, or before the eyes of, some other person whom he can impress, into whom he can "eject" the admiration or submissiveness he felt when learning the act.

The actual "ejective" phase of self-development appears to first develop in the second year of life. At that age, the child seems to attribute feelings to others and to show things to, and communicate with, others. At the end of the second year, a "negativistic crisis" (Ausubel, 1957) typically occurs. This is a phase in which self and other are sharply differentiated and the difference between copying the self and copying (or obeying) the other are sharply distinguished. An example of the counter-imitation of this era is a 2½-year-old's consistent response of "Not goodbye," when someone said "Goodbye" to him.[5]

Interestingly, however, it is just at this age of "independence" that the child acquires a need for an audience, a need reflected in "look at me" or attention-seeking behavior. Indeed, it is striking to notice that "look at me" behavior often is a phase of imitative acts at this developmental level. The father takes a big jump, the same 2½-year-old imitates, and then demands that the father look at him just as he looked at the father in imitating. Imitation immediately placed the child in the model's role, and led him to eject into the adult his own capacity for admiration.

Thus Baldwin would account for the "show-and-tell" behavior of the 3-4-year-old as the reverse form of the sharing involved in the initial imitative act. Imitation, then, generates social sharing at both the learning and the practicing phase. Seeking to act competently almost always requires another person for the imitative young child. First, the child needs another self as a model of what to do. Second, because he has learned from a model, he needs to practice what he has learned on another self, e.g., to be a model to another.

Much of the show-and-tell behavior of the preschool child shades over into "private" or "egocentric" speech (Kohlberg, Yaeger & Hjertholm, 1968) which accounts for about a third of the preschool child's verbal output. Mead would explain such speech by the need to tell another person what one is doing in order to establish its meaning for the self, a meaning which requires "taking the role of the other" toward the self's activity. According to Mead, the self needs an audience to be a self, to establish the meaning and value of its own action. Eventually, this audience becomes an internal and abstract "generalized other," but first it is the concrete other of the egocentric dialogue.

In spite of these differences in emphasis, Baldwin and Mead would agree that the preschool child's need to show and tell others about his activities reflects the egocentric "ejection" of the subjective component of the bipolar self upon another to establish the meaning of the self's activity, an interpretation far different from the usual "dependency motive" interpretations of attention-seeking.

An experiment by Emmerich and Kohlberg (1953) provides some crude support for Baldwin's analysis in that it suggests the bipolarity of the imitative and the audience-seeking and egocentric-speech tendencies in the child. The study is discussed further in Section XIII in that it indicated both of two experi-

---

[5] This negativism about imitation and obedience is paralleled by a negativism about receiving help, the insistence on "doing it oneself." A typical expression was the same child's insistence that a coat be put back on him so he could take it off himself after it had been removed by a helpful adult.

mental conditions, prior negative criticism by an adult E and prior helpfulness, equally led to high imitation by kindergarten children in contrast to a no-interaction condition. These conditions which led to high imitation were, however, the exact opposite of those which led to high audience-seeking and egocentric speech. The "no prior interaction" condition elicited the most such speech in contrast to both of the conditions eliciting imitation. This negative association between the situations eliciting imitation and those eliciting social speech was reflected in negative correlations between situational change scores in the two types of social behavior. Children who went down in social speech (compared to a pretest baseline) were high in imitation, those who went up in such speech were low in imitation ($r = -.34$). This negative association between the situational conditions eliciting imitation and the conditions eliciting audience-seeking speech does not mean that children who imitate do not engage in social speech. In fact the two go together as developmental or personality dispositions, as Baldwin's analysis (as well as others) suggests. The correlation between pretest audiencing speech and subsequent imitation was .45. The negative association was rather between the occasions for audiencing and imitative behavior as bipolar tendencies, not between the two of them as general social dispositions.

Age-developmental studies suggest that look-at-me attention-seeking precedes the seeking of approval from others. It is clear that the child who shows off to the adult the act he has just learned from him will not seek the adult's approval. As the child matures, he recognizes that imitation of the act does not make him as competent as the model, and that performance of one competent act still leaves the adult a generally superior performer. As the child acquires a stable sense of the superiority of the older model, "look at me" after imitation becomes the request for approval, "did I do it right?" Baldwin's (1906) account, then, suggests that much of the need for approval is born from the fact that most of the child's accomplishments are imitative. Almost everything the young child strives to do or accomplish is something he sees another person do first and which he learns, in part, imitatively. The young child's accomplishments, his talking, walking, dressing himself, toileting, etc., are all activities that he sees others do and knows they can do. Because they are his models for activity, their approval of his performance counts.[6]

Following Baldwin, then, we may propose that the motivational basis of social reinforcement is to be found in the child's imitative tendencies, his tendencies to engage in shared activities. The child's "look at me" behavior is not so much a search for adult response as it is a search for confirmation of social or imitative learning. Insofar as the desire for approval arises developmentally out of "look at

---

[6] The interpretation just advanced reverses social-learning accounts of the relations between imitation and social approval. Gewirtz (1969) notes, like Baldwin, that almost every behavior which socialization requires is a behavior children see others do first. Accordingly, says Gewirtz, when a child is rewarded for a step in socialization, he is also being rewarded for imitating, and so a generalized habit of imitating is born. In a subsequent section, we consider this argument in more detail.

me" behavior, it, too, is not a sign of some more concrete reward which the child seeks. As we elaborate in a subsequent section, the child's dependence on social reinforcement is heaviest at the developmental stage where he is concerned with "doing things right" but has no clear internal cognitive standards of what is right and so must rely on the approval of authorities to define "right" behavior. The child's initial desires to perform competently, to succeed, rest on intrinsic competence motivation. The infant struggles to master a task without the least concern for adult reward for performing the task, and without the least concern for the adult's judgment as to whether or not he is doing it right. Social development up until age 6-7 is not a matter of internalizing "extrinsic" social reinforcement into intrinsic competence motivation; rather it is a process of growing sensitivity to external social definers of standards of competence, and in that sense an increased sensitivity to "extrinsic" social reinforcement. This increased sensitivity, in turn, is the result of a growing sense of dependence upon having a social model of performance. The tendency to imitate, to seek a model of performance, itself rests primarily upon intrinsic competence motivation, upon the "need" to act or function. The child's fundamental motive in imitation is expressed in the familiar cry, "what can I do?" Relying on models to do something interesting and effective, he comes to feel increasingly that he must rely also on them to tell him "how he is doing." In this view, competence motivation engenders imitation which engenders social dependency through an increased sense of discrepancy between the child's own activities and the norms embodied in the activities of his models.

In Baldwin's account, the development of the imitative process into social dependency, the need for approval, is also part of the development of imitation into "identification," into the combination of attachment, admiration, and desire for normative guidance which forms a focus of the child's attitude toward his parents. Identification as discussed by Baldwin is a constellation of attitudes similar to that termed "satellization" by Ausubel (1957). Ausubel distinguishes between an imitative "incorporatory" attitude and a "satellizing" attitude. An incorporative child is a general imitator, he is always ready and eager to imitate any interesting or prestigeful model, because such imitation is a primitive form of self-aggrandizement, of getting something the model has or sharing his prestige. In contrast, the satellizing child is loyal to his past modelings of his parents and to their expectations, and will pass up the opportunity to copy the new prestigeful response of the model. In fact, Ausubel et al. (1954) predicted and found that "imitative" or "suggestible" copying of the preferences of a prestigeful model was negatively correlated with satellizing attitudes toward parents.

The distinctions between an "incorporatory" and a "satellizing" attitude are suggested by the following examples:

Incorporatory — Boy, aged 4, to male adult interviewer, "You're twice as big so you have twice as much brains. I'm going to knock your brains out, and then they'll go in my brains and I'll be twice as smart."

Satellizing — Boy, aged 12, asked about his father: "I'd like to be like my father because I think of him as nice and I was brought up by him and learned the things he taught me so I could be a good boy because he always taught me to be good."

Boy, aged 15: "I try to do things for my parents, they've always done things for you. I try to do everything my mother says, I try to please her. Like she wants me to be a doctor and I want to, too, and she's helping me to get up there."

It is clear that the examples cited illustrate different cognitive and moral levels of thought. Since the four-year-old's thinking is concrete and physicalistic, becoming like another involves a transfer of body contents.[7] In contrast, the older boy's conceptions are based on psychological likenesses through processes of teaching and conformity to expectations. Furthermore, the admired quality of the model has shifted from power and smartness to moral goodness.

These identification statements are "moral" in a double sense. First, the content of what is to be shared with, or learned from, the parent is a moral content. The parent both models and expects the good. The boy wants to be like the model in the ways expected by the model. Second, the reasons for identifying with the parent are moral. The boy wants to be like the parent because the parent is good, and the boy wants to be good. More specifically, however, to become good is to give something to the parent to whom one owes something, because what the parent wants is for the child to be good.

As we discuss later, the development of such "moral identifications" presupposes the development of moral thought already discussed. At the same time, however, Baldwin (1906) points out that these identifications rest on a sense of a shared self built up because the child feels he shares with the adult everything that he has learned from him. This sense of a normative shared self Baldwin terms "the ideal self" and equates it with moral conscience. As we have seen, Baldwin says that the bipolar self involves an active, assertive, controlling self and a passive, submissive, imitative self. The child may be either as occasion arises. With a younger child or a parent in a permissive mood, the child himself defines what is to be done and the other is merely an object to be manipulated, an agent in terms of whom the action may be carried out. With an older person or in a novel situation, the child expects to be the object in terms of which action determined by the other is carried out.

Whether the self determining the child's action is the other (the adult) or the child himself that is "selfish," it is a bipolar self, not a shared or sharing self. The act of adjusting to or obeying the adult need not imply an experience of self-control and unselfishness by the child since the self controlling the child and demanding sacrifice of his wishes is not his own self. Though the child's action may be determined by the dominating self of the other, still that other self is conceived by the child in its own image as a basically impulsive or need-gratifying self (insofar as motives are assigned to it at all). The experience of unselfish

---

[7] In our opinion, it is the concrete bodily nature of the young child's thought and the resulting magical and destructive notion of becoming like another by physical possession which makes early identification "incorporative," rather than such identification being the result of the child's domination by oral libido.

obligation requires that the two selves be identified or unified with one another, an integration which is not achieved by motives to imitate or obey in themselves.

How does such a concept of a shared self which wants to be good and to conform to rule arise? The experience required, says Baldwin, is one in which the child perceives the parent as putting pressure on the child to conform to something outside the parent. Such an experience is not bipolar since the parent wants the child to be like himself vis-a-vis his attitude toward the rule. The parent's self is seen as simultaneously commanding (the child) and obeying (the rule). Thus initiating action and conforming are seen as both parts of the same self, a self-controlling self.

Such conformity to a third force might simply be perceived by the child as indicating that a third person dominates the parent as the parent dominates the child. However, the fact that such pressure to conform goes on in the absence of the third person or authority tends to give rise to the concept of a generally conforming self. In addition, the fact that the conformity is shared in the family or group gives rise to a sense of a common self which the child is to become.

Originally such a general or ideal self is largely in the image of the parents. It is ideal to the child, it is what he is to become, but it is largely realized in the parents. This does not mean that there is no differentiation of parents from the rule; the parents are seen as obeying the rule. It does mean that the image of a good, conforming self which obeys the rules tends to be in the parent's image.[8]

In summary, Baldwin holds that in the years three to eight, the child develops from seeing interaction as governed by bipolar self-other relations to seeing it as governed by rules. These rules are shared by both members of the self-other dyad. As "ejected" into others in the course of action, they are what Mead (1934) termed "the generalized other," the common rules and attitudes shared by the group. As these rules are felt as governing the self, but as being imperfectly known and followed by the self, they are the "ideal self." The sense of the rule-following self, "the ideal self," is more personal and more closely equated with the parent than is the system of rules themselves, "the generalized other."

Baldwin's concepts imply that as the child develops a sense of himself as a "good boy" governed by shared rules, his relations to others are increasingly dominated by a sense of himself as a "good boy" whose relations of sharing with others (especially those close to him) are based on this common "goodness," this common "ideal self." His non-moral forms of self-aspiration (his desire to be a powerful, strong, clever self) are neither ideal nor a basis for sharing, and in that sense are not an "ideal self." Given the formation of an ideal self, then, it determines forms of social relationship as well as regulating moral behavior.

---

[8] By experience of conflict between models and by perception of their failure to incarnate the rule, the self which is the child's model becomes recognized as abstract and impersonal and is embodied as conscience, according to Baldwin (1906). In this sense, however, a morality of principle is still based on identification, but an identification with a set of principles (or a principled self) rather than another person.

As an example of the role of the ideal self in social relations, one might cite the state of "being in love" as conventionally (or romantically) defined. All psychological analyses of love, including the psychoanalytic, agree that it involves a relationship of identification (or sharing between selves) involving idealization of the other, and a sense of being governed by an unselfish or sacrificial concern for the love object. In other words it involves a sense of sharing based on the ideal self, not the concrete self.[9]

In spite of the obvious scope and suggestiveness of Baldwin's and Mead's theories of the role of imitation and role-taking in the function of the social self, these theories have been almost completely neglected by research child psychologists. The remainder of this chapter will attempt to elaborate these concepts, to compare them with more familiar psychoanalytic or social-learning concepts, and to document them in terms of research findings.

IX. GENERAL COMPARISON OF COGNITIVE-DEVELOPMENTAL, PSYCHOANALYTIC AND SOCIAL-LEARNING CONCEPTS OF IDENTIFICATION

It is apparent that Baldwin's cognitive-developmental view of moral development and identification has similarities to the psychoanalytic view in which moral "internalization" is the result of a process of parental "identification," i.e., a motivated transfer of norms outside the self-system into the boundaries of the self-system, a process located in the years four to eight by both Baldwin (1906) and Freud (1938).

In the cognitive-developmental account, however, the notion of "moral internalization" does not imply a simple and literal transfer, incorporation, or internalization of something outside the ego to something inside. Assimilation of the "outside" to "inside" depends upon the structural reorganization of the external norm and upon structural reorganization of the self assimilating the norm. At the earlier stages of valuing (Stage 1), cultural standards and values are oriented to as labels of good and bad external physical events and actions (e.g., punishment and other bad happenings) and the self's pursuit of values lies in the avoidance of "bad" physical events and objects. By Stage 3, cultural standards are conceived of as "internal" in the sense that they are defined as internal psychological dispositions or virtues in the self and moral expectations

---

[9] The role of "ideal self" identifications in social relations is clearest at the "good boy–good girl" stage of morality. It is not surprising to find that girls achieve good girl (Stage 3) morality earlier than boys and persist in it longer, so that most adult Stage 3 persons are female (Kohlberg, 1969). Girls move to this position faster (and perhaps stay there longer) because they are forced to differentiate the prestige of goodness from the prestige of power in defining their own roles. In any case, girls focus upon a "good girl" ideal-self morality and this focus is associated with an emphasis on love relationships of the sort described, often prefigured in an idealized relation to the father, first found in girls at age 7-8, rather than in the "Oedipal" (3-5) period (Kohlberg, 1965, 1966b).

(and virtues) in others, and the self is defined as "someone trying to be a good person." At this conventional level, however, values are still seen as depending upon some actual social relations of sharing, upon a concrete social order with actual shared expectancies. The standard is contingent upon its being held and maintained by others, and upon approval and disapproval by others. Only at the stage of principle, rather than at the stage of identification with authority, are norms oriented to as fully internal, in the sense of resting upon a basis of self-selection (and ideal universality or the capacity to be shared) rather than upon actual sharedness.

The cognitive-developmental view holds that the development of morally relevant identifications is a relatively advanced phase of development of the imitative process, and accordingly, that a theory of identification with parents must be part of a much broader account of the development of imitative processes in general. Psychoanalytic theories of parent identification are obviously unsuitable to deal with the bread-and-butter phenomena of imitation which constitute the basis of much of the child's ordinary situational and reversible social learning. As Bandura points out in this volume,

> According to the (neo-psychoanalytic) theories of identification reviewed, in order to get a boy to emulate a baseball player such as Mickey Mantle, it would be necessary for the youngster to develop an intense attachment to the brawny model who would then withhold affectional responsivity. Or the youngster would have to develop strong incestuous desires towards Mrs. Mantle and hostile rivalrous feelings toward the slugger (p. 233).

Of course, psychoanalytic theories of identification were not designed to account for such phenomena of imitation, and presuppose a sharp distinction between identification as a process of structural change in the personality and ordinary imitation. Occasionally psychoanalytic writers use examples of the child's daily imitations as exemplifying principles of identification (e.g., Anna Freud's [1946] child who plays dentist out of "identification with the aggressor"), but in so doing run the risk of the absurdities Bandura mentions. Essentially, psychoanalytic identification theory has no detailed way of dealing with daily imitation and presupposes a theoretical discontinuity between processes of imitation and processes of identification.

In the research literature (Kohlberg, 1963a), it has been customary to distinguish between identification (as structural change) and imitation according to the following empirical criteria of structure:

1. In identification, modeling is generalized and trans-situational. A variety of behaviors and roles are reproduced in a variety of situations. In imitation, modeling is of specific behaviors in specific situations.
2. In identification, modeling is persistent and occurs in the absence of the model.
3. In identification, performance of the modeled behavior appears to be

motivated intrinsically. It persists in the absence of any obvious reinforcement to which it is instrumental.

4. In identification, performance of the modeled behavior is relatively
   irreversible or non-extinguishable even when it is non-reinforced or
   punished.

In research practice, these distinctions between identification and imitation
have been assumed rather than observed, in the sense that a paper and pencil
measure of similarity between the child's self-concept and his concept of his
parent is assumed to have the structural properties mentioned, while an experimental measure of imitation of a strange experimenter is assumed not to have
these properties. Given the fact that distinctions between identification and
imitation have been assumed rather than studied, it is fair to say, as Bandura does
in this volume, that a review of the research literature gives no support for the
notion of two distinct realms or processes of modeling, one of "deep" identification and the other of superficial imitation. Bandura, as well as Aronfreed and
Gewirtz, argue that the distinctions between imitation and identification are not
distinctions between processes but rather represent a continuum of stimulus,
response, and reinforcement generalization of processes of imitative learning
which have the same basic social-learning antecedents whether they are situation-
specific or whether they appear to be generalized and functionally autonomous.

The cognitive-developmental approach would agree with these writers in
seeking theoretical continuity between the two and in rejecting general theories
of identification which cannot directly handle the phenomena of imitation. The
developmentalist diverges from the social-learning analyst in holding that while
many of the *functions* and causal antecedents of imitation and identification are
continuous, the cognitive-*structure* characteristics of phenomena of imitation and
identification are different and discontinuous.[10] In considerable part, the differences customarily implied by the terms "imitation" and "identification" are
differences in the developmental level of structure implied by the two terms. In
distinguishing between continuity of function and discontinuity of structure, the
developmentalist is employing a familiar strategy. Stages of morality, stages of
intelligence, etc., all imply a continuity of function (e.g., moral value-judgment)
together with a discontinuity of the structures (moral stages) fulfilling those
functions. Piaget (1951) has attempted to employ this strategy to define the
early stages of imitation. In Piaget's view imitation is defined functionally

---

[10] It is evident that either the psychoanalytic or the cognitive-developmental conceptions of identification-internalization presuppose a self-concept or ego with boundaries. Since
associationistic social learning postulates no self-system, the concept of identification cannot
be meaningful within it. In Aronfreed's (1969) treatment, "internalization" refers to the
operation of a variety of learning mechanisms (some cognitive, some simple conditioning)
which can lead to relatively permanent response-patterns, but does not presuppose an ego
or identification processes. The cognitive-developmental theory assumes, like psychoanalysis,
that the ego's judgment of perceived similarity between self and other are basic structural
components of attitudes of identification, but, unlike psychoanalysis, assumes these are
conscious cognitive judgments.

(primacy of accommodation over assimilation) in a continuous fashion, but each new stage of intelligence or cognition leads to new stages of imitation.

The cognitive-developmental view of identification differs from the psychoanalytic in the following regards:

1. Identification is viewed as a cognitive-structural stage of more general imitative or social-sharing processes.
2. Accordingly it is not uniquely dependent upon particular motives and ties only present in the early parent-child relationship.
3. Identifications are not totally fixed, irreversible, or "internalized." Identifications are "solutions" to developmental tasks which may change in object or nature with new developmental tasks.

It was said that the cognitive-developmental account distinguishes identification (generalized enduring modeling and perception of a portion of the self as shared with the parents) from imitation, but makes the distinction relative and one of developmental structure, rather than of dichotomous processes. In the cognitive-developmental account, however, enduring tendencies to model are only one component of a larger constellation of attitudes termed "identification" or "satellization." The constellation includes the following components:

a) tendencies to imitate the parent or other model,
b) emotional dependency and attachment to the parent,
c) tendency to conform to the parent's normative expectations,
d) perceived similarity to the parent,
e) idealization of the parent or of his competence and virtue,
f) vicarious self-esteem derived from the parent's competence or status,
g) ability to derive self-esteem from the parent's approval and so to forego other sources of prestige or competence, with associated security of self-esteem, moderate level of aspiration, etc.

This constellation is believed to develop more or less gradually in the "latency" years (4-10) in most (but not all) "normal" children, and to wane or decline with the growth of independence in adolescence. Accordingly the constellation is a major component in the definition of a later childhood stage of ego development in the theories of Baldwin, Ausubel, Loevinger and myself.[11]

The existence of such a constellation of attitudes has received considerable support from the research literature. Correlations between affectional attachment responses (wanting to be with the parent), imitation responses, perceived similarity responses, and awarding of authority and competence are consistently reported in the literature and are all related to parental nurturance (evidence reviewed in Kohlberg, 1966b). These attitudes toward parents (though not

---

[11] The major alternative focus for defining this era of social development has been Piaget's (1948) and H. S. Sullivan's (1953) focus upon development of "Stage 2" peer attitudes of egalitarian competition, cooperation, and exchange as opposed to the development of "Stage 3" attitudes of identification, approval-seeking, loyalty, and gratitude toward parents. I have argued that both develop in this era, but that there is typically a hierarchical and unified (rather than conflicting) relation between these two foci of development.

specifically to the same-sex parent) are also correlated with acceptance of the conventional moral code or of parental moral expectations, and to self-report measures of adjustment (evidence reviewed in Kohlberg, 1963a, 1966b). Furthermore, it seems fairly clear that whatever major "positive" or "socialized" contribution to development is made by identification dispositions is based on this constellation. While perceived similarity and affectional reactions to parents are jointly tied to acceptance of the moral code and to self-rated adjustment, measures of dispositions to play adult or same-sex role are not (evidence reviewed in Kohlberg, 1963a, 1966b). In other words, it is not so much that moral content is internalized by identification as it is that the identifying attitude is a "moral" attitude of conformity to shared expectations.

We have referred to satellizing or developmental identification as a constellation of attitudes of attachment, imitation, and conformity to the expectations of the model. This is because definite causal priorities are not definitely implied by a cognitive-developmental identification theory. Insofar as these three attitudes are linked in other theories, such causal sequences are assumed. Anaclitic identification theory (Sears, 1957) assumes a sequence in which (1) parental nurturance (and nurturance withdrawal) causes (2) identification (modeling) which causes (3) the internalization of parental moral expectations. While single causal sequences are oversimplified, the developmental view stresses that the desire to model the adult leads to attachment and social dependency, rather than the reverse, a theme taken up at length in Section XIV.

The cognitive-developmental concept that imitative attitudes support and stimulate a dependency relationship is quite different in its implication than are psychoanalytic theories of identification which suppose that it is primarily a form of substitution for the relationship to the other person by acting upon the self in the role of the other. As a relationship of sharing with another person, developmental identification is not as fixed, "internalized," or self-directed as is implied by psychoanalytic concepts. In its moral implications, satellizing identification leads to a "semi-internalized" conformity to expectations and concern about disapproval based on a sense of sharing these expectations, not to an "internalized" self-critical and self-punitive "superego." (As noted previously, it is linked to a conventional rather than a fully internalized moral orientation.) Furthermore, satellizing identifications are not the unilateral cause of the formation of conventional "good boy" morality. In actuality, the structure of these identifications partially presupposes conventional moral concepts and attitudes. Such identifications, however, support conventional morality, give it specific content, and deepen its affective significance. A somewhat superficial analogy may be drawn between relations to parents and relations to a personal god in moral development. Children of varying religions (Catholic, Protestant, Jewish, Muslim, Buddhist, atheist) go through the same sequence of moral stages. As they pass through these stages, religious relations are redefined. (As an example a Stage 2 Protestant boy says, "The best rule is to be a good Christian. You be good to God and He'll be good to you." Of being a "good son" he also says, "If you do things for your father, he'll do things for you.") Attitudes toward God, in turn, support moral attitudes, particularly at the conventional levels of morality. This is because they give the child the feeling that someone besides himself really cares that he is good, i.e., that he has someone with whom to share his moral expectations of himself. Similarly, once relations to parents have been defined in moral-identificatory terms, they tend to support moral attitudes because they provide a matrix of generalized support and care about the child's being good. While "society" or other authorities expect the child to "be good," the child is only one of many for everyone but his parents.[12]

From the cognitive-developmental viewpoint, then, it is impossible to conceive of such basic and near-universal features of personality development as morality as being directly caused by parent identification. There are too many developmental and cultural forces tending to produce "normal" morality to see these attitudes as contingent on special unique relationships to parents. As we elaborate later, the role-taking opportunities required for moral development need not be specifically familial nor need they imply identification in any specific sense. Accordingly, our view is that identifications do not cause moral (or sex-role) internalization but develop in parallel with them, and help to support moral or sex-role attitudes. Cognitive-developmental changes in conceptions of moral rules and social-sex roles are causative forces in the formation of parent identifications as much or more than the reverse. The research evidence supporting the cognitive-developmental (as opposed to the psychoanalytic) conception of the role of identification in psychosexual and moral development will be briefly considered at the end of this chapter, after a consideration of the imitative process and its development.

X. COGNITIVE-STRUCTURAL STAGES
OF IMITATION-IDENTIFICATION

A discussion of stages in the cognitive organization of imitation, must start by noting that all imitations, including its early forms, are cognitive, as Aronfreed's and Bandura's chapters very convincingly argue. Bandura's studies demonstrate no-trial observational learning and storage by preschoolers of complex new behavior patterns of models. Developmental studies such as Piaget's (1951) document the same characteristics as are true of later infant imitation. It is evident that such acquisition and the resulting generalized and autonomous

---

[12] It may be the loss of this support of the parent's special concern about the child's being good which leads to "regression" to instrumental hedonism on leaving home in some of the college-age population (Kramer, 1968). Decline in attitudes of identification with parents, as well as decline in religious attitudes, appears to characterize both regression to preconventional morality and progression to principled morality in a college population (Haan et al., 1969). If no one else one cares about cares whether the self is good, one tends to fall back upon self-chosen goals and standards, whether these are amoral or morally principled. In the latter case, one cares about the principle, however, rather than about "being a good self."

enactment of an absent model's behavior presupposes what Aronfreed (1969) terms a "cognitive template" and Bandura (1969) "an image" guiding imitation. Such a "cognitive template" is involved in much or most of the ordinary phenomena of infant imitation, such as is involved in language learning.[13]

The cognitive prerequisites of imitative behavior are further suggested by the fact that it is difficult or impossible to teach highly *generalized* imitation by instrumental-learning procedures to most lower animals like rats (Solomon & Coles, 1954). In contrast, cognitively higher animals, e.g., primates, readily display generalized imitative behavior and imitative learning (Warden & Jackson, 1935).

While some associationistic (or social-learning) theories of imitation, like those of Aronfreed (1969) and Bandura (1969), recognize the cognitive skill components in imitation acquisition, they fail to recognize stages of imitation, i.e., radical reorganizations of the imitative act due to changes in its cognitive structure. With regard to infancy, Piaget's (1951) observations have led him to define the following stages of imitation:

1. *Pseudo-imitation because of lack of differentiation between stimuli produced by self and other (Intelligence Stage 2)* (1-3 months). Stimuli made by other which are similar to those the child makes himself and which provide feedback to prolong the child's own circular reactions will prolong or elicit the child's response, e.g., crying by another child will prolong or trigger the child's own crying.

2. *Pseudo-imitation to make an interesting spectacle last (Intelligence Stage 3)* (3-7 months). The child will employ a schema already in his repertoire to maintain a like schema of action modeled by the adult. If the adult imitates what the child is doing (putting out his tongue), the child will repeat his own act to "make" the adult continue in this interesting activity.

3. *Imitation of new models (Intelligence Stage 4)* (7-10 months). The child will imitate a visually perceived movement by the adult for which he has only kinesthetic or auditory but not visual feedback, e.g., matching a visually perceived mouth movement of the adult. He will also imitate new schemas by trying out various known schemata which gradually become closer to the model. No effort is made to reproduce models too remote from his own schema, but some novelty in the modeled activity is required.

---

[13] In the Piaget (1951) framework an image of action is a rather late-developing (age 1) representational schema, one that itself presupposes imitation for its genesis. Before imitation involves copying novel responses, Piaget terms it "pseudo-imitation." A discussion of whether or not imitation is "cognitive" presupposes some distinction between "genuine" and pseudo-imitation (Gilmore, 1967). One condition for defining genuine imitation is that the subject has attended to cues of similarity and difference between his behavior and the model's. A second is that the behavior pattern is actually acquired from observation of the model rather than being learned in other ways. Much of what has been studied experimentally as "imitative learning" is not imitation in this sense, but is simply the gradual increase of performance of similar responses under reinforcement, without real specification of the conditions of original acquisition of the responses.

4. *Imitation of unfamiliar models (Intelligence Stage 5)* (10-18 months). The child will imitate visually perceived new movements of parts of the body not visible to it. Imitation of the new is systematic experimental groping toward the new model as in active imitation of new speech sounds not in the child's repertoire.
5. *Deferred imitation (and playful "making believe" one is another) (Intelligence Stage 6)* (after 18 months). Imitates a new action when the model is no longer present. As an example, the child imitates a temper tantrum of another child, not at the time, but the next day (the imitator never having had a temper tantrum herself).

Piaget's observations of these five stages of imitation are sufficiently accurate to generate a test of infant development which is stage-sequential in the sense of defining a cumulative Guttman scale (Hunt & Uzgiris, 1967). Among other dimensions characterizing this developmental scale are the dimensions of increased situational generality, independence of the presence of the model, and independence of an overt eliciting stimulus customarily used in distinguishing between imitation and identification. At the first stages of imitation the infant simply repeats specific responses made by another which are already in his repertoire and which are modeled before his eyes. At Piaget's final stages of sensorimotor imitation (by age 2) the child will play at being an absent person in the sense of deliberately enacting a set of behaviors characterizing another person. This is the first developmental approximation of identification-like behavior.

From the Piaget point of view sensorimotor cognitive organization is more or less completely developed by age 2 but the processes of cognitive organization characterizing maturity at the sensorimotor level must be repeated again at the symbolic-conceptual level, a process completed (at the level of concrete concepts) at about age 7-8 with attainment of the logic of classes, relations, and number. With regard to identification, the final stage of sensorimotor imitation launches the child into the beginnings of identification, i.e., the symbolic equations of the self with another (rather than the equations of an act of the self with an act of the other). From the Piaget point of view, the psychoanalytic descriptions of identification fantasies involving "magical" or logically impossible transformations of identity belong to this symbolic but prelogical era of thought (2-5). Early in this period the child first "fantasies," enacting roles other than his own, and then gradually learns (or develops) a firm sense of the limits of his own identity, i.e., that he can't change sex or age-status, that he can't take his father's place, etc. Associated with (1) clear establishment of the limits of his physical identity is the growth of (2) selectively modeling persons similar in identity, (3) selectively modeling in terms of attributes of admired models which can be shared because they are teachable psychological skills and virtues rather than physical attributes and symbols, and (4) awareness that possible sharing is through exhibiting the model's norms of goodness with regard to the child's own role activities rather than directly imitating the grown-up role activities.

These trends were illustrated by the quotations explaining Baldwin's theory

84

and Ausubel's concept of "satellization." They all imply a trend to structure imitative processes in terms of conceptions of structured roles, i.e., of categories of persons in defined relations to one another with normatively defined functions. These role conceptions themselves depend upon "concrete operations," i.e., the logic of classes and relations.

The developmental trends in cognitive structuring of modeling and identity concepts in the years 4 to 8 just enumerated have formed the basis of a general theory of psychosexual development in these years which I have propounded (Kohlberg, 1966b). The theory explains a large number of age-developmental trends and sequences which seem to occur regardless of any vicissitudes of particular parent-relations. The theory may be summarized as follows:

1. The concrete, physicalistic, and symbolic nature of the child's thought and interests leads him to conceive of interpersonal relationships in terms of body actions and to define social roles in terms of physical characteristics and differences. The elaboration of the physical bases of sex-role concepts in the concrete thought of the child leads to a core of common meaning of these concepts, regardless of cultural and family variations in sex-role definition.

2. Accordingly, there are "natural" developmental trends or sequences in sex-role attitudes, trends not directly structured by cultural teaching, which are the products of cognitive development. Because of the universal physical dimensions of sex-role concepts and because of culturally universal developmental transformations in modes of conceptualizing, it is plausible to expect some relatively invariant developmental trends in sex-role concepts and attitudes.

3. The fact that sex-role concepts have physical dimensions suggests that the formation of a sex-role identity is in large part the comprehension and acceptance of a physical reality rather than a process primarily determined by sexual fantasies, social reinforcement, or identification with models. The child's basic sex-role identity is largely the result of self-categorization as a male or female made early in development. While dependent on social labeling, this categorization is basically a cognitive reality judgment rather than a product of social rewards, parental identifications, or sexual fantasies. The reality judgments, "I really am and will always be a boy" or "I really am and will always be a girl," are judgments with a regular course of age-development relatively independent of the vicissitudes of social labeling and reinforcement. This course of age-development is dependent upon complex modes of cognitive organization and development. The stabilization of sex-role identity implied in the judgment, "I really am and will always be a boy," is dependent upon the types of cognitive reorganization discussed by Piaget (1947) as "conservation of the identity of physical objects" and is not completed until age 6-7 at the time that other forms of physical conservation are fully stabilized.

4. The motivational forces implied in such reality judgments are general "drive-neutral" motives of effectance, or competence, which orient the child both toward cognitive adaptation to a structured reality and toward the maintenance of self-esteem. Accordingly sex-typed preferences in activities and

social relationships (masculinity-femininity) are largely the product of such reality judgments of sex identity. The boy, having labeled himself as male, goes on to value masculine modes because of the general tendency to value positively objects and acts consistent with one's conceived identity.

5. To a large extent, the value of social reinforcers to the child is determined by his sex identity rather than the reverse. As opposed to a social-learning sequence, "The boy wants rewards, the boy is rewarded by boy things, therefore, he wants to be a boy," a cognitive theory assumes a sequence, "The boy asserts he is a boy. He then wants to do boy things; therefore, the opportunity to do boy things and the presence of masculine models is rewarding."

6. The tendency to value positively and imitate self-like objects tends to radiate out in the child's development in the form of imitation and liking for the same-sex parent. The boy's preferential attachment to the father as against the mother proceeds from, rather than causes, basic sex-role identity and basic tendencies to imitate the father preferentially. It depends not only upon a prior stable gender identity (point 3 above) and masculine values (point 4 above), but upon the formation of abstract cognitive categories of likeness involved in the boy's inclusion of his father in a category of "we males."

7. The effect of father-identification (in the case of boys) is, then, not to cause the child to desire and ascribe to generalized sex-role stereotypes and a basic gender identity, but to aid in defining the masculine role in more individualistic terms related to the father's particular role definitions. This does not make the boy more "masculine" but it may serve to make the boy more conforming to parental expectations. In particular it may lead the child to define his masculine role aspirations in more "moral" and more achievement-oriented terms as opposed to the more physicalistic power terms found in the young child's sex-role imagery. Same-sex parent identification is less cause than consequence of natural trends of self-categorization and sex-role stereotyping. Its developmental function is primarily to channel relatively crude sex-role aspirations and stereotypes into culturally conforming and "moral" role aspirations.

The fact that the developmental changes in imitation and identification just discusssed are cognitive-structural has been well documented. Piaget (1951) and Hunt and Uzgiris (1967) document point-to-point relationships between stages of imitation and general stages of sensorimotor intelligence. The cognitive nature of stabilization of gender identity, of same-sex modeling and same-sex attachment behavior has been documented by showing its relatively invariant relationships to mental age as opposed to other factors (Kohlberg & Zigler, 1967). The formation of normative "good boy" identifications with parents is correlated with maturity of moral judgment (in turn, correlated with mental age), so it, too, is in considerable part a cognitive-structural development.

We have just sketched some of the age-developmental cognitive-structural changes through which the imitative process proceeds. These changes are paralleled by clear developmental changes in sheer amount of imitation in experimental situations. During the age of 2-3 there is a well-documented "negativistic" period (Ausubel, 1957). In the period from 3-5 there is a regular increase in conformity to suggestion or instruction, which is accompanied by an increase in imitativeness (Kohlberg & Zigler, 1967). In a study discussed further in Section XII, Kuhn and Langer (1968) found only 20 per cent of 3-year-olds imitated an adult E in a "neutral" experimental condition (children told they could do what they wanted) in which 80 per cent of 4-year-olds imitated. Indeed the 3-year-olds imitated as much (20 per cent) under a condition where they were told *not* to imitate as they did in a neutral condition.

From the period of 5-8 there is a regular decline in imitativeness of an adult model under "neutral" experimental conditions, (Kohlberg & Zigler, 1967) so that 8-year-olds superficially appear much like the 3-year-olds in disposition to imitate. The trends mentioned are again largely a function of cognitive maturity, of mental rather than chronological age. In the 3-4 period where imitation is developmentally increasing, bright children imitate more than average children, whereas bright children imitate less in the 6-8 period when imitation is declining (Kohlberg & Zigler, 1967). Similar findings are reported by others comparing retarded and average school-age children.

As we document further in Section XII, this curvilinear trend partly reflects changes in definitions of what is good or right or conforming behavior in ill-defined situations. The 4–5-year-old takes the adult's example as his cue to what he wants the child to do, the 6–7-year-old child is aware that "copying someone else's work isn't good," "you should do your own work," etc. When a group of twelve 4-year-olds were asked about copying, none said it was bad, whereas a majority of a group of twenty-four 6-year-olds did (Kohlberg, unpublished interview data). This in turn reflects a growing orientation to stable normative patterns of an "ideal self." According to our viewpoint, this developmental decline in imitativeness does not reflect the disappearance of the modeling process, but rather its transformation into more structured identifications with normative models as reflected in "good boy" concepts. The findings of Ausubel et al. (1954, that *low* imitation in school-age children was correlated with *high* identification with parents or high satellizing attitudes supports this interpretation.

In summary, then, the developmental trends in modeling processes in the years 3 to 8 broadly summarized by Baldwin (1906) under the name of "the formation of an ideal self" and by Ausubel as "satellization" have a detailed cognitive-structural base in the general development of concepts of roles and rules in this period discussed by Piaget (1947). While much of the particular content and intensity of these identifications is given by individual family experience, much is also universally derived from the common basic meanings of age and sex-roles at a given cognitive stage.

XI. THE MOTIVATION FOR IMITATION IS INTRINSIC—EFFECTANCE AND INTEREST AS DETERMINING IMITATION

While few would question that early imitation entails cognitive patterning and skill components, cognitive-developmental theories also hold a "cognitive" theory of the motivation of imitation, a theory of the same sort as that involved in explaining curiosity, and exploratory and mastery behavior. The conditions leading to such behaviors are best conceived along the lines of Piaget's (1952b) notions of assimilation, White's (1959) notion of competence or effectance motivation, and Hunt's (1963) notions of information-processing motivation.

Effectance theories of motivation have always been difficult to grasp because they do not assume any "pushes," "drive states," "needs" or other definite sources of activity. They assume that one does not need to ask for specific deficit states to explain why the organism is active, any more or (perhaps) less than one needs to ask for specific states to explain why the organism is at rest. Like operant analyses, it assumes a motivational analysis is one of (a) the conditions under which this, as opposed to that, activity occurs, and (b) of the directed quality of the action. This directed quality, it believes, cannot be defined in terms of goals or end states which are distinct from the activities or the behavior structures seeking them (or from the situation in which the organism finds itself), but must be defined in terms of forms of relation between the action and its results (or between the act and the object), forms suggested by words like "mastery." It is this refusal to separate the act and the "reinforcer" which discriminates theories of effectance motivation not only from drive theory but from driveless accounts of motivation in terms of external reinforcement. The general rationale for effectance concepts of motivation is most lucidly presented by White (1959). In terming an effectance concept of the motive for imitation "cognitive," we do so because effectance concepts are most clearly required for cognitive activities, which are very hard to account for in terms of "drives" or "reinforcers." It is almost impossible to discuss the "energetic" and the patterning or "structural" characteristics of cognitive activities independently of one another. The "motivational" characteristics of an object arousing curiosity and the activities upon the object terminating curiosity are defined by the relation of the cognitive-structural characteristics of the object to the cognitive-structural characteristics of the child's behavior patterns, relations definable in terms of structural match or balance. If an object fits a schema or behavior structure, but does not fit it too well, it arouses exploratory or mastery behavior, as has been documented repeatedly since the days Baldwin (1895) first formulated the notion of "assimilation" and "schema." The assumption that the motivation of imitative behavior is best explained by effectance theory, then, is the assertion that the primary conditions which arouse imitation are a moderate degree of mismatch between the child's behavior structure and the behavior of the model (or later between the behavior structure of the child and the structure of the situation as this mismatch may be reduced by imitating the model), and the conditions which terminate it are a better state of match, balance, or "mastery" between the child's behavior and the model's (or between the child's behavior and the situation).

We shall attempt to elaborate the foregoing view of the motivation for imitation by working from some facts. The first fact is that much imitation appears to be intrinsically motivated, in the sense of having no obvious external reinforcer for which the imitative act is instrumental or contingent. Much apparently non-reinforced imitation is discussed by Bandura (1969) under the heading of "vicarious reinforcement," since none of his studies involve directly reinforcing the child for imitating. One cannot, however, explain his findings of imitation of nurturant or powerful models in terms of vicarious reinforcement, since power leads to imitation but consumption of resources does not (Bandura, Ross & Ross, 1963c). Furthermore, Bandura gets a high level of imitation in his control groups exposed to his non-nurturant or powerless models.

As an example, in one study Bandura and Huston (1961) had an adult make nurturant responses to one group of preschool children while the children played with toys, while ignoring a second group. The adult then made various irrelevant non-aggressive (e.g., marching) and aggressive gestures (knocking down a rubber doll) while performing a simple task which the child then performed. In the nurturant condition, almost all the children imitated the adult (100 per cent on aggression, 65 per cent on marching). What is also striking, however, is that in the control condition, a great deal of imitation occurred also (80 per cent on aggression, 25 per cent on marching). The imitation in the control group is not to be attributed to socially learned generalized imitativeness of young children. The discrepancy between the 100–80 per cent aggression and the 65–25 per cent marching makes that clear enough. Even the 65–25 per cent of children marching is high, however, compared to the findings from other studies. Anyone who (like the author, Kohlberg & Zigler, 1967) has attempted to get preschool children to imitate an experimental model will realize it is not that easy. Bandura's success in eliciting imitation is due to the interesting and zany things he has his adult models do. An adult goose-stepping around the room shouting "March, march, march!" or pummeling a Bobo doll is clearly a fascinating spectacle to the child. If the adult is not crazy and seems at all encouraging ("nurturant") the child is likely to follow suit.

If preschool children often like to imitate interesting behaviors with no extrinsic reinforcement consequences, infants are even clearer in this desire. This is demonstrated by the standard results achievable with infant tests of imitation, such as those developed by Valentine (1942), and by Hunt and Uzgiris (1967) following Piaget (1951). A stranger elicits these imitative behaviors one by one without following them with any clear reinforcement. Yet the tests work regardless of the prior social reinforcement history of the infant but cannot be made to work with nonimitative species. Any observer of these imitation tests with infants will note two qualitative characteristics of early imitation which further bespeak its basic independence of extrinsic reinforcers. First, it customarily occurs in a play context, rather than in the context of being a means to some external goal. Second, early imitation clearly displays a joy in the reproduction of irrelevant details of the model's action. There seems to be a desire to exactly replicate for its own sake, rather than simply to match to some degree of similarity associated with reinforcement. In other words, the similarity sought is not as a discriminative cue associated with reinforcement, as in a "matching to sample" response, but is sought without regard to a criterion of similarity.

Because early imitation often appears to be intrinsically motivated, because it is species-specific or characteristic of some gregarious species (e.g., primates), and because it is so universal within the species, it has often been taken to be instinctive. There are certain telling characteristics of imitation, however, which do not fit our usual concepts of instinct. The first characteristic is the flexibility of the behavior patterning or structuring of imitative acts. The behavior patterns referred to by the word "imitation" are far from fixed; there is no specific patterned action which is imitative nor is there any fixed specific releaser stimulus for imitative behavior. The characteristic of imitation is the absorption of new behavior patterns from the environment. Our characterization of early imitation as cognitive is itself a statement that its patterning is not instinctive or innate. Not only is imitation flexible and cognitive rather than being instinctively fixed and blind, but its forms change with cognitive-structural growth. The second "non-instinctual" characteristic of imitation is the flexibility of the motivational conditions for the performance of imitative acts. Instinctive behaviors are repeatedly performed, with durations of exhaustion followed by periods of readier elicitation. In contrast, imitative behavior is exploratory and playful rather than being repetitive and compulsive. While there is an emphasis on exact reproduction of the model, this reproduction is not repeated in the same way over long periods of time. Typically, the child imitates a behavior only as long as it is novel and interesting, and then he goes on to imitate something else. This characteristic "seeking of novelty" in the conditions eliciting imitative behavior is as inconsistent with an instinct notion as it is with the operant notion that an imitative act will be repeated as long as it is followed by some extrinsic reinforcer.

The reasons we have just advanced for rejecting the idea that imitation is instinctive are also reasons why we are led to reject Aronfreed's (1969) affect-conditioning theory of the motivational conditions for imitative behavior. As opposed to social reinforcement theories, the cognitive-developmental approach agrees with Aronfreed that the (motivational) "foundations of imitative learning appear to lie in the conditions of the child's observations (of the model) rather than in the modification of the child's overtly emitted behavior by positive or aversive external outcomes" (p. 280). However, it does not appear plausible to define the "conditions of observation" leading to imitation as a contiguity between the behavior of the model and a strong affective state in the child. In the first place, the infant frequently imitates the behaviors of adults who are not emotionally important to him, as the construction of a baby test of imitation by a strange examiner indicates. Second, when he does imitate, the behaviors imitated are often not those immediately associated with affectively significant events, as baby tests of imitation of gestures with little affective charge document. Third, the affect-conditioning model suggests a repetitive or compulsive character to imitative behavior which is quite different from that usually

90

found. As noted, behaviors tend to be imitated or reproduced only as long as they are novel.

Having rejected instinct, reinforcement, and classical conditioning accounts of the motivation for early imitation, what positive account of the conditions for imitation may be given? We may start with the simple generalization that the one common condition of stimuli that are imitated is that they are interesting. One simple cue to interest value is attention, so that anything which leads an action to be attended to may be sufficient to lead to its being imitated. Many of the dimensions of interest or attention have been catalogued by Berlyne (1961) under such headings as complexity, novelty, etc. The statement that the motivational conditions for imitation are cognitive, then, implies that they are not found in fixed intraorganismic needs, but in "objective" dimensions of the stimulus which make it interesting. These dimensions or conditions are not located purely in the stimulus, however, since they also include its match to the child's behavior structure, as is implied by dimensions like "novelty," or by the dimension of similarity of the model to the self (e.g., that it is a person being imitated). In general, if a person does something interesting, the infant tries to assimilate it to his own behavior capabilities; he tries to see if he can do it too. If the behavior is not interesting or if the child, through repetition, is sure he can do it, he is unlikely to imitate the behavior.

One way of looking at Piaget's (1951) stages of imitation is as a series of progressions in the kinds of events which elicit imitation. Following Baldwin's (1895) fundamental insights, Piaget defined imitation and its development in terms of the growing complexity of "circular reactions."

The fundamental unit of directed behavior in infancy is a circular reaction, that is, a patterned action which produces feedback stimuli which are the natural elicitors of the act in question. The first and simplest circular reactions are those innately wired to produce such a reaction (sucking which itself produces the tactile pressure on the mouth which naturally elicits sucking, or clenching the fist which produces the pressure on the child's palm naturally eliciting further clenching). These behaviors, then, naturally lead to cycles of repetition, and soon generate integrations in which activities in one modality (waving the hand) lead to sensory feedback in another modality (the spectacle of a moving hand) which leads to repetition of the activity in the first modality, repetitions with functional value (developing eye-hand coordination). This is termed "primary circular reaction," and is in turn followed by a stage of "secondary circular reaction" (the feedback from the act is from its effect in moving an external object), "tertiary circular reaction," etc. These progressive complications of the circular reaction define Piaget's (1952b) stages of sensorimotor intelligence. As stages of circular reaction, they define an active tendency to repeat any behavior pattern with a "circular" feedback stimulation output.[14] Postulating an active tendency

---

[14] This active tendency toward repetition is in a sense like the Freudian (1938) "repetition compulsion" without the instinctual underpinnings.

toward repetition, it was Baldwin's (1895) further genius to see that the basis for the child's imitating another was no different than the basis for imitating himself. If a child by accident performed a behavior leading to an interesting result, he would desire to repeat it. To do so, he must copy his own behavior. The situation is no different if another performs the interesting behavior. Insofar as repetition rests upon accommodation to, or copying of, a model or stimulus pattern, then, it is imitation. Expressed in slightly different terms, almost anything which might lead the child to repeat a novel behavior pattern he emitted could lead him to repeat the behavior pattern of another. A specification of the motivational conditions for imitation, then, does not imply a special imitative motive, but derives from the conditions leading to the reproduction of any interesting behavior pattern.

We have so far discussed the interest value of the act to be imitated in terms of dimensions of the structure of the act itself, such as its complexity and novelty. A large part of the interest value of many imitated actions, however, rests upon the effects of the act upon other objects. When the infant repeats one of his own acts which has interesting consequences, an operant analysis will claim that the consequences serve as a "reinforcer" for the act. As already mentioned, however, exploratory or playful acts do not appear to be under the stable control of definite reinforcers. An interesting light, sound, or movement resulting from a playful act soon ceases to be interesting, and ceases to function to maintain the behavior. Furthermore, while the effect of the child's actions maintains his behavior, the relation between behavior and effect does not look Skinnerian under close scrutiny. Close observation of infant learning suggests that the goal state is not defined directly by either external or internal stimuli ("reinforcers"), but is defined by a *relation* of mastery between the act and its effects. In other words, the effects of the child's behavior are only reinforcing if they are caused by the self's action, while the self's action is only satisfying if it leads to effects, to mastery. As an example (Piaget, 1952b), the infant's kicks start a toy bird swinging and the child delightedly kicks "to make the bird swing." One cannot call the external event itself (swinging of the bird) a reinforcer of kicking, since it is not the external event which is the "reinforcer," but its relation to the act of kicking, a relation of causality or mastery. If the adult makes the bird swing, this leads to renewal of the kicking to reestablish the connection. It is quite difficult for reinforcement theory to explain why the infant kicks when he is already being reinforced for lying still. Furthermore, as mentioned, the swinging of the bird is not a stable reinforcer; the infant soon loses interest when he has assimilated it (established its relation to his own behavior).

This example (Piaget's infant kicking to make the bird swing) is used by Piaget as an example of a "secondary circular reaction." It may also be described as an assimilation of an interesting event. Basically, early imitation of another is also assimilation of an interesting event. This interest may be generated either by the form of the model's act, or by its striking consequences. This simple formulation in terms of assimilation of the interesting is most clearly applicable to infant imitation. However, it is also applicable to much preschool imitation, as was mentioned earlier in connection with Bandura's studies.

XII. SOCIAL REINFORCEMENT AND IMITATION AS A FORM OF NORMATIVE CONFORMITY

In this volume, Gewirtz suggests that imitation is a generalized response based on reinforcement for making responses similar to those of others. He notes that while adults may not systematically intend to reward and support imitative behavior, almost all the socialization demands of the adult involve expecting the child to make responses or develop skills like those already displayed by other people, by older members of the group. Accordingly, Gewirtz says, any reward for socialization achievement is also a reward for imitating. In our discussion of Baldwin, we observed that he, too, notes the omnipresent connection between the child's social achievements and his imitative tendencies, but uses this connection between achievement and imitation to explain approval-seeking (i.e., social reinforcement effects), rather than deriving imitation from it. Baldwin's approach rests on the theory that both early imitation and early mastery of basic skills are motivated by intrinsic competence or effectance tendencies. Children in orphanages try to walk, talk, etc., as well as try to imitate with a minimum of social reinforcement. According to the cognitive-developmental interpretation, the fact that the child's achievements are imitative engenders a concern for social approval, as the child comes first to need another self (or an audience) as confirmation of his achievement and then to systematically ascribe superior competence to the adult model or audience. In other words, "intrinsically" motivated imitation should come under the control of social reinforcers increasingly with age-development (up to about age 5-6), rather than originating from such reinforcement.

There are three points to the interpretation we have just advanced. The first is that the ordinary social reinforcement effects upon imitation (or any other task) behavior in the child are based upon the child's "primary competence motivation," upon his generalized desire for task success. This intrinsic desire for success is mediated by external social definitions through social reinforcement. But the desire for success is not the desire for the concrete reinforcers administered. By this we mean that it is more correct to say that the child wants to secure rewards or approval as a sign that he has performed the task competently rather than to say that the child wants to perform competently in order to obtain situational rewards or approval. The role of reinforcers is primarily that of cognitively redefining success in terms of social standards rather than through directly strengthening an associated response.

The second point of our interpretation is that there is an age increase in the child's concern about external social definitions of correct performance, in his "need" for approval, up until about age 6-7. The third (and most questionable) point is that this development is mediated by the imitative process itself, in addition to being mediated by the child's growing awareness of the limits of his own competence. While the second point receives some documentation from social learning studies (Stevenson, 1965), this documentation is sketchy, because of the indifference of most research students of social reinforcement to developmental variables. The third point has not been considered at all in research studies.

Accordingly, the remainder of this section will attempt to document the first point. It carries the following implications:

a) Social reinforcement affects children's imitation primarily because it has informational value, i.e., because the reward is perceived as indicating that the child's response is correct or in accordance with a standard in the mind of a person more competent than the self. A schedule of social reinforcement functions primarily as a long-winded instruction or definition of the right answer; it does not function like a food pellet to a rat. If the situation is one in which a social reinforcer does not symbolize a judgment of normative conformity, the social reinforcer ceases to function.

b) One or no-trial extinction of imitation "learned" under social reinforcement will occur under conditions where the child is given relevant information that the situation or rules are "new" or changed.

c) In some cases, social reinforcement functions as the equivalent of a direct instruction to imitate. Where more subtle mediation of imitation by the desire for task success appears, it is primarily in situations in which the definition of the rules of the game are ambiguous.

d) The preschool child's general cognitive ambiguity about the rules of the game encourages both imitation and susceptibility to reinforcement which does not appear to be "normative" or instructional to the adult. Because young children have few clear cognitively defined standards or information concerning correct performance, they do not clearly discriminate between correct performance and being rewarded, and hence are more likely to appear to be governed by extrinsic and arbitrary social reinforcement contingencies.

The first implication is that the effectiveness of social reinforcers is contingent on the child's interpretation of them as a symbol of a competent judgment, of correct performance. To illustrate, a social-learning analyst actually installed in a preschool a machine which emitted a tape-recorded vocalization, "That's good," after a bar was pressed, under various schedules of reinforcement. After an initial amused run on the machine, clearly motivated by the desire for novelty, the machine lay dormant, its reinforcing power spent. Obviously, "That's good" did not stand for a social judgment. Another illustration is suggested by Bandura's studies of "vicarious reinforcement." Models receiving social reinforcement were imitated in the Bandura and MacDonald's (1963) study of the modeling of moral judgment. However, in another study adult models who were given concrete social "rewards" (candy, ice cream, etc.) were not imitated more than those who were not rewarded. The most likely interpretation is that the non-imitated models did not receive their rewards in a way in which they could be viewed as indicating correct performance.

The fact that the effectiveness of social reinforcement depends upon a normative context has been obscured by the preschool child's readiness to assume a normative context, a "rule" on which the reward is based, where none exists. As an example, in a study (Kohlberg, 1969) children were told a story in which a boy faithfully watched his baby brother and was punished by his mother on her return (or abandoned the baby but was rewarded by the mother on her return). Most 4-year-olds (though knowing obedient baby-sitting was "good") said the punished boy was bad for obediently baby-sitting. Most 5-year-olds said the boy's baby-sitting was good but he was a bad boy because "he must have done something bad to get punished" and went through a variety of cognitive contortions to balance the act and the sanction. By age 7, about half of the children were able to completely disentangle "goodness" or the rule from reinforcement and to say the child was good and there must be something foolish or bad about the mother to punish him (still maintaining cognitive balance but of a more differentiated justice-balance sort). This demonstration of the extent to which "arbitrary" social reinforcement carries a normative meaning for the preschool and kindergarten child suggests that a very arbitrary social reinforcement schedule will still owe much of its power to its ability to define the child's act as good or bad (or as successful or unsuccessful). When concrete reward and punishment are still equated with being good or bad, the value of physical or social rewards administered by an authority is as much due to their assumed connection with competent and correct performance as is the value of correct performance due to its association with physical reinforcers. Furthermore, it is the informational value of reinforcement as defining correct performance which probably leads to any durable generalized effects it might have. Accordingly, the effects of arbitrary and concrete reinforcement would be expected to have more enduring effects at an age where they are confused with the normative, and in a situation where the normative is ambiguous.[15]

An experimental example of this point is provided by a study of Bandura, Ross and Ross (1963b), who found children were much more likely to imitate the aggressive behavior of Rocky, the bully, if Rocky was successful in beating up his victim and taking his toys than if he was defeated. In the successful condition, 60 per cent of the children said that they would like to be like Rocky "because he was a fighter, he got good toys." While not attributing virtue to Rocky, they said his victim was "a crybaby, didn't share, was mean, dumb, etc." This is hardly surprising when it is found that most children of this age (4-6) not only say that the "good guys win" but explain that you can tell who are the "good guys" in TV shows because they win (Kohlberg, 1965). Bandura (1969) accounts for this

---

[15] To illustrate, children aged 9 to 16 were asked if they would "change their mind" about a moral judgment question for 50 cents in the Kohlberg (1958, 1969) study. Moral Stage 1 subjects tended to say, "Yes, because you know the answer, you have the answers in the back of the book (from which the questions were read)." Stage 2 subjects tended to say, "I'd take the 50 cents and tell you I'd changed my mind." Children above Stage 2 tended to say they would not change their minds.

cognitive balancing as *ex post facto* verbal cognitive dissonance reduction, i.e., rationalization for imitation the children want to do anyhow for vicarious rewards. In contrast, our interpretation makes it causative and postulates that Bandura would not get this "vicarious reinforcement effect" with children over seven who are more able to differentiate goodness from arbitrary success.

We have claimed that more enduring effects of social reinforcement are contingent on their normative-informational components. One cannot doubt that a concrete reward or prize engenders more immediate incentive to perform than a mere verbal acknowledgment that the child's response is correct. The effect of a concrete reward as an added incentive may lead to more or faster learning as well as performance. However, there is little reason to think that a concrete reward engenders a longer-range disposition than does a sign of social approval, given that either reinforcer leads to any learning or behavior change. While the child may perform more eagerly to get a physical prize than to be told he is right, long-range maintenance of the behavior depends on the cognitive stability of the child's definition of the behavior as "good" or "right." The effects of reward depend for their stability on either the expectation of future reward or on the redefinition of successful or good behavior. As already mentioned, the two tend to be equated by young children, who only form generalized expectations of reward if they think the behavior is generally considered good by adults. The child understands that whether or not he gets candy for a performance is highly specific to the situation and the adult, and that the more generalized component of his learning is that of whether the act is good or bad.

An example of the cognitive flexibility or reversibility of imitative learning under concrete reward is provided by a study of Turiel and Guinsburg (1968). The situation used by Turiel was the "conventional" Miller and Dollard (1941) instrumental imitation situation in which the child watches a model find candy under one of two boxes. When the child was told that the E had put two candies under one box, he engaged in "no-trial imitation." When he was told that the E had put one piece of candy under each box, he engaged in "no-trial" counter-imitation (went to the other box). If the child imitated for many rewarded trials under the imitation-reward condition, he would nevertheless immediately stop imitating as soon as he was told the second candy had been placed under the alternative box. The point is, of course, that prior rewards for imitation, direct or vicarious, are irrelevant where the situation can be directly defined cognitively. Past rewarded imitation will only be maintained where it is appropriate to the situational "rules of the game" or where "the rules of the game" are cognitively ambiguous.

In summary, we have claimed that the more durable effects of social reinforcement in young children (aged 3-8) are the result of the informational value of such reinforcement in normatively defining the "successful" or "right" response. Only from such a perspective do studies of "vicarious reinforcement" effects, such as those of Bandura (1969) and his colleagues on imitation, make sense. The concept of vicarious reinforcement presupposes cognitive processes of observational learning and is objected to on these and other grounds by Gewirtz (1969). While presupposing cognitive processes, vicarious reinforcement concepts assume these processes are irrational. Such an irrational cognitive component is implicit not only in theories of vicarious reinforcement, but in Whiting's (1960) "status envy" theory that identification is based on the desire to consume the resources possessed or consumed by the model.

In general, it is not "rational" to believe that doing what the model does will lead to getting the rewards the model gets. Turiel's study (Turiel & Guinsburg, 1968) clearly indicates that if you provide the child with information that allows him to infer that he will not get the reward the model received, the child will not imitate. The only conditions under which "vicarious reinforcement" will lead to modeling with some persistence are the conditions in which vicarious reinforcement is taken by the child as indicating that the model made the "right" or successful response. This, in turn, is contingent upon the normative context of the situation, and upon the prior beliefs about the good held by the child. Where the child's normative standards are confused and externalized, a rather arbitrary reinforcement pattern will still be interpreted normatively.

The fact that vicarious social reinforcement has a "normative" rather than a "pellet" effect on modeling is indicated by the studies on the imitation of the self-administration of rewards (Bandura & Kupers, 1964; Bandura & Whalen, 1966; Bandura, Grusic & Menlove, 1967). These studies indicate that the child will imitate a model's self-denial in giving himself physical rewards for performance in a game that a model has imposed upon himself, but that this imitation is partly contingent on perceiving the model rewarded for his self-denial. Bandura's interpretation, in terms of vicarious reinforcement, supposes that the child through no-trial observational learning foregoes the unlimited and concrete reinforcers he could give himself for the sake of the "pie in the sky" of the limited and "vicarious" reinforcement of the model. In fact, the reinforcement effect only makes sense as defining the normatively correct pattern of reward for the game, i.e., as indicating that the model is following the rules.

We have discussed the fact that much imitation is motivated by the desire to succeed by following "the rules of the game," and that much of the effect of social reinforcement upon imitation depends upon this desire, rather than upon a past reinforcement history or upon fixed needs. The major "motivational" conditions determining experimental imitation, then, are the rules of the game of the task situation as this is determined by the conditions of instruction on the one hand, and the cognitive-developmental status of the child on the other. This conclusion is very convincingly documented in a study by Kuhn and Langer (1968). In this study, preschool children were exposed to an adult model who performed three acts (putting marbles in a bowl, putting them in a circle, and building with blocks). The children were then given one of seven instructions ranging from 1. explicit instruction to imitate a stressed act of the model ("While I'm gone you put the marbles in the bowl just like I did. I'll have a prize for you when I come back."), to 4. "neutral" condition ("You can do anything you want while I'm gone. I'll have a prize for you when I come back."), to 7. instructions not to imitate the stressed act ("When I'm gone, be sure not to do what I did. When I come back, I'll have a prize for you.").

The results for the stressed act indicated that the "neutral" condition was treated like an instruction to imitate. Under the "explicit" instructions (Conditions 1-3), 100 per cent of a group of 4-year-olds imitated the stressed act. In the "neutral" condition, 80 per cent of the children imitated the stressed act. Essentially, none of the children imitated the stressed act under the negative instruction condition. With regard to "incidental imitation" (i.e., imitation of the two acts of the experimenter not mentioned in the instructions), the results were equally clear. In the neutral condition, 80 per cent of the children engaged in incidental imitation. In the next most neutral condition ("You don't have to put the marbles in the bowl like I did."), there was 50 per cent imitation. In all other conditions of instruction, there was no substantial incidental imitation (less than 20 per cent imitated) even where the children were instructed to imitate the stressed act. These results clearly indicate that the children only engaged in incidental imitation when they were puzzled as to what they were supposed to do. If they knew what to do, whether told positively (imitate the stressed act) or negatively (don't imitate the stressed act), they did not engage in incidental imitation.

It is unlikely that this tendency of 80 per cent of 4-year-olds to incidentally imitate in the neutral condition was due to any generalized disposition to imitate based on prior social reinforcement for imitating. If such were the case, one would expect the children to incidentally imitate when they were told to directly imitate, since this indicated that the situation was one of reinforcement for imitation. Furthermore, one would expect more individual variation than occurred. The individual differences found were purely cognitive-developmental. Most 3-year-olds failed to imitate directly (20 per cent) in the neutral condition (as noted earlier) and they also failed to imitate indirectly in this or any other condition. In other words, they had not yet developed a conception that "when in doubt, do what the model does."[16]

In the Kuhn and Langer (1968) study, almost all of the variance in imitative behavior was accounted for, a rare feat in experimental social psychology. Almost all the variation can be accounted for in terms of variation in the cognitive ambiguity of the instructions and the cognitive maturity of the child, variation which cannot be explained by drive or reinforcement concepts of motivation and habit.

The Kuhn and Langer study indicates how one kind of cognitive ambiguity, that of the definition of the task, determines amount of imitation. The study suggests a continuity between the determinants of childhood imitation (e.g., ambiguity in task definition) and those studied by social psychologists of adult-

---

[16] That the age effect in question is primarily a function of cognitive maturity is suggested by the Kohlberg and Zigler (1967) study in which all age differences in imitation were largely mental rather than chronological age effects.

hood interested in the conditions of conformity to group norms as mediated by the behaviors or judgments of others. In other contexts, the child's cognitive uncertainty as to his capacity to succeed in the task, independently, is an equally powerful determinant of imitation. This is demonstrated by a study of Turnure and Zigler (1964). Normal children, aged 8, were given two measures of imitation, the Miller and Dollard (1941) measure of looking for a toy under the same box as a child stooge, and Emmerich and Kohlberg's (1953) measures of making sticker designs like those of an adult E. Before the imitation tasks, the children were given some prior tasks. Half were told by the E that they were doing well on the tasks (success), half that they did poorly (failure). After the success condition, none of the children imitated at all in either task, after the failure condition a slight majority imitated on both tasks. Obviously individual differences irrelevant in the success condition (since no one imitated) determined the split between imitators and non-imitators in the failure condition. These individual differences, however, themselves seem largely individual differences in expectations of task success. Turnure and Zigler (1964) ran a retarded group of the same mental age[17] through their experimental procedures. About half of the retarded children imitated under the success condition, while 90 per cent imitated under the failure condition. Turnure and Zigler present evidence suggesting that this greater proneness to imitate is due to a history of experiences of failure and uncertainty about independent task performance. Accepting this interpretation, it would appear that Turnure and Zigler have predicted and accounted for all the variance in their dependent variable, imitation, by one independent variable (success-failure expectation) since they were able to predict variability from 0 per cent imitation in one group to 90 per cent imitation in another.

Like the Kuhn and Langer (1968) study, the Turnure and Zigler study indicates that most of the variance in many experimental imitation studies is determined by the child's desire to successfully perform the task, as this is mediated by varying definitions of task success. The fact that failure experiences in a prior task generate imitation in a subsequent task is not derivable from an operant analysis, but requires an explanation in terms of the cognitive redefinition of the self's capacities in the task situation.

Like the other studies discussed in this section, the Turnure and Zigler (1964) study indicates that most of the variations in amount of imitative behavior in experimental situations with rules (tasks or games) is to be explained in terms of variations in the normative value of the model, i.e., in the extent to which the experimental situation defines the model behavior as indicating the "right answer" for the child to give to the task, and in the extent to which it defines the child's independent or imitative behavior as likely to yield the right answer

---

[17] By using a mental age control, the study presumably eliminates a further source of the greater imitativeness of retardates relative to controls of the same chronological age, the earlier discussed tendency of less cognitively mature children to imitate more.

to the situation. This interpretation encompasses the experimental findings on the effects of prior task reinforcement (Turnure and Zigler, 1964) as well as the effects of direct and vicarious reinforcement upon imitative behavior. Taken together with the findings on the interest value of the model's act discussed previously, this interpretation accounts for the bulk of the reported experimental findings on imitation in young children.[18] The remaining findings, those on the status characteristics of the model in relation to those of the child, are taken up in the next section.

XIII. STATUS OF THE MODEL AND THE CHILD: COMPETENCE AND SIMILARITY AS DETERMINANTS OF IMITATION

We have considered so far the motivational conditions for imitation as they reside in the interest-value of the act and in the appropriateness of imitative behavior to the situation (its social reinforcement parameters). We shall now consider the conditions of imitation as they reside in the personality or status of the model, i.e., in the quality of his relationships to the child, to other persons, or to the larger social structure. A consideration of the status conditions of imitation takes us closer to the concerns of traditional psychoanalytic and neo-psychoanalytic theories of identification, e.g., theories which invoke the model's love withdrawal, his aggressiveness, his power, his possession of envied resources, etc., as major determinants of the child's modeling.

Almost all of the theories of identification just listed have assumed a strong deficit-state motivation for identification, i.e., either the model's infliction of pain-anxiety (identification with the aggressor, A. Freud, 1946; Sarnoff, 1951), the model's withdrawal of love (anaclitic identification, A. Freud, 1946; Sears, 1957), or the model's control or withholding of someone or something else desperately wanted by the child (status envy identification, Whiting, 1960). The reason for this focus on strong deficit states becomes clearer if it is recognized, as Whiting (1967) has pointed out, that these theories are really designed to account for illogical fantasy identifications, such as identification with the opposite-sex role. The theories more or less assume some magical thought processes involved in identification, i.e., a magical equation of self and other. One may term such equations magical since they are "incorporative," i.e., they involve the notion of "being the other" or "absorbing him," not becoming like another person distinct from the self through approximating his behavior. In other words, they assume that the reason for identification is either to do away with another causing the self pain (defensive identification), or to "be the other" so that the self can love

---

[18] The studies which suggest more mechanistic Skinnerian interpretations of imitation learning have been conducted with grossly retarded (Baer et al., 1967), or autistic children (Lovaas, 1967) who have not reached preschool cognitive maturity and do not seem to display the "natural" imitativeness discussed in the previous section, which was said to increase with such cognitive maturity.

or hate itself as it has the other from whom one is separated. The processes involved in identification have been assumed to be illogical in another sense, the sense of being equations of the self with others whom one cannot "really" become, or like whom it is maladaptive to become. Finally the processes involved have been assumed to be illogical in the sense of leading to self-other equations of a painful or self-punishing sort, e.g., in the creation of a "superego."

The two notions of strong deficit state and magical thought process are interlocked, since presumably some strong deficit state must be a motivator for magical cognitive processes. In other words, psychoanalytic and neo-psychoanalytic theory has assumed that identification is illogical, i.e., a defense, and hence must be a reaction to an intense pain experience or a negative drive state. The defensive character of identification is assumed not only by its illogical character, but by its presumed fixity, rigidity, or persistence in the face of situational inappropriateness.

As we discuss in more detail subsequently, while psychoanalytic and neo-psychoanalytic identification theories were designed to account for the pathological and the structurally fixed, actual research applications of the theories have been to the phenomena of ordinary imitation or to self-conscious perception of similarity to one's parents or one's parents' sex-role. Neither of these sets of phenomena reveal anything rigidly fixed since perceived similarity measures of identification are not fixed or longitudinally stable (the boy who is heavily father-identified one year is not the next, Kohlberg, 1965). Also, neither of these sets of phenomena involve anything directly illogical or pathological since there is nothing, per se, more illogical or pathological about thinking one has values or personal traits like the father than the mother.[19] With regard to sex role, the process by which a child acquires an identification with his own role is not the process by which he acquires an "illogical" or "pathological" identification with the opposite-sex role, as our cognitive-developmental theory stressed. Since studies of sex-typing in preschool and school children include few children with definite opposite-sex identification, but only children more and less "mature" in development of a logical or conforming identity, these studies also are irrelevant to distress-defense theories of identification.

In light of what has been said, it is not surprising to find that reviews of the findings of research studies of imitation and perceived similarity provide little support for the neo-psychoanalytic theories mentioned (Kohlberg, 1963a; Bandura, 1969). More specifically they suggest the following qualifications about these theories:

1. *Anaclitic theory.* While prior nurturance (and perhaps nurturance-withdrawal) are correlates of imitation-identification in a number of studies, they are not stronger determinants than a number of others.

---

[19] There is no positive correlation between measures of perceived similarity with the opposite-sex parent and measures of "maladjustment" or "neuroticism" in women and only a slight one in men.

As elaborated earlier, "positive atmosphere" effects seem to best fit these findings, e.g., that the instructions and examples of liked persons are more readily assimilated than those of disliked persons.

2. *Identification with the aggressor.* Few studies have found any "identification with the aggressor" effects. The few studies finding such effects can be best interpreted in terms of the concept that "the aggressor" is perceived as powerful, competent and sex-appropriate (masculine). In any case, the theory does not account for general-power competence effects.

3. *Status envy theory.* Bandura et al. (1963c) found that the experimental owner of resources was imitated, not the consumer of the resources. Admiration of the power of the "owner" rather than envy of the consumer was presumably, therefore, the determinant of imitation.

As theorists concerned with identification have focused more specifically on the phenomena of childhood imitation, sex-typing, and perceived similarity to parents, they have increasingly converged on a notion of power as the central status attribute in modeling. This central focus is to be found in the theories of Brim (1958), Kagan (1958), Maccoby (1959), Parsons and Bales (1955), and Mussen and Rutherford (1963). In contrast to neo-psychoanalytic theories, these theories do not assume identification to be an incorporation of the other, but view it as a process of role-playing, i.e., of enacting the role of the other. The theories assume that roles are packages of behavior performed by classes of persons, so that playing the other's role does not imply magically equating the body or identity of the self with the other, nor does it imply that one plays the other's role in order to "magically" give oneself what the other gives or to magically do away with the other. The most elaborated of these theories (Brim, 1958; Maccoby, 1959) start from G. H. Mead's (1934) analysis of the bipolar or complementary role-taking process. In interacting with another, the child must implicitly take the other's role. Under certain circumstances, covert role-taking will lead to overt role-playing. In some cases, the absence of the other will make playing his role realistic or appropriate. As an example, it is sometimes found that on the death of a father, the widow or son will not only take over the father's functions but will play out stylistically and interpersonally the particular role of the father, a role they had long taken implicitly in interacting with him. In other cases, the role of the other will be played out as fantasy, a playing out which may promote competence in the child's playing of his own role with the other (Maccoby, 1959). From this perspective, it is logical to assume that the basic conditions for taking and playing the role of the other are that the consequences of interaction with the other are important to the child. If the other person controls resources on which the child depends, and access to these resources is contingent on playing a certain role to the other or in correctly anticipating the other's role, then the child should "identify with" or play out the other's role under appropriate "free" conditions. It is evident this type of analysis of identification as role-playing or role-practice is fitted to deal with the child's selective enactment of familiar roles (other than his own) in an unstructured situation, such as family doll-play. It is not, however, a theory of general conditions under which a child will learn a behavior or attitude of a model or wish to be like another person, including conditions in which he had not had a history of complementary role interaction with that person.

When one considers the general characteristics of models which elicit imitation, it becomes apparent that power is too narrow a term for the attributes of favored models. As Bandura's (1969) Mickey Mantle example suggests, any form of competence by a model in any (or no) direct relationship to the child may elicit imitation. While power is one index of competence, it is only one of many. As long as this is true, boys will continue to prefer to be like big league ball players or inventive scientists to being like generals or senators or bankers. The cognitive-developmental theory, then, would propose that there are as many qualities of an emulated model as there are perceived forms of competence. In addition to sheer perceived competence, the perception of similarity to, or relevance of, the model to the self is the other major status determinant of imitation-identification.

The statement just made is, in effect, a direct derivative of the notions of the primary competence motivation for imitation discussed in previous sections. The motive for imitating is not a peculiar or special one, as identification theories have assumed. The reason for imitating is to do the competent, "smart," right, or effective thing. Insofar as the model's status is an index of his competence, it tends also to be an index of the competence or "rightness" of his action. Insofar as this is the case, one need not assume that the enactment of the model's behavior is instrumental to some further equation of the self and the model, and hence need not assume that this equation involves magical thinking. The assumption is rather that the power and competence of the model leads the child to see the specific act modeled as competent (or "big boy") and so makes it gratifying to perform, because he likes to perform competent acts, which make him feel more competent. It does not assume that the child's modeling indicates the desire to introject the model, to magically share his powers, or to act toward the self as the model has.

We have discussed so far the status determinants of imitation in a way which would account for an adult's tendency to copy the tennis style of a tennis star, or the writing style of a Freud. The account, however, raises a number of issues about the development of concepts of competence and their relations to modeling. Piaget and Baldwin discuss early infant motivation in terms of assimilation of the interesting and circular reaction. As the infant's cognitive structuring of the self and the world progresses, the assimilation of the interesting becomes a definite motive to master, to be competent, to demonstrate power or control over events. Such a development presupposes a differentiation between the self (as a locus of agency) and the other (as a locus of agency), a sense of causal relation, and a differentiation of what the self causes from what others cause. These differentiations in concepts of objectivity and causality develop in sequential order and are completed by the end of the second year of life (Piaget, 1954). At this point, the desire for mastery is reflected in the need to do things oneself. A typical incident is a two-year-old's frustration at putting on his coat, followed by a temper tantrum if his mother tries to help him. The temper tantrum indicates that the child clearly differentiates what he can cause from what others can do, and as a result only what he can do leads to a sense of "mastery."

We have pointed to the cognitive development of a self-other differentiation in causality as transforming effectance motivation, the assimilation of the interesting, into a definite desire for power and control over things and people. At first it would seem that such competence strivings would lead only to independent and negativistic rather than imitative behavior. It is clear, however, that such a striving for power and control is a precondition to perceiving superior power and control in a model, and imitating as a result. At an early stage of lack of differentiation of self and world, the child may not imitate the adult's act which generates interesting consequences (swinging the birds) because he will "believe" that he generated those consequences himself. At a later stage, however, he will imitate the adult to gain the assurance that he, too, can generate those consequences. At the stage of negativism, the child makes an even sharper differentiation of what he can do and what the other can do. Before this period it is typical that the child feels satisfied if the act is completed with the aid of the mother or someone else like the self.[20] At the negativistic stage insistence on independence in the performance of an act is independence in performing an act "imitatively" learned from others. In our example, "putting on the coat myself" is still an imitation of the mother's care-taking act. So "independence," "doing things oneself," is still an expression of competence motivation which generates further imitation.

The negativistic crisis, then, heralds the clear awareness that there is something more competent and powerful in being the model than in imitating. This first leads to the "look-at-me behavior," the need to turn around the imitator-imitated roles described in connection with Baldwin's (1906) theory. It also leads to an increasing selectivity of models on the grounds of relative power and competence. With growing awareness of relative competence and power, the child will award some generalized capacity or power to adults or others regardless of the particular consequences of the adult's specific act. At this point the child takes "on faith" the fact that the adult's act is a demonstration of power and competence and imitates it in order to make sure that he, too, can do the "grown up" or "big boy" thing being modeled.

The cognitive-structural developments in the differentiation of the competence of self and other just discussed are largely responsible for the growing

---

[20] It is this undifferentiated feeling of mastery which psychoanalysis termed "primary identification with the mother" and "feelings of omnipotence" and which Ausubel (1957) terms "executive dependency associated with volitional independency." The lack of differentiation of causal agency, however, is actually not limited to the mother, as these terms suggest.

generalized imitativeness of adult models found in the years 3 to 6, and discussed in Section X. In the period from 5 to 8, there is further cognitive development in concepts of competence which leads to selective imitation of good and skillful, as opposed to older and more powerful, models and to a selective modeling of good and skillful behavior by the model (as opposed to other aspects of his behavior). These trends were discussed in Section X, and related to the development of concrete-operational conceptualization of role relations and attributes. In terms of concepts of competence, we shall merely stress here that the change is from physicalistic to psychological-normative notions of the relative competence of individuals. During the earlier (3-5) period, the child assimilates the superior skill and virtue of individuals to their age-status, which is defined in terms of physical size and strength. An earlier quoted example was the boy who discussed the adult's task skill as a product of "bigger body, bigger brain." Children under five do not tend to be able to distinguish age from size, and assume that physically growing up automatically leads to possessing adult competence, just as their own growing up has led them to no longer be that worst of all categories, "babies." By the early school years, the child has discriminated physical attributes of competence (being big and strong, and owning things) from "psychological" attributes of competence ("being smart," "knowing things," "doing things right," "being good") which represent the fitness of behavior to a normatively defined role with a status in a social order (Kohlberg, 1965, 1969). Associated with this differentiation is a more refined and disciplined imitation of the "good" and "smart" way of doing things of the model rather than a simple sharing of the activity.

Associated with this differentiation of competence from age-size is a growing differentiation of the competences appropriate to males and females. At the preschool level, sex differences are more or less equated with age differences. Insofar as the sexes are different, it is because males are physically bigger and stronger than females, just as grown-ups are bigger and stronger than children (Kohlberg, 1966b). As an example, four-year-old Philip told his mother, "When you grow up to be a Daddy, you can have a bicycle too (like Daddy's)." As "virtues" or forms of competence are discriminated from age-size, these virtues become increasingly sex-typed. In the years from 4 to 7, girls develop a clear perception that feminine competence and status are based on being "attractive" and "nice," rather than on being powerful, aggressive, and fearless. (Boys come to make grossly similar distinctions, in learning to differentiate the qualities of the "good guys" and the "bad guys," both of whom are alike in physical attributes.)

There are, then, major developmental shifts in status-dimensions of the model leading to imitation. These shifts are not due to the formation of new motives for imitation, but are due to cognitive-structural transformations in conceptions of role-competence. These cognitive changes lead to a rechanneling of primary competence motivation into varying channels of selective imitation. A single example may clarify the point. Psychological discussions of "ownership of resources" have a simple cash meaning in the world of the American child. When asked, "who is the best one in the family," a majority of 24 middle- and lower-class six-year-old boys and girls replied "the father," and give as the single most frequent reason "because he makes the money" (Kohlberg, 1965). In contrast, a minority of four-year-old children choose father as "best," and none give "making money" as a reason for choice of "best one in the family." The response that father is the best one in the family forms the highest step in an age-developmental cumulative Guttman scale of appreciation of the father's cash function which includes the following items or the following order of increased maturity:[21]

1. Father chosen as the one most needed to buy things in the store.
2. Father chosen as most needed in the family in general.
3. Father chosen as best one in the family.

This development in awareness of economic functions of the father closely parallels the following logical development of a general understanding of economic roles which is stage sequential (Guttman scaleable) and is closely linked to Piaget's (1947) stages of logical development (Strauss, 1954; Danziger, 1958):

1. *Preconceptual* (Age 3-4). Money is not recognized as a symbol of value different from other objects and it is not understood that money is exchanged in purchase and sale transactions. Money is not recognized as necessary for gaining all objects from stores, i.e., as necessary for having food.

2. *Intermediate* (Age 4-5). Children recognize that money transfer is required in stores, but do not recognize that the transfer is an exchange of equal economic value. The exchange of work or job for salary is not understood, nor is the scarcity of money understood. Money is thought to come from a store or the bank without any exchange or input required. The mother is as much or more the supplier of money and goods than the father because she goes to the bank and gets the money, and goes to the store and buys the food.

3. *Concrete operational* (Age 6-8). Children recognize money transactions as involving a logical relation of reversible, reciprocal, and equal exchange of values. They understand that the storekeeper must pay money to others for his goods, they understand the work-salary exchange, and the scarcity or "conservation" of money. Accordingly, the child recognizes the need and importance of the father's work-role ("otherwise the family will die or starve").

The logical and sequential nature of the development of the valuing of the father's economic function indicates that it is not a cultural learning of the male-dominant and materialistic values of the American culture, but is a natural cognitive development (in families with a sexual division of labor in economic

---

[21] Obviously, the scale is derived from children in intact families with non-working mothers.

roles). This cognitive development in definitions of family power and prestige, in turn, is a determinant of modeling. At age 4-5, physicalistic sex stereotypes are critical in differentiating mother and father roles (Kohlberg, 1965, 1966b). While fathers are perceived as bigger, stronger, and more aggressive than mothers by age 4-5, social power and prestige are not clearly typed in favor of the father until 6-7 (Emmerich, 1961; Kohlberg, 1965). This, in turn, is linked to the father's economic and work functions, as already discussed.

The developmental tendency to award greater authority to the father-role leads in turn to a developmental increase in modeling the father in the ages (4-7) mentioned. This tendency is true for girls as well as boys.[22]

To close the cognitive-developmental circle, bright children are advanced on all the trends mentioned, including the trend for boys and girls to increasingly orient to the father as a model.

The fundamental assertion of the present section has been that the general characteristic of the model's status leading to imitation is his role-appropriate competence as this is perceived by the child, and that this perception undergoes cognitive-developmental transformations. While this generalization is so prosaic as to scarcely require documentation, it does cast light on the findings of studies of social-power effects on imitation which are otherwise puzzling. In particular, these studies indicate the following points:

a) Interpersonal power over the child is only an aspect of general competence which is the determining status attribute for modeling.

b) The import of power for the child's modeling is contingent upon whether power is a role-appropriate form of competence, an issue determined by the child's sex-role stereotypes.

With regard to the first point, Van Manen (1967) found that adolescent children's value-similarity to the father was not correlated with the father's dominance over the boy or the father's dominance over the mother. The boy's identification, however, was correlated with the father's external occupational competence (job success and satisfaction as perceived by father, mother, and in part, "objectively"). Sixty-six per cent of the children of the 80 fathers dissatisfied with their jobs were low in value agreement with their fathers, as compared to only 7 per cent of the children of the remaining 225 fathers.

With regard to the second point, paternal dominance over the spouse (Hetherington, 1965; Hetherington & Frankie, 1967) has been found to correlate markedly and clearly with boys' same-sex parent imitation-identification as measured in a quasi-experimental setting. These same studies indicated that there was no relationship between maternal dominance and girls' same-sex parent identification. Dominance is a form of competence in fathers because it is role-appropriate (as perceived by children) but it is not a form of competence in mothers.

---

[22] In the case of the girls this modeling is not part of a global desire to be like the father, but is due to the notion that he knows the right way to do things better than the mother, is smarter, etc.

These findings clarify various puzzles in social-learning experiments on imitation. As an example, among 16 experimental groupings in the Bandura et al. (1963c) study of control of resources, the single highest modeling effect was that found for boys to imitate a male adult who was ignored by a female adult who dispensed rewards to the boy subject. The rewards were candies, cookies, etc., typically dispensed by "mother figures." The boys in this condition tended to criticize the lady dispenser and sympathize with the ignored male (e.g., "She doesn't share much, she's greedy. John played bravely even though she didn't share."). Even in preschool, when feminine power violates sex stereotypes of feminine givingness and when masculine impotence coincides with masculine "virtue" and "bravery," it seems to be sex-typed virtue and not bare power which leads to imitation

In addition to the role appropriateness of the model's competence, a cognitive-developmental theory would stress that the relevance of the model's role to the child's own is a major determinant of imitation. A major determinant of relevance is the degree of similarity between the child and the model. At an adult level, this has been documented by Stotland and his colleagues (Stotland, Zander & Natsoulas, 1961). At the childhood level, and at the level of gross sameness of role, it is so basic as to have been ignored. We noted that at the earliest stage of imitation, the child only "imitates" the behavior of others which is already in his repertoire, i.e., the infant's repetition of other's actions and his repetition of his own actions are indistinguishable. At later stages, novel behavior of others is repeated, but with an increasing sensitivity to the like-self quality necessary for another to serve as model. While the infant may imitate physical things and animals, this is presumably because the boundaries of self as animate and human are not clearly distinguished from the not-self as inanimate or non-human. In any case, by age 5, prolonged imitation of the non-human is considered pathological. By age 5, the sameness of sex of child and model has also become a most basic determinant of modeling, as discussed previously. After age 5, there is also a fairly steady increase of imitation of peers, as compared to an adult, in spite of recognition of the superior competence of adults[23] (Kohlberg & Zigler, 1967). The importance of similarity as a determinant of modeling is not only highly important by age 6, but it is a focus of generalized awareness. In one study (Kohlberg, 1965, 1966b) children aged 4 to 8 were shown animal pictures in sets composed of four animals of the same species, two of which were of the same color. The child was then asked, "Which animals do the same (specified) activity?" and "Which animals like each other?" Over 70 per cent of the responses of children 5 and over named the same-colored animals for both these sets of questions, although four-year-olds did not choose the same-colored animals beyond the level of chance (33 per cent). This growing self-consciousness about

---

[23] This tendency is, of course, task-relative. In an instructional setting with a right answer, adults are preferentially imitated; in a value-preference situation, peers are preferentially imitated.

similarity is suggested by the response of a seven-year-old boy after his four-year-old brother had just expressed a preference for a male baby-sitter. When the younger boy was asked why he wanted a boy, his older brother intervened to say, "because he's a boy, himself, of course."

While similarity is a major determinant of imitation, it is only one of many determinants of the model's relevance to the child's imitation. The concept of similarity is itself a cognitive-classificatory development of the concrete-operational period. Before the period of categorical-classificatory thought, feelings of "likeness" may be based as much on proximity, familiarity, and dependency as upon similarity in role, status, or attribute. As an example, it is not until about age 6 that the boy preferentially imitates his father even though he preferentially orients to boys as opposed to girls at an earlier age (Kohlberg, 1966b). Before this, the young boy tends to feel his mother is most like him because feelings of social closeness at young ages are based more on association than upon judgments of similarity. As conceptual relations between persons become based on attributes of similarity and class membership, so do definitions of social ties.

As an example, when children were asked to put family dolls together with the ordinary concept-formation instruction ("Put the ones together that go together"), it was not until age 5 that a majority of children grouped the dolls on the basis of similarity (boys together, mothers together, etc.). Before this, dolls were primarily grouped associatively ("the boy and girl go together because they play together"). At age 5-6, then, categorization (object-sorting) and generalized preference in imitation (same-color animals choose each other) develop together. With age and IQ controlled, significant correlations were found between object-sorting classification, same-color choice on the animal test, and doll-play imitation of the same-sex parent, indicating the cognitive roots of a growing same-sex orientation of imitation.

Of the determinants of relevance other than similarity, prior interaction with the model is perhaps most important. Many of the effects of prior experimenter nurturance or reward upon the child's imitation may be understood in these terms. As an example, a study by Emmerich and Kohlberg (1953) involved three groups of kindergarten children. In the first or nurturance group, children were given help and praise by the experimenter in a puzzle task; in the second or conflict group, children were given help but blamed and criticized in the task; and in a third group the children were ignored by the experimenter during their work on the puzzle. The experimenter then joined the child in a sticker-kit design-making session in which the child's tendency to copy the experimenter's designs could be measured. The results were a significantly lower amount of imitation for the children who had been ignored (0.4 imitative designs) than for either of the other two conditions (3.0 and 3.2 imitative acts respectively). There were no differences between the children who were nurtured and those who were criticized and blamed.

What seemed to count was the mere fact of interaction, whether that interaction was negative or positive. Thus, an interpretation of the nurturance condition as causing responses like the E's to acquire secondary reinforcement value seemed ruled out. In both conditions of high interaction, it seemed that the experimenter's helping and evaluating activity defined him as someone who was a relevant norm-setter for shared activities in the situation. Whether help and evaluation of the child were positive or negative, the experimenter defined himself as an evaluator, guide and participant in the child's activities. If the experimenter fairly explicitly defines himself as a norm-setter in shared activities with the child, it seems obvious that he is more likely to be imitated than if he does not.

In summary, then, the findings on selective imitation of models may be best explained in terms of the child's perception of the models' competence and of their relevance to his own role. The age-development of selective preference for models may be explained in terms of the cognitive development of the child's concepts of role competence, and in his conceptions of dimensions of relevance such as similarity.

XIV. THE DEVELOPMENT OF SOCIAL DEPENDENCY AND ATTACHMENT

In Sections VIII and IX, we sketched a conception of identification in which imitation was one component of a cluster of attitudes of perceived similarity, dependency, attachment, approval-seeking, and moral conformity toward the parent. We said that all the correlational studies supported the existence of such a cluster of attitudes toward parents. We questioned the neo-psychoanalytic sequence designed to account for these correlations and pointed out that Baldwin's (1906) theory suggested that under at least some conditions, this sequence might be turned on its head. The alternative sequences proposed are as shown in Figure 6.5.

Examples of the cognitive-developmental sequence appear in the formation

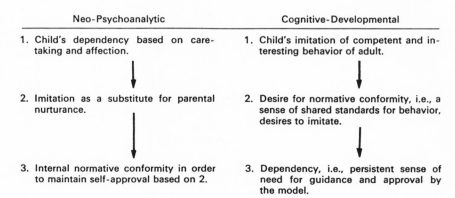

Neo-Psychoanalytic	Cognitive-Developmental
1. Child's dependency based on care-taking and affection.	1. Child's imitation of competent and interesting behavior of adult.
2. Imitation as a substitute for parental nurturance.	2. Desire for normative conformity, i.e., a sense of shared standards for behavior, desires to imitate.
3. Internal normative conformity in order to maintain self-approval based on 2.	3. Dependency, i.e., persistent sense of need for guidance and approval by the model.

FIGURE 6.5.

of adolescent or adult relations of dependency-identification, where these have no basis in extensive prior interaction and care, and where there is no sexual basis for the relation. A familiar case to the reader is the identification of a student with a same-sex teacher. Such relations are based on the competence and interest value of the teacher's behavior generating (or joining with a prior) desire to be like, or to be in a role like, the teacher, which in turn generates a need to share his normative attitudes and obtain his guidance, approval, etc. This sequence, familiar enough in young adulthood, is also apparent in childhood relations to older same-sex figures. The seven-year-old boy quoted earlier, who explained that his younger brother wanted a male baby-sitter "because he was a boy himself" went on to say that he (the seven-year-old) wanted a male baby-sitter because "a girl can't teach me anything."

The sequence just described also best fits the available evidence on the development of the boy's orientation to the father in the years from 4 to 8 (Kohlberg, 1966b). The development of the boy's attachment and identification with the father is of particular interest because it is the first strong attachment which cannot be explained in terms of the physical caretaking or social instinct theories so frequently introduced in discussions of the mother-child tie. The existence of the shift has been documented in studies with various social classes and ethnic groups, using various measures which all show preschool boys as somewhat female-oriented in doll-play and experimental tests of social dependency toward adults and parent figures, and show a shift to male-oriented preference at about age 6 (Kohlberg, 1966b). While all identification theories postulate such a mother-father shift for the boy, none provide a very adequate mechanism for it. It does not seem that the shift could be a result of the fact that the father actually becomes the primary nurturer and rewarder in these years while the mother ceases to be, while the psychoanalytic account in terms of castration anxiety raises many difficulties in accounting for a positive shift in dependency.

The cognitive-developmental explanation of a developmental shift in the boy's orientation to his parents is straightforward. The theory would claim that the child learns to sex-type himself and his activities during the second and third year. By the age of 3 to 4 the boy knows quite well he is a boy and prefers "boy things" to "girl things" simply because he likes himself and that which is familiar or similar to himself. Up to this point in his development, he has remained mother-oriented, however. Tending now to prefer masculine activities, he seeks a model for these activities. Thus he is led to select his father rather than his mother as a model. Imitation in turn leads to emotional dependency upon the father. The sequence can be diagramed as shown in Figure 6.6.

The existence of such a sequence was confirmed in a semi-longitudinal study of boys aged 4 to 8 (Kohlberg, 1966b; Kohlberg & Zigler, 1967). Like other studies, this study indicated that there was a clear preference[24] for appropriately

---

[24] "Clear" male preference on these tests denotes over 60 per cent of the choices or responses of the age group went to the male object or figure.

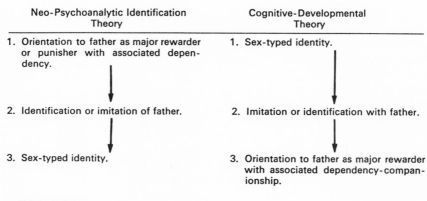

FIGURE 6.6.

sex-typed objects and activities by age 3 (on Brown's [1956] IT Scale and the Sears et al. [1965] Pictures Test), a clear preference for imitating the male figure by age 5 (on Hartup's [1962] measure of imitating the doll father as against the doll mother and on the measure of imitating a male E more than a female E), and a clear preference for orienting social dependency to the male at age 6 (on Ammons & Ammons [1949] measure of relative choice of father and mother doll as agent of nurturance and on a measure of amount and "dependency" of talk to a male, as opposed to a female, E).

The age at which an individual child advanced through this sequence varied considerably. One of the major determinants of speed of movement was cognitive maturity. As a group bright boys, aged 4 (mental age 6), displayed male preference in dependency and imitation as well as in sex-typing whereas average boys did not display male dependency preference until age 6[25] (Kohlberg & Zigler, 1967). Regardless of the boy's speed in moving through the sequence, however, he moved through it in the same order, i.e., the tests mentioned defined a cumulative Guttman scale. All but 3 of 48 boys fell into one of the four scale-type groups (passes all preference tests, passes sex-typing and imitation but not dependency tests, passes sex-typing tests only, fails all tests).

The existence of such a sequence and its relation to cognitive maturity is extremely difficult to explain in terms of any other theory of identification. All the usual theories that might account for the measured shifts from mother to father between the ages of 4 and 6 seem to be ruled out by a study by C. Smith (unpublished, summarized in Kohlberg, 1966b). Half of the subjects of the study, all Negro boys, came from father-absent homes, half from father-present

---

[25] Bright boys go through the sequence faster than average boys because: (a) they cognitively stabilize a gender identity faster (as in the "conservation of sex-role" test), (b) they become aware of general relations of similarity faster, i.e., become aware that they and their fathers are both male sooner (as in the concept-formation test), and (c) become aware of the competence of male adults sooner (as in awareness of the father's economic role).

homes. These groups in turn were equally divided by age (5 and 7) and by IQ (average and mildly retarded). The boys were administered the same tests as in the Kohlberg and Zigler (1967) study. The age trends for both father-absent and father-present Negro boys of average IQ were quite similar to those found in an average IQ middle-class white population. By age 7 almost all boys had 100 per cent masculine choice on the IT Scale and a clear majority were father, as opposed to mother, oriented on the identification measures. At age 5 identification choice was mixed (about 50 per cent) and masculine sex-typing was incomplete. Clear IQ effects were found in both father-absent and father-present groups, similar to those found in middle-class children (Kohlberg & Zigler, 1967). Mildly retarded boys aged 7 were more like their mental age counterparts (the average IQ boys aged 5) than they were like their chronological age counterparts (the average IQ boys aged 7). In sum, general cognitive and social development is leading the father-absent boys to develop attitudes of "identification" toward non-existent fathers which are grossly similar to those father-present boys develop toward their own fathers.

These findings indicate that the age-developmental trend toward father identification cannot be explained by any of the usual theories, such as anaclitic theory (an actual increase in nurturance and reward by the father), imitation theory (fear of retaliation by the father for sexualized attachment to the mother), social reinforcement theory (mother shifts to rewarding the boys for imitating the father). All these theories assume a present and active father.[26]

In the case of the boy's identification with the father (or with a teacher) we have stressed a definite sequence in which a similar identity precedes imitation, which precedes dependency-attachment. We have done so to stress the fact that the element of the identification-cluster which appears to be the developmentally simplest and earliest in the child, social dependency (the need for proximity, help, and response), is not, in general, the first and prior element in the formation of human bonds.[27] The case of the development of the boy's identification with the father in the years 4 to 8 is artificial, however, since the cognitive-development requirements of this particular development slow its component down into a definite sequential order. Where developing cognitive abstractions are not involved in slowing down the steps in identification, its different components tend to develop more or less simultaneously.[28]

---

[26] The fact that these theories do not explain sex-typed preference or the child's sense of gender identity goes without saying, since such a sex-typed identity is established before, or in the absence of, a preferential identification with the father and even in the absence of a father at all.

[27] To recur to the earlier example, the student who displays early help-seeking or instrumental dependency to a teacher is most unlikely to form any social or stable attachment, unlike the student who follows the identification sequence.

[28] As an example, girls, too, seem to increase, though less markedly, in father identification in the 4 to 7 period, partly because of increased awareness of the prestige or competence of the father's role. In this development, there seems to be no particular sequence in the relative increase of imitation and dependency components of identification.

We have stressed the boy-father identification to establish the fact that: (1) the formation of human social bonds or attachments requires components of past shared-identity (similarity) and of the disposition to share and learn new behavior patterns (imitation), and (2) therefore, the motivational determinants of attachment are in large part those discussed already as determinants of imitation. These considerations allow us to sketch out briefly a general cognitive-developmental theory of attachment which contrasts markedly with social learning, psychoanalytic, and ethological theories of attachment. (A comprehensive survey of these theories and the relevant research data is provided by Maccoby, 1969.)

Our theory holds that the motivation of social attachment, like the motivation of imitation, must be primarily defined in terms of effectance or competence motivation. The interest value of the activities of the other, his competence and social value, the relevance of his competence to the self's own action, and the general degree of similarity or like-mindedness of the self and other are all major determinants of dependency or attachment as we have shown they are for imitation-identification. All these conditions have repeatedly been found to be important by social psychologists concerned with studying adult affiliation, friendship formation, marriage, and leader-follower relations.

As studied by social psychology, a social attachment or bond is conceived of as a relationship of sharing, communication, and cooperation (or reciprocity) between selves recognizing each other as other selves. In contrast, all popular child psychological theories have denied that experience of, and desire for, sharing and communication between selves are the primary components of a human social bond. Their model of the child's attachment to others has been based on a model of an attachment to a physical object, or to a physical source of physical pleasure or pain. The "physical object" concept of social attachment is equally basic to Freudian (1938) theory (cathexis of the physical body of the other), to secondary drive and reinforcement theory (presence and response of the other is associated with care-taking reinforcement and so becomes a secondary reinforcer, i.e., the presence of the bottle or the breast is desired because it is associated with hunger reduction), and to ethological "social instinct" theory which implies that clinging responses are imprinted on the body of the mother as the baby chick is imprinted on a physical decoy (Bowlby, 1958; Harlow, 1959).

If, in contrast to physical theories, one takes the desire for a social bond with another *social self* as the primary "motive" for attachment, then this desire derives from the same motivational sources as that involved in the child's own strivings for stimulation, for activity, mastery, and for self-esteem. Social motivation is motivation for shared stimulation, for shared activity, and shared competence and self-esteem. Social dependency implies dependency upon another person as a source for such activity, and for the self's competence or esteem. The basic nature of competence motivation, however, is the same whether self or the other is perceived as the primary agent producing the desired stimulation, activity, or competence, i.e., whether the goal is "independent mastery," social mastery (dominance), or social dependence. The differences between the two are differences in the cognitive structures of the self-other relationships involved.[29]

In our discussion of Baldwin's theory of the bipolar social self (Section VIII), we indicated the exact sense in which the same desire to master an activity or situation would at one time lead the child to imitative following, at another to dominating "showing off," at a third to independent "doing it myself." We cited research showing that imitation and "verbal dependence" were tendencies correlated with one another and with brightness and active mastery in preschool children. The research showed that while these tendencies were positively correlated in children, they were negatively correlated in situations, some situations being appropriate for imitation, others for verbal dependency, others for independent mastery. These situational definitions were in turn related to the cognitive-developmental status and self-concept of the child. The polarity between active mastery and passive dependence is, then, not a polarity between two motives but a polarity of social-situational and self-definition. (A generally passive-dependent child is not one with a stronger motive for a social bond; if he were, he would engage in more of the independent behavior which would win him social approval.)

The more physicalistic models have found favor in considering early attachment, because of the physical dependency of the infant and his apparent similarity to infants in lower species with more definite or rigid instincts. It is clear, however, that there is no such definite attachment to the mother in the infant before the age of six months, i.e., there are no separation reactions before this period (Yarrow, 1964; Schaffer & Emerson, 1964). This casts suspicion on mechanistic imprinting or conditioning accounts which are plausible for the early forming attachments of lower species.

Human (and perhaps primate) attachments, even in the first two years of life, reflect the fact that they are attachments to another self or center of consciousness and activity like the self, i.e., that they are "identifications."

This fact of human attachment implies the following characteristics:

1. *Attachment involves similarity to the other.* Attachment is only to another person, not toward physical objects. The distinctive sign of instinctual imprinting in lower species is that a decoy object may be imprinted. In baby monkeys, there may be an attachment to a blanket or cloth figure, but it is not a social attachment,

---

[29]An account of social ties in terms of competence motivation and resulting desires for sharing does not deny the importance of sex, aggression, and anxiety in human relations. It does deny that drives provide the basic source of human social attachment. Were human attachments dependent upon instinctual drives, they would have the unstable periodicity, the promiscuity of arousing objects, the narcissistic quality which drives typically have, not only in mammals but in humans. Even the most attached male is capable of fantasy sexual arousal by someone to whom he is not attached, and is capable of sexual drive reduction in nonsocial onanistic ways. Sexual lust is anchored by a social attachment of sharing which makes it love; without such sharing, it is not a cause of attachment. As dryly stated by Kinsey et al. (1953), "In a socio-sexual relationship, the sexual partners may respond to each other and to the responses made by each other. For this reason, most persons find socio-sexual relationships more satisfactory than solitary sexual activities."

as the Harlows (Harlow & Harlow, 1962) discovered. Whether "contact-comfort" blankets or oral drive-reducing bottles are involved, neither creates a social attachment.

2. *Attachment involves love or altruism toward the other,* an attitude not felt toward bottles or cloth mothers. Altruism, of course, presupposes the "ejective" consciousness of the feelings and wishes of the other, i.e., empathy or sympathy.

3. *Attachment and altruism presuppose self-love.* The striving to satisfy another self presupposes the capacity or disposition to satisfy one's own self. Common sense assumes that the self (as body and center of activity) is loved intrinsically, not instrumentally (i.e., not because the body or the body's activities are followed by reinforcement or drive reduction). It is this nucleus of self-love which is involved, also, in organizing attachment to others.

4. *Attachment involves a defined possessive bond or relation linking the self and the other.* This is most clear when the bond is least "selfishly" possessive, as in the parent's attachment to his child. The difference between the attachment of the parent and that of the nurse or foster mother to the child illustrates this component.

5. *Attachment presupposes the desire for esteem in the eyes of the other or for reciprocal attachment.* In other words, it presupposes self-esteem motivation and the need for social approval, again presupposing ejective consciousness.

To summarize, a human social bond presupposes a relation to another self, a relation which involves various types of sharing and of identification between the self and the other.

We have stressed the cognitive structures and self-esteem motivations found prerequisite for post-infant human attachment by social psychology. The rudiments of these prerequisites are also evident in primate and infant attachments. With regard to mammalian attachments, it is striking that the social species are also (a) the more cognitive species, (b) the more imitative species, and (c) the more playful (primary competence motivated) species. The fact that these attributes are primary to monkey sociality is suggested by the Harlows' (Harlow & Harlow, 1962) studies of monkey socialization. First the studies indicate that monkey attachment is neither the result of drive reduction nor of imprinting in any mechanistic sense. Associations of a wire "mother" with hunger-satisfaction do not lead to attachment to the wire "mother" or to anything else. Cloth "mothers" will be clung to by baby monkeys for "contact comfort" in quasi-instinctual fashion, but this does not generate later social attachment either to the cloth "mother" or to other monkeys any more than does experience with wire mothers. The fact that satisfaction of contact-comfort needs and early "imprinting" of these needs on a cloth mother does not generate any forms of social behavior in the monkey is indicated by the absence of social behavior or attachment in adult monkeys to either their cloth "mothers" or to other monkeys. If contact comfort does not generate social attachment by "imprinting" mechanisms neither does sheer visual exposure to other monkeys (in other cages) generate attachment or lead to social "imprinting," though it does lead to prepatterned responses.

What Harlow has found to be sufficient for the formation of monkey attachments and for "normal" adult social and sexual behavior is social interaction with peers in play. What elements of play interaction are important has not been specified, though it is clear the elements are more than body contact, visual exposure, and drive reduction. It is very likely that it is the social quality of the interaction that is important, where "social" is taken as reciprocity or sharing of behavior. In general, even simple social play and games have the character of either complementarity-reciprocity (I do this, then you do that, then I do this) or of imitation (I do this, and you do this, too). In either case there is a shared pattern of behavior, since reciprocal play is a sort of reciprocal imitation ("you follow me, then I follow you"). One cannot claim that such sharing creates "the ejective consciousness" in the monkey, but the contrast between films of mother monkeys without childhood social experience and those who have had such experience suggests something like "ejective consciousness" in the normal monkey mothers. The socially deprived monkey mothers simply treat their infants as disturbing physical things, in marked contrast to the normal monkey mothers.

Turning to the human data, the widespread notion that a specifically maternal early caretaking relationship is essential for basic social development has borne up poorly under careful research scrutiny (Yarrow, 1964). Where early maternal deprivation has a deleterious effect on social development, it is part of a more general "package" of insufficient stimulation, cognitive as well as social, leading to retardation rather than irreversible "damage," and leading to cognitive, as well as emotional retardation (Casler, 1961; Dennis & Najarian, 1957). While adolescents and adults with long histories of social deprivation, of mistreatment, and of transfer from institution or foster home to foster home seem deficient in a capacity for social attachment, there is no clear evidence that these effects are due to infant deprivation, rather than to later negative influences in their life. In particular, insofar as deprivation or institutionalization have deep social effects, it seems to be due to the absence of stable and pleasurable social interaction, rather than a lack of maternal caretaking which produces weakened social ties. A. Freud and Dann's (1951) report of the deep identifications and attachments between young children which developed in a Nazi concentration camp without maternal caretaking suggest, at a deeper human level, the normal social attachments which peer interaction and sharing cause at the monkey level in Harlow's (1959) studies.[30]

---

[30] Insofar as early social environments cause schizoid and autistic withdrawals from social interaction which are not genetic, the effect appears not to be a sheer deprivation effect so much as an effect of nonresponsive and nonreciprocal mothering. As White (1963) suggests, it is the feeling of noncontrol, incompetence, of not having a predictable and reciprocal effect on the human environment which is probably the experiential agent in the autistic child's focus upon things, not people, as objects for interaction.

We have pointed out that the evidence suggests that positive social attachments develop out of intrinsic motivation to engage in social interaction and the intrinsic pleasure of social interaction, regardless of specific body instincts and drives. We have also said that the evidence suggests that this aspect of ego development has a natural developmental course and robustness in early life, so that, like other aspects of ego development, it is responsive to a much wider variety of functionally equivalent types of social stimulation than is suggested by doctrines of "mother love." We shall now trace a few of the steps in the development of social attachment implied by this account.

As was the case for stages of imitation, age-developmental progressions of attachment are generated by cognitive-structural changes. In the infant period, this is indicated by the work of Decarie (1965). Decarie found (a) close age parallels between Piaget progressions in physical object concepts and social object-relations or psychoanalytic ego-stages, and (b) correlations between the two such that infants advanced on one scale were advanced on the other. For various reasons, it is more plausible to assume that cognitive advance is the more basic or causal factor in this parallelism, though there is some reason to think that the cognitive advance is reflected earlier in the social-object world than in the physical-object world. In the preschool period, this is suggested by my own work on father-attachment just summarized. Our sketch of the age-development of attachment stresses the following strands in cognitive-developmental theories of ego-development:

1. The Piagetian development of the concept of the mother as a permanent, causally independent but familiar object (completed by age 2).
2. The development of the child's conception of the parent (or older sibling) as having a mind, intelligence or will different than, and superior to, the child's own mentality or will, but one which he can share through processes of learning, conformity, and winning affection (completed by age 6-7). This development is termed "satellization" by Ausubel (1957), formation of "ideal self" by Baldwin (1906). The cognitive developments involve (a) the ability to make comparative judgments of competence, (b) the differentiation of the child's own mind and perspective from that of others, (c) development of conceptions of shared ascribed social identities of sex, age and kinship, and (d) the development of conceptions of shared rules.
3. The development of conceptions of reciprocity, of choice, of shared but relative self-chosen and individual values and identities (completed in adolescence); and the development of intimacy, friendship and love as discussed by Erikson (1950) and Sullivan (1953).

It is obvious that our account assumes that intense and stable attachment (love) is a mature end-point of ego-development, not a primitive tendency. A careful analysis of the research on age differences in response to separation and object-loss (Branstetter, 1969) supports this assumption.

As was the case for imitation, we must commence our account by noting that social objects are first responded to more than physical objects because they are much more interesting. It is evident that other people are especially interesting to infants and that this interest is due primarily to the fact that people look familiar and yet they are complex stimulus objects constantly engaging in interesting activities having some relationship to the infant's own activities. While some of the most interesting things done by social objects are to care for the needs of the infant, these activities fall into a much larger class of interesting activities.[31] The fact that the motivational conditions for early social responses are general information-processing conditions is suggested by recent findings on the determinants of attention and smiling to human-face schemata, e.g., "stimuli that resemble the infant's schema will maintain his attention with the greatest intensity. Stimuli that very closely match or have no relation to his schema will hold his attention for a much shorter time" (Kagan, 1968). In addition, however, the sudden recognition of the familiar (whether faces or other configurations) elicits smiling, because it leads to a rapid assimilation of an uncertain experience (Piaget, 1952b).[32] In this sense, the child's early social smile is functionally continuous with much of his later smiling and laughter at funny stimuli, i.e., stimuli which are first incongruous but suddenly "fall into place" in a somewhat unexpected way, as all theories of humor emphasize.

We have stressed the role of assimilation of the familiar and interesting in one positive social response, the smile. Failure to assimilate the unfamiliar and incongruous seems to be responsible for another early "attachment" response, the 8-12-month reaction of "stranger anxiety" (Morgan & Ricciutti, 1968). Before the appearance of stranger anxiety, all human faces tend to be assimilated to the familiar "mother" schema. The clear failure to fit the schema seems to induce stranger anxiety. After "normal" stranger anxiety has subsided in development (e.g., after 1 year) the donning of a mask by the mother will elicit a similar reaction of anxious response to incongruity in the apparently familiar (though the sheer presentation of a mask will not).[33] We do not yet know enough either about the infant's schema development or about the general conditions of schema-stimulus match to specify what is the optimal amount of incongruity to

---

[31] Wolff (1965) notes that attentiveness to external stimuli in very young infants was lowest when the infant was hungry or otherwise viscerally excited. The account which follows assumes that the infant's "social responses" are part of this broad attentiveness to the outside world, rather than that the child attends to the outside world only when something external meshes with a visceral drive-state.

[32] The notion that smiling to human faces is due to an association with feeding satisfaction has been disproved. Association of face-schema with bottle feeding reduced, rather than increased, smiling to a schema of the face in orphanage infants (because it made it overly familiar) (Wilson, 1962). The notion that the human face constitutes a specific "innate releasing mechanism" for an instinctive smiling response also seems untenable, since a large variety of complex stimuli will elicit smiling (Wilson, 1962).

[33] Just as smiling to a face has been reviewed as involving an innate releasing mechanism, stranger anxiety has been viewed as an innate "flight" response terminating the period of "imprinting" or attachment (Schaffer, 1966). Not only does the onset of stranger anxiety not terminate the potential for attachment, but it disappears in a way instinctive flight responses do not.

produce pleasurable attention and what is an overload of incongruity producing distress. However, the burgeoning work on infancy clearly suggests that early "social" responses will be understood in terms of the broad picture of assimilative reactions to patterned stimuli rather than in terms of specific prepatterned, maturationally unfolding responses to innate releasing stimuli for "attachment" or "flight," or by histories of conditioning (Ricciutti, 1968).

The implication of what has been said so far is that the infant's "social attachment" responses in the first eight months are simply part of his responsiveness to patterned external stimulation, rather than being genuinely "social" or forming the necessary groundwork of later human ties. We have claimed that preference for his parent over a stranger, so-called "stranger anxiety," is a negative response to the unfamiliar. In this regard it seems no more "social" than his anxiety about being placed in a strange room as opposed to a familiar room. Ainsworth (1963, 1964) suggests that it forms part of a sequential pattern of attachment behaviors, but neither her work nor that of Decarie (1965) has succeeded in arriving at a sequential or cumulative scale of social or mother "object relations" which clearly indicates any patterning not due to the sequential patterning of infants' responses to physical objects based on general Piagetian principles of cognitive development. The stages of the infant's construction of permanent independent physical objects have close parallels in the child's growth of awareness of the permanence and independence of social objects like the mother, as Decarie (1965) has documented. The age at which the child first shows stranger-anxiety and separation responses is the age (6-9 months) at which he first shows awareness of the permanence of physical objects (Decarie, 1965; Schaffer and Emerson, 1964). It is obvious that the permanent existence of the mother is a precondition to missing her. The open question is whether there are steps in the formation of a mother attachment which indicate something more than the child's general cognitive growth in response to external objects whether physical or social. If not, there is no reason to assume that early experience should have a basic effect on capacities for later social attachment unless early deprivation or trauma were so extreme as to retard responsiveness to external stimuli and cognitive development in general.

We have claimed that the 9-month response to the socially unfamiliar is in itself not "social" since it is no different from the child's response to the unfamiliar in general. The child's early separation responses may represent something more specifically social than this, however. The fact of object constancy indicates the beginning of a growth of selfness, a discrimination between the self and outer objects. While the mother must be recognized in some sense as an outer object to be missed when she is not present, she is also more self-like than other outer objects, as psychoanalytic theories of infancy have always stressed.

In a certain sense, the mother may be a part of the child to be missed as a part of his body might be missed. Separation and stranger anxiety, then, may not only be a reaction to an unfamiliar situation, but to the change or loss of a more or less permanent self. While a mother-infant identification may not be responsible for separation reactions in the first year of life, it seems clearly involved in reactions in the second year of life. By the second year of life, there is a self-other differentiation at the level of bodies but not of minds and wills. While "ejective consciousness" is established in the second year of life, the child's confusion between his own perspective on objects or mental reactions and those of others (termed egocentrism by Piaget [1947]) continues in quite gross form until age 5-7. Before the two-year-old's "negativistic crisis" signals awareness of a differentiation of wills and agencies, the child feels no sense of incompetence or weakness in either imitating others, obeying others (i.e., in being the agent of another's will), or in being helped by others (i.e., in the other being an agent of his will). In the second year of life, then, there is a sense in which the psychoanalytic notion of a primary identification or undifferentiated symbiotic bond with the mother is an accurate characterization of social relationships.[34]

Insofar as this is the case, this tie is not social; it involves neither acts of sharing nor love for the other nor the desire for love. This is brought out in Ausubel's (1952, 1957) account of the development of identification-attachment. According to Ausubel, in this undifferentiated phase, the infant conceives of the caretaker as a mere extension of his own wishes and actions, as an executive arm. Accordingly the infant's dependency upon the parent is essentially an instrumental or executive dependency rather than a volitional dependency, i.e., it is not a willingness to subordinate his actions to the wishes or responses of the parent. It does not imply any orientation to the psychic state of the mother, i.e., no desire to share psychic states, no altruism about her state, and no concern about being loved (as a psychic state in the other, important for self-esteem). Ausubel believes that growing cognitive differentiation of self and other and growing awareness of the superior power of the parents precipitates a third-year negativistic crisis typically resolved by accepting a satellite role in the family. The satellizing child gives up a sense of self-esteem based on his own power and achievement (and a controlling executive dependency over the mother which extends his sense of power to what he can get the mother to do) for a sense of vicarious self-esteem as the result of vicarious sharing of parental superiorities and as the result of being loved and being positively evaluated by parents and others. Both identification and volitional dependency are motivated by needs for self-esteem in a satellite role. The need to be loved does not precede identification but is contemporaneous with it in a total process of cognitively realistic ego devaluation where love, acceptance and attractive adult role models are available.

Ausubel's crisis-oriented typological account is useful as a dramatic sketch of the development of identification, compressing into a single conflict and a

---

[34] Bowlby (1958) and others have exaggerated the specificity and depth of the symbiotic clinging attachment to the mother in the second year of life, however. A recent carefully controlled study of the reactions of infants (age 1½ to 3) to hospitalization involved comparisons of mother-absent, "substitute-mother" volunteers, and rooming-in groups. While many of the mother-absent infants showed intense distress, there were no differences between the real and substitute-mother groups in distress reactions (Branstetter, 1969).

single relationship a process of social development going on in the first eight years of life. The account is limited, not only by condensing too much development into the resolution of a single crisis, but by its neglect of the positive experiences of, and motives for, sharing. Shared goals, shared norms and shared esteem are derived by Ausubel from a clash which leads the child to give up a unilateral primary "egoistic" will and sense of competence or self-esteem for a unilateral "derived" sense of goals and sense of self-esteem, rather than from more positive, unconflicted and egalitarian experiences of sharing.

In particular, both Ausubel and the psychoanalytic accounts of second-year sociality stress a negative mother-child symbiosis expressed in a physical clinging and a demandingness which results from the child's seeing the mother as a physical extension of himself. In addition, however, the child in the second year of life clearly takes a delight in sharing through imitation, reciprocal play and communication (e.g., pointing things out to the other). It is this type of experience, rather than clinging, which clearly indicates that other people are people to the infant, not security blankets or "cloth mothers" to be clung to in unfamiliar situations. The bridge between the physical and the social is suggested by the infant's response to his own mirror-image (Dixon, 1957). The eight-month-old child's interest in his mirror "twin" is based largely on the fact that his mirror twin "imitates" him. The infant acts repetitively to get the mirror twin to "imitate" his movements. According to Dixon, however, the infant is far more interested in his real twin than in his "mirror twin," and this interest is largely connected with simple imitative games in which each takes turns imitating and eliciting imitaton from the other.

Social objects early become a special focus of attention and recognition because they do more interesting things. They become differentiated from physical things because a major vehicle for interacting with them is to imitate them rather than to manipulate them. Social objects not only do interesting things, but these interesting activities may be shared and made one's own by imitation or by reciprocal interaction. By the second year of life, most children are tagalongs behind their older siblings, following siblings more than they follow their mothers. They tag along because what their older siblings do is interesting, more interesting than the parent's sedate activities. They follow along, not to watch, but to imitate and participate in these activities. The motivation for this "tagging-along" is effectance motivation, the motivation behind the perennial question, "What is there to do?" and the satisfaction of the motive is through imitation of the interesting. In large part, then, the child is dependent upon the other as a model for his own activities, and the motivation for this dependence is the motivation for imitation we have discussed before. It is also clear that the two-year-old is not attached to the older brother he slavishly imitates in the sense that he is to his mother; when in a state of insecurity or need, the two-year-old quickly turns to his mother, not his brother. We argued earlier, however, that sheer physical need for the presence and services of the other does not in itself generate social bonds because it does not involve a motive to share between self and other or to be guided by the response of the other. It is an open question whether the child's symbiotic relation to his mother constitutes a more basic or favorable base than do his relations to peers and other adults for the cultivation of a desire to share, and a "satellizing" renunciation of nonshared wishes and sources of self-esteem for shared ones which is basic to the formation of later stable social bonds.[35]

The ego-development theories of Baldwin (1906), Piaget (1948), Ausubel (1957), and Loevinger (1966) suggest that the child's further development of social ties and his development of moral attitudes become different sides of the same coin. M. Blatt (unpublished research) has found that children's conceptions of love and friendship go through stages parallel to my moral judgment stages. It is not until the onset of Stage 3, "good boy" morality, at age 6-7 that the child expresses the desire to be liked independently of being given rewards; expresses the desire to do something for someone he likes; feels being a friend of, or being liked by, someone prestigeful gives him derived self-esteem; or thinks that he likes his parent or friend, even though they are momentarily frustrating him. At this point, the child's social tie to his parent becomes the satellizing moral identification previously discussed. The development of attachment and love past satellization to intimacy must be left for subsequent treatment.

XV. IDENTIFICATION AND PSYCHOPATHOLOGY

We have claimed that specific identifications with specific parent figures may: (a) speed up (or slow down) development in natural moral or psychosexual sequences,[36] and (b) may give particular stages of development specific content and affective significance. The child's stage of development in turn colors or gives specific significance to the child's relationships to his parents. We have claimed, however, that specific identifications with specific parent figures are neither necessary nor sufficient conditions for normal moral or psychosexual development.

The need to explain general trends of both moral and sex-role development in terms independent of specific parent-child ties or identification is indicated by research findings reviewed elsewhere (Kohlberg, 1963a, 1964, 1966b).

1. Children and young adults are no more like their parents in level of morality or of masculinity-femininity than they are like a random parental indi-

---

[35] It must be stressed that psychoanalytic, ethological, or S-R theories basing later dependency or attachments on mother-infant relations in the first two years are not as yet based on any substantial research findings. The facts are more to the contrary. As a single example from many, Kagan and Moss (1962) found a correlation of only .33 between affectional dependency in the first three years of life and at ages 6-9, and a similar correlation of .33 between anxiety at loss of nurturance across the same periods.

[36] As an example, if the child's family world fits a Stage 1 conception that the right thing is to avoid punishment and to be obedient, he is likely to remain at that stage longer than others, though not to remain there forever. At age 13, parental use of physical punishment correlates significantly with Stage 1 thinking. Nevertheless, almost all Stage 1 3-year-olds eventually move out of Stage 1, after leaving home if not before (Kohlberg, 1969).

vidual of the same social class. All reported studies indicate no correlation between the masculinity-femininity of the child and the masculinity-femininity of their same-sex parents (Terman & Miles, 1936; Mussen & Rutherford, 1963; Angrilli, 1960). There is no significant correlation between the stage or level of moral maturity (as defined by my methods) of male adolescents or young adults and that of their fathers (Holstein, 1968; Kramer, 1968). While "principled" mothers are more likely to have "conventional" children than less-advanced mothers, this is not due to identification mechanisms. If it were, conventional mothers should have more conventional-level children than principled mothers (Holstein, 1968).

2. Measures of identification (perceived similarity) with the same-sex parent do not clearly and consistently relate to moral and sex-role maturity or to moral and sex-role "internalization" (i.e., to acceptance of conventional moral and sex-role attitudes and standards). With regard to sex role, measures of girls' femininity tend to correlate with measures of identification with the opposite-sex parent rather than the same-sex parent. Measures of boys' masculinity correlate with measures of identification with the same-sex parent at most, but not all, age periods. With regard to morality, low significant correlations are found between parent identification measures and acceptance of the conventional moral code. These are not sex-specific, e.g., measured identification with the same-sex parent is not more clearly related to moral attitudes than is identification with the opposite-sex parent. These correlations may be best explained along the lines of the findings on warmth and liking, e.g., that if the child likes his parent, he tends to agree with him and learn more from him as reflected in both moral attitude measures and perceived similarity measures.

3. There is no generalized "identification-internalization factor" in children's personality. Measures of moral and of sex-role attitudes or development are not correlated with one another. Measures of identification do not correlate well with one another. Measures of identification at one age do not predict to measures of identification at another age.

4. The presence of a same-sex parent is not necessary for normal moral or psychosexual development. Children in the kibbutz and children from father-absent households are little different from children of intact families in all measured or observed aspects of "normality" or development of sex-role, as well as of moral, attitudes and behavior.[37]

There is a widespread misunderstanding of the research findings as indicating "the importance of the father for the development of the boy's sex-role

---

[37] Differences appear where intactness of the family represents the general "badness" or deviance of the parents and the environment as in the Gluecks' (Glueck & Glueck, 1950) studies of delinquency in which divorce, parent-conflict, criminality and neglect of children form part of a bad-environment package. Where some control of these correlates of a single-parent household is attained in a research design, the actual presence of a specific parent does not appear salient. One study, however, that of Hoffman and Saltzstein (1967), does report more internalized moral judgment and guilt in father-present boys than in a sample of father-absent boys matched for IQ and social class (Hoffman, 1969).

identity." In fact, no study has shown any marked differences between father-absent and father-present boys with regard to measures of masculine-feminine attitudes (Terman & Miles, 1936; Barclay & Cusumano, 1965; C. Smith summarized in Kohlberg, 1966b). A naturalistic longitudinal study by McCord, McCord and Thurber (1962) indicated no difference between father-absent and father-present families in incidence of effeminacy or homosexuality in boys.

While these findings clearly contradict any theory that claims that particular identifications or good parent relations are necessary for normal social development, there are some findings suggesting that bad parent relations are retarding or disrupting of such development. As an example, McCord et al. (1962) found intact families with strong marital conflict produced "effeminate" boys more frequently than either the conflict-free or the father-absent families. Hetherington (1965) and Hetherington and Frankie (1967) also find the sons of extremely submissive fathers to be low on sex-typing and on father imitation compared to the sons of high dominant fathers. The sons of dominant fathers appeared to be no different from a random population, or even from C. Smith's father-absent population, however (Kohlberg, 1966b). In other words, while markedly bad, deviant, or conflictful mother-father relations produce disturbances in sex-role attitudes, exposure to a "good" or conforming mother-father interaction is neither necessary for normal sex-role development (since it does not favor father-present over father-absent boys) nor does it even favor normal sex-role development (since highly masculine and dominant fathers are no more likely to have masculine sons than are fathers in the middle range).

In the moral area, the findings of the Gluecks (Glueck & Glueck, 1950) clearly indicate that delinquent boys are much more likely to come from markedly "bad" families, according to any criterion of "badness." But again, a specific relation to a specific good parent is neither necessary nor sufficient for normal or advanced moral development, since father absence, father's moral level, and use of "good" child-rearing techniques, however defined, do not predict to such maturity (Kohlberg, 1969).

The contrast between the relatively clear findings on effects of deviantly bad parents and the lack of findings on the effects of parent absence (or of normal variations in child-rearing practices) upon socialization is theoretically important for several reasons.[38] Limiting ourselves to identification theory, we pointed out that psychoanalytic identification theory (especially identification with the aggressor notions) was designed to account for illogical, pathological, or deviant identifications. We pointed out that a theory as to why boys want to be boys is not a theory as to why a boy wants to be a girl in some generalized sense; nor is an explanation of why boys want to be good in general, an explanation of why a particular boy seems to want to be bad or sees himself as bad in some generalized

---

[38] The practical implications of this conclusion imply a revolution in current social work and mental health services for children now addressed to helping the child under the presupposition of preserving his relation to a "bad" but intact family.

sense. While we cannot conclude that boys low in masculinity or delinquent boys have formed a definite deviant "opposite-sex" or "bad" identification modeled on a parent, it is at least possible that some of the effects of bad families are due to this mechanism.

There is at present, little definite reason to view "opposite-sex identification" as a valuable explanation of sexual psychopathology, since homosexuals are not clearly more "opposite-sex identified" than heterosexuals (Kohlberg, 1966b). With regard to some forms of moral psychopathology, however, deviant parental identifications seem more directly relevant. Freud's (1938) reasoning that pathological feelings of being blamed by others (paranoia) and of self-blame (depression) require a notion of fixed self-blaming structure, somewhat ego-alien but at the same time internalized within the psyche and based on identification, still seems convincing. Self-criticism and self-punishment by definition require identification in the broad sense of taking the role of the other, and severe forms of self-punishment and self-blame must be modeled in some sense on parental reactions in young childhood since the parent is ordinarily the only agent who engages in intensive punishment and blaming activities. Explanations of pathological guilt (i.e., guilt in the absence of serious transgression of self-accepted standards) suggest a base in idiosyncratic family and childhood experience, explanations of normal guilt (guilt over transgressions of self-accepted moral standards) do not.

Unfortunately, it is premature to attempt explanations of psychopathological identifications because there are almost no data concerning them except clinical case studies. The research literature is irrelevant to such questions except under the dubious assumption that measures of developmental lag in sexual or moral attitudes, or low scores on verbal measures of conformity to conventional moral or sex-role standards reflect pathological identifications (e.g., that a low score on an M-F test is a measure of a cross-sex identification of an illogical or pathological sort). A consideration of theories of psychopathological identification requires the kind of developmental and longitudinal data on psychopathology not now available. The analysis of such data may provide more of an integration of psychoanalytic and cognitive-developmental concepts than this chapter has suggested.

REFERENCES

AINSWORTH, M. D. Development of infant-mother interaction among the Ganda. In B. Foss (Ed.), *Determinants of infant behavior*. Vol. II. London: Methuen, 1963.

AINSWORTH, M. D. Patterns of attachment behavior shown by the infant in interaction with his mother. *Merrill-Palmer Quarterly*, 1964, 10, 51-58.

AMMONS, R., & AMMONS, H. Parent preference in young children's doll-play interviews. *Journal of Abnormal and Social Psychology*, 1949, 44, 490-505.

ANDERSON, J. Development. In D. Harris (Ed.), *The concept of development*. Minneapolis: Univer. of Minnesota Press, 1957.

ANDERSON, J. The prediction of adjustment over time. In I. Iscoe & H. Stevenson (Eds.), *Personality development in children*. Austin: Univer. of Texas Press, 1960.

ANGRILLI, A. F. The psychosexual identification of preschool boys. *Journal of Genetic Psychology*, 1960, 97, 329-340.

ARONFREED, J. The nature, variety, and social patterning of moral responses to transgression. *Journal of Abnormal and Social Psychology*, 1961, 63, 223-241.

ARONFREED, J. The concept of internalization. In D. A. Goslin (Ed.), *Handbook of socialization theory and research*. Chicago: Rand McNally, 1969. Chapter 4.

AUSUBEL, D. P. *Ego development and the personality disorders*. New York: Grune & Stratton, 1952.

AUSUBEL, D. P. *Theory and problems of child development*. New York: Grune & Stratton, 1957.

AUSUBEL, D. P., ET AL. Perceived parent attitudes as determinants of children's ego structure. *Child Development*, 1954, 25, 173-183.

AZRIN, N., & LINDSLEY, O. R. The reinforcement of cooperation between children. *Journal of Abnormal and Social Psychology*, 1956, 52, 100-102.

BAER, D., PETERSON, R., & SHERMAN, J. The development of generalized imitation by programming similarity between child and model as discriminative for reinforcement. *Journal of Experimental Analysis of Behavior*, 1967, 10, 405-416.

BALDWIN, J. M. *Mental development in the child and the race*. New York: Macmillan, 1895.

BALDWIN, J. M. *Social and ethical interpretations in mental development*. New York: Macmillan, 1906.

BALDWIN, J. M. *Thoughts and things or genetic logic*. 3 Vols. New York: Macmillan, 1906-11.

BALDWIN, J. M. *Genetic theory of reality*. New York: Putnam's, 1915.

BANDURA, A. Social-learning theory of identificatory processes. In D. A. Goslin (Ed.), *Handbook of socialization theory and research*. Chicago: Rand McNally, 1969. Chapter 3.

BANDURA, A., GRUSIC, JOAN, & MENLOVE, FRANCES. Some social determinants of self-monitoring systems. *Journal of Personality and Social Psychology*, 1967, 5, 449-455.

BANDURA, A., & HUSTON, A. C. Identification as a process of incidental learning. *Journal of Abnormal and Social Psychology*, 1961, 63, 311-319.

BANDURA, A., & KUPERS, CAROL. Transmission of patterns of self-reinforcement through modeling. *Journal of Abnormal and Social Psychology*, 1964, 69, 1-9.

BANDURA, A., & MACDONALD, F. The influence of social reinforcement and the behavior of models in shaping children's moral judgment. *Journal of Abnormal and Social Psychology*, 1963, 67, 274-281.

BANDURA, A., ROSS, D., & ROSS, S. Transmission of aggression through imitation of aggressive models. *Journal of Abnormal and Social Psychology*, 1963, 66, 3-11. (a)

BANDURA, A., ROSS, D., & ROSS, S. A comparative test of the status envy, social power and secondary reinforcement theories of identificatory learning. *Journal of Abnormal and Social Psychology*, 1963, 67, 527-534. (b)

BANDURA, A., ROSS, D., & ROSS, S. Vicarious reinforcement and imitative learning. *Journal of Abnormal and Social Psychology*, 1963, 67, 601-607. (c)

BANDURA, A., & WHALEN, CAROL. The influence of antecedent reinforcement and divergent modeling cues on patterns of self-reward. *Journal of Personality and Social Psychology*, 1966, 3, 373-382.

BARCLAY, A., & CUSUMANO, D. Effects of father absence upon field-dependent behavior. Paper delivered at meeting of the American Psychological Association, September, 1965.

BECKER, H. *Outsiders: Studies in the sociology of deviance.* New York: Free Press, 1963.

BECKER, W. Consequences of different kinds of parental discipline. In M. Hoffman & L. Hoffman (Eds.), *Review of child development research.* Vol. 1. New York: Russell Sage Foundation, 1964.

BERLYNE, D. *Conflict arousal and curiosity.* New York: McGraw-Hill, 1961.

BERLYNE, D. *Structure and direction in thinking.* New York: Wiley, 1965.

BLATT, M. The effects of classroom discussion programs upon children's level of moral judgment. Unpublished doctoral dissertation, Univer. of Chicago, 1969.

BOWLBY, J. The nature of the child's tie to his mother. *International Journal of Psychoanalysis,* 1958, 39, 350-373.

BRANSTETTER, E. Separation reactions in hospitalized children with and without substitute mothers. Unpublished doctoral dissertation, Univer. of Chicago, 1969.

BRIM, O. G., JR. Family structures and sex-role learning by children. *Sociometry,* 1958, 21, 1-6.

BRONFENBRENNER, U. The role of age, sex, class, and culture in studies of moral development. *Religious Education,* 1962, 57, 3-17.

BROWN, D. G. Sex-role preference in young children. *Psychological Monographs,* 1956, 70, No. 14.

BURTON, R. V., MACCOBY, ELEANOR, & ALLINSMITH, W. Antecedents of resistance to temptation in four-year-old children. *Child Development,* 1961, 22, 689-710.

CASLER, L. Maternal deprivation: A critical review of the literature. *Monograph of the Society for Research in Child Development,* 1961, No. 26.

CATTELL, R. B. *Personality and motivation: Structure and measurement.* Yonkers, N.Y.: World Book, 1957.

CHILD, I. Socialization. In G. Lindzey (Ed.), *Handbook of social psychology.* Cambridge: Addison-Wesley, 1954.

CHOMSKY, N. Language and the mind. *Psychology Today,* 1968, 1 (9), 48-51, 66-68.

COWEN, P., LANGER, J., HEAVENRICH, J., & NATHANSON, M. Has social learning theory refuted Piaget's theory of moral development? Unpublished manuscript, 1968.

CROWLEY, P. M. Effect of training upon objectivity of moral judgment in grade-school children. *Journal of Personality and Social Psychology,* 1968, 8, 228-233.

DANZIGER, K. The development of children's economic concepts. *Journal of Genetic Psychology,* 1958, 47, 231-240.

DECARIE, THERESE G. *Intelligence and affectivity in early childhood.* New York: International Universities Press, 1965.

DENNIS, W., & NAJARIAN, P. Infant development under environmental handicap. *Psychological Monographs,* 1957, 71, No. 7 (Whole No. 436).

DEWEY, J. Experience and conduct. In C. Murchison (Ed.), *Psychologies of 1930.* Worcester: Clark Univer. Press, 1930.

DIXON, J. C. Development of self-recognition. *Journal of Genetic Psychology,* 1957, 91, 251-256.

EMMERICH, W. Family role concepts of children ages six to ten. *Child Development,* 1961, 32, 609-624.

EMMERICH, W. Continuity and stability in early social development. *Child Development,* 1964, 35, 311-333.

EMMERICH, W., & KOHLBERG, L. Imitation and attention-seeking in young children under conditions of nurturance, frustration, and conflict. Unpublished mimeographed paper, Univer. of Chicago, 1953.

ERIKSON, E. *Childhood and society.* New York: Norton, 1950.

FREEDMAN, J. L. Long-term behavioral effects of cognitive dissonance. *Journal of Experimental Social Psychology*, 1965, 1, 145-155.

FREUD, ANNA. *The ego and the mechanisms of defense*. New York: International Universities Press, 1946.

FREUD, ANNA, & DANN, SOPHIE. An experiment in group upbringing. In R. Eissler et al. (Eds.), *The psychoanalytic study of the child*. Vol. 6. New York: International Universities Press, 1951.

FREUD, S. *The basic writings of Sigmund Freud*. New York: Modern Library, 1938.

FROMM, E. *Man for himself*. New York: Rinehart & Co., 1955.

GESELL, A. The ontogenesis of infant behavior. In L. Carmichael (Ed.), *Manual of child psychology*. New York: Wiley, 1954.

GEWIRTZ, J. L. Mechanisms of social learning: Some roles of stimulation and behavior in early human development. In D. A. Goslin (Ed.), *Handbook of socialization theory and research*. Chicago: Rand McNally, 1969. Chapter 2.

GILMORE, B. Toward an understanding of imitation. Unpublished manuscript, Waterloo Univer., 1967.

GLUECK, S., & GLUECK, E. *Unraveling juvenile delinquency*. New York: Commonwealth Fund, 1950.

GOTTESMAN, I. Heritability of personality: A demonstration. *Psychological Monographs*, 1963, 77, No. 9.

GREEN, B. A method of scalogram analysis using summary statistics. *Psychometrika*, 1956, 21, 79-88.

GRIM, P., KOHLBERG, L., & WHITE, S. Some relationships between conscience and attentional processes. *Journal of Personality and Social Psychology*, 1968, 8, 239-253.

GRINDER, R. Relations between behavioral and cognitive dimensions of conscience in middle childhood. *Child Development*, 1964, 35, 881-893.

GUTTMAN, L. The basis for scalogram analysis. In S. A. Stougger et al., *Measurement and prediction*. Princeton: Princeton Univer. Press, 1954.

HAAN, N., SMITH, M. B., & BLOCK, J. The moral reasoning of young adults: Political-social behavior, family background and personality correlates. *Journal of Personality and Social Psychology*, 1969 (in press).

HARLOW, H. Love in infant monkeys. *Scientific American*, 1959, 200, 68-74.

HARLOW, H., & HARLOW, MARGARET. Social deprivation in monkeys. *Scientific American*, 1962, 207 (5), 136-146.

HARTSHORNE, H., & MAY, M. A. *Studies in the nature of character*. Columbia Univer., Teachers College. Vol. 1: *Studies in deceit*. Vol. 2: *Studies in service and self-control*. Vol. 3: *Studies in organization of character*. New York: Macmillan, 1928-30.

HARTUP, W. W. Some correlates of parental imitation in young children. *Child Development*, 1962, 33, 85-97.

HARVEY, O. J., HUNT, D., & SCHROEDER, D. *Conceptual systems*. New York: Wiley, 1961.

HETHERINGTON, E. MAVIS. A developmental study of the effects of sex of the dominant parent on sex-role preference, identification and imitation in children. *Journal of Personality and Social Psychology*, 1965, 2, 143-153.

HETHERINGTON, E. MAVIS, & FRANKIE, G. Effects of parental dominance, warmth and conflict on imitation in children. *Journal of Personality and Social Psychology*, 1967, 6, 119-125.

HOBHOUSE, L. T. *Morals in evolution*. London: Chapman & Hall, 1906.

HOFFMAN, M. Moral development. In P. Mussen (Ed.), *Manual of child psychology.* New York: Wiley, 1969.

HOFFMAN, M., & SALTZSTEIN, H. Parent discipline and the child's moral development. *Journal of Personality and Social Psychology,* 1967, 5, 45-57.

HOLSTEIN, CONSTANCE. Parental determinants of the development of moral judgment. Unpublished doctoral dissertation, Univer. of California, Berkeley, 1968.

HULL, C. *Principles of behavior.* New York: Appleton-Century, 1943.

HUNT, J. McV. *Intelligence and experience.* New York: Ronald Press, 1961.

HUNT, J. McV. Motivation inherent in information processing and action. In O. J. Harvey (Ed.), *Interaction.* New York: Ronald, 1963.

HUNT, J. McV., & UZGIRIS, I. An ordinal scale of infant development. Unpublished manuscript, Univer. of Illinois, Urbana, 1967.

JAMES, W. *Principles of psychology.* New York: Holt, 1890.

KAGAN, J. The concept of identification. *Psychological Review,* 1958, 65, 296-305.

KAGAN, J. The many faces of response. *Psychology Today,* 1968, 1, No. 8, 22-27.

KAGAN, J., & MOSS, H. *Birth to maturity.* New York: Wiley, 1962.

KAPLAN, B. The study of language in psychiatry. In S. Arieti (Ed.), *American handbook of psychiatry.* Vol. 3. New York: Basic Books, 1966.

KESSEN, W. (Ed.) *The child.* New York: Wiley, 1965.

KINSEY, A., ET AL. *Sexual behavior in the human female.* Philadelphia: W. B. Sanders, 1953.

KOHLBERG, L. The development of modes of moral thinking and choice in the years ten to sixteen. Unpublished doctoral dissertation, Univer. of Chicago, 1958.

KOHLBERG, L. Moral development and identification. In H. Stevenson (Ed.), Child psychology. *62nd Yearbook of the National Society for the Study of Education.* Chicago: Univer. of Chicago Press, 1963. (a)

KOHLBERG, L. The development of children's orientations toward a moral order: 1. Sequence in the development of moral thought. *Vita Humana,* 1963, 6, 11-33. (b)

KOHLBERG, L. Stages in conceptions of the physical and social world. Unpublished monograph, 1963. (c)

KOHLBERG, L. Development of moral character and ideology. In M. L. Hoffman (Ed.), *Review of child development research.* Vol. 1. New York: Russell Sage Foundation, 1964.

KOHLBERG, L. Psychosexual development, a cognitive-developmental approach. Unpublished mimeographed manuscript, Univer. of Chicago, 1965.

KOHLBERG, L. Cognitive stages and preschool education. *Human Development,* 1966, 9, 5-17. (a)

KOHLBERG, L. A cognitive developmental analysis of children's sex-role concepts and attitudes. In E. Maccoby (Ed.), *The development of sex differences.* Stanford, Calif.: Stanford Univer. Press, 1966. (b)

KOHLBERG, L. Moral and religious education and the public schools: A developmental view. In T. Sizer (Ed.), *Religion and public education.* Boston: Houghton-Mifflin, 1967.

KOHLBERG, L. Preschool education: A cognitive-developmental approach. *Child Development,* 1968 (in press).

KOHLBERG, L. *Stages in the development of moral thought and action.* New York: Holt, Rinehart & Winston, 1969.

KOHLBERG, L., YAEGER, J., & HJERTHOLM, E. The development of private speech: Four studies and a review of theory. *Child Development,* 1968 (in press).

Kohlberg, L., & Zigler, E. The impact of cognitive maturity on sex-role attitudes in the years four to eight. *Genetic Psychology Monograph*, 1967, 75, 89-165.

Kohn, N. Performance of Negro children of varying social class background on Piagetian tasks. Unpublished doctoral dissertation, Univer. of Chicago, 1969.

Kramer, R. Moral development in young adulthood. Unpublished doctoral dissertation, Univer. of Chicago, 1968.

Krebs, R. L. Some relationships between moral judgment, attention and resistance to temptation. Unpublished doctoral dissertation, Univer. of Chicago, 1967.

Kuhn, D., & Langer, J. Cognitive-developmental determinants of imitation. Unpublished manuscript, 1968.

LaCrosse, J., & Kohlberg, L. The predictability of adult mental health from childhood behavior and status. In B. Wolman (Ed.), *Handbook of psychopathology*. New York: McGraw-Hill, 1969.

Langer, J. Disequilibrium as a source of cognitive development. Paper delivered at the meeting of the Society for Research on Child Development, New York, March 21, 1967.

Lehrer, L. Sex differences in moral behavior and attitudes. Unpublished doctoral dissertation, Univer. of Chicago, 1967.

Lippett, R., & White, R. The effects of social climates. In R. Barker, J. Kounin & H. Wright (Eds.), *Child behavior and development*. New York: McGraw-Hill, 1943.

Loevinger, J. The meaning and measurement of ego development. *American Psychologist*, 1966, 21, 195-217.

Lorenz, K. *Evolution and the modification of behavior*. Chicago: Univer. of Chicago Press, 1965.

Lovaas, O. I. A program for the establishment of speech in psychotic children. In J. Wing (Ed.), *Childhood autism*. Oxford: Pergamon Press, 1967.

Maccoby, Eleanor. Role-taking in childhood and its consequences for early learning. *Child Development*, 1959, 30, 239-252.

Maccoby, Eleanor. Social attachment. In P. Mussen (Ed.), *Manual of child psychology*. New York: Wiley, 1969 (in press).

MacFarlane, J., Allen, L., & Honzik, N. *A developmental study of behavior problems of normal children between 21 months and four years*. Berkeley: Univer. of California Press, 1954.

MacKinnon, D. W. Violation of prohibitions. In H. A. Murray (Ed.), *Explorations in personality*. New York: Oxford Univer. Press, 1938. Pp. 491-501.

McCord, J., McCord, Joan, & Thurber, Emily. Some effects of paternal absence on male children. *Journal of Abnormal and Social Psychology*, 1962, 64, 361-369.

McDougall, W. *An introduction to social psychology*. London: Methuen, 1908.

Mead, G. H. *Mind, self, and society*. Chicago: Univer. of Chicago Press, 1934.

Milgram, S. Behavioral study of obedience. *Journal of Abnormal and Social Psychology*, 1963, 67, 371-378.

Miller, N., & Dollard, J. *Social learning and imitation*. New Haven: Yale Univer. Press, 1941.

Morgan, G., & Ricciutti, H. Infant's responses to shapes during the first year. In B. M. Foss (Ed.), *Determinants of infant behavior*. Vol. 4. London: Methuen, 1968.

Mussen, P., & Rutherford, E. Parent-child relations and parental personality in relation to young children's sex-role preferences. *Child Development*, 1963, 34, 589-607.

Parsons, T., & Bales, R. F. *Family, socialization and interaction process*. Glencoe, Ill.: Free Press, 1955.

PARTEN, M., & NEWHALL, S. M. The development of social behavior in children. In R. Barker, J. Kounin & H. Wright (Eds.), *Child behavior and development*. New York: McGraw-Hill, 1943.

PAVLOV, I. P. *Lectures on conditioned reflexes*. New York: Liveright, 1928.

PECK, R. F., & HAVIGHURST, R. J. *The psychology of character development*. New York: Wiley, 1960.

PIAGET, J. *The child's conception of the world*. New York: Harcourt, Brace, 1928.

PIAGET, J. *The psychology of intelligence*. London: Routledge, Kegan Paul, 1947.

PIAGET, J. *The moral judgment of the child*. Glencoe, Ill.: Free Press, 1948. (Originally published in 1932)

PIAGET, J. *Play, dreams, and imitation in childhood*. New York: Norton, 1951.

PIAGET, J. *Les relations entre l'affectivitie et l'intelligence dans le development mental de l'enfant*. Le course de Sorbonne psychologie. Paris: Centre de Documentation Universitaire, 1952. (Mimeographed) (a)

PIAGET, J. *The origins of intelligence in children*. New York: International Universities Press, 1952. (b)

PIAGET, J. *The construction of reality in the child*. New York: Basic Books, 1954.

PIAGET, J. The general problems of the psychobiological development of the child. In J. M. Tanner & B. Inhelder (Eds.), *Discussions on child development: Proceedings of the World Health Organization study group on the psychobiological development of the child*. Vol. IV. New York: International Universities Press, 1960. Pp. 3-27.

PIAGET, J. Cognitive development in children. In R. Ripple & V. Rockcastle (Eds.), *Piaget rediscovered: A report on cognitive studies in curriculum development*. Ithaca, N. Y.: Cornell Univ. School of Education, 1964.

PIAGET, J. *On the development of memory and identity*. Worcester, Mass.: Clark Univer. Press, 1968.

PINARD, A., & LAURENDEAU, M. *Causal thinking in children*. New York: International Universities Press, 1964.

REST, J. Developmental hierarchy in preference and comprehension of moral judgment. Unpublished doctoral dissertation, Univer. of Chicago, 1968.

REST, J., TURIEL, E., & KOHLBERG, L. Relations between level of moral judgment and preference and comprehension of the moral judgment of others. *Journal of Personality*, 1969.

RICCIUTTI, H. Social and emotional behavior in infancy: Some developmental issues and problems. *Merrill-Palmer Quarterly*, 1968, 14, 82-100.

RIESEN, A., & KINDER, E. *The postural development of infant chimpanzees*. New Haven: Yale Univer. Press, 1952.

RIESMAN, D. *The lonely crowd*. New Haven: Yale Univer. Press, 1950.

RUMA, E., & MOSHER, P. Relationship between moral judgment and guilt in delinquent boys. *Journal of Abnormal Psychology*, 1967, 72, 122-127.

SARNOFF, I. Identification with the aggressor: Some personality correlates of anti-Semitism among Jews. *Journal of Personality*, 1951, 20, 199-218.

SCHACHTER, S. The interaction of cognitive and physiological determinants of emotional state. In L. Berkowitz (Ed.), *Advances in social psychology*. Vol. I. New York: Academic Press, 1964.

SCHAFFER, H. R. The onset of fear of stranger and the incongruity hypothesis. *Journal of Child Psychology and Psychiatry*, 1966, 7, 95-106.

SCHAFFER, H. R., & EMERSON, P. E. The development of social attachment in infancy. *Monograph of the Society for Research in Child Development*, 1964, 29, Serial No. 94. Pp. 1-77.

SEARS, R. R. Identification as a form of behavior development. In D. B. Harris (Ed.), *The concept of development*. Minneapolis: Univer. of Minnesota Press, 1957.

SEARS, R. R. Relations of early socialization experience to aggression in middle childhood. *Journal of Abnormal and Social Psychology*, 1961, 63, 466-493.

SEARS, R. R., RAU, L., & ALPERT, R. *Identification and child-rearing*. Stanford, Calif.: Stanford Univer. Press, 1965.

SHIRLEY, MARY. *The first two years*. 2 vols. Minneapolis: Univer. of Minnesota Press, 1933.

SIGEL, I., & HOOPER, F. (Eds.) *Logical thinking in children: Research based on Piaget's theory*. New York: Rinehart & Winston, 1968.

SOLOMON, R., & COLES, R. A case of failure of generalization of imitation learning across drives and across situations. *Journal of Abnormal and Social Psychology*, 1954, 49, 7-13.

STEVENSON, H. Social reinforcement of children's behavior. In C. Spiker (Ed.), *Advances in child development*. Vol. II. New York: Academic Press, 1965.

STOTLAND, E., ZANDER, A., & NATSOULAS, T. Generalization of interpersonal similarity. *Journal of Abnormal and Social Psychology*, 1961, 62, 250-258.

STRAUSS, A. The learning of social roles and rules as twin processes. *Child Development*, 1954, 25, 192-208.

SULLIVAN, C., GRANT, M. Q., & GRANT, J. D. The development of interpersonal maturity: Application to delinquency. *Psychiatry*, 1957, 20, 373-385.

SULLIVAN, H. S. *An interpersonal theory of psychiatry*. New York: Norton, 1953.

TERMAN, L. M., & MILES, C. C. *Sex and personality studies in masculinity and femininity*. New York: McGraw-Hill, 1936.

TURIEL, E. An experimental test of the sequentiality of developmental stages in the child's moral judgment. *Journal of Personality and Social Psychology*, 1966, 3, 611-618.

TURIEL, E. Developmental processes in the child's moral thinking. In P. Mussen, J. Langer & M. Covington (Eds.), *New directions in developmental psychology*. New York: Holt, Rinehart & Winston, 1969.

TURIEL, E., & GUINSBURG, G. The cognitive conditions for imitation without reinforcement. Unpublished manuscript, 1968.

TURNURE, J., & ZIGLER, E. Outer directedness in the problem solving of normal and retarded children. *Journal of Abnormal and Social Psychology*, 1964, 69, 427-436.

VALENTINE, C. W. *The psychology of early childhood*. London: Methuen, 1942.

VAN MANEN, GLORIA. An interpersonal theory of deviance: A test of general theory. Unpublished doctoral dissertation, Univer. of Chicago, 1967.

WARDEN, C., & JACKSON, T. Imitative behavior in the rhesus monkey. *Journal of Genetic Psychology*, 1935, 46, 103-125.

WERNER, H. *The comparative psychology of mental development*. Chicago: Wilcox & Follett, 1948.

WHITE, R. Motivation reconsidered: The concept of competence. *Psychological Review*, 1959, 66, 297-333.

WHITE, R. Ego and reality in psychoanalytic theory. *Psychological Issues*, Vol. III, No. 3. New York: International Universities Press, 1963.

WHITING, J. W. M. Resource mediation and learning by identification. In I. Iscoe & H. W. Stevenson (Eds.), *Personality development in children*. Austin, Tex.: Univer. of Texas Press, 1960. Pp. 112-126.

WHITING, J. W. M. The concept of identification. Paper delivered at the meeting of the Society for Research in Child Development, New York, March 21, 1967.

WILSON, J. An experimental investigation of the development of smiling. Unpublished doctoral dissertation, Univer. of Chicago, 1962.

WITKIN, H. A. Social influences in the development of cognitive style. In D. A. Goslin (Ed.), *Handbook of socialization theory and research.* Chicago: Rand McNally, 1969. Chapter 14.

WOLFF, P. H. The development of attention in young infants. New York Academy of Sciences, *Transactions,* 1965, 118, 783-866.

YARROW, L. J. Separation from parents during early childhood. In M. L. Hoffman & L. W. Hoffman (Eds.), *Review of child development research.* New York: Russell Sage Foundation, 1964. Pp. 89-136.

Journal of Abnormal and Social Psychology
1963, Vol. 67, No. 3, 274–281

INFLUENCE OF SOCIAL REINFORCEMENT AND THE BEHAVIOR OF MODELS IN SHAPING CHILDREN'S MORAL JUDGMENTS [1]

ALBERT BANDURA AND FREDERICK J. McDONALD

Stanford University

This experiment was designed to test the relative efficacy of social reinforcement and modeling procedures in modifying moral judgmental responses considered by Piaget to be age-specific. 1 group of children observed adult models who expressed moral judgments counter to the group's orientation, and the children were reinforced with approval for adopting the model's evaluative responses. A 2nd group observed the models but received no reinforcement for matching their behavior. A 3rd group of children had no exposure to models but were reinforced for moral judgments that ran counter to their dominant evaluative tendencies. Following the treatments, the children were tested for generalization effects. The experimental treatments produced substantial changes in the children's moral judgment responses. Conditions utilizing modeling cues proved to be more effective than the operant conditioning procedure.

Most of the literature and theorizing in the area of developmental psychology has been guided by various forms of stage theories (Erikson, 1950; Freud, 1949; Gesell & Ilg, 1943; Piaget, 1948, 1954; Sullivan, 1953). Although there appears to be relatively little agreement among these theories concerning the number and the content of stages considered to be necessary to account for the course of personality development, they all share in common the assumption that social behavior can be categorized in terms of a predetermined sequence of stages with varying degrees of continuity or discontinuity between successive developmental periods. Typically, the emergence of these presumably age-specific modes of behavior is attributed to ontogenetic factors rather than to specific social stimulus events which are likely to be favored in a social learning theory of the developmental process.

The stage and social learning approaches differ not only in the relative emphasis placed

[1] This investigation was supported in part by Research Grant M-5162 from the National Institutes of Health, United States Public Health Service.

The authors wish to express their appreciation to Florence Mote, Charles Carver, and Nathan Kroman for their aid in arranging the research facilities, and to Peter Gumpert for his assistance with the statistical analyses. We also wish to express our gratitude to the many students who served as experimenters and as models in this project.

upon time schedules or reinforcement schedules in explaining the occurrence of changes in social behavior, but also in the assumptions made concerning the regularity and invariance of response sequences, and the nature of response variability. Stage theories, for example, generally stress intraindividual variability over time, and minimize interindividual variability in behavior due to sex, intellectual, socioeconomic, ethnic, and cultural differences. To the extent that children representing such diverse backgrounds experience differential contingencies and schedules of reinforcement, as well as exposure to social models who differ widely in the behavior they exhibit, considerable interindividual behavioral variability would be expected. Similarly, the sequence of developmental changes is considered in social learning theory to be primarily a function of changes in reinforcement contingencies and other learning variables rather than an unfolding of genetically programed response predispositions.

Despite the considerable attention devoted to theoretical analyses of the learning process, a comprehensive theory of *social learning* has been relatively slow in developing. By and large, current principles of learning have been based upon investigations involving simple fractional responses which are neither social nor developmental in nature, and often with animals as subjects. Although recent years have witnessed a widespread application of learning principles to developmental psychology, the experimentation has been primarily confined to operant or instrumental conditioning of responses that are modeled on the fractional responses elicited in experimentation with infrahuman organisms (for example, manipulating plungers, pressing bars, levers, buttons, etc.). Moreover, a good deal of this research has been designed to reduce complex social learning to available simple learning principles, rather than to extend the range of principles and procedures in order to account more adequately for complex social phenomena.

It is generally assumed that social responses are acquired through the method of successive approximations by means of differential reinforcement (Skinner, 1953). The effectiveness of reinforcement procedures in shaping and maintaining behavior in both animals and humans is well documented by research. It is doubtful, however, if many social responses would ever be acquired if social training proceeded solely by this method. This is particularly true of behavior for which there is no reliable eliciting stimulus apart from the cues provided by others as they performed the behavior. If a child had no occasion to hear speech, for example, or in the case of a deaf-blind person (Keller, 1927), no opportunity to match laryngeal muscular responses of a verbalizing model, it would probably be exceedingly difficult or impossible to teach a person appropriate linguistic responses.

Even in cases where some stimulus is known to be capable of eliciting an approximation to the desired behavior, the process of learning can be considerably shortened by the provision of social models (Bandura & Huston, 1961; Bandura, Ross, & Ross, 1961, 1963). Thus, in both instances, imitation of modeling behavior is an essential aspect of social learning.

In the experiment reported in this paper a social learning theory combining the principles of instrumental conditioning and imitation was applied to a developmental problem that has been approached from a stage point of view.

According to Piaget (1948), one can distinguish two clear-cut stages of moral judgment demarcated from each other at approximately 7 years of age. In the first stage, defined as *objective responsibility*, children judge the gravity of a deviant act in terms of the amount of material damages, and disregard the intentionality of the action. By contrast, during the second or *subjective responsibility* stage, children judge conduct in terms of its intent rather than its material consequences. While these stages are predetermined (for example, Piaget reports that young children are relatively incapable of adopting a subjective orientation and he was unable to find a single case of objective morality in older children), the factors responsible for the transition from one stage to the other are not entirely clear. Presumably, the principal antecedent of objective judgmental behavior is the "natural spontaneous and unconscious egocentrism" of child thought reinforced to some extent by adult authoritarianism, which produces submissiveness and preoccupation with external consequences. As the child matures, however, he gains increasing autonomy, his relationships become based upon mutual reciprocity and cooperation giving rise to the emergence of subjective morality.

The purpose of the present investigation was to demonstrate that moral judgment responses are less age-specific than implied by Piaget, and that children's moral orientations can be altered and even reversed by the manipulation of response-reinforcement contingencies and by the provision of appropriate social models.

In this experiment children who exhibited predominantly objective and subjective moral orientations were assigned at random to one of three experimental conditions. One group of children observed adult models who expressed moral judgments counter to the group's orientation and the children were positively reinforced for adopting the models' evaluative responses. A second group observed the models but the children received no reinforcement for matching the models' behavior. The third group had no exposure to the models but each child was reinforced whenever he expressed moral judgments that ran counter to his dominant evaluative tendencies. Thus the experimental design permitted a test of the relative efficacy of social reinforcement, the behavior of models, and these two factors combined in shaping children's moral judgments.

It was predicted, for reasons given in the preceding sections, that the combined use of models and social reinforcement would be the most powerful condition for altering the children's behavior and that the provision of models alone would be of intermediate effectiveness. Since the presence of a strong dominant response limits the opportunity for reinforcement of an alternative response which is clearly subordinate, it was expected that social reinforcement alone would be the least effective of the three treatment methods.

METHOD

Subjects

A total of 78 boys and 87 girls ranging in age from 5 to 11 years served as subjects in various phases of the study. They were drawn from two sources, a Jewish religious school and an elementary public school serving predominantly middle-class communities. The research was conducted on week ends in the religious school and on weekdays in the public school facility. Female students from Stanford University served in the roles of experimenters and models.

Stimulus Items

Following the procedure employed by Piaget (1948), the children were presented with pairs of stories each of which described a well-intentioned act which resulted in considerable material damage, contrasted with a selfishly or maliciously motivated act producing minor consequences. The children were asked to judge, "Who did the naughtier thing?" and to provide a reason for their choice. An illustrative stimulus item, taken from Piaget, is given below:

1. John was in his room when his mother called him to dinner. John goes down, and opens the door to the dining room. But behind the door was a chair, and on the chair was a tray with fifteen cups on it. John did not know the cups were behind the door. He opens the door, the door hits the tray, bang go the fifteen cups, and they all get broken.

2. One day when Henry's mother was out, Henry tried to get some cookies out of the cupboard. He climbed up on a chair, but the cookie jar was still too high, and he couldn't reach it. But while he was trying to get the cookie jar, he knocked over a cup. The cup fell down and broke.

Six of the story items employed in the present experiment were identical with those developed by Piaget except for minor modifications in wording or content to make the story situations more appropriate for American children. In addition, a set of 36 new paired items was devised to provide a sufficient number of stories so as to obtain a fairly reliable estimate of children's moral judgments at three different phases of the experiment, i.e., base operant test, experimental treatment, and posttest. In each of these story situations which were modeled after Piaget's items, intentionality was contrasted with serious consequences. These items were carefully pretested on a sample of 30 children in order to clarify any ambiguities, to gauge the children's interpretations of the seriousness of the depicted consequences, and to remove any irrelevant cues which might lead the children to judge depicted actions in terms other than intentions or consequences.

Except for the assignment of the six Piaget items to both the operant test and the posttest set, for reasons which will be explained later, the remaining stories were distributed randomly into three different groups.

Design and Procedure

A summary of the overall experimental design is presented in Table 1.

Operant level of objective and subjective responses. In the first phase of the experiment, the children were individually administered 12 pairs of stories to furnish measures of the operant levels of objective and subjective moral judgments at the various age levels. These data provided both a check on Piaget's normative findings and the basis for forming the experimental treatment groups.

Experimental treatments. On the basis of operant test performances, 48 children who were decidedly subjective in their moral orientation (Mean percentage of subjective responses = 80), and 36 who gave high base rates of objective responses (Mean percentage of objective responses = 83) were selected from the total sample to participate in the second and third phases of the experiment. The children in each of the two classes of moral orientation were equally divided between boys and girls. They were also further categorized into younger and older children and then assigned at random to one of three experimental treatment conditions. Thus the experimental groups were balanced with respect to age and sex of child.

In the *model and child reinforced condition,* both the model and the child were administered alternately 12 different sets of story items with the model receiving the first story, the child the second one, and so on. To each of the 12 items, the model consistently expressed judgmental responses in opposition to the child's moral orientation (for example, objective responses with subjective children,

TABLE 1

SUMMARY OF THE EXPERIMENTAL DESIGN

Experimental groups	Step 1 Assessment of operant level of objective and subjective moral responses	Step 2 Experimental treatments	Step 3 Posttreatment measurement of subjective and objective moral responses with models and reinforcement absent
Subjective moral orientation I (*N* = 16)	Step 1	Model emits objective responses and positively reinforced; child reinforced for objective responses.	Step 3
II (*N* = 16)	Step 1	Model emits objective responses and positively reinforced; child not reinforced for objective responses.	Step 3
III (*N* = 16)	Step 1	No model present; child reinforced for objective responses.	Step 3
Objective moral orientation IV (*N* = 12)	Step 1	Model emits subjective responses and positively reinforced; child reinforced for subjective responses.	Step 3
V (*N* = 12)	Step 1	Model emits subjective responses and positively reinforced; child not reinforced for subjective responses.	Step 3
VI (*N* = 12)	Step 1	No model present; child reinforced for subjective responses.	Step 3

and vice versa), and the experimenter reinforced the model's behavior with verbal approval responses such as "Very good," "That's fine," and "That's good." The child was similarly reinforced whenever he adapted the model's class of moral judgments in response to his own set of items. To control for any intermodel variability in length or content of evaluative responses, the subjective and objective responses for the models' test items were prepared in advance.

The procedure for children in the *model reinforced, child not reinforced condition,* was identical with the treatment described above with the exception that the children received no reinforcement for matching the moral judgment responses of their respective models.

In the *model absent, child reinforced condition,* no model was present; the experimenter simply administered the 24 story items to the child and reinforced him with verbal approval whenever he produced an evaluative response that ran counter to his dominant orientation.

The time elapsing between the operant testing and the experimental phase of the study ranged from 1 to 3 weeks with the majority of the children receiving the experimental treatment after a 2-week period.

A total of nine experimenter-model pairs participated in the treatment phase of the experiment. To control for possible differences in experimenter or model influences across conditions or sex groups,

each pair was assigned groups of subjects in triplets, i.e., boys and girls taken from each of the three treatment conditions.

Students who served as the experimenters' assistants brought the children individually from their classrooms to the experimental session and introduced them to their experimenters. The experimenter explained that she would like to have the child judge a second set of stories similar to the ones he had completed on a previous occasion. In the conditions involving the presence of models, the experimenter further explained that she was collecting normative data on a large sample of people, including both children and adults, and to expedite matters she invited the adult subjects to appear at the school so that the items could be administered to both groups simultaneously. To add to the credibility of the situation, the experimenter read to the model the same instructions the child had received in the operant test session, as though the model was a naive subject. The experimenter then read the story situations to the model and the child who were seated facing the experimenter, delivered the social reinforcement whenever appropriate, and recorded the responses.

It was found in the preliminary pretesting of the stories that they were sufficiently structured with respect to the intentionality-consequences dichotomy so that children's identification of the naughtier story character was virtually a perfect predictor

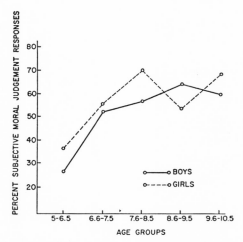

FIG. 1. Mean percentage of subjective moral judgment responses produced by boys and girls at different age levels.

that the children would provide the corresponding subjective or objective reasons for their choices. Since there is some evidence that reinforcement given immediately is considerably more effective than when delayed (Mahrer, 1956), the reinforcement value of the experimenter's approval would have been considerably reduced if administered following the children's explanations, not only because of the delay involved but also because many responses, some relevant others irrelevant, occur during the intervening period, thus making it difficult to specify the behavior being reinforced. For this reason, the experimenters reinforced the children immediately following correct choice responses, and again after they gave the appropriate explanations.

The measure of learning was the percentage of objective judgmental response produced by the subjective children and the percentage of subjective responses performed by the objectively oriented subjects.

Posttest. Following the completion of the treatment procedure, the child reported to another room in the building. Here a second experimenter presented the child with 12 additional stories to obtain further information about the generality and stability of changes in judgmental responses when models and social reinforcement were absent. The experimenter simply read the stories to the child and recorded his verbal responses without comment.

In view of Piaget's contention that moral judgments are age-specific and considerably resistant to out-of-phase changes, it was decided to repeat, in the posttest, the Piaget items included in the set of operant test stories. If the interpolated social influence experience succeeded in altering children's evaluative responses, such findings would throw

considerable doubt on the validity of a developmental stage theory of morality.

Different sets of experimenters conducted each of the three phases of the study, with a total of 10 experimenters participating in the posttesting. The utilization of different rooms and different sets of experimenters provided a more stringent test of generalization effects than if the same experimenters had been used throught the investigation.

The experiment was concluded with a brief interview designed to assess the child's awareness of the behavior exhibited by the model, the social reinforcers administered by the experimenter, and the response-reinforcement contingency in the experimental situation.

RESULTS

Since the data disclosed no significant differences in operant levels or in responsivity to the social influence procedures for children drawn from the two different school settings, the data were combined in the statistical analyses.

Judgmental Responses as a Function of Age

The mean percentage of subjective moral judgment responses for boys and girls at 1-year intervals are presented in Figure 1. The normative data based on the present sample of children show that subjectivity is positively associated with age ($F = 4.84$, $p < .01$), but unrelated to sex differences at any age level. It is evident from these findings, however, that objective and subjective

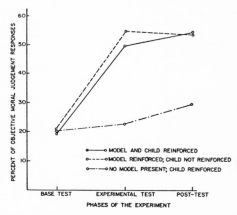

FIG. 2. Mean percentage of objective moral judgment responses produced by subjective children on each of the three test periods for each of three experimental conditions.

judgments exist together rather than as successive developmental stages. Most young children were capable of exercising subjective judgments, and a large majority of the older children exhibited varying degrees of objective morality.

Influence of Reinforcement and Modeling Cues

Figure 2 presents the curves for the acquisition and the generalization of objective moral judgment responses by subjective children in each of the three experimental conditions. Results of the analysis of variance performed on these data are summarized in Table 2. The main effects of experimental conditions and phases, as well as their interaction effects, are highly significant sources of variance. Further comparisons of pairs of means by the t test reveal that subjective children who were exposed to objective models, and those who were positively reinforced for matching their models moral judgments, not only modified their moral orientations toward objectivity, but also remained

TABLE 2

ANALYSIS OF VARIANCE OF OBJECTIVE MORAL JUDGMENT RESPONSES PRODUCED BY SUBJECTIVE CHILDREN

Source	df	MS	F
Conditions (C)	2	5,226.2	3.24*
Sex (S)	1	1,344.4	<1
C × S	2	3,671.4	2.28
Error (b)	42	1,612.1	
Phases (P)	2	9,505.8	35.46**
P × C	4	1,430.3	5.34**
P × S	2	203.8	<1
P × C × S	4	747.6	2.79*
Error (w)	84	268.1	

* $p < .05$.
** $p < .001$.

objectively oriented in their post-experimental judgmental behavior (Table 3).

The provision of models alone, however, was as effective in altering the children's moral judgments as was the experimental condition combining modeling cues with social reinforcement. As predicted, the experimental conditions utilizing modeling procedures proved to be considerably more powerful than

TABLE 3

COMPARISON OF PAIRS OF MEANS ACROSS EXPERIMENTAL PHASES AND BETWEEN TREATMENT CONDITIONS

Scores	Base Test versus Experimental Phase	Base Test versus Posttest	Experimental Phase versus Posttest
	t	t	t
Within conditions			
Objective treatment			
Model and Reinforcement	5.31****	5.74****	<1
Model	5.84****	5.74****	<1
Reinforcement	<1	1.52	<1
Subjective treatment			
Model and Reinforcement	3.12***	3.09**	<1
Model	4.10***	2.69*	1.87
Reinforcement	2.04	<1	1.99

Scores	Model + Reinforcement versus Model	Model + Reinforcement versus Reinforcement	Model versus Reinforcement
Between conditions			
Objective treatment			
Experimental phase	<1	2.81**	3.34***
Posttest	<1	2.68**	2.61**
Subjective treatment			
Experimental phase	<1	1.11	1.13
Posttest	<1	2.81**	2.15*

* $p < .05$.
** $p < .02$.
*** $p < .01$.
**** $p < .001$.

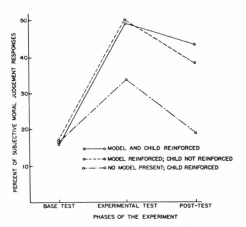

FIG. 3. Mean percentage of subjective moral judgment responses produced by objective children on each of three test periods for each of three experimental conditions.

was operant conditioning alone, which produced a slight increase in objective judgmental responses but not of statistically significant magnitude (Table 3).

Some additional evidence for the efficacy of the behavior of models in accelerating the acquisition process is provided in the finding that only 9% of the children who were exposed to the objective models failed to produce a single objective response; in contrast, 38% of the subjects in the operant conditioning group did not emit a single objective response despite obtaining twice as many acquisition trials.

The significant triple interaction effect shows that modeling combined with reinforcement exerted a greater influence on girls than on boys whereas, relative to girls, boys were more responsive to modeling cues when reinforcement was absent.

The acquisition and generalization data for objective children treated subjectively are presented graphically in Figure 3.

Analysis of variance of this set of scores reveals that the experimental treatments were highly influential in modifying the children's orientations from objective to subjective morality (Table 4). Although the differences between the three experimental groups did not reach statistical significance, evidently

the two conditions utilizing modeling procedures were the principal contributors to the main treatment effect. Comparison of pairs of means across phases yielded no significant differences for the operant conditioning group. The modeling conditions, on the other hand, produced significant and relatively stable increases in subjective moral judgment responses (Table 3).

DISCUSSION

The results of the present study provide evidence that subjective morality increases gradually with age, but fail to substantiate Piaget's theory of demarcated sequential stages of moral development. Children at all age levels exhibited discriminative repertoires of moral judgments in which both objective and subjective classes of responses exist concurrently. A recent study by Durkin (1961) provides some additional support for the specificity of children's moral judgment behavior.

The utility of Piaget's stage theory of morality is further limited by the finding that children's judgmental responses are readily modifiable, particularly through the utilization of adult modeling cues.

In most experimental demonstrations of modeling effects the model exhibits a given set of responses and the observer reproduces these responses in substantially identical form in similar or identical stimulus contexts (Bandura, 1962). The findings of the present study reveal, however, that a general class

TABLE 4

ANALYSIS OF VARIANCE OF SUBJECTIVE MORAL
JUDGMENT RESPONSES PRODUCED BY
OBJECTIVE CHILDREN

Source	df	MS	F
Conditions (C)	2	1,869.2	1.76
Sex (S)	1	2,821.3	2.66
C × S	2	208.6	<1
Error (b)	30	1,059.9	
Experimental phases (P)	2	7,057.5	16.38**
P × C	4	422.1	<1
P × S	2	99.4	<1
P × C × S	4	132.9	<1
Error (w)	60	430.9	

** p < .001.

of behavior may be readily acquired through observation of social models and consequently, the observer responds to new stimulus sensations in a manner consistent with the model's predisposition even though the subject had never observed the model respond to the same stimuli. These results illustrate the potency of modeling cues for shaping generalized patterns of social behavior.

The failure of operant conditioning procedures alone in altering moral judgment behavior is not at all surprising considering that the desired responses were much weaker than the competing dominant class of moral judgments. In many cases, particularly in the objective treatment condition, the subordinate responses occurred relatively infrequently; consequently there was little opportunity to influence them through reinforcement. In fact, the absence of a statistically significant conditions effect for children who experienced the subjective treatment largely resulted from several of the subjects in the operant conditioning group who happened to emit subjective responses on early trials and increased this behavior under reinforcement.

It is apparent, however, from both sets of data that operant conditioning procedures are particularly inefficient when there are strong dominant response tendencies and the desired alternative responses are only weakly developed or absent. In such cases, the provision of models who exhibit the desired behavior is an exceedingly effective procedure for eliciting from others appropriate matching responses early in the learning sequence and thus accelerating the acquisition process.

The results of the present study fail to confirm the hypothesis that a combination of reinforcement and modeling procedures constitutes a more powerful learning condition than modeling alone. Several factors might have accounted for the lack of differences between these two treatment conditions. In some cases the mere exposure to modeling cues produced rapid and complete changes in moral orientations and consequently the addition of reinforcement could not contribute any performance increments. This interpretation, however, does not fully account for the data since the majority of children were

not performing at or near the ceiling level. Results from a series of experiments of social learning by means of imitation provide an alternative explanation (Bandura, 1962). These studies suggest that the process of response acquisition is based upon contiguity of sensory events and that reinforcement may function primarily as a performance related variable. In the present investigation the models' responses were highly consistent and sufficiently distinctive to insure observation and imitative learning. The experimenters' positive evaluative statements, however, may have served as relatively weak reinforcers. Had more highly desired incentives been employed as reinforcing agents, it is very likely that the addition of reinforcement would have significantly enhanced the children's reproduction of the modeled judgmental orientations.

REFERENCES

BANDURA, A. Social learning through imitation. In M. R. Jones (Ed.), *Nebraska symposium on motivation: 1962.* Lincoln: Univer. Nebraska Press, 1962. Pp. 211–269.

BANDURA, A., & HUSTON, ALETHA C. Identification as a process of incidental learning. *J. abnorm. soc. Psychol.,* 1961, 63, 311–318.

BANDURA, A., ROSS, DOROTHEA, & ROSS, SHEILA A. Transmission of aggression through imitation of aggressive models. *J. abnorm. soc. Psychol.,* 1961, 63, 575–582.

BANDURA, A., ROSS, DOROTHEA, & ROSS, SHEILA A. Imitation of film-mediated aggressive models. *J. abnorm. soc. Psychol.,* 1963, 66, 3–11.

DURKIN, DOLORES. The specificity of children's moral judgments. *J. genet. Psychol.,* 1961, 98, 3–13.

ERIKSON, E. H. *Childhood and society.* New York: Norton, 1950.

FREUD, S. *An outline of psychoanalysis.* New York: Norton, 1949.

GESELL, A., & ILG, F. L. *Infant and child in the culture of today.* New York: Harper, 1943.

KELLER, HELEN. *The story of my life.* New York: Doubleday, 1927.

MAHRER, A. R. The role of expectancy in delayed reinforcement. *J. exp. Psychol.,* 1956, 52, 101–106.

PIAGET, J. *The moral judgment of the child.* Glencoe, Ill.: Free Press, 1948.

PIAGET, J. *The construction of reality in the child.* New York: Basic Books, 1954.

SKINNER, B. F. *Science and human behavior.* New York: Macmillan, 1953.

SULLIVAN, H. S. *The interpersonal theory of psychiatry.* New York: Norton, 1953.

(Received July 2, 1962)

THE SOCIALIZATION OF ALTRUISTIC AND SYMPATHETIC BEHAVIOR: SOME THEORETICAL AND EXPERIMENTAL ANALYSES

Justin Aronfreed[1]

The focus of this volume is on certain forms of human social behavior which are widely interpreted as the expression of altruistic and sympathetic dispositions. I am going to confine my own contribution primarily to some theoretical and experimental analyses of the origins of these dispositions—more particularly, to an analysis of the affective and cognitive mechanisms through which they are originally acquired. The purpose of the analysis is to show that an adequate psychological conception of altruism and sympathy cannot be mounted without a broader developmental perspective into the process of socialization. I would like to begin the analysis by calling to your attention some of the problems which are associated with any attempt to specify the criteria for the identification of altruistic and sympathetic actions. Then I would like to make a few general observations, of a developmental and even comparative nature, which follow from these problems of criteria. Finally, I want to use the naturalistic socialization of children as a context in which to place two different types of experimental inquiries into children's acquisition of their dispositions toward altruism and sympathy.

[1]Vivian Paskal was a warm and intelligent collaborator in the experiments which are outlined in the latter part of this paper. Her untimely death in January of 1969 has only temporarily delayed the plans for co-authored reports of the full empirical details of the experiments.

Perhaps the most significant way of characterizing the consequences of socialization is to say that children become capable of their own internalized control over their behavior. Their acquired patterns of social behavior begin to show, quite early in the course of development, many signs of persistence even in the absence of explicit rewards or punishments. The fact that children do come to maintain certain forms of conduct, under conditions which would not support their expectation of direct external reinforcement, and sometimes even without the presence of agents of socialization, is a phenomenon of major importance for an understanding of altruism and sympathy. It indicates that children are able to monitor their behavior in the absence of control by actual or anticipated external outcomes which have immediate consequences for themselves. If we assume that the child's choices among behavioral options must have some consequences which are reinforcing, in order to account for any stability in the maintenance of the choices, it then follows that the child's direct experience of rewards and punishments is at least partially dispensable as the medium of reinforcement.

I have suggested elsewhere, in more detailed analyses of the phenomena of internalization (Aronfreed, 1968a,b), that internalized control of the child's behavior rests on the coupling of potentially reinforcing changes of affectivity to internal monitors. These internal monitors are sometimes directly inherent in the feedback from the behavior itself. But they take their move powerful form in cognitive representations which are highly mobile with respect to both the child's behavior and its immediate external environment. Because the child's capacity for cognitive representation becomes relatively independent of any direct correlation to overt action, or to the observable consequences of action, it assumes anticipatory as well as reactive functions in the control of the child's behavior. For the purposes of this volume, I want only to point out that a broad conception of the mechanisms of internalization is required for an understanding of the specific character of altruistic and sympathetic actions. I am also going to argue that the inference of empathic or vicarious mediation of affectivity is the central criterion for the identification of altruism and sympathy.

Altruism and sympathy cannot be identified as distinct forms of behavior. They may be more accurately identified as dispositional components of actions. Moreover, their identification requires close attention to the conditions under which an act occurs, rather than merely a knowledge of the consequences of the act. In the case of altruism, for example, the altruistic act sometimes has been analyzed as though its critical feature were the absence of reinforcing (or valued) consequences for the actor (Durkheim, 1951, pp. 217-240). However, the fact that an act has no directly rewarding external consequences for the actor does not imply that the act functions entirely without reinforcing consequences. From the point of view of the requirements for a more general conception of internalized control of behavior, we would do better to assume that altruistic acts are indeed governed by the affective value of their anticipated outcomes, and that they often do have reinforcing consequences for the person who carries them out. Even when an altruistic act may have a directly experienced aversive outcome for the actor, the value of its total set of outcomes can nevertheless be preferred to the value of the outcomes of another less altruistic alternative.

The assumption that altruistic behavior does have reinforcing consequences is not to be taken as equivalent to an assertion which can be found in a number of recent analyses of altruism—the assertion that altruistic action can be treated as a form of social exchange (Gouldner, 1960; Homans, 1961; Thibaut & Kelly, 1959). The concept of altruism can more usefully be restricted to the choice of an act which is at least partly determined by the actor's expectation of consequences which will benefit another person without benefit to himself. But the expected consequences for the other person are not necessarily without affective (and reinforcement) value for the actor, even though directly beneficial outcomes for the actor are not specified by the altruistic component of the act.

When the consequences of an act for another person are concrete and visible, their affective value for the actor may be mediated by his capacity for empathic or vicarious response to social cues which immediately transmit the other person's experience (for example, to expressive cues which may convey the affective state of the other person). Alternatively, the actor may experience the empathically or vicariously reinforcing affective consequences of altruistic behavior through his capacity to give a cognitive representation to the effects of the behavior on another person. The affective support for the altruistic act therefore does not require that the effects of the act be directly observable. Of course, the affective value that is attached to such cognitive representations will sometimes be filtered through the normative self-evaluative systems which people may apply to their actions. But changes of self-esteem or other consequences of self-evaluation cannot have a criterial status in the specification of the affective or cognitive mechanisms of altruistic behavior. A concept of altruism must focus on a component of behavioral control that is directed to effects which will be produced in the experience of another person. Regardless of whether such effects are directly observable or are given a cognitive representation by the actor, the altruistic component of their affective value must be transmitted by the actor's empathic or vicarious experience. Empathic or vicarious control is 'the criterion of the truly altruistic act.

Although empathic or vicarious experience is also a prerequisite of sympathetic behavior, a concept of sympathy must be distinguished from a concept of altruism in certain other respects. The concept of sympathy often has been used to refer to a complex of affective and cognitive dispositions toward empathic or vicarious experience (Allport, 1954; Asch, 1952, pp. 171–172; Heider, 1958, pp. 277–282; McDougall, 1908, pp. 150–179). But its more behaviorally

immediate usage is in reference to a disposition to relieve the distress of others—
a disposition which appears to influence the behavior of all of the primate species
(DeVore, 1965) as well as the behavior of many other species, and which is most
prevalent in the behavior of mothers toward their offspring. To state the criterion for the presence of this disposition in human social behavior, we may say
that an act is sympathetic to the extent that it is elicited through the actor's
empathic or vicarious affective response to the actual or anticipated distress of
another person. An act cannot be identified as sympathetic, of course, merely
because it has the effect of relieving another person's distress. It might have been
motivated, for example, by the actor's simultaneous experience of the same distressful events, or even by the actor's anticipation of aversive consequences
which he will directly experience as a result of his failure to come to the aid of
another.

The requirement of empathic or vicarious distress specifies that sympathetic behavior is under aversive affective control. A sympathetic component of
an act, therefore, has a narrower potential affective base than does an altruistic
component, since altruism may be under either positive or aversive affective control. However, the contingencies of reinforcement for sympathetic behavior are
less restrictive than are the contingencies for altruistic behavior. A sympathetic
act may be altruistic to the extent that it is controlled by the anticipated consequence of the reduction of empathic or vicarious distress which the actor will
experience when another person's distress is relieved. Altruistic components may
be present, for example, in some recent demonstrations of the conditions under
which both children and college students will display sympathetic actions (Buss,
1966; Lenrow, 1965; Rosenhan & White, 1967; Schopler & Bateson, 1965). But
sympathetic actions also are very often under the control of the anticipation of
direct social rewards, or of subsequent reciprocity from another person, even
though the disposition toward sympathy itself requires a capacity for empathic
or vicarious experience of distress. Observations in naturalistic settings have
shown that the sympathetic behavior of children frequently is predicated on
their expectation of social approval or of mutual benefits in a shared difficulty
(Isaacs, 1933; Murphy, 1937). The sympathetic act can be dependent, then, on
external outcomes which are to be directly experienced by the actor. In contrast,
independence of such outcomes is a criterion for the altruistic component of an
act.

Since empathic or vicarious experience is taken to be a prerequisite of
both altruism and sympathy, I would like to summarize here, in an abbreviated
form, a more extended analysis of the essential properties of this experience
(Aronfreed, 1968a). There is actually an interesting distinction which can be

made between the concepts of empathic and vicarious. Empathy might be used for a person's affective response to the expressive behavioral cues of another person's affective experience, whereas vicarious experience might be a more appropriate term when a person's affect is elicited by information about the external events which have an impact on another person. The distinction may be very useful in the observation and experimental analysis of social behavior. But it can be overlooked in a rough outline of the larger problems which are posed in an account of altruistic and sympathetic dispositions. Accordingly, I will use the single term *empathy* here to denote an individual's affective experience when it is elicited by social cues which transmit information about the corresponding affective experience of another person—either by expressive cues which are direct indices of another person's affective state, or by other kinds of cues which convey the affective impact of external events upon another person.

It should be noted that the concept of empathy is tied to observations which allow the inference that a person's affectivity is elicited by the observation (or cognitive representation) of social cues which transmit another person's *experience.* The requirements of this inference would not be met merely by a demonstration that one person's behavior had been influenced by observation of the rewarding or punitive outcomes of another person's behavior. A great many such demonstrations have been conducted with both children and adults as subjects (Bandura, 1965; Bandura, Grusec, & Menlove, 1967; Bruning, 1965; Craig, 1967; Ditrichs, Simon, & Greene, 1967; Kanfer & Marston, 1963; Lewis & Duncan, 1958; Marston, 1966; Rosekrans, 1967; Rosekrans & Hartup, 1967; Walters, Parke, & Cane, 1965; Wheeler & Smith, 1967). In none of these demonstrations is it possible to distinguish between the observer's affective response to the perception of another person's experience and the observer's more direct response to the information that is carried in the observed reward or punishment itself. The same difficulty of interpretation is present in the findings of experiments which have been addressed to the question of whether mere observation of another person's aggression will strengthen or reduce an observer's subsequent disposition toward aggression (Bandura, Ross, & Ross, 1963; Berkowitz & Geen, 1966; Feshbach, 1961; Rosenbaum & deCharms, 1960; Wheeler & Caggiula, 1966).

More persuasive demonstrations of empathic experience can be found in the results of experiments which have used peripheral autonomic indices of an observer's anxiety or distress in response to either expressive or objective cues of another person's pain or distress (Bandura & Rosenthal, 1966; Berger, 1962; Haner & Whitney, 1960; Lazarus, Speisman, Mordkoff, & Davidson, 1962; Miller, Caul, & Mirsky, 1967). However, these latter experiments have not been designed to demonstrate how empathic experience functions in the control of overt social behavior. Empathic affective control of choices of action can perhaps be examined most convincingly when the social cues which are used to elicit empathic control are made the contingent outcomes of the observer's own overt performance of an act. It would then be possible to assess the value of these outcomes for control of the observer's behavior, even though they have no directly rewarding or punitive consequences for the observer.

Since the specific qualitative properties of a change of affective state are determined by its cognitive housing, empathic reactions will require some common elements between the cognition of the observer and the cognition of the person whose experience is being observed. For this reason, it is usually quite difficult to identify truly empathic control of an observer's behavior. For example, a child's reactions to another person's expressive affective cues, or to the impact of external events upon that person, often may be partially attributable to its experience of the observed social stimuli as impinging directly upon itself— perhaps because of some generalization of affectivity from the child's direct experience of the stimuli in the past, or because the child perceives the stimuli as signals which portend correlated events of corresponding affective value that it will experience directly. But the concept of empathy is used too broadly to have any utility unless it is restricted to that component of an observer's affectivity which is elicited by the perception of another person's experience, and which is independent of the perception of social stimuli as having an impact on one's self. The application of such a criterion clearly must rest on experimental operations or conditions of observation which permit certain kinds of inferences to be made about the observer's cognition of concrete social cues. It is interesting to note that the criterion is not met, for example, by experiments which have demonstrated response indices of an observing animal's aversion to the distress cues of another animal (Church, 1959; Miller, 1961; Miller et al., 1967). These demonstrations have been conducted under conditions in which the distress cues might have retained their original conditioned value as signals of directly aversive experience for the observer.

Bearing in mind these suggested criteria of empathic experience, we can now turn our attention more closely to the problem of the identification of altruistic and sympathetic acts. Comparative psychologists sometimes have suggested that the higher species of animals may have innate dispositions toward altruism and sympathy—particularly in their reactions to the distress of others (Hebb & Thompson, 1954; McBride & Hebb, 1948). More recently, a number of ethologists have argued that evolutionary selection in animals will favor a certain amount of behavior that is altruistic in the sense that it benefits others, even at some cost in survival to the altruistic individuals—for example, alarm calls at the approach of predators (Hamilton, 1964; Maynard Smith, 1965; Wynne-Edwards, 1962). Campbell (1965) has proposed that humans also may have unlearned altruistic dispositions which are selected for their adaptive value in meeting environmental stress. While some of the kinds of behavior in question might well be classified as sympathetic—for example, reactions to the distress of the young—it is very doubtful that a concept of altruism gains anything when it is applied indiscriminately to any behavior that may benefit another member of the same species. It is reasonable to suppose that grooming, retrieval, and some other behavior patterns of the higher animals might be forerunners of human altruistic behavior. But the distinctive utility of a concept of altruism would be much diluted if we were to treat these types of animal behavior as equivalent to the more highly internalized altruistic acts of which human beings are capable. For example, the extensive grooming behavior of many primates (DeVore, 1965) is not properly described as altruistic, because it is usually reciprocal and is sometimes a source of edible insects for the groomer. Correspondingly, cleaning, retrieval, and other components of nurturance of the young may have directly experienced pleasurable or distress-reducing consequences for the female adults of many species.

Altruism is a more useful concept when it is limited to contingencies from which it can be inferred that the behavior of one individual is controlled by the anticipation of its consequences for another individual. The problem of the identification of altruism in the behavior of animals also hints at the need for caution in the application of concepts of both altruism and sympathy to observations of human social behavior. The act of helping another person to attain desirable ends, for example, or the act of relieving another person's distress, may be controlled by the expectation of social approval or of subsequent reciprocal assistance, or by the sense of contract or equity which is acquired from previous experience as the recipient of help. Likewise, the conditions under which people are likely to respond with aid to the circumstances of others who are ill or in danger may often be influenced primarily by their anticipation of potential external social reactions to their initiative, their effectiveness, or their good judgment. The fact that help or aid has been extended to another person obviously does not, therefore, require us to assume that the observed behavior is controlled by altruistic or sympathetic dispositions. A very considerable part of the problem of interpretation here clearly arises out of our inability to classify the relevant behavior on the criteria of either its form or its consequences. Classification must rest on inferences about the affective and cognitive determinants of the behavior.

The magnitude of the problem of the identification of altruistic and sympathetic components in social behavior is indicated by the ambiguity of numerous experimental observations of the dispositions of children to share possessions with or extend aid to their peers (Doland & Adelberg, 1967; Fischer, 1963; Hartshorne, May, & Maller, 1929; Hartup & Coates, 1967; Lenrow, 1965; Murphy, 1937; Rosenhan & White, 1967; Ugurel-Semin, 1952; Wright, 1942). The same ambiguity is apparent in demonstrations of the behavior with which adults produce beneficial consequences for others (Berkowitz & Daniels, 1964; Berkowitz & Friedman, 1967; Darlington & Macker, 1966; Goranson & Berkowitz, 1966; Schopler & Matthews, 1965). Similar demonstrations have been carried out with other primates (Crawford, 1941; Mason, 1959; Mason & Hollis, 1962; Nissen & Crawford, 1936). And some investigators have attempted to show that there are analogous dispositions in rats (Holder, 1958; Ulrich, 1967). With the exception of the studies which are reported by Lenrow (1965) and by Rosenhan and White (1967), it is very difficult to determine whether an altruistic status should be assigned to the behavior that has been observed in these demonstrations. In a number of instances, the behavior is reinforced by direct and explicit rewards. In other cases, the behavior appears as part of a cooperative effort to produce beneficial outcomes for both self and other. And virtually all of the remaining demonstrations with human subjects are conducted under conditions which cannot be used to separate the altruistic component of the observed behavior from strong implicit incentives for the expectation of social approval.

Some experiments with both humans and other primates are particularly effective illustrations of the difficulty of establishing the presence of an altruistic component in cooperative behavior or sharing (Boren, 1966; Daniels, 1967; Horel, Treichler, & Meyer, 1963). These experiments uniformly show that cooperative behavior breaks down when it no longer has direct and fairly immediate reciprocal reinforcing consequences for one of the partners. Experiments which have been designed to demonstrate the aversive reactions of monkeys to the distress of their peers also are difficult to interpret as evidence of either altruistic or sympathetic dispositions (Masserman, Wechkin, & Terris, 1964; Miller, Banks, & Ogawa, 1963; Miller et al., 1967). It cannot be determined that the behavior with which the monkeys reduce or prevent the distress of a peer actually has an altruistic or sympathetic character, because there is little evidence to support the inference that the behavior is empathically controlled by its consequences for the peer. The design of the experiments makes it equally plausible that the subjects are acting to avoid stimulation (either electric shock or distress cues) which they experience as directly aversive to themselves. The results of other experiments with rats (Lavery & Foley, 1963; Rice & Gainer, 1962), in which the subjects were given opportunities to terminate either white noise or the distress squeals of a peer, also tend to confirm the suspicion that acts which reduce the distress of another are not necessarily empathically motivated, but may be controlled instead by the directly aversive experience of distress cues by the actor-observer.

From the point of view of the developmental psychology of socialization, the ingredients of altruistic and sympathetic behavior can be divided into two basic classes of phenomena. The first class establishes the child's capacity for empathic experience. It consists of the coupling of changes in the child's affectivity to social cues which transmit information about the experience of others. Some of these social cues can then serve as motivational elicitors of the child's altruistic and sympathetic dispositions. Other kinds of social cues can begin to function as empathically reinforcing outcomes of the child's overt acts. The origin of the child's empathic reactions can be found in contingencies of socialization which have certain essential properties of a paradigm for the conditioning of changes of affective state. The prerequisite contingencies for this conditioning process may take a number of different forms (Aronfreed, 1968a). But their common and crucial feature—a feature that is indigenous to the child's earliest social experience—is an initial temporal association between cues which transmit the affective experience of others and closely related events whose affective value is directly experienced by the child. As a result of this temporal contiguity, the cues which transmit the experience of others will acquire their own independent value for the elicitation of changes in the child's affectivity, under conditions where they are no longer perceived by the child as signals of other events which it will experience directly. These social cues must be concretely observable in order to function in the earliest period of socialization. But they can gradually be given a cognitive representation that also exercises affective control over the child's behavior.

The second basic class of phenomena in the socialization of altruistic and sympathetic behavior lies within the establishment of the instrumental value of overt acts. The child often finds the outcome value of overt acts of altruism or sympathy in its empathic experience of the effects of the acts upon others. The empathically reinforcing effects of an altruistic or sympathetic act may take the form of social cues which are directly observable contingent outcomes of the act. Or the effects may have their value transmitted, even when they are not observable, through their cognitive representation by the child. Of course, as was noted earlier, an act may have a sympathetic component even when its reinforcing consequences are directly experienced rather than empathically mediated—that is, the sympathetic component of an act does not confer upon it an altruistic status.

The act may be motivated in part by the expectation of direct rewards or mutual benefits.

Behavior-contingent learning is one path for the establishment of the instrumental value of a child's altruistic and sympathetic actions. In the behavior-contingent paradigm of learning (Aronfreed, 1968a), the child would find that its overt performance of certain actions could produce either pleasurable or distress-reducing outcomes in the experience of others. These outcomes in turn would elicit the child's own empathically reinforcing changes of affective state. Opportunities for the child's behavior to be brought under the control of such outcomes pervade the socialization process. In the socialization of sympathetic behavior, for example, dispositions which the child already has begun to acquire—such as giving, sharing, or the expression of affection—may be more selectively channeled into sympathetic action when the child finds that they can be instrumental to the reduction of another person's distress. The reinforcing reduction of empathic distress that the child experiences, when it observes social cues which indicate relief of another person's distress, will also attach some potentially reinforcing change of affectivity to the intrinsic correlates of the actions with which it has reduced the other person's distress. And as the child's cognitive capacities expand, the intrinsic affective value of sympathetic acts may come to be carried in the child's cognitive representation of their consequences for others. The maintenance of the child's sympathetic behavior will then have acquired some independence both of its directly experienced consequences for the child and its directly observable consequences for others.

The speed and accuracy with which altruistic and sympathetic dispositions often appear in the behavior of the young child, together with the rapid spread of these dispositions toward a variety of real and surrogate social objects, indicates that behavior-contingent learning will provide only a very partial account of their origins. Imitative modeling and other forms of observational learning may make an even more important contribution to the emergence of the child's altruistic and sympathetic behavior (Aronfreed, 1969). The opportunity for observational learning of the form and value of sympathetic behavior, for example, would occur whenever the child observed another person's sympathetic actions in conjunction with its own direct or empathic experience of relief of distress. It might be expected that the most frequent and potent foundation of this learning in the child's social experience would be the many occasions on which the child is the recipient of actions that others direct to the relief of its own distress. The result of such experience would be an attachment of intrinsic affective value, corresponding to relief of distress, at first to the child's cognitive representation of the sympathetic actions of others, and then to the representational correlates of its own potential repertoire of sympathetic behavior. The child could then reduce its empathic distress, in response to the perceived or anticipated distress of another, by reproducing the sympathetic actions which it had learned by observation. And since the child's representation of a sympathetic act, and of its consequences, would already have acquired some internalized distress-reducing value on the basis of past observational learning, its overt performance of the act could have reinforcing consequences which were to some degree independent of directly observable effects on others.

The learning of altruistic behavior can be demonstrated in the findings of an experiment which was conducted by the author and Vivian Paskal (Aronfreed & Paskal, 1965). Six- to eight-year-old girls were used as subjects, and an adult female acted as the agent of socialization. The experimental paradigms of socialization consisted of two immediately successive phases, which were respectively designed to control the following processes: first, the attachment of a child's empathic positive affectivity to the expressive cues of a corresponding affective state of the adult agent; second, the establishment of the altruistic value of an overt act that the child could use instrumentally to produce the agent's expressive cues. During the initial phase of socialization, the agent sat close enough to the child to allow body contact. She demonstrated the operation of a choice box which automatically dispensed a small candy as the outcome of the movement of one lever and a 3-second red light as the outcome of the movement of another lever. Each outcome was programmed so that it would occur unpredictably, however, on only 60% of the occasions on which the appropriate lever was moved. The child merely watched while the agent varied her choices equally between the two levers over the course of 20 trials. The agent displayed no reaction when her choices did not produce explicit outcomes. Nor did she show any reaction when her choices produced candy. But when one of her choices activated the red light, she displayed one of three patterns of behavior which represented variations in the contingencies between her expressive cues and her behavior toward the child. These variations were constructed to support the inference that the reinforcement value of the agent's expressive cues, when they were later used as outcomes of the child's own choices among alternative acts, during the second phase of socialization, could be attributed to their conditioned elicitation of the child's empathic positive affective experience.

In the basic experimental paradigm, the children were repeatedly exposed to a very close relationship in time between the agent's expressive cues of pleasure and their own direct experience of the agent's affection. Whenever the agent's choice of a lever activated the red light, she stared at the light and smiled. Simultaneously, the agent gave one of four exclamations in a pleased and excited tone of voice. All of these exclamations were roughly equivalent to: "*There's the light!*" The agent's exclamation terminated her expressive cues. It was followed immediately by a firm hug of the child, for which the agent used one arm. At the same time, she inclined her head toward the child and displayed a very broad direct smile. The physical affection and social warmth were emitted as though they were the spontaneous overflow of the agent's pleasurable reaction to the light. Two control paradigms were used to eliminate different segments of the contingencies which occurred in this experimental paradigm. In one of the control paradigms, children were exposed only to the agent's expressive affective cues (and were given no experience of affection from the agent); whereas in the second control paradigm, the children experienced only the agent's affection (and were not given the opportunity to observe the agent's preliminary expressive cues).

The second phase of socialization consisted of a performance task which was designed as a common test of the effects of the three paradigms of the first phase. During the second phase, the child herself operated the choice box over a great many trials. The agent used a pretext to deactivate the red light on the face of the box, the illumination of which had sometimes been the outcome of her choices during the first phase. The agent now sat directly across from the child, facing the rear of the box. Her gaze was fixed on another red light that was visible only to her. The child was told of the presence of this auxiliary light, and also was told that it could be illuminated by her choice of the light-producing lever. The child was further informed that she could keep all candies which came out of the box (but that she could not eat them until completion of the task). While the child was engaged in the performance of the task, the agent remained impassive when the child's choice of a lever produced no explicit outcome. The agent was likewise unreactive when the child's choice produced candy for herself. But whenever the red light was illuminated by the child's choice of the appropriate lever, the agent would smile while staring at the light, and would at the same time exclaim: "*There's the light!*" Thus, the agent emitted the same cues which she had used to express her pleasure during two of the three paradigms of the initial phase. The child therefore found herself in a position where she had to choose repeatedly between an act that could produce candy for herself and an act that could produce only observably pleasurable consequences for another person. The situation therefore simultaneously tested both the child's altruistic disposition and her empathic responsiveness.

Variations in the contingencies of experience during the first phase of the paradigms had a strong effect on the children's choices during the test for altruism. It will be recalled that the basic experimental paradigm initially placed the agent's expressive affective cues in very close conjunction with the child's direct experience of affection. The children who had been exposed to this contingency were significantly more willing to surrender opportunities to obtain candy, during the test for altruism, than were the children whose earlier experience had included only an association between the red light and the agent's expressive cues of positive affect (without physical affection). They also showed significantly more altruism than did the children who had been exposed previously only to physical affection in association with the red light (without the expressive cues which the agent then used during the test task). The majority of the children who had been in the basic social conditioning paradigm in fact produced the light for the agent more frequently than they produced candy for themselves. In the case of each of the control paradigms, however, the children typically chose the candy-producing lever more frequently.

For the children in the basic experimental paradigm, the establishment and demonstration of the value of the agent's expressive affective cues was a variant of a more general procedure that is commonly used to establish and test the acquired positive reinforcement value of a "neutral" stimulus. However, the expressive cues and the child's direct experience of affection were paired under contingencies which were analogous to those of a Pavlovian conditioning paradigm. Since the child was only an observer during these contingencies, the pairing was not contingent on its overt performance of the critical act. There are some experiments with animals which also appear to demonstrate that the positive secondary reinforcement value of a stimulus can be acquired under Pavlovian contingencies—that is, where the pairing with the unconditioned stimulus is not produced by the subject's overt behavior (Ferster & Skinner, 1957; Kelleher & Gollub, 1962; Knott & Clayton, 1966; Stein, 1958). The performance test for altruism was an index of the potential reinforcement value that had been acquired by the agent's expressive cues. It was apparent that these cues had acquired some empathic affective value for the children who initially had been exposed to the basic conditioning paradigm.

The relationships among the different contingencies of the three initial paradigms, and their relationship in turn to the contingencies of the subsequent performance paradigm, were devised with the aim of assuring that differences among the groups in their altruistic test behavior could not easily be attributed merely to differences in the children's perception of approval when the agent reacted to their choices with expressive cues of pleasure. Since the agent's expressive cues were unrelated to the children's overt behavior during the initial paradigms, but were made contingent on the overt choices of all of the children during the test, it seems clear that the experimental effect could not have been the result of the already established value of the cues as evidence of direct social approval. It is also of some interest to note that the agent's cues of pleasurable affect appeared to have a highly durable value for the reinforcement of the altruistic choices of children in the experimental group. These children made essentially as many altruistic choices during the second half of the test trials as they did during the first half. The inconsistent scheduling of both the expressive cues and the agent's affection, with respect to the agent's choices during the initial phase and the child's choices during the test, possibly may account for the fact that the value of the cues showed such strong resistance to extinction. The findings of other experiments with children also have suggested that the acquired positive secondary reinforcement value of a stimulus event can be maintained independently for longer periods of time when the event is scheduled inconsistently during extinction, and when the event originally was associated with a more "primary" event that was used as an inconsistent outcome of behavior (Myers & Myers, 1963; Myers, 1960; Myers & Myers, 1966).

The author and Vivian Paskal also have used experimental paradigms of socialization in a more detailed examination of the mechanisms for children's learning of sympathetic behavior (Aronfreed & Paskal, 1966). This experiment was conducted with seven- and eight-year-old girls as subjects. And an adult female was again the agent of socialization. The experimental paradigms were constructed around three distinct but immediately successive phases of socialization. The first phase was designed to condition a child's distress to the observed distress cues of another person. The second phase gave the child the opportunity to observe the sympathetic actions with which the agent relieved the child's own distress. The last phase placed the child in a situation where it could respond sympathetically to the distress of another child. Five separate sequences or experimental groups were used to vary the contingencies of socialization within one phase at a time. During each phase of any of the sequences, the child classified a number of small toys which were replicas of real objects. She was assigned the task of classifying each toy in accordance with whether she thought it most appropriate for a house, a dog, or a school. Twelve discrete toys were classified in each of the three phases. And the set of toys was changed for each new phase. The child showed her classification of each toy by pushing down one of three levers on a choice box. The word which labeled the category appeared on a panel above each lever. The middle lever was used for the dog category, and the toys were selected to make its use inappropriate, so that it would ordinarily be chosen very infrequently or not at all. Since choices of the middle lever were not instrumental to the task of classification, it became possible to use them as an index of sympathetic behavior during the third or test phase of all of the experimental sequences.

The first of the five experimental sequences was designed as the prototype of the contribution of both empathy and observational learning to children's acquisition of sympathetic behavior. A summary of its three phases can be used to describe the essential ingredients of the same phases within any of the sequences. The first phase was devised to be a paradigm of the original acquisition process for the establishment of a child's empathic affective response to the expressive cues which indicate another person's distressful experience. The crucial contingencies for conditioning of the child's empathic experience were introduced in a temporal contiguity between the agent's observable distress cues and the child's own direct experience of aversive stimulation. Both the child and the agent wore earphones, on the pretext of having to monitor periodic noise from within the choice box. The child was told that the noise in the agent's earphones would be even louder than the noise in her own earphones. Following six of the child's 12 classifications of toys, she heard through her earphones a highly aversive loud noise which had a duration of 7 seconds. The occurrence of the noise was unpredictable across trials, and was not determined by the child's choice. The noise began at a point well into the intertrial interval that followed the classification of a toy. The agent began to show cues of distress (apparently because of the noise in her own earphones) by placing her head in her hands 3 seconds before the onset of the noise. Her distress cues continued throughout the duration of the noise.

The second phase was designed to give the child the opportunity to form a cognitive representation of an act–outcome contingency that was observable in the agent's sympathetic actions toward the child. The agent now wore no earphones and therefore showed no evidence of distress. As soon as the child had classified each toy, the agent operated another choice box to show how she would classify the same toy. She had told the child beforehand that she might be able, while she was using her own choice box, to turn off the noise that the child would still sometimes hear through her earphones. When the child had finished her classification of each toy, the agent would begin her classification by poising her finger above one of the two outer levers in the array of three on her choice box. The outer levers represented house and school, and were clearly the only correct choices for almost all of the toys. After 2 or 3 seconds of apparent thought, the agent did actually choose one of the two outer levers on six of the 12 trials. On the remaining six trials, however, the child at this point began to hear the noise through her earphones. The noise remained at the same highly aversive intensity as had been used during the first phase, in order to maximize the distress-reducing value of the agent's sympathetic actions toward the child. As had been true earlier, the noise was unpredictable across trials and unrelated to the child's choice. It lasted only for 3 seconds, at which point the agent pushed the middle lever on her choice box, and at the same time said that she was choosing the middle lever in order to turn off the noise. Her action in fact did terminate the noise. It was clear that she had reduced the child's distress by temporarily giving up the task of making a correct classification.

The third phase of the first sequence was constructed as a test of whether the subject had acquired a disposition to reproduce the previously observed sympathetic actions of the agent. The subject was given a number of opportunities to reduce her empathic experience of distress, in response to the distress cues of another child, by making the same choice (of the middle lever) as the agent had made earlier in order to reduce the subject's own direct exposure to the noise. The contingencies of this phase also were arranged so that elimination of the other child's distress cues would be a potentially reinforcing outcome of the subject's choices. The subject's sympathetic dispositions thus could be brought under the control of external events which provided both the empathic motivation and the empathic reinforcement for her behavior.

Another girl was introduced as a new subject for the third phase. The new girl actually had been a subject earlier, and then had been trained to the role of a more or less innocent dummy. She was now to emit distress cues at critical junctures in the test of the primary subject's sympathetic dispositions. The primary subject was given the task of classifying each toy, following its classification by the dummy, by using the levers on the second choice box—the same role that the adult agent had performed during the preceding phase. Only the dummy now wore the earphones, so that the subject was no longer vulnerable to the direct experience of aversive stimulation. The agent sat behind the subject as an observer. Dummy and subject made their successive choices without incident in the classification of six of the 12 toys. But on the remaining six trials, the dummy placed her head in her hands, in response to a low signal from her earphones, just when the subject was about to make her own choice. The dummy's distress cue was the same, of course, as the one that the agent had emitted originally during the first phase of the socialization sequence. If the subject now chose the middle lever—the same sympathetic choice which the agent had made to reduce the subject's own distress during the second phase—the dummy would immediately terminate her distress cue by raising her head in response to the termination of the low signal in her earphones. But if the subject made a task-oriented, nonsympathetic choice of one of the two outer levers, the dummy would maintain her distress cue for a duration of 5 seconds after the subject had made her choice (such a choice would therefore be deprived of empathically mediated reinforcement).

The four remaining experimental sequences were designed primarily as a series of controls on the basic contingencies which had been used in the three phases of the first sequence. But they were also structured to support certain key inferences concerning the affective and cognitive mechanisms in the acquisition of sympathetic behavior. The second sequence was identical to the first, with the exception that the agent's distress cues were not paired with the aversive noise that the child heard during the first phase. Although the noise occurred at the same six intertrial intervals at which it had occurred for the first sequence, the agent's distress cues were emitted only during the noiseless intervals which followed the remaining six trials. This sequence exposed the children, of course, to the same frequencies of occurrence of noise and distress cues as had been used in the first sequence. But the children were not exposed to the temporal contiguity which was required for the conditioning of empathic distress.

The third experimental sequence differed from the first only in one feature of the second phase, where the noise that the child occasionally heard was sharply reduced to a very mild intensity (in contrast to the first sequence, in which the noise continued to be highly aversive). It was expected that the third sequence would be relatively ineffective in establishing the child's disposition to reproduce the agent's sympathetic actions, since it minimized the potential distress-reducing value of the actions for the child. The fourth and fifth experimental sequences introduced two levels of reduction of the social cues which were used, during the third phase of the first sequence, to elicit and reinforce the children's sympathetic choices. During the third phase of the fourth sequence, the dummy wore earphones but emitted no distress cues. In the third phase of the fifth sequence, the dummy did not even wear the earphones.

Differences among the effects of the five sequential paradigms strongly confirmed the contribution of the mechanisms of both empathic conditioning and observational learning to the acquisition of sympathetic behavior. In all of the sequences, the children were highly task oriented in their classification of the toys across the twelve trials of each of the first two phases. They would choose the task-inappropriate middle lever (classification in the dog category) only once or twice. But during the third phase, the children from the basic first sequence moved to a marked preference for the middle lever. Half of them chose the middle lever on six or more trials—that is, at least on all of the occasions on which the dummy emitted distress cues. With few exceptions, the remainder of the children from the first sequence showed a sharp increase in the frequency of their choice of the middle lever. They typically now made a sympathetic choice four or five times (among the six trials on which the dummy showed distress cues), and each time forfeited the opportunity to make a correct classification.

The children from all of the other four sequences continued to show a strong task orientation during the test for sympathetic behavior. Although some of the children made small increases in the frequency of their choice of the middle lever (particularly those from the fourth sequence), the frequency distributions of their choices during the third phase were generally quite similar to the corresponding distributions for the first two phases. There was a powerful and highly reliable difference between the effect of the first sequence and the effect of each of the other sequences, when all sequences were compared with respect to the shifts, between the first two phases and the test phase, in the frequencies of the children's choices of the middle lever. The distributions of frequency shifts in choices of the middle lever were very similar among the groups of children from the second through the fifth sequences—although the children from the fourth sequence departed somewhat from this pattern in a rather interesting way.

The difference between the effects of the first and second sequences shows that the empathic experience of distress is a prerequisite for the establishment of sympathetic behavior. During the first phase of the second sequence, the agent's distress cues and the children's direct experience of aversive stimulation were not placed under contingencies which would condition the children's distress to observation of the cues alone. These children showed little sympathetic behavior during the test phase. Even though they previously had many opportunities to observe the sympathetic action which the agent had directed toward them, and even though the same action was easily available for their choice, they seldom chose to use it to relieve another child's observable distress. Clearly, reproduction of the agent's sympathetic actions was not elicited merely by the knowledge that another child was now experiencing distress. The children's behavioral expressions of sympathy appeared to require some empathic reinstatement of the conditions of affective experience under which the agent's actions originally had acquired value for them.

The absence of sympathetic behavior among children from the third sequence indicates that the sympathetic actions of children from the first sequence were not simply attributable to a generalized disposition to be influenced by observation of the previous choices of an adult. Such a generalized disposition would not account for the difference between the two groups even if we were to assume that its behavioral expression was narrowed, under the conditions of the test situation, by the further requirement that the subject experience empathic distress in response to the cues from the dummy. This requirement would not have been realized for children from the second sequence, who were not exposed to the contingencies for conditioning of empathic distress during the

first phase of the experiment. But children from both the first and third sequences did experience the contingencies which were designed to attach their
empathic responsiveness to the distress cues of the agent, and which would also
have made them responsive to the distress cues of the dummy. Certainly both of
these groups had equal access to the sheer informational value of the observation
of which actions the agent could most effectively direct to their own welfare
during the second phase of the experiment. Both groups were therefore in an
equal position to know that reproducing the agent's actions would reduce the
dummy's distress during the test. The single difference between the experiences
of the two groups occurred in the intensity of the aversive stimulation to which
they were exposed during the second phase. The agent's sympathetic actions
terminated a highly aversive noise for children in the first sequence, but only a
mild noise for children in the third sequence. It therefore seems necessary to
conclude that the effect of this difference was to give different amounts of acquired value to a sympathetic act which the children could potentially reproduce
in their own behavior, during the test situation, in order to reduce their empathic
reaction to the dummy's distress. Although both groups had the same opportunity for observational learning of sympathetic act—outcome contingencies, their
behavioral reproduction of the observed sympathetic actions seemed to be determined by the magnitude of the change of affectivity which they originally
had experienced when the actions had been directed toward themselves.

The relatively unsympathetic behavior of the children from the fourth and
fifth sequences, during the test phase, confirms the obvious functional value of
the dummy's distress cues as elicitors of the children's sympathetic dispositions.
Unlike the children from the first sequence, the children from the last two sequences did not show sharp increases in the frequency of their choice of the
action with which the agent previously had reduced their own distress, even
though their exposure to the contingencies for empathic conditioning and the
opportunity for observational learning had been identical during the first two
phases. Of course, the importance of external distress cues in the affective control of the children's sympathetic behavior was also apparent in the fact that the
children from the first sequence generally confined their choice of the middle
lever to the six trials on which the dummy emitted distress cues. These findings
make it clear once again that the second phase of the experiment provided only
the basis for observational learning of the actions and consequences which could
be produced by a sympathetic agent. The children's own dispositions to reproduce these actions required the affective control of their empathic experience of
distress.

There are some other aspects of the experimental findings which reveal
that onset and termination of the dummy's distress cues, while crucial to the

choices of children from the first sequence during the test, were not the only determinants of their sympathetic behavior. As was pointed out earlier, the experience of children from the third sequence would have given them the empathic motivation to terminate another child's distress cues, and also the necessary information about the distress-reducing consequences of a choice of the middle lever. Yet when they were given the opportunity to use their potentially sympathetic resources, they did not show a significant increment in their frequency of choice of the middle lever. Their failure to do so suggests the inference that the same act had acquired some additional intrinsic value for children from the first sequence, who earlier had experienced the relief of their own relatively intense (rather than mild) distress in direct conjunction with the observation of the agent's sympathetic actions. Because the difference between the effects of the two sequences cannot be attributed to the children's control of external outcomes in the dummy's distress cues, it seems plausible to conclude that the children's potentially sympathetic actions differed in the amount of inherent value that the actions had acquired as representations of an earlier external sample of behavior.

There was another indication of representational control over the value of sympathetic behavior in the behavior of children from the fourth sequence. Despite their maintenance of a fairly strong task orientation during the test for sympathetic behavior, these children showed discernible increments in the frequency of their choice of the middle lever. Their behavior was in fact closer to that of children from the first sequence than was the behavior of the children from any of the other control sequences. It was especially interesting to note that they chose the middle lever, during the test situation, reliably more often than did the children from the fifth sequence, whose dummies wore no earphones as well as emitted no distress cues. Of course, since the dummy did not emit distress cues for the children in the fourth sequence, the children distributed their choices of the middle lever more or less unpredictably among the 12 test trials. It seems likely that their choices were under the control of their cognitive representations of the distress-reducing (or distress-avoiding) consequences of their actions for another child who was wearing the earphones. Their behavior suggested that the internalized affective value of a sympathetic act also can be mediated in part by the cognitive representation of outcomes of the act.

During a verbal inquiry that followed most of the experimental sessions, the children gave introspective reports which provided some additional evidence of the role of cognitive representation. Among the children in the three groups which received distress cues from the dummy, almost all perceived the cues as indicators of loud noise in the dummy's earphones. However, many of these children seemed unable or unwilling to report a clear recognition that their choices of the middle lever would have relieved the dummy's distress. Among the children in the first sequence, reported awareness of this contingency was a highly reliable predictor of maximal sympathetic behavior. Among the children in the second and third sequences, reported awareness of the contingency was unrelated to their behavior.

REFERENCES

Allport, G. W. The historical background of modern social psychology. In G. Lindzey (Ed.), *Handbook of social psychology.* Vol. 1. *Theory and method.* Cambridge, Mass.: Addison-Wesley, 1954, Pp. 3–56.

Aronfreed, J. *Conduct and conscience: The socialization of internalized control over behavior.* New York: Academic Press, 1968. (a)

Aronfreed, J. The concept of internalization. In D. A. Goslin (Ed.), *Handbook of socialization theory and research.* Chicago: Rand-McNally, 1969. (b)

Aronfreed, J. The problem of imitation. In L. P. Lipsitt & H. W. Reese (Eds.), *Advances in child development and behavior.* Vol. 4. New York: Academic Press, 1969.

Aronfreed, J., & Paskal, V. Altruism, empathy, and the conditioning of positive affect. Unpublished manuscript, University of Pennsylvania, 1965.

Aronfreed, J., & Paskal, V. The development of sympathetic behavior in children: An experimental test of a two-phase hypothesis. Unpublished manuscript, University of Pennsylvania, 1966.

Asch, S. E. *Social psychology.* Englewood Cliffs, New Jersey: Prentice-Hall, 1952.

Bandura, A. Influence of models' reinforcement contingencies on the acquisition of imitative responses. *Journal of Personality and Social Psychology,* 1965, 1, 589–595.

Bandura, A., Grusec, J. E., & Menlove, F. L. Some social determinants of self-monitoring reinforcement systems. *Journal of Personality and Social Psychology,* 1967, 5, 449–455.

Bandura, A., & Rosenthal, T. L. Vicarious classical conditioning as a function of arousal level. *Journal of Personality and Social Psychology,* 1966, 3, 54–62.

Bandura, A., Ross, D., & Ross, S.A. Imitation of film-mediated aggressive models. *Journal of Abnormal and Social Psychology,* 1963, 66, 3–11.

Berger, S. M. Conditioning through vicarious instigation. *Psychological Review,* 1962, 69, 450–466.

Berkowitz, L., & Daniels, L. R. Affecting the salience of the social responsibility norm: Effects of past help on the response to dependency relationships. *Journal of Abnormal and Social Psychology,* 1964, 68, 275–281.

Berkowitz, L., & Friedman, P. Some social class differences in helping behavior. *Journal of Personality and Social Psychology,* 1967, 5, 217–225.

Berkowitz, L., & Geen, R. G. Film violence and the cue properties of available targets. *Journal of Personality and Social Psychology,* 1966, 3, 525–530.

Boren, J. J. An experimental social relation between two monkeys. *Journal of the Experimental Analysis of Behavior,* 1966, 9, 691–700.

Bruning, J. L. Direct and vicarious effects of a shift in magnitude of reward on performance. *Journal of Personality and Social Psychology,* 1965, 2, 278–282.

Buss, A. H. Instrumentality of aggression, feedback, and frustration as determinants of physical aggression. *Journal of Personality and Social Psychology,* 1966, 3, 153–162.

Campbell, D. T. Ethnocentric and other altruistic motives. In D. Levine (Ed.), *Nebraska symposium on motivation.* Vol. XIII. Lincoln, Neb.: University of Nebraska Press, 1965.

Church, R. M. Emotional reactions of rats to the pain of others. *Journal of Comparative and Physiological Psychology,* 1959, 52, 132–134.

Craig, K. D. Vicarious reinforcement and noninstrumental punishment in observational learning. *Journal of Personality and Social Psychology,* 1967, 7, 172–176.

Crawford, M. P. The cooperative solving by chimpanzees of problems requiring serial responses to color cues. *Journal of Social Psychology,* 1941, 13, 259–280.

Daniels, V. Communication, incentive, and structural variables in interpersonal exchange and negotiation. *Journal of Experimental Social Psychology,* 1967, 3, 47–74.

Darlington, R. B., & Macker, C. E. Displacement of guilt-produced altruistic behavior. *Journal of Personality and Social Psychology,* 1966, 4, 442–443.

DeVore, I. (Ed.) *Primate behavior: Field studies of monkeys and apes.* New York: Holt, Rinehart & Winston, 1965.

Ditrichs, R., Simon, S., & Greene, B. Effect of vicarious scheduling on the verbal conditioning of hostility in children. *Journal of Personality and Social Psychology,* 1967, 6, 71–78.

Doland, D. J., & Adelberg, K. The learning of sharing behavior. *Child Development,* 1967, 38, 695–700.

Durkheim, E. *Suicide.* Glencoe, Ill.: Free Press, 1951.

Ferster, C. B., & Skinner, B. F. *Schedules of reinforcement.* New York: Appleton-Century-Crofts, 1957.

Feshbach, S. The stimulating versus cathartic effects of a vicarious aggressive activity. *Journal of Abnormal and Social Psychology,* 1961, 63, 381–385.

Fischer, W. F. Sharing in preschool children as a function of amount and type of reinforcement. *Genetic Psychology Monographs,* 1963, 68, 215–245.

Goranson, R. E., & Berkowitz, L. Reciprocity and responsibility reactions to prior help. *Journal of Personality and Social Psychology,* 1966, 3, 227–232.

Gouldner, A. W. The norm of reciprocity: A preliminary statement. *American Sociological Review,* 1960, 25, 161–178.

Hamilton, W. D. The genetical evolution of social behavior. I and II. *Journal of Theoretical Biology,* 1964, 7, 1–16, 17–52.

Haner, C. F., & Whitney, E. R. Empathic conditioning and its relation to anxiety level. *American Psychologist,* 1960, 15, 493. (Abstract)

Hartshorne, H., May, M. A., & Maller, J. B. *Studies in the nature of character.* Vol. 2. *Studies in service and self-control.* New York: Macmillan, 1929.

Hartup, W. W., & Coates, B. Imitation of peers as a function of reinforcement from the peer group and rewardingness of the model. *Child Development,* 1967, 38, 1003–1016.

Hebb, D. O., & Thompson, W. R. The social significance of animal studies. In G. Lindzey (Ed.), *Handbook of social psychology.* Vol. 1. *Theory and method.* Cambridge, Mass.: Addison-Wesley, 1954. Pp. 532–561.

Heider, F. *The psychology of interpersonal relations.* New York: Wiley, 1958.

Holder, E. E. Learning factors in social facilitation and social inhibition in rats. *Journal of Personality and Social Psychology,* 1958, 51, 60–64.

Homans, G. C. *Social behavior: Its elementary forms.* New York: Harcourt, Brace & World, 1961.

Horel, J. A., Treichler, F. R., & Meyer, D. R. Coercive behavior in the rhesus monkey. *Journal of Comparative and Physiological Psychology,* 1963, 56, 208–210.

Isaacs, S. *Social development in young children.* London: Routledge & Kegan Paul, 1933.

Kanfer, F. H., & Marston, A. R. Human reinforcement: Vicarious and direct. *Journal of Experimental Psychology,* 1963, 65, 292-296.

Kelleher, R. T., & Gollub, L. R. A review of positive conditioned reinforcement. *Journal of the Experimental Analysis of Behavior,* 1962, 5, 543-597.

Knott, P. D., & Clayton, K. N. Durable secondary reinforcement using brain stimulation as the primary reinforcer. *Journal of Comparative and Physiological Psychology,* 1966, 61, 151-153.

Lavery, J. J., & Foley, P. J. Altruism or arousal in the rat? *Science,* 1963, 140, 172-173.

Lazarus, R. S., Speisman, J. C., Mordkoff, A. M., & Davison, L. A. A laboratory study of psychological stress produced by a motion picture film. *Psychological Monographs,* 1962, 76(34, Whole No. 553).

Lenrow, P. B. Studies of sympathy. In S. S. Tomkins & C. E. Izard (Eds.), *Affect, cognition, and personality: Empirical studies.* New York: Springer, 1965. Pp. 264-294.

Lewis, D. J., & Duncan, C. P. Vicarious experience and partial reinforcement. *Journal of Abnormal and Social Psychology,* 1958, 57, 321-326.

McBride, A. F., & Hebb, D. O. Behavior of the captive bottle-nose dolphin, *Tursiops truncatus. Journal of Comparative and Physiological Psychology,* 1948, 41, 111-123.

McDougall, W. *An introduction to social psychology,* London: Methuen, 1908.

Marston, A. R. Determinants of the effects of vicarious reinforcement. *Journal of Experimental Psychology,* 1966, 71, 550-558.

Mason, W. A. Development of communication between young rhesus monkeys. *Science,* 1959, 130, 712-713.

Mason, W. A., & Hollis, J. H. Communication between young rhesus monkeys. *Animal Behaviour,* 1962, 10, 211-221.

Masserman, J. H., Wechkin, S., & Terris, W. "Altruistic" behavior in rhesus monkeys. *American Journal of Psychiatry,* 1964, 21, 584-585.

Maynard Smith, J. The evolution of alarm calls. *American Naturalist,* 1965, 99, 59-63.

Miller, N. Acquisition of avoidance dispositions by social learning. *Journal of Abnormal and Social Psychology,* 1961, 63, 12-19.

Miller, R. E., Banks, J. H., & Ogawa, N. Role of facial expression in "cooperative-avoidance conditioning" in monkeys. *Journal of Abnormal and Social Psychology,* 1963, 67, 24-30.

Miller, R. E., Caul, W. F., & Mirsky, I. F. Communication of affects between feral and socially isolated monkeys. *Journal of Personality and Social Psychology,* 1967, 7, 231-239.

Murphy, L. B. *Social behavior and child personality: An exploratory study of some roots of sympathy,* New York: Columbia University Press, 1937.

Myers, J. L., & Myers, N. A. Effects of schedules of primary and secondary reinforcement on extinction behavior. *Child Development,* 1963, 34, 1057-1063.

Myers, N. A. Extinction following partial and continuous primary and secondary reinforcement. *Journal of Experimental Psychology,* 1960, 60, 172-179.

Myers, N. A., & Myers, J. L. Secondary reinforcement as a function of training and testing schedules. *Child Development,* 1966, 37, 645-652.

Nissen, H. W., & Crawford, M. P. A preliminary study of food-sharing behavior in young chimpanzees. *Journal of Comparative Psychology,* 1936, 22, 383-419.

Rice, G. E., Jr., & Gainer, P. "Altruism" in the albino rat. *Journal of Comparative and Physiological Psychology,* 1962, 55, 123-125.

Rosekrans, M. A. Imitation in children as a function of perceived similarity to a social model and vicarious reinforcement. *Journal of Personality and Social Psychology,* 1967, 7, 307–315.

Rosekrans, M. A., & Hartup, W. W. Imitative influence of consistent and inconsistent response consequences to a model on aggressive behavior in children, *Journal of Personality and Social Psychology,* 1967, 7, 429–434.

Rosenbaum, M. E., & deCharms, R. Direct and vicarious reduction of hostility. *Journal of Abnormal and Social Psychology,* 1960, 60, 105–111.

Rosenhan, D., & White, G. M. Observation and rehearsal as determinants of pro-social behavior. *Journal of Personality and Social Psychology,* 1967, 5, 424–431.

Schopler, J., & Bateson, N. The power of dependence. *Journal of Personality and Social Psychology,* 1965, 2, 247–254.

Schopler, J., & Matthews, M. W. The influence of the perceived causal locus of partner's dependence on the use of interpersonal power. *Journal of Personality and Social Psychology,* 1965, 2, 609–612.

Stein, L. Secondary reinforcement established with subcortical stimulation. *Science,* 1958, 127, 466–467.

Thibaut, J. W., & Kelley, H. H. *The social psychology of groups.* New York: Wiley, 1959.

Ugurel-Semin, R. Moral behavior and moral judgment of children. *Journal of Abnormal and Social Psychology,* 1952, 47, 463–474.

Ulrich, R. Interaction between reflexive fighting and cooperative escape. *Journal of the Experimental Analysis of Behavior,* 1967, 10, 311–317.

Walters, R. H., Parke, R. D., & Cane, V. Timing of punishment and the observation of consequences to others as determinants of response inhibition. *Journal of Experimental Child Psychology,* 1965, 2, 10–30.

Wheeler, L., & Caggiula, A. R. The contagion of aggression. *Journal of Experimental Social Psychology,* 1966, 2, 1–10.

Wheeler, L., & Smith, S. Censure of the model in the contagion of aggression. *Journal of Personality and Social Psychology,* 1967, 6, 93–98.

Wright, B. A. Altruism in children and the perceived conduct of others. *Journal of Abnormal and Social Psychology,* 1942, 37, 218–233.

Wynne-Edwards, V. C. *Animal dispersion in relation to social behavior.* New York: Hafner, 1962.

CHAPTER 3

Moral Development from the Standpoint of a General Psychological Theory

Justin Aronfreed

Introduction

It is characteristic of anything really complex about the human condition that it offers a severe test of both the power and the breadth of a psychological theory. As in the case of any other science, each theoretical perspective in psychology is necessarily built on a limited realm of observation and experiment. And different perspectives vary in the degree to which they focus on observations that are basic or general enough to be extended to other realms. Of course, any robust psychological theory wants to demonstrate its vigor on aspects of human behavior other than those for which it was specifically designed. But the pressure of social reality seems to offer an especially strong temptation for a point of view to expand in splendid isolation when the domain of expansion is special or essential to human affairs. There the tendency often is to overextend concepts which should have been used more modestly, or else to succumb to the most obvious surface features of human action and thought, without sufficient regard for the more fundamental analysis that is required to advance knowledge. Among the social and philosophical issues that exercise a fatal attraction on psychological theory, it is doubtful whether any has been more seductive than the question of man's status as a moral creature. I will try in this brief essay to outline some of the ways in which the problem of understanding moral development illuminates the larger problems of a general psychological construction of the child (and the adult).

Psychoanalytic theory may fairly be considered the first fully psychological theory of moral development. Like other theorists among philosophers as early as Augustine, S. Freud (1927; 1936; Chap. 8) tried to distinguish between the functions of knowledge and feeling in the operation of an internalized conscience. Freud's conception of the superego was also sensitive to the massive behavioral expressions of conscience, which often appeared not to require rational thought or even voluntary decision. However, the direction taken by psychoanalytic theory was not well suited to a more integrative account of the affective, cognitive, and behavioral ingredients of the child's acquisition of conscience.

The ideological force of the theory, with its emphasis at first on "instincts" and later on an inner emotional life, tends to separate if from whatever empirical and conceptual progress has been made within other paradigms of psychological science. It is particularly difficult to find meeting points between psychoanalytic theory and more contemporary knowledge of the processes of learning and development in children. Our current paradigms tend toward a more refined picture of the child's plasticity in transactions between his predispositions and his experience of the external world.

Behavioristic theories of learning have also been elaborated into a strong point of view about the origins of social conduct. The earliest extensions of these theories were little more than extrapolations from the patterns of learning displayed by animals (Holt, 1931; N. E. Miller & Dollard, 1941; Thorndike, 1911). However, later versions escalated their observational base to human social behavior and its antecedents in childrearing (Mowrer, 1960, chap. 3; Sears, Maccoby, & Levin, 1957, chap. 10; J. W. M. Whiting & Child, 1953, chap. 11). They also went well beyond an account of the immediate effects of external rewards and punishments, in an attempt to explain how internalized monitors of conduct could become independent of direct social reinforcement. These later versions even have a discernible second generation, which has used experimental paradigms of children's "social learning" to argue that the internalization of conscience can be understood as the shaping of the child's behavior by such processes as imitative modeling and self-generation of reinforcing events (Bandura & Walters, 1963; Kanfer & Phillips, 1970; Mischel, 1966).

Although these learning-theoretical approaches generally assume that their mechanisms of learning will cope with the transmission of values from socializing agents to children, they do not specify any developmental analysis of either the cognitive or affective dimensions of values.

Social-learning theories, even in their most sophisticated extensions, restrict values to the role of an inferred cognitive mediator of overt behavior. They do not really address the question of how values gain control over the child's actions. And since these theories also do not examine the nature of representational thought, they can hardly be expected to illuminate the contribution that moral judgment makes to the development of conscience.

The conceptual tradition that concerns itself most specifically with moral judgment has been the qualitative description of the substance and structure of different types of thinking about the rules governing human interactions. Durkheim (1961) may have been the first to offer, early in the twentieth century, a thoroughly psychological as well as sociological treatment of moral thought in this tradition. His analysis of the child's internalization of normative values deserves more attention than it has received from psychologists who are interested in the most highly developed forms of human cognition. The distinctions that Durkheim made among different orientations to moral rules were based primarily on an implicit notion of changes in the child's perspective on the relationship between himself and others. But the later expressions of this tradition placed the varieties of moral thought explicitly in a framework of sequential stages of cognitive development, which were conceived of as qualitatively distinct structures.

Piaget's investigations (1932; Lickona, Chap. 12) of children's conceptions of rules of conduct led him to the view that there are two major stages in the development of moral thought (after an initial stage in which the very young child shows only certain stereotypes of concrete action). Piaget characterized the first stage as a moral heteronomy of absolute and rigid judgments oriented toward multiple sources of external authority. The second stage he described as a more autonomous and relativistic subscription to principles obtained through social contract. Kohlberg (1969b, 1971b) has advanced a far more systematic and elaborate classification of sequential stages of moral development, which he describes in Chapter 2. Based on respondents' rationales for choices of acts in hypothetical story-situations, his system distinguishes six stages of moral thought, which reduce in turn to the three essential types of *preconventional, conventional,* and *principled.*

In contrast to the focus of "social-learning" theories on the internalized control of the overt behavioral surface of conduct, cognitive theories of moral development are based on verbal indices of changes in the thinking processes which underlie the child's choices among alternative actions. It is especially clear in Kohlberg's system that the developmental stages of moral judgment differ not only in the substance of their axioms of legitimacy or justification, but also in the type and power of the reasoning applied to the axioms. Developmental-cognitive approaches to the acquisition of conscience provide a welcome antidote to a behavioristic paradigm in which an act is regarded as "moral" by virtue of its conformity to an external norm. Since representational thought is far richer in structure and potential variety than are the mere acts of conduct which can be subjected to normative definitions of conformity or deviance, it follows that the moral status of an act cannot be determined without knowing the categories and operations of value through which it has been processed.

At the same time, stages of moral thought are markedly deficient as a complete account of the development of the child's conscience. Although their systematic exposition is sometimes set forth under the claim of affective or motivational as well as cognitive criteria, their essential base of evidence in fact reduces to different types of reasoning. But knowledge is not equivalent to action. And the richest cognitive map of the child's moral domain does not specify the affective mechanisms that are required in order for reasoning to control behavior. The power of affective components in the internalization of conscience is well demonstrated in the great repertoires of human conduct which are molded by the rewards and punishments of socialization, yet come to be independently maintained in a automatized or stereotyped manner. Common observation as well as introspection can raise some very serious questions about whether any significant amount of moral decision-making enters into the internalized control of conduct for most human beings (despite the fact that various states of moral knowledge may be available to them). Moreover, even when the control of conduct takes place through evaluative cognition, it may more typically rest on representational thought that is not structured in truly moral categories. Accordingly, the conception of the child as a miniaturized moral philosopher leaves something to be desired when one takes a larger psychological view of the full range of manifestations of conscience.

There is the further consideration that most of the relevant evidence for moral stages is not in the form of longitudinal succession within the individual, but consists rather of increments and declines of specific stages over cross-sectional groups of respondents of different ages, together with a high incidence of mixed but adjacent stages within the prescribed order (Kohlberg, 1963a; Kohlberg & Kramer, 1969). The interpretation of the evidence therefore tends to drain into an oversimplified typology of character, in which a premium is placed on the stages regarded as "higher" or more "mature." Aside from the sheer cognitive power that is obviously required for a respondent's formulation of the higher stages, the reasons offered for such a system of classification do not go persuasively beyond a commitment to a philosophical position. And in such an evolutionary framework, it is sometimes difficult to distinguish natural philosophy from moral philosophy. The difficulty is not resolved by demonstrations that the different stages have some correlation with variations in the actual behavior of respondents in situations of apparent moral conflict (Kohlberg, 1969b). It is easy enough to find a behavioral situation that divides the value categories of one stage from those of another. Adding behavioral components to character portraits cannot be a substitute for theoretical and empirical analysis of the nature of the bonds between thought and action.

An Illustrative Experiment

I have offered elsewhere (Aronfreed, 1968c) some detailed experimental and conceptual analyses of the socialization process and its transformation into the internalized control of conduct. These analyses aim at both the affective and cognitive mechanisms that underlie the child's acquisition and maintenance of conscience. The mechanisms are required to account not only for the internalized residues of the child's direct experience of reward and punishment, but also for the enduring behavioral and representational products of imitation, of empathic or vicarious learning, and of other transmission processes which rest on the observation of social models. For our purpose here, which is to illustrate how an understanding of the development of conscience needs a more fundamental psychological base, it will be sufficient to describe briefly one line of work. This work examines the effectiveness of punishment learning in producing internalized suppression of the child's punished behavior. Although punishment learning is usually seen as bearing upon only one aspect of conscience, its analysis can be made to include many of the central issues in a general account of moral development.

The choice of punishment learning as an illustration may serve also to dilute a long-standing and uncritical ideological conviction that children do not learn well in its dominion. It is in fact doubtful that socialization ever takes place without those inherently aversive events which a child must perceive as contingent on his own actions and intended by others to suppress his behavior. When punishment is defined broadly enough to include rejection, disapproval, and other kinds of "psychological" discipline—and not just the more obvious physical or verbal attacks—it can be clearly seen to be an inevitable part of childrearing. The pervasiveness of punishment, rather than the question of its social desirability, is a proper starting point for scientific investigation.

The experiment I shall outline here is given only in the most basic features of its methods and results. It is conducted with boys and girls ranging roughly from 8 to 10 years of age. And the results are the same for both sexes. The details of experimental method, and the numerous variations of conditions and parameters, have been extensively described elsewhere (Aronfreed, 1968a).

The experiment begins with a training period in which the individual child is presented, over a series of ten successive trials, with different pairs of very small toy replicas of real and familiar common objects. Although the toys vary from one trial to another, one of the toys in each pair is always highly attractive, while the other is relatively unattractive and nondescript. In each trial the child is asked to pick up the toy that he wants to tell about, to hold it briefly in his hand, and then to tell something about the toy when requested to do so. Somewhere within this sequence of behavioral components, the child is punished during any trial on which he chooses the attractive toy. The punishment consists of verbal disapproval ("*No!*") and deprivation of candy by the experimental agent of socialization, without any further explanation (other than that implied in the original instructions, which simply warn the child that some choices are not permitted, without specifying which ones).

The timing of the punishment with respect to the onset and termination of a transgression sequence varies in four steps, which represent distinct experimental training conditions. But the timing remains consistent over trials for the subjects within any one of these conditions. In contrast, the subject is always permitted to choose and tell about an unattractive toy without punishment. Although the children invariably begin with choices of the attractive toys, they learn very quickly in this type of training. Almost all of them begin to choose the unattractive toy after only one or two punishments. And they continue to do so throughout the trials.

The really interesting observation occurs during a common test for internalization, which directly follows all four of the different training conditions. The child is left alone on a carefully prepared pretext, under conditions which free him of any apparent risk of surveillance. Again he is confronted with a pair of small toys. The attractive toy is a minute glass, in which salt descends from an upper to a lower chamber (it is extremely difficult for children to resist the urge to handle this object). And the unattractive toy is more nondescript than ever.

It is now possible to see the internalized power of the behavioral suppression that punishment has induced during training. The strength of the suppression, as indexed by covert monitors of the occurrence and latency of a transgression, is highly predictable from the four training variations in the timing of punishment. For example, after the training condition in which punishment is introduced quite early in the sequential components of the act of transgression (while the child is still reaching), the majority of children never touch the attractive toy during the test for internalization. Other children in this condition succumb to temptation only after a long period of resistance. But for virtually all children who have been punished *during* training at the latest point in the act of transgression (after telling about the toy), handling of the attractive toy usually begins almost immediately when the experimental agent leaves the room. Intermediate values in the timing of punishment during training also produce reliably distinct strengths of suppression during the test for internalization.

After the experimental session is over, the children are questioned about their choices of toys during both training and test. Almost none of them can verbalize anything that even approaches an evaluative standard. In trying to account for their actions, they refer uniformly only to the danger of external punishment (in the presence of the agent). This result can hardly be surprising when we consider its parallels in the socialization process in natural settings. Many of the initially dominant behavioral dispositions of very young and even preverbal children can be effectively suppressed only by the aversive outcomes transmitted in the reactions of their parents. And even when parental reactions are not so explicit as to fit the ordinary meaning of punishment, they may be aversive enough that the child's behavior continues to be suppressed in the parents' absence. Yet it is often quite clear that children at this early age do not have a standard of judgment capable of differentiating punished actions from unpunished alternatives—particularly in view of the complexity of the distinctions to be made not only among actions, but also among their situational determinants and possible consequences, in the definition of a transgression. One need only observe the infant who can just crawl as he reaches for an electrical outlet, yet refrains from touching it because of a few past experiences with the reactions of other people (even though no one is now visibly present). It is sobering also to consider that essentially the same experimental effect on internalized suppression can be obtained with dogs (Solomon, Turner, & Lessac, 1968).

Of course, the experiment described was not designed to produce an internalized suppression that would last over a long period of time, without the benefit of any further external reinforcement. The long-term maintenance of internalized control based on punishment will often require a distribution of the child's experience over a far greater period of time, along with many opportunities to probe surveillance and response from his social environment. What the experiment does reveal is something about the basic mechanisms of (Pavlovian) conditioning through which punishment begins to induce control of conduct in the absence of external monitors. The experiment is in fact designed to support the inference that punishment attaches anxiety to certain *internal* monitors, which are correlated with the occurrence of transgressions, and that these internal monitors then become capable of exercising some affective control over the child's behavior.

What is the nature of these internal monitors which come to govern the child's conduct? The critical experimental finding is that punishment is most effective when it is used early in the onset of transgression. This finding confirms an expectation that the internalized strength of suppression will be determined by the magnitude of anxiety that has been conditioned specifically to internal *precursors* of a transgression. The precursors of a punished act may consist, for example, of behavioral cues which are produced by the child's own motoric orienting actions. But they may also take the far more interesting form of cognitive processes which range from the simplest representational images to the most complex evaluative structures (such as moral principles). If anxiety can be attached to such monitors, and if these monitors can assume a temporal position in which they precede a punished act, it becomes possible to see how suppression of the incipient act may be later motivated even when there is no longer an objective danger of punishment. During the socialization process, un-punished alternatives to the punished act will conversely acquire some intrinsic value for reduction or inhibition of anxiety.

An Apparent Paradox

A fairly simple experiment confronts us, then, with something of a paradox in its apparent relevance to the development of conscience. It demonstrates the child's internalization of control over conduct, without our having provided any verbal evaluation or even categorical representation of his transgression. The demonstration thus confirms the obvious: Human beings are highly conditionable animals, whose social habits often assume an autonomy and permanence unburdened by any evaluative thought processes. At the same time, we have every reason to suppose that the substance of thought can enter powerfully into a child's internalized control over his own behavior. The mere presence of a mental representation of action, as a monitor for some independence of social reaction, would be only a first step toward cognitive control. It need not imply that the child also has an evaluative structure in which to place the representation. But children do acquire categories of value, moral and otherwise; and these categories can develop into internalized structures which are sensitive to large realms of social experience.

Just as it is clear that many behavioral manifestations of an internalized conscience do not require moral judgment, it is likewise clear that moral values can sometimes be significant determinants of conduct. Values cannot be regarded as merely a form of knowledge or reflection that has a passive relationship to conduct. We are left with the question of how it is possible for *both* conditioning *and* moral knowledge to contribute to the organization of conduct—and to its at least partial independence of the individual's expectation of social reward or punishment. An attempt to answer this question will allow us to begin to see the generality of the theory required for an account of the acquisition of conscience.

I want to suggest that one requirement of an answer to the question posed above is the recognition that moral judgment turns out to be a rather specialized capacity, as soon as one tries to set any interesting criteria as to when a value may be called moral. Although moral judgment may bear upon some choices of conduct for most human beings, it may actually represent a very small part of the total range of cognitive and affective resources through which socialization induces the child's internalized control over his conduct. I have emphasized at first the kind of internalization process that proceeds without the benefit of evaluative thought. But even the organized structures of value that the child acquires—though they may permit him to evaluate his actions with great independence of external control—can be built around many concepts other than moral ones. The larger issue, then, is how the child's representational capacities enter into the internalization process. And the question of how moral judgment enters is a derivative one. Of course, we know very little about the acquisition processes through which the cognitive competence of children develops. And we know even less about how this competence interlocks with social experience to produce internalized structures of value.

The power of cognitive mediation of internalized control over conduct—even when it takes the form of the simplest verbal representations—can be illustrated with the results of some further variations of the punishment-training experiment described earlier. The method used in the additional variations is exactly the same as that used in the original experimental conditions (Aronfreed, 1968a), except for the following modifications:

During the training trials of all of the new variations, punishment is delayed until six seconds after the child's completion of a transgression (choosing and picking up the attractive rather than the unattractive toy). This interval of delay of punishment was the third of the four timing variations used in the original experiment. In the absence of any verbalized reasons for the occurrence of punishment, the delay had produced a relatively ineffective suppression during the test for internalization that immediately followed the training. In comparison, the use of punishment as soon as a child reached for an attractive toy during training had made the children very resistant even to any handling of the attractive toy when they were later left alone. Now the experimental agent of socialization introduces, into the delayed-punishment condition, a verbalized cognitive structure which the child can use to represent certain properties of the transgression. During the initial instructions, and together with each occurrence of punishment, the agent states that certain toys are *"hard to tell about"* and are therefore *"only for older boys (girls)."* The agent's verbalization is preceded by the verbal disapproval (*"No!"*) and coterminous with the deprivation of candy, so that it will be interwoven with components of punishment.

It will be observed that the agent injects a cognitive structure of ease versus difficulty into the child's choice of which toy to tell about. But this structure does not specify any particular category of toy. Nor is it especially rational or appropriate (and purposely so) for a distinction between attractive and unattractive toys. Nevertheless, the verbal provision of this structure during punishment training induces more effective suppression of handling of the attractive toy during the test for internalization. Children who are exposed to this form of training show more prolonged internalized suppression than was shown by children who were trained without cognitive structure (but under the same delay of punishment) in the original experiment. And most of the children who are given cognitive structure are able to verbalize the standard of ease versus difficulty, when they are asked after the experiment to explain their predominant choices of unattractive toys during training.

Another training variation injects the same cognitive structure of ease versus difficulty into the child's choice within each pair of toys. But it focuses the agent's explanation of punishment on the child's *intention*. Each time that a transgression occurs, the agent coordinates punishment with a statement that the child had *"wanted"* to pick up a toy that was *"hard to tell about."* This focus on intention produces a very effective suppression during the test for internalization, in spite of the fact that punishment is substantially delayed. Children trained under this cognitive focus on intention show a strength of internalized suppression which is fully comparable to that shown by children who were punished during training immediately upon reaching for an attractive toy (under the original condition of no provision of cognitive structure). A great many of these intention-trained children never handle the forbidden toy during the test for internalization. The remainder do so only quite late in the ten-minute test period.

Most readers will find the results of these experimental variations perfectly consonant with their expectations: Children should show better internalized control of their conduct when their transgressions are defined by verbal explanation, and particularly when the explanation sensitizes them to their own intentions. Presumably the provision of verbal structure in socialization gives the child a richer cognitive representation of the nature and conditions of transgression. But how does this cognitive representation—even when it includes a dimension along which a transgression may be evaluated (as in the case of the experimental treatment)—come to be able to actually control the child's behavior? Why does it not merely remain transfixed in representational thought? The experimental results begin to suggest, I think, that representational thought assumes its

power over conduct because of the affective loadings which become attached to the representations themselves.

When internalization is based on punishment training, we would expect an aversive affective state to be "conditioned" to those cognitive representations of the child which are initially contiguous with the occurrence of punishment. Correspondingly, a reduction or inhibition of this affective state would become attached to the representations that are contiguous with avoidance of an anticipated or uncertain punishment. The aversive state may be experienced with different qualities—for example, fear, shame, or guilt—depending on the cognitive structure in which it is housed (Aronfreed, 1968c, chap. 9). But here we may continue to think of the aversive state as anxiety, with respect to its generalized motivational properties.

If the child's cognitive representations of actions were as immobile as the proprioceptive cues inherent in the actions themselves, then the anxiety attached by punishment to these representations would also be locked to the precise points at which the punishment had occurred for previous transgressions. Thus internalized anxiety might be mobilized only at a point well past the completion of a transgression. However, the child's representation of an act is undoubtedly far more mobile than are the behavioral cues in the overt initiation and commitment of the act. Cognitive representation can be induced by verbal socialization long after the actual occurrence of a transgression; and yet such representation may also later assume an anticipatory relationship to the same transgression. Accordingly, the child's evaluation of a punished act can come to activate anxiety at the point of an incipient transgression, even though evaluative standards may have been transmitted by others only in conjunction with punishment that originally occurred after transgressions already had been committed. And the anxiety can serve to motivate suppression of the incipient transgression, without the continued support of external surveillance or threat of punishment.

The fact that a verbal medium of socialization makes the precise timing of a child's punishment less critical, in yielding an effective internalized suppression of transgression, is entirely in accord with what we find in the natural setting of the home. If the internalized behavioral consequences of parental punishment were dependent only on Pavlovian mechanisms for the conditioning of anxiety directly to the child's overt acts, the punishment could hardly make much contribution to the later suppression of an incipient transgression. It is rather unusual for parents to have the opportunity to react to a child's potential transgression before it is committed. Yet their punishment is generally quite effective, even though it occurs almost always after the completion of a transgression—and could therefore not attach much anxiety directly to the behavioral precursors of the transgression. We can attribute this effectiveness to the representational medium that is structured by the verbalization of parents. The adequacy of this medium for evaluative cognition will vary greatly, of course, across different agents of socialization. But even its more primitive forms will provide a representation to which some anxiety can be attached, and which is mobile with respect to the point of onset or anticipation of a subsequent transgression.

The results of some other variations of experimental conditions, beyond those already described, provide further confirmation of the importance of an attachment of affective value to whatever representations the child is expected to use for his own evaluation and control of transgressions. For example, after training that consistently separated the point of punishment on each trial from the point at which the experimental agent verbalized a cognitive structure (of ease versus difficulty in telling about toys), the strength of suppression was much weaker on the internalization test, in which the agent was absent,

than it had been after the training conditions where punishment was always contiguous with the agent's verbalization. Similar effects were obtained with the introduction into training of still other variations that provided a cognitive focus on the child's intentions in choosing an attractive toy (as described earlier). When the precise temporal location of punishment was varied for different groups of children over the several behavioral components of a transgression—for example, reaching for an attractive toy, picking it up, or then telling about it—the strength of internalized suppression following training was far greater if punishment immediately coincided with the behavioral component that the agent always identified verbally as the prohibited aim of the child's intention.

These findings clearly indicate that the power which verbal representation gives to the child's internalized control is a function of contiguity in time between social transmission of the representation and other correlated events which have a significant affective value for the child (in this case, punishment and punishment avoidance). We are again compelled to infer that the attachment of changes of affective state to representation is what gives the child's evaluative cognition its control over conduct.

Affective Mediation of Cognitive Control

The conception of the affective and cognitive mechanisms of internalization that I have advanced thus far is not peculiar to the child's aversive experience of transgression and punishment. It appears to be equally applicable to experimental and theoretical analyses of the socialization of altruism and sympathy (Aronfreed, 1970), of self-criticism (Aronfreed, 1964), and more generally of internalized choices of conduct based on reward (Aronfreed, 1968c, chap. 5). Nevertheless, it may not be accidental to the very nature of socialization that the clearest picture of the child's acquisition of internalized control has emerged from empirical studies of the effects of punishment on his initially predominant behavioral dispositions (see also, for example, Parke & Walters, 1967; Walters, Parke, & Cane, 1965).

Insofar as the experiments described include the role of cognitive representation in the socialization process, they are very short indeed of the general theoretical requirements for an understanding of moral development. They do not tell us what, for example, are the properties of a cognitive structure (much less a moral structure). They do not reveal how such a structure organizes the categories of value in which potential acts of conduct can be classified. And they certainly do not resolve the question of how such categories are transmitted in the first place. Of course, we would need to know a great deal more about the development of children's conceptual thinking (than we now do), in terms of basic acquisition and storage processes, in order to project either experiments or theories to the realm of moral judgment. But what the analysis does provide is some appreciation of the pervasiveness of internalized affective states in the control of conduct, together with the implication that the child's representational monitors of his own conduct must also work through affective pathways.

These conclusions do not mean merely that conscience consists of thoughts and feelings. The evidence shows specifically that a moderate amount of verbalization of standards to the child, particularly when it focuses on his intentions, will yield much more effective internalized control than might be expected if the control depended on the coincidence between overt action and punishment. And, secondly, there are very strong indications that the representations transmitted by verbalization must, in order to be effective, be given an affective value by a fairly precise association with the punishment.

The emphasis here on the importance of affective mechanisms in the child's internalized control of conduct is in no way intended to underplay the significance of moral cognition. The reasons for conduct, and not only its behavioral conformity, are critical ingredients of the individual's social experience. But there has been so much recent (and justifiable) investment in the child's capacity to represent the world in thought, and to form complex rules and concepts, that we are in some danger of overlooking the affective learning which is also required to translate knowledge into social behavior. And the most general kind of interest in the socialization process must recognize that societies do not transmit only knowledge. They also transmit motivations to compel action.

Repetition does not dull our astonishment at the resources of moral perception that young children can verbalize in social situations that they know well. These resources sometimes include an understanding not only of the consequences of their actions, but also of their obligations to particular other people, and even of the relevance of their intentions—when these components are being considered with respect to their own concrete actions, rather than from the perspective of the more hypothetical and abstract situations that Piaget (1932) and others have posed to them. Only the more naive among us would also be surprised to observe that these cognitive resources of children (and of adults as well) are often not realized in their actual conduct. The discrepancies between knowledge and action simply reflect once again that the affectivity generated by a child's evaluation of potential alternative acts may be insufficient to direct the choices known to have the greater valuation on a moral dimension. Further increments of socially rewarding or aversive experience may be necessary to attach a greater magnitude of affect to the child's categories for the moral status of these choices.

However, though it may be useful for theoretical analysis, separating the cognitive and affective components of an evaluative representation has a certain artificiality. The child's classification of an act (under the constraints of its context) within a judgmental category is a cognitive coding. This classification is not sufficient to define the *value* of the act. A workable definition of what we might wish to mean by values would surely specify some inherent affective components as well as a cognitive substance. The nature and intensity of these affective components is what we should expect to be critical in permitting values to exercise control over the child's behavior. Obviously the affective mediation between thought and action will be complex and highly variable across different situations and different areas of conduct. It is therefore perfectly sensible that many investigators have uncovered less than startling consistency when they have tried simply to correlate overt behavioral indices of the child's conduct with various verbalized expressions of his conscience (Hartshorne & May, 1928; M. L. Hoffman, 1970a; Kohlberg, 1969b; Terman et al., 1925).

I once attended a conference on moral education at which I was much surprised by the interactions between philosophers and psychologists on the question of how to teach moral decision-making to children (Aronfreed, 1971). One of the arguments advanced was that moral reasoning ought to be used to overcome the "emotional prejudices" implanted by early experiences in the home. A counterargument, from the perspective advanced in this chapter, would be that moral education must build upon the strong affective dispositions acquired in early experience —that affective values are, as it were, the ultimate axiomatic base upon which moral principles can engage the child's conduct among and toward others. If the wrong emotions (by whatever criterion) have been attached to certain actions during childhood, then affective reeducation and not just moral reeducation will be required. The consequences of aggression, the fidelity of words to actions, and the distribution

and possession of objects of value are observable events around which socialization takes place every day in a child's life. There are a massive number of opportunities for the child to experience these events in affective media which are pleasurable or aversive—though these media are often far more subtle than explicit rewards and punishments. Both the affective and cognitive residues of these early experiences will yield fundamental dispositions for which later moral principles can only be an elaboration rather than a replacement.

The priority of the most basic affective and cognitive ingredients of early socialization is apparent in the few points of agreement among the findings of numerous studies that have attempted to assess the relationship between the disciplinary practices of parents and various indices of their children's internalized control of conduct (Allinsmith, 1960; Aronfreed, 1961; Bandura & Walters, 1959; Burton, Maccoby, & Allinsmith, 1961; M. L. Hoffman & Saltzstein, 1967; MacKinnon, 1938; Sears, Maccoby, & Levin, 1957, chaps. 7, 10; Sears, Whiting, Nowlis, & Sears, 1953; J. W. M. Whiting & Child, 1953, chap. 11). The findings are clearest in respect to the child's internalization of reactions to his own committed transgressions. But they also apply to the child's internalized dispositions to suppress the occurrence of transgressions.

What emerges from these studies is that children show more effective internalization when their parents use what are often termed "psychological" forms of discipline. I have suggested that these disciplinary habits be called *induction* because they inscribe a pattern of learning that induces internalized monitors of the child's anxiety in response to an anticipated or committed transgression (Aronfreed, 1961; Saltzstein, Chap. 14). One key component of this category of discipline is simply the parent's use of explanation or reasoning. But a second and somewhat independent component, which indicates the importance of affective context, is the parent's focus on withdrawal of affection (and its restoration for the child's termination or correction of prohibited behavior). The power of this affective component would obviously depend on the establishment of the parent's affection as a base of value. And it is interesting to note that many studies have reported evidence of weak internalization among children whose parents are unusually lacking in nurturance toward them (Bandura & Walters, 1959; Bronfenbrenner, 1961; J. McCord, McCord, & Howard, 1963; W. McCord, McCord, & Howard, 1961; Sears, Maccoby, & Levin, 1957, chap. 10; J. W. M. Whiting & Child, 1953, chap. 11).

In placing such a heavy burden on affective mechanisms in the development of conscience, I am not implying that we know very much about the properties of specific affective states or about how these properties can be differentiated in their control of the child's behavior. A specification of the varieties of emotion or affectivity would be another requirement for a more general theory of moral development. Affect is used here as a construct with which to make some theoretical sense out of both common observation and experimental analysis of the phenomena of conscience. We have recognized the obvious distinction between aversive and pleasurable affective states. We have seen the explanatory value of the ease of conditionability of changes of affective state to cognitive representation as well as to overt action. And we have shown that the attribution of motivating and reinforcing properties to affective states can be used as part of an account of the child's internalization of control over conduct. What we have not done is to go beyond these rather primitive properties into the cognitive structures or housings which give different affective states their specific features of qualitative experience—although an attempt to begin such an analysis has been made elsewhere (Aronfreed, 1968c, chap. 9).

Further Requirements: Cognitive Transactions

I have as yet given little attention to one other requirement of a more general theory of the psychological processes in moral development: an understanding of the forms of social experience, and of the mechanisms of transition, which produce different qualitative organizations or "stages" of moral judgment. Such an understanding will depend, of course, on our broader state of knowledge of the development of children's thought and language. Any conception of a developmental sequence of types of reasoning based on moral values must be derived from a larger conception of changes in the cognitive resources with which the child codes or processes his social experience, in the categories with which he represents that experience, and in the operations or transformations of thought which he is able to impose on those categories.

The study of basic phenomena in cognitive development has become a heavy and rewarding contemporary investment of developmental psychologists. Readers who are not as familiar with it as they might wish can consult the latest edition of *Carmichael's Manual of Child Psychology* (Mussen, 1970). But it is clear that the conceptual and empirical state of the science is only beginning to touch upon the mechanisms of change which mediate transitions between different levels of cognitive capacity in the child. And it is quite certain that the study of moral judgment has not yet moved beyond the description of qualitatively distinct expressions of thought in children of different ages.

A psychological theory that addresses moral values (or any other kind of value system) must be concerned with cognitive and affective dispositions of considerable breadth and stability. An individual's values are rarely constructed around a few very specific or isolated acts of conduct, or around a highly limited set of external social contexts. A system of values will ordinarily give representation to complex interrelationships among a wide spectrum of alternative actions, the conditions under which the actions can occur, and the possible outcomes of the actions. That children do acquire the cognitive structures which are the substrate for a value system, and that such structures can mediate the highly differentiated behavioral controls of which human beings are capable, are remarkable accomplishments in the light of what current theories of learning seem able to digest.

One reason for the absence of a theory of how children acquire values is the lack of an intellectually engaging psychological conception of the nature of values. I pointed out earlier that values are not merely cognitive schemas. They must carry affective loadings of varying quality and magnitude in order to add *value* to their representational power to control behavior. But there is also a very considerable problem in formulating the cognitive properties of values. For heuristic purposes here we might treat a system of values as being, in its representational aspects, a hierarchical system of categories for classification of social actions (or objects), in which some criterial markers are subordinated to the priority of others. The structure of such a categorical system would be inherent in the relationships among the categories, in the presence of critical dimensions along which events could be multiply ordered, and in other fixed properties of the classification scheme. The different operations of thought which could be imposed on this representational base would then constitute the evaluative processes of moral judgment.

The most widely cited investigations of children's moral judgment have not yet concerned themselves with the basic cognitive processes underlying the acquisition and functioning of values. These studies are still engaged in the descriptive assessment of developmental stages in the criteria which the child applies to the evaluation of conduct. Although Piaget (1932)

did include some evidence of children's conceptions of rules in an actual game of marbles, these descriptive studies generally elicit the child's verbalized evaluation of an action, together with his explanation or justification, in a hypothetically posed situation. Among children in Western societies at least, the results of this method of inquiry commonly disclose an ordered sequence in the evaluative structures of conscience. The structures are distinguished from one another in part by the child's criteria of value, in part by the qualitative organization of his thinking, and in part by the type of reasoning he applies. And the order in which the different moral conceptions are acquired appears to be reliably correlated with developmental time, even though they are not consistently fixed to specific ages.

In general, the developmental changes in children's expressions of moral thought may be characterized as transitions along a continuum moving from an externalized to an internalized orientation toward the resolution of problems of conduct. Piaget's description (1932) of these changes is well known (see Lickona, Chap. 12). It has often been replicated by other investigators, though sometimes with only partial or uncertain confirmation. Kohlberg's system (1963a, 1971b) of classification probes more deeply and broadly into the child's thinking, produces a larger mass of verbal data, and is based on a somewhat more integrative view of the child's criteria of value across a number of different kinds of situations of moral conflict. Kohlberg's observations in Chapter 2 suggest that the child's first organized pattern of moral thought focuses on rewards or punishments, and is followed by an intermediate (and very common) type of thought which justifies choices of conduct by reference to the maintenance of authority or to the conventional requirements of social approval. Finally, Kohlberg notes that the most advanced type of moral thinking employs more abstract principles of justice which are oriented toward the welfare of others in a "social contract," or toward the categorical intuition of whether an action is right or wrong.

Because these shifts in children's moral conceptions seem to have an invariant developmental sequence, both Piaget and Kohlberg have been tempted to assume that they represent a succession of developmentally preprogrammed cognitive stages—with the corollary (not too well suppressed) assumption that social experience serves mainly as a generalized and not highly determinant nutriment or catalyst. Among the difficulties attached to this view is its neglect of the nature of the learning that might give rise to the transformations of thought. There appears to be little interest in going beyond the speculation that changes in the child's moral thought arise from an interaction between his intrinsic dispositions toward cognitive growth and the expansion in the variety of his potential social roles. In this evolutionary perspective, moral judgment moves from lower to higher stages in a natural order. And if the sequence fails to reach its final stage, we are left with the problem of whether we should infer an "unnatural" or socially undesirable source of developmental arrest.

The conception that the child carries an intrinsically ordered incipient program of moral development, which unfolds under the stimulation of social experience, confronts a number of problems of evidence from other sources. We can only briefly summarize these problems here (a more thorough exposition can be found in Aronfreed, 1968c, chap. 10). To begin with, middle-class and working-class children in Western societies are often found to differ in the speed and extent of their developmental shifts in moral thought. The amount of change with advancing age among working-class children is sometimes so small as to seem trivial when compared with the very substantial and long-term differences between the two social classes. These class differences persist to some degree, interestingly enough, even when the

effect of intelligence is statistically removed through the conventional standardized indices.

Secondly, children drawn from non-Western societies sometimes do not show, as they become older, the same decline of an externalized orientation of moral judgment. In some cross-cultural studies, a more highly internalized orientation toward the evaluation of conduct never does develop; rather, an externalized orientation appears to be the terminal point of acculturation. A third problem is the finding by some investigators that young adults in our own society can show a great variety of moral orientations. Their differences in moral perspective are correlated with their subscription to certain religious, political, or other ideologies. Such differences are not sensibly ordered on a developmental continuum. Finally, we must take account of the radical changes of values which occasionally take place among adults under the stress of very unusual experiences—for example, in prisoner-of-war or concentration camps. These changes may either parallel or reverse those which occur in developmental time during childhood.

In addition to the evidence cited above, the findings of a number of studies indicate that children's verbalizations of moral thinking undergo significant shifts under the impact of brief exposures to the social influence of alternative models. All of the evidence points to one conclusion: that although the child's structures of moral value may be successively reorganized around different rules or principles in the course of development, he nevertheless remains able to draw on more than one type of evaluative structure. Since the different structures appear to be able to displace one another to some extent (even after some have been subordinated to others over developmental time), it would seem that none of them is actually lost as a result of cognitive development. Of course, one would very much like to know just what kinds of cognitive mechanisms would permit one type of moral value to predominate over others, and yet allow others to become more salient under specified conditions. But common observation must make it obvious that these phenomena exist. Because fully developed adults can apply more than one criterion to the evaluation of conduct, many social situations will induce them to think and react in ways that are beneath their maximal capacity for moral reasoning (or sometimes in ways that are beneath any reasoning at all).

The question of whether stages of moral development can be illuminated by closer analysis of underlying cognitive processes remains to be addressed. It can be best illustrated by an incident of which I am inordinately fond: A 7-year-old girl showed herself to be quite capable of gross physical violence toward her younger brother, even though her intended action was arrested at the last moment by her awareness of my presence. When the incident came up casually in a later conversation, she also showed a clear capacity to expose her intended action to a moral examination. Not only did she spontaneously express her understanding of an obligation not to hurt her brother, but she also verbalized her own disapproval of having wanted to react so strongly to a petty affront. What she said might be taken as evidence of only the beginnings of moral perception. But it can hardly be doubted that she had a moral principle of conduct at her command.

The young lady who is the heroine of this incident will certainly acquire more abstract cognitive structures as she grows older. And she will therefore attain correspondingly more complex moral rules, which integrate many different features of an act and its consequences. She will also become more complex in her language and in her operations of thought on the physical world. Greater abstraction and complexity are in the very nature of development. And it may well be that the substance of moral values is only one of many representational systems on which cognitive development simultaneously works its transformations. We might then consider the possibility that the thinking of young children already shows most of the fundamental properties of moral judgment. The fundament of their moral conceptions may well be the product of rather specific, though almost universal, forms of social experience. And the subsequent stages through which their moral thought moves may reflect successive impositions upon this substantive moral base—impositions that represent advances in the power of reasoning, and in the abstraction and organization of criteria.

To make the argument above even more explicit, I am suggesting that the basic cognitive and affective substance of moral value is formed fairly early in the socialization process, and that it remains relatively stable thereafter. But it does become subordinated to increasingly differentiated structures and increasingly powerful operations of thought. This distinction between substance and form may be useful in understanding whatever cross-cultural regularities may exist in moral development. The fundamental substantive dimensions of moral value may well vary from one society to another. Yet there may also be some uniformities in the forms or structures which children's cognitive operators allow them to impose sequentially on any categorical substance. Of course, these same operators could also be imposed on many other systems of representation which the child obtains from his transactions with the social and physical world, quite irrespective of any moral content. Thus, one would expect an analysis of the transformations of the child's thought in the moral domain to uncover much the same pattern as can be seen in his conceptions of time, space, or physical quantity. Indeed, there is now some initial evidence of just such parallelism (Kohlberg, in press). The implication is clear: The stages that can be discerned in moral development are subsidiary to more general shifts in the child's cognitive power. And these structural changes are not in themselves intrinsically moral; their moral status resides only in the substantive base of values upon which they operate.

There are a number of limitations, then, on the heuristic value of the conception of moral development as moving through a universal sequence of stages. The first qualification is that a number of different evaluative structures, varying in their power and complexity, are apparently available to the conscience of the ordinary person. The transformations between stages therefore either are reversible or else leave preceding stages functionally intact. Furthermore, it is distinctly possible that any universality in the acquisition of conscience is to be found in changes of cognitive capacity rather than in changes of the basic substance of moral values. The children of any society may acquire an increasingly abstracted and internalized moral orientation (up to the point of support from whatever cognitive devices the society provides). Many members of Western societies may be motivated to use their cognitive capacities to arrive at principled values of self-direction which go beyond the more obvious kinds of external constraints. In other societies, however, elaborate and abstract principles of conduct may be constructed around values which take a much more externalized perspective on human relationships; an excellent example can be found in Erikson's description (1950) of the moral focus of Yurok society on values of cleanliness and economic exchange.

These limitations are boundary conditions which must be honored by any conception of the development of moral thought. They are perfectly consistent with the view that the child's moral cognition does undergo structural and qualitative transformations. And they do not contradict evidence that the attainment of some rules of moral value may be prerequisite to the attainment of others. But we need to recognize that the boundary conditions present large problems for a conception of discontinuous stages of moral judgment. What we now know about moral judgment and conduct might be better contained by the view that they evolve from continuities in the interaction between the child's cognitive capacity and his social experience. Cognitive change in itself will be a critical determinant of how the child receives his social experience. An external program of socialization will not induce more complex or autonomous moral principles in a child who does not have the requisite cognitive capacity. Conversely, cognitive development is too general a phenomenon to account specifically for the substance of moral values. An understanding of how conscience is acquired will therefore depend on a knowledge of how concrete experiences of socialization both induce and capitalize on the structural changes in children's thinking.

A Cognitive Social-Learning Approach to Morality and Self-Regulation[1]

Walter Mischel and Harriet N. Mischel

Introduction

In this chapter we will consider some of the main constructs of a cognitive social-learning position (Mischel, 1973) and examine how they apply to the psychological analysis of moral judgments, moral (prosocial) conduct, and self-regulation.

Parts of this discussion will focus on the *processes* through which moral and self-regulatory patterns are acquired, evoked, maintained, and modified (e.g., Bandura, 1969; Mischel, 1968). An adequate approach to complex human behavior also requires attention to the psychological products within the individual of cognitive development and social learning experiences. Therefore we will also consider some of the *person variables* that are the consequences of the individual's social and biological history and that in turn mediate how new experiences influence subsequent behavior. Such person variables and their interaction with conditions are crucial for an understanding of how behavior becomes organized and patterned within individuals, as well as how certain

developmental sequences tend to become normative for the social community. Consequently, the present discussion will include the role of such person variables, and of person-situation interactions, in a cognitive social-learning view of morality and self-regulation.

Human beings not only generate behaviors but also categorize, evaluate, and judge them. Thus a comprehensive psychological analysis of "morality" must consider *judgments* about moral behavior as well as the determinants of moral *behavior* itself. To adequately discuss moral judgment and behavior it will also be necessary to deal with the topic of self-regulation. Moral judgment, moral conduct, and self-regulation at first glance may seem to be separate topics, but from the present perspective a comprehensive psychological approach to any one of them requires considering the others. Moral judgment, moral conduct, and self-regulation all involve man's efforts to deal with good and bad, right and wrong. Moral judgment concerns the *evaluation* of good–bad (right–wrong) and of what one "ought to do"; moral conduct and self-regulation concern the processes and behaviors relevant to the *achievement* of the good and the avoidance of the bad and thus of realizing (or falling short of) one's moral ideals.

In a psychological analysis of morality it is also necessary to distinguish two components: the individual's *competence* (capacity) to generate prosocial behaviors, and the motivational (incentive) variables for their *performance* in particular situations. This difference between competence and performance mirrors the basic distinction made between acquisition (learning) and performance in social learning formulations (e.g., Bandura, 1969; Mischel, 1968, 1971). Acquisition or learning depends mainly on cognitive-sensory processes (although it may be facilitated by incentive or reinforcement conditions). The products of acquisition are a person's competencies, that is, the repertoire of what the individual *can* do, and encompass what he knows, and the skills, rules, and cognitive capacities which he has acquired and which permit him to generate (construct) behaviors (Mischel, 1973). In contrast, performance depends on motivational variables and incentive conditions, as will be discussed in later sections.

In sum, a comprehensive psychological approach to morality needs to include the individual's conceptions of what he "should" do (his moral judgments, good–bad evaluations) as well as the moral conduct and self-regulatory behaviors required to achieve moral ideals. The present analysis will include all three of these topics. It will also distinguish the determinants of the individual's competence for moral judgment and conduct from the motivational (performance) variables that influence whether or not he enacts and achieves the behaviors of which he is capable in particular situations.

In the present paper we will consider, first, the topic of moral competence. Thereafter conditions relevant to the performance of moral conduct and the achievement of self-regulation will be discussed. Finally we will deal with some basic issues in the organization and inter-relations of moral judgment, moral conduct, and self-regulation.

Moral Competence

In the course of development, and by means of both direct and observational learning, each person acquires information about the world and his relationship to it. As a result of cognitive maturation and continuous social learning, the individual acquires an increasingly large potential for generating organized behavior. The existence and importance of observational (cognitive) learning have been demonstrated clearly (Bandura, 1969a; Campbell, 1961), but it is less certain how to construe what is acquired. The phenomena include such diverse learnings as the structure (or construction) of the physical world (Piaget, 1954); the social rules, conventions, and principles that guide conduct (Aronfreed, 1968c; Kohlberg, 1969b); and the personal constructs generated about self and others (G. Kelly, 1955). These acquisitions have been discussed by some psychologists in terms of information processing and information integration (e.g., N. H. Anderson, 1972; Bandura, 1971a; Rumelhart, Lindsay, & Norman, 1971), and by others in terms of schemata and cognitive templates (e.g., Aronfreed, 1968c), while still others have invoked a series of discrete, sequential developmental stages, each characterized by distinctive cognitive structures (Kohlberg, 1969b).

THE CONCEPT OF COGNITIVE AND BEHAVIORAL CONSTRUCTION COMPETENCIES

The concept of *cognitive and behavioral construction competencies* encompasses the great variety of man's psychological acquisitions and refers to the diverse cognitions and behaviors that the individual is capable of constructing. The term *constructions* emphasizes the constructive fashion in which information appears to be retrieved (Neisser, 1967) and the active organization through which it seems to be categorized and transformed in the course of its processing (Bower, 1970; Mandler, 1967, 1968). There is little doubt that instead of mimicking models or emitting unedited copies of earlier observations, every person constructs (generates) his renditions of "reality" in a highly selective fashion. Research on modeling effects, for example, has consistently indicated that the products of observational learning involve novel organization of information by the observer and rule-governed performances, rather than mirroring of observed responses (Bandura, 1971c; Mischel & Grusec, 1966). The concept of construction competencies is intended to emphasize the person's *cognitive activities* (the operations and transformations that he performs on information), rather than the finite cognitions and responses that he "has" in a more passive, static, sense.

Each individual acquires the capacity to construct a great range of potential behaviors—moral, immoral, and amoral; and different individuals acquire different behavior construction capabilities in different degrees. Obviously there are enormous differences between people in the range and quality of the cognitive and behavioral patterns that they can generate in any domain. To assess an individual's potential for the construction of a particular behavior, incentives can be offered for the most complete, adequate performance that he can achieve on tasks sampling the behavior of interest. The assessment conditions for this purpose are identical to those in achievement testing (Wallace, 1966). The same tactics can be employed to assess what subjects "know" (i.e., the cognitive constructions they can generate, for example, about principles of justice and ethical conduct) and what they are capable of doing (as in the achievement of particular patterns of moral conduct, such as helpfulness toward others and resistance to temptations). To assess what they had acquired from observing a model, children were later offered attractive incentives contingent upon their reproducing the model's behavior (Bandura, 1965b; Grusec & Mischel, 1966). The data indicated that the children had acquired a great deal of information by observing the model and were capable of reconstructing this knowledge in detail, but only when they were given appropriate incentives for doing so.

CORRELATES OF COGNITIVE COMPETENCE

In spite of their long neglect by traditional personality theories, cognitive-intellective competencies are highly relevant to understanding most of the phenomena of personality in general and of prosocial behavior in particular. This relevance is reflected in the important, persistent contributions of indices of intelligence to the obtained networks of personality correlations (Campbell & Fiske, 1959; Mischel, 1968). Cognitive competencies (as tested by mental age and IQ tests) tend to be among the very best predictors of "honesty" in conduct (Hartshorne & May, 1928) and of later social and interpersonal adjustment (J. Anderson, 1960). Brighter, more competent, people presumably experience more success (interpersonally and through work achievements) and hence are more positively assessed by themselves and by others on the evaluative good–bad dimension so ubiquitous in trait ratings (Vernon, 1964). As noted elsewhere (Mischel, 1973), competence and achievement also may be reflected in the substantial "first factor" pervasively obtained on such tests as the MMPI (J. Block, 1965), often interpreted as connoting "adjustment" at the positive end and maladaptive character structure at the negative end. Cognitive achievements and intellective potential, as measured by mental age or IQ tests, are being given a central role in current cognitive-developmental theories (Kohlberg, 1969b) and appear to be important aspects of such concepts as *moral maturity, ego strength,* and *ego development*. Finally, indices that are strongly correlated with cognitive-intellective competence—such as age and the demographic variables of socioeconomic level and education—also tend to be among the best predictors of the adequacy of social functioning (Robins, 1972).

The importance of "sheer cognitive power in the operation of conscience" (Aronfreed, 1968c, p. 265) is also supported by studies that have found intelligence to be significantly correlated with the complexity of the information that children can deal with in their judgments of conduct (e.g., Kellmer Pringle & Edwards, 1964; Whiteman & Kosier, 1964). For example, the child's increasing capacity for verbal complexity seems to be a crucial determinant of age-related changes in the ability to utilize the principle of intentionality in the appraisal of other people's conduct (Breznitz & Kugelmass, 1967). Thus there is a triad of associations: Indices of the growth of conscience tend to be correlated with independent measures of the child's intelligence as well as with his age (Abel, 1941; R. C. Johnson, 1962; Kohlberg, 1964; MacRae, 1954).

Many age-related changes in conceptual styles and cognitive competencies have been identified and often have been interpreted to reflect fixed maturational sequences of cognitive development (e.g., Baldwin, 1967; Piaget 1926b). But a growing body of empirical evidence also suggests that these age-related cognitive patterns are modifiable when subjects are exposed to relevant cognitive and social-learning experiences designed to alter them (Bandura & Harris, 1966; Odom, Liebert, & Hill, 1968; Carroll, Rosenthal, & Brysh, 1969; T. L. Rosenthal & Whitebook, 1970; T. L. Rosenthal, Zimmerman, & Durning, 1970; Siegler, Liebert, & Lie-

bert, 1973). These studies suggest that such cognitive skills as linguistic construction and conceptual organization of a set of stimuli are amenable to change through observational learning and reward procedures. Cognitive competencies specifically relevant to moral reasoning and conduct also have been shown to be modifiable in the same manner (Bandura & McDonald, 1963; Cowan et al., 1969; Prentice, 1972). Thus widespread age-related changes in both cognitive competencies and preferred cognitive styles may reflect age-correlated alterations in the social-learning variables salient at different points in development (to be discussed in later sections) as well as maturational changes in cognitive capacities—perhaps in almost inextricable interactions.

MATURITY IN MORAL REASONING

As noted before, judgments of right–wrong comprise an important aspect of morality. An evaluative dimension consistently emerges when people rate each other's traits and attributes (or assess themselves), as well as when they rate meanings of words and events. On the semantic differential, for example, a primary evaluative (good–bad) factor accounted for about half to three-quarters of the extractable variance (Osgood, Suci, & Tannenbaum, 1957). The same evaluative factor also was found pervasively in trait ratings of persons (e.g., Mulaik, 1964; Vernon, 1964). There is little doubt that good–bad evaluations are a basic ingredient of human judgment, but there is much less agreement about the nature and determinants of such judgments, especially with regard to morality.

Most challenging and controversial is the view that moral judgment, and specifically moral reasoning, involves the child's passage through a series of successive stages characterized by increasing degrees of maturity in the mode of organizing the social and moral order (Piaget, 1932; Kohlberg, 1963a, 1969b).[2] To help test this contention, Kohlberg (1958, 1969b) has provided an increasingly popular measure of maturity in moral reasoning. On this test the subject is confronted with a set of conflict-inducing moral dilemmas, and his answers are scored for their level of "moral maturity." This measure and the theorizing related to it have become increasingly influential in conceptions of morality (as the contents of the present volume attest).

Unfortunately, the Kohlberg measure of maturity in reasoning about moral dilemmas does not permit one to separate the type of moral reasoning of which the respondent is capable from the moral reasoning which he favors (or which he prefers to use). To separate *competence* in moral reasoning from *performance* (or preference) it would be necessary for the test to encourage all subjects to display the "best" (highest, most mature) moral reasoning that they are capable of generating. This could be achieved by offering incentives for maximum performance (as on other achievement tests). Without such a procedure one cannot determine whether a subject's performance reflects the most mature moral reasoning that he *can* generate or the degree to which he uses (prefers) different types of moral reasoning in the dilemmas sampled or (as most likely occurs) some indeterminate mix of both. One cannot be sure from the test, for example, whether a "Stage 3" subject who displays a dominant "good boy" orientation does not know more abstract principles which go beyond approval seeking, or whether he may "have" such concepts but prefer not to verbalize them when reasoning about moral dilemmas.[3]

Since subjects often use moral reasoning at levels judged to be above their current stage, it would be implausible to view their assigned stage as an index of their current maximal competence. As Kohlberg (1969b, p. 387, fig. 6.4) reports, on the average somewhat less than 50 percent of a subject's moral judgments fit a single stage, the remainder being dis-tributed in the form of a normal curve encompassing the stages both above and below the modal one. Similarly, Bandura and McDonald (1963, p. 280) found that children at all ages (from 5 to 11 years) "exhibited discriminative repertoires of moral judgment" (i.e., used reasoning at various stages). Among college students "not one of the subjects studied employed moral reasoning that was exclusively rated at any single level of development" (Fishkin, Keniston, & MacKinnon, 1973, p. 114). To the extent that a subject uses *any* moral judgments at levels higher than the level he is assigned to by his modal score, one must conclude that he is capable of constructing such judgments but normatively prefers not to make them. Thus the assigned stage of "maturity" in moral judgment may be seen to reflect *preferred* modes of justifying moral conduct, and not necessarily to indicate the subject's cognitive limits. Moreover, the heterogeneity across situations of both moral reasoning and moral conduct which may be displayed by an individual assigned to any given stage requires explanation. From the present perspective, such intraindividual differences, as well as differences between individuals, may be understood in terms of each person's unique social-learning history and experiences; they reflect the interaction of the products of cognitive development and social learning with the specifics of the immediate psychological situation in which behavior is generated.

Some Determinants of Moral Conduct and Self-Regulation

The individual who knows how to behave competently in prosocial, constructive, ways is *capable* of such behaviors, but whether or not he enacts them at any given time (or chooses less virtuous courses of action) depends on specific motivational and performance considerations in the psychological situation. So far we have considered what the individual is capable of doing, that is, his competencies and abilities. But the person who is capable of the most virtuous moral conduct may also be capable of aggressive and morally despicable action. To go from competence and potential behaviors to actual performance, from construction capacity to the construction of behavior in specific situations, requires attention to the determinants of performance. In this regard, the variables of greatest interest are the person's expectancies and subjective values.

EXPECTED RESPONSE CONSEQUENCES

It often helps to know what an individual can do, but to predict specific behavior in a particular situation one must consider the individual's specific expectancies about the consequences of different behavioral possibilities in that situation (e.g., Mischel & Staub, 1965). The subject's own behavior-outcome expectancies guide his selection of behaviors from among the enormous number which he is capable of constructing within any situation.

In part, expectancies about environmental contingencies may be based on direct experience (e.g., Rotter, 1954, 1972). Yet behavior-outcome expectations depend not only on the outcomes one has obtained for similar behavior in similar situations but also on the consequences one has observed occurring to other people. Information about the outcomes of other people's behavior may provide valuable information about the probable consequences to oneself for trying similar behavior.

After one has observed that other people ("models") obtain positive consequences for a response pattern, one tends to act more readily in similar ways. For instance, if a child sees other children receive encouragement and praise for, let us say, helpfulness and generosity at play, his own tendency to behave altruistically in similar situations will increase. Conversely, when social models are punished

for their behavior (e.g., for aggressing), observers tend to become more inhibited about displaying similar behavior (Bandura, Ross, & Ross, 1963a). However, when incentives are later offered for imitating the aggressive model, children who had initially seen the model punished give evidence of as much imitation learning as children who had seen the model unpunished or rewarded (Bandura, 1965b). It may be concluded that the children in all conditions had learned the model's behavior equally well; the observation of different consequences, however, had inhibited or facilitated their later performance of the behavior.

Modeling cues and vicarious response consequences have been shown to influence performance measures of both moral reasoning (Bandura & McDonald, 1963; Cowan et al., 1969; Prentice, 1972) and prosocial behavior (Bryan & Test, 1967; Rosenhan, Moore, & Underwood, Chap. 13; Staub, 1973). In the present view, these effects were probably mediated by alterations in the observers' expectancies regarding the desirability (consequences) of their displaying behavior similar to the behaviors that they saw modeled and rewarded. Even reactions to frustration, which often tend to be aggressive, are likely to become prosocial and cooperative when the positive consequences for such constructive behaviors are enhanced and made salient. For example, when domineering, hyperaggressive children were exposed to modeling situations that depicted positive consequences for cooperativeness in response to interpersonal conflicts, their own behavior became increasingly cooperative even in a follow-up assessment one month later (Chittenden, 1942). Bandura (1973) has documented in detail the often subtle and complex ways in which anticipated response consequences may facilitate antisocial aggressive behavior or lead to prosocial alternatives.

Although laboratory studies provide the most conclusive demonstrations of the close links between the occurrence of behavior and expected consequences, naturalistic observations serve to further document the social implications. Consider, for example, the collective modeling of airline hijackings (Bandura, 1973). While air piracy was unknown in the United States until 1961, successful hijackings of Cuban airliners to Miami were followed by a wave of hijackings, reaching a crest of eighty-seven airplane piracies in 1969. The phenomenon was given fresh impetus by news of a hijacker who successfully parachuted from an airliner with a large sum of extorted money, but hijackings in the United States finally seemed to end when new security procedures greatly reduced the likelihood of success.

In sum, one does not have to enact particular behaviors in order to learn their consequences; modeling cues and vicarious as well as direct consequences of performances influence subsequent behavior. One does not have to be arrested for embezzling to learn some of its consequences; one does not have to be searched personally to learn of airport security arrangements and the penalty for concealed weapons; nor does one have to rescue a drowning child to discover the positive consequences of such an act. Information that alters the person's anticipations of the probable outcomes to which a behavior will lead also changes the probability that he will engage in the behavior. Modeling cues (both live and symbolic) provide an extremely effective way of changing an observer's behavior-outcome expectancies, and thus enhancing or inhibiting the behaviors involved.

Modeling cues and vicarious response consequences may have powerful effects on performance, but not all models are equally effective for all people. The attributes of the observer (e.g., Bandura & Walters, 1963; Turiel, 1966) and of the model (e.g., prestige, status, power, similarity to the observer), as well as the model's relationship with the observer (e.g., nurturance and warmth), will affect the likelihood that the modeled behavior will be influential

(Grusec & Mischel, 1966; Mischel & Liebert, 1967). For example, children tend to adopt the performance standards displayed by adult models who are rewarding and powerful, but tend to reject the same standards when they are modeled by adults who are low in those attributes (Mischel & Grusec, 1966). Similarly, children with nurturant caretakers who had modeled helpfulness in both live and symbolic distress situations were later themselves more helpful and consistently altruistic (Yarrow, Scott, & Waxler, 1973). These experimental findings are congruent with naturalistic and field studies reporting some correlations between the affection and nurturance of the parents and the prosocial behavior (e.g., "consideration") of their children (M. L. Hoffman & Salzstein, 1967) and suggest that parental nurturance tends to be conducive to children's prosocial behavior especially when it is combined with judicious control (see Staub, 1973).

"Direct training" for prosocial behavior may encompass a wide variety of experiences such as role playing, role exchange, and reasoning to encourage responsibility, empathy, and consideration for others (Staub, 1973). Experiences of this type presumably help to sensitize the individual to the consequences of his behavior for other people and not merely for himself. Not surprisingly, concern for others seems to be learned most effectively when more than moral exhortations are involved. Cross-cultural research suggests that children's altruistic–egoistic tendencies may depend most strongly on the degree to which the children are actually involved in the maintenance of the family's welfare. Children tended to be more altruistic in their behavior when the culture required them to assume more interpersonal obligations and responsibilities, such as caring for younger siblings and animals (J. W. M. Whiting & B. Whiting, 1969). Increasing responsibilty for the welfare of others tended to generate increasing altruism. In the present view, the assignment of such responsibilities and their successful execution serve to generate enduring expectancies regarding the positive consequences of mutually helpful behaviors, and hence tend to increase their likelihood. Just as aggression tends to feed on aggression (Berkowitz, 1973b), so does a person's future prosocial behavior thrive on his past prosocial behavior.

Opportunities to practice prosocial behavior and to observe or experience its positive consequences facilitate the future occurrence of similar behavior, but it is also easy to use "rewards" unwisely in socialization. A major purpose of socialization is to wean the individual from external controls and rewards so that his behavior becomes increasingly guided and supported by intrinsic gratifications, that is, satisfactions closely connected with the prosocial activity itself. Therefore it is essential to use incentives judiciously and only to the extent necessary to initiate and sustain desired prosocial behavior.

SUBJECTIVE VALUES

Even when different people share similar expectancies, they may choose different patterns of behavior because of differences in the *subjective values* of the outcomes that they expect (Mischel, 1973; Rotter, 1954). For example, given that all persons expect approval from peers to depend on verbalization of particular value judgments, there may be differences in the frequency of such verbalizations due to differences in the perceived value of obtaining peer approval. Similarly, while approval from peers for a particular behavior pattern in a particular situation may be more important for one individual than parental approval, these values may be reversed for a second person and irrelevant for a third.

The subjective (perceived) value for the individual of particular classes of events (his stimulus preferences and aversions) is an important determinant of behavioral choices. *Subjective value* refers to stimuli that have acquired the power to induce positive or negative emotional states

in the person and to function as incentives or reinforcers for his behavior. The subjective value of any stimulus pattern may be acquired and modified through instructions and observational experiences as well as through direct experiences (Bandura, 1969a) and obviously may change substantially in the course of development. The highest subjective values of a 40-year-old may have little appeal for his young child, and vice versa.

The *affective value* (valence) of any stimulus depends on the exact conditions—in the person and in the situation—in which it occurs. The many variables known to affect the emotional meaning and valence of a stimulus include its context, sequencing, and patterning (Helson, 1964); social comparison processes (Festinger, 1954); and the cognitive labels the person assigns to his own emotional arousal state (Schachter & Singer, 1962).

Even when subjective values for particular activities are shared, individuals may differ in how they tolerate (and respond to) deviations from these values either in their own behavior or in the conduct of others. For example, to the surprise of many sociologists, members of the lower class (gang and nongang) and of the middle class, both black and white, were found to endorse similar values "in principle"; but individuals from these different subcultures differed in the degree to which they tolerated behavioral deviations from the prosocial norms that they all abstractly endorsed (Gordon et al., 1963). Such differences in tolerance are presumed to be partly a function of differences in people's self-regulatory systems. These systems are discussed next.

SELF-REGULATORY SYSTEMS

Tests of moral maturity (i.e., moral reasoning) focus on how the individual solves hypothetical moral dilemmas in story situations, but the successful realization of moral choices in real life often depends on the faithful execution of long-term commitments that demand high levels of self-control. Moral conduct requires the individual to adhere behaviorally to reciprocal commitments and obligations even (or especially) under extremely difficult conditions, and not merely to endorse them in principle. Such prolonged self-control sequences involve more than abstract problem solving and right–wrong decision making; they hinge on the individual's ability to regulate his own behavior in the face of strong temptations and situational pressures for long periods and without the aid of any obvious external rewards and supports. As noted at the start of this chapter, self-control is an important aspect of morality, for without it moral ideals cannot be realized. Indeed, some philosophers suggest that *all* virtues are forms of self-control (Von Wright, 1963, chap. 7). To go from moral thought to moral conduct requires self-regulation.

Although behavior is controlled to a considerable degree by externally administered consequences for actions, each person also regulates his own behavior by self-imposed goals (standards) and self-produced consequences. Even when there are no external constraints and social monitors, individuals set standards for themselves and criticize or commend their own behavior depending on how well it fits their expectations and standards. The notion of self-imposed standards has figured in Rotter's "minimal goal" construct (1954) and more recently in conceptions of self-reinforcing functions (Bandura, 1971c; Kanfer, 1971; Kanfer & Marston, 1963; Mischel, 1968, 1973).

A fundamental quality of self-regulatory systems is the subject's adoption of *contingency rules*, which guide his behavior in the absence of and sometimes in spite of immediate external situational pressures. Such rules specify the kinds of behavior appropriate (expected) under particular conditions, the performance criteria (standards, goals) that the behavior must achieve, and the consequences of achieving or failing to reach these standards. Different individuals may differ, of course, in each component of self-regulation, depending on their unique earlier histories or their more recent experiences (e.g., situational information).

Research on goal setting and self-reinforcement has demonstrated some of the components in self-regulation (e.g., Bandura & Perloff, 1967; Bandura & Whalen, 1966; Mischel & Liebert, 1966). These studies reveal that even young children will not indulge in freely available immediate gratifications; instead they follow rules that regulate conditions under which they may reinforce themselves. Far from being hedonistic, children, like adults, make demands of themselves and impose complex and often stringent contingencies upon their own behavior. These self-imposed criteria are grounded in the observed standards displayed by salient models, as well as in the individual's direct socialization history (e.g., Bandura & Walters, 1963; Mischel & Liebert, 1966).

When modeling cues and direct tuition for a pattern of standards are congruent they tend to facilitate each other, and when they conflict (as often occurs in life) the observer's behavior is affected jointly by both sources (e.g., Mischel & Liebert, 1966; Rosenhan & White, 1967). Thus an observer is most likely to adopt modeled standards for behavior when the standards used by the model for himself are consistent with the standards used by the model to train the child. When there is a discrepancy between what is practiced and what is preached, observers are more likely to adopt the least stringent standards available for behavior. Mischel and Liebert (1966), for example, found that when models imposed stringent standards for behavior upon children and displayed similarly rigorous standards in their own self-evaluation, all children subsequently adopted these high standards. But when the models permitted and encouraged lenient standards in the children, the youngsters were uniformly lenient with themselves, even when the models had been stringent in their own standards.

After the individual has set his standards (terminal goals) for conduct in a particular situation, the route toward their realization may be long and difficult. In that case, progress may be mediated extensively by covert symbolic activities, such as praise and self-instructions, as the individual reaches subgoals en route. When reinforcing and noxious stimuli are imagined, their behavioral consequences may be the same as when such stimuli are presented externally (e.g., Cautela, 1971). These covert activities serve to maintain goal-directed work until the performance reaches or exceeds the person's terminal standards (e.g., Meichenbaum, 1971). Progress toward goal attainment also may be aided by self-generated distractions and cognitive operations through which the person can transform the aversive self-control situation into one that he can master effectively (e.g., Mischel, Ebbesen, & Zeiss, 1972; Mischel & Moore, 1973; Mischel, Moore, & Zeiss, 1973). When important goals are attained, positive self-appraisal and self-reinforcement tend to occur, whereas the individual may indulge in psychological self-lacerations and self-condemnation if he fails to reach significant self-imposed standards.

People can readily perform *cognitive transformations* on stimuli (Mischel, 1974), focusing on selected aspects of the objective stimulus; such selected attention, interpretation, and categorization may substantially influence how any stimulus affects their behavior (see also Geer, Davison, & Gatchel, 1970; Schachter, 1964). The significant role of cognitive transformations in self-regulation is demonstrated in research on the determinants of how long preschool children will actually sit still alone in a chair waiting for a preferred but delayed outcome before they signal with a bell to terminate the waiting period and settle for a less preferred but immediately available gratification (Mischel, 1974; Mischel, Ebbesen, & Zeiss,

1972). The results reveal that the same child who may terminate his waiting in less than half a minute on one occasion may be capable of waiting for long periods on another occasion a few weeks earlier or later, if cognitive and attentional conditions are conducive to delay.

Studies on cognitive transformations during delay have also helped to clarify the role of attention in self-control. As early as 1890, William James noted a relationship between attention and self-control, and contended that attentional processes are the crux of the self-control phenomena usually subsumed under the label "will" (or since James's time under the concept "ego strength"). In James's words (1890), "Attention with effort is all that any case of volition implies. The essential achievement of will is to attend to a difficult object" (p. 549). Beginning with the research of Hartshorne and May (1928) some correlations have been found between indices of moral behavior and measures of attention or resistance to distraction on mental tests (Grim, Kohlberg, & White, 1968). Such correlations have led to the suggestion that a person's ability to resist temptation may be facilitated by how well he attends to a task. Yielding to temptation in most experimental paradigms hinges on the subject's becoming distracted from the main task to which he is supposed to be attending. In such paradigms a subject's ability to focus attention *on* the task and to resist distraction may automatically make it easier for him to resist such temptations as cheating, as Grim, Kohlberg, and White (1968) have noted.

Findings on the role of attention during delay of gratification, however, reveal another relationship: *Not* attending to the goal (potential reward) was what facilitated self-control most dramatically (Mischel, Ebbesen, & Zeiss, 1972). More detailed analyses of attentional mechanisms during delay of gratification showed that the crucial variable is not *whether* the subject attends to the goal objects while delaying, but *how* he focuses on them (Mischel, 1974). It was found that through instructions the child can cognitively transform the reward objects that face him during the delay period in ways to either permit or prevent effective delay of gratification. For example, if the child is left during the waiting period with the actual reward objects (pretzels or marshmallows) in front of him, it becomes difficult for him to wait for more than a few moments. But through instructions he can cognitively transform the reward objects in ways that permit him to wait for long periods (Mischel & Baker, 1975). If he cognitively transforms the stimulus to focus on its nonarousing qualities, for example, by thinking about the pretzel sticks as little brown logs, or by thinking about the marshmallows as round white clouds or as cotton balls, he may be able to wait for long time periods. Conversely, if the child has been instructed to focus cognitively on the consummatory (arousing, motivating) qualities of the reward objects, such as the pretzel's crunchy, salty taste or the chewy, sweet, soft taste of the marshmallows, he tends to be able to wait only a short time (Mischel, 1974). By knowing the relevant rules of cognitive transformation and utilizing them during self-control efforts, individuals may be able to attain considerable self-mastery in pursuit of their goals, even in the face of strong countervailing situational pressures.

Affective states also influence the person's self-control and self-reactions. After positive (as compared to negative) experiences, individuals become much more benign toward both themselves and others. After success experiences or positive mood inductions, for example, there is greater selective attention to positive information about the self (Mischel, Ebbesen, & Zeiss, 1973), greater noncontingent self-gratification (Mischel, Coates, & Raskoff, 1968; Moore, Underwood, & Rosenhan, 1972), and greater generosity (Isen, Horn, & Rosenhan, 1973).

The organization of self-regulatory behaviors also requires attention to the individual's priority rules for determining the sequencing of behavior and stop rules for the termination of a particular sequence of behavior. Like other complex human actions, prosocial, morally relevant behaviors depend on the execution of lengthy interlocking sequences of thought and behavior. The concept of plans as hierarchical processes that control the order in which an organism performs a sequence of operations (G. A. Miller, Galanter, & Pribram, 1960) seems applicable. Introspectively, we do seem to generate plans. And once a plan is formed and adopted (to marry, to divorce, to report suspicions about another's immoral act to authorities, to resist the draft, to join a protest movement), a whole series of subroutines follows. While the concept of plans is intuitively plausible, it has not yet led to the necessary personality-oriented cognitive research. Helpful first steps toward the study of plans are the concepts of behavioral intentions (Dulany, 1962), intention statements and contracts (Kanfer et al., 1974). Self-instructions and intention statements are likely to be important aspects of the individual's plans and the hierarchical organization of his self-regulatory behavior.

In sum, a comprehensive approach to prosocial behavior must take account of the individual's self-regulatory systems. These systems include (1) the rules that specify goals or performance standards in particular situations; (2) the consequences of achieving or failing to achieve those criteria; (3) the self-instructions and cognitive stimulus transformations required to achieve the self-control necessary for goal attainment; and (4) the organizing rules (plans) for the sequencing and termination of complex behavioral patterns in the absence of external supports and in the presence of external hindrances.

AGE-RELATED CHANGES

In the present view, age-related changes in the individual's moral judgments and his prosocial and self-regulatory patterns reflect correlated changes in the interaction between his growing cognitive and behavioral competencies and the social-learning variables salient at different points in his experience. Early in the child's life, the consequences for moral and immoral behavior tend to be defined and presented in a concrete, tangible, immediate fashion. When a mother is socializing her toddler not to hurt his siblings, she is likely to say such things as "Don't! That's not nice! If you do that again I'll have to (specific threat)." Or she might praise good behavior with, "Now Johnny's being a good boy; nice Johnny." She is certainly unlikely to express abstract rules about general moral principles to her barely verbal child.

The young child's moral understanding comes to reflect the regime of personal constraints, of punishments and approvals, of rules and conventions, which are modeled and upheld by parents, peers, and other significant persons at different points in his development. Similarly, the child's changing prosocial conduct reflects the changes in his expectancies, subjective values, and self-regulatory systems caused partly by his changing competencies and experiences. The specific shifts in these socialization patterns with age and developmental progress during early childhood probably have considerable similarity to the first few moral stages conceptualized by Kohlberg (1969b). For example, the most primitive phases of moral reasoning (in their orientation to retaliation for wrong doing and to the assessment of transgressions in terms of their objective magnitude) tend to mirror the practices to which the child is exposed earliest in the socialization process.

The young child does not have good control over his own behavior and tends to interpret both positive and negative outcomes as the result of factors outside himself (Mischel, Mailer, & Zeiss, 1973). Moreover, the magnitude of the young child's transgressions is often unintended and unanticipated, as when a poke at a milk bottle produces a spill that badly upsets an adult. Not surprisingly, at this point in socialization the youngster learns that the damaging consequences of an act, rather than its motivations, signal the probable occurrence and magnitude of punishment. But with the growth of cognitive and behavioral competence, the child learns to hold himself increasingly responsible for his own behavior. He becomes more sensitive to the fact that cues about intentions, often conveyed verbally ("I didn't mean it!"), determine the response consequences for an act. While a parent may punish the older child's transgression if it seems voluntary, punishment is less likely and less severe if the act is judged to be accidental. Expectancies about behavior-outcome relations gradually become moderated by a host of social cues, including those for inferring the intentions motivating behavior (i.e., its perceived causes). Over time a person's reactions to a physical blow from another will depend on whether it was perceived as accidental or deliberate. Similarly, whether praise and attention will have a positive effect on the recipient or will generate suspicion (and a rebuff) depends on whether the behaviors are perceived as sincere or as ingratiating (Jones, 1964).

The relations between socialization practices and the child's age and cognitive competencies are not arbitrary; they probably reflect a continuous interaction of the child's increasing cognitive competencies with the priorities and practices of socializing agents. It is essential for a mother to prevent young Johnny from injuring his sibling, even when she does not have the time, and Johnny does not have the capacity, to reason about the moral bases of this constraint; therefore she must rely on specific admonitions and punishments. Later in socialization, when the child's cognitive and verbal skills expand, the justification for right and wrong courses of action tends to be increasingly based on rules—first of an arbitrary authority-oriented type but gradually of a more abstract and reasoned nature.

Consider, for example, the differences in how a 12-year-old delinquent from a lower socioeconomic-class family and a professor in an Ivy League college might handle moral dilemmas in ways that result in the delinquent's being assigned to Stage 2 or 3 of Kohlberg's scale of moral maturity, while the professor is likely to reach higher levels. To understand the differences between these two people it is necessary to take account of the differences in their cognitive and verbal skills as well as in the ways in which moral issues and conduct are represented and treated in their respective experiences. In part, the delinquent youngster and the professor differ in the cognitive and linguistic maturity with which they can conceptualize and articulate "reasons." That is likely to be the case regardless of whether the issues about which they are asked to reason are moral dilemmas or morally irrelevant—for example, esthetic judgments about why they prefer particular paintings, books, movies, or music. When justifying either his moral reasoning or his esthetic preferences (or any other choice, morally relevant or not) the professor is likely to deal in "higher" abstractions (e.g., about justice, about beauty), to invoke more generalized rules (e.g., about reciprocity in ethics, about harmony in esthetics) than will the twelve-year-old. The latter is likely to be not only more concrete but also more self-centered and peer-centered in his explanations.

Some of the differences between the juvenile delinquent and the professor reflect their different cognitive capacities; but it is also essential to consider the enormous differences in the consequences which they expect and value for different courses of action and for different verbalizations, and their different self-regulatory systems. For example, both the delinquent and the professor may be partly motivated by expected consequences such as the approval of their relevant peer group and their own self-esteem. But such a sense of approval and self-esteem may require strict conformity to the group's conventions for the delinquent; for the professor it may be

contingent on adherence to reciprocity, consistency, and appeals to abstract universal principles. For the professor, moral reasoning oriented explicitly toward approval from others and adherence to conventional authority is unlikely to be rewarding, unlikely to be valued, and thus unlikely to be used. His moral reasoning will probably be structured and justified in far more impersonal, "unselfish," abstract terms, with generalizations about universal principles (which would produce a much higher moral maturity score). But while the particular consequences to which the professor and the delinquent are especially alert may be different, and while they may justify their choices at different levels of abstraction and verbal sophistication, both will be guided by a concern with the external and self-administered outcomes expected from the available alternatives.

In sum, in the present view, age-related changes in the style and content of moral reasoning and conduct reflect changes in the individual's cognitive and verbal capacities (e.g., the ability to deal with abstract concepts) in interaction with the social-learning variables salient for him at different points in the life cycle. The specific manner in which socialization variables interact with the individual's cognitive capacities in different ways at different points in the development of prosocial behavior has been documented elsewhere (see Aronfreed, 1968c). To the degree that the development of cognitive competencies follows a sequential course (e.g., in the direction of greater verbal and abstract concept-formation skills), some universality may also be found in the age-related sequence of indices of morality across cultures. But while moral judgments may generally move from a focus on immediate consequences to more temporally distant concerns, and from concrete justifications to more abstract general rules and principles, their content will depend on the culture in which the individual develops. The increasing cognitive and verbal competencies of the child follow an age-related sequence which in turn is reflected in age-related changes in moral reasoning. But it would not be parsimonious to believe that the latter reflects more than the growth of cognitive competencies interacting with socialization practices.

While there is considerable controversy about the possible existence and specific content of any "universal" hierarchy of moral judgment (Alston, 1971; Aronfreed, 1968c; Kohlberg, 1971a), there is widespread agreement about what is *not* an index of high levels of moral maturity. Specifically, even when the outcome of an act is judged as "good" by an evaluator, the actor is less likely to be judged as having "high moral maturity" when he seems to be motivated by obvious immediate, tangible gratifications, rather than altruistic concerns. In the course of development the perceived subjective intent (motivation) attributed to the actor replaces the objective outcome of the behavior as a main determinant of evaluative moral judgments (Weiner & Peter, 1973).

Psychological theorists, just like laymen, also base judgments about the goodness of an act on the actor's inferred intentions, not merely on its outcome. When it is easy to identify the specific situational incentives or pressures that seem to motivate behavior, there is no reason to credit the performer with moral maturity, with advanced ego development, or with altruistic motivations. For example, to help another person either in order to get an apparent reward for oneself, or because one is under duress to give aid is generally not considered an act of moral virtue or maturity. Behavior that is obviously related to immediate rewarding or punishing consequences for the actor can be easily explained without recourse to any internal moral or ego regulators. But when there are no obvious justifications for an act, the popular explanation changes quickly. Why does a child refrain from attractive pleasures even in the absence of external constraints? Why does one

berate oneself for enacting, or even fantasizing, behaviors that others cannot detect? Why does one aid another even when doing so is painful and costly to oneself? Why does one share one's bounty with others even when not pressured to be so generous? These are the kinds of questions that have led to the construction of mediating systems as explanations. These questions also point to some of the conditions under which behaviors are more likely to be judged as moral, good, and "self-controlled"—conditions in which the outcomes of a behavior are evaluated as good but the motivation for the action does not seem adequately explained by immediate incentives and constraints in the actor's situation.

A tendency to judge either "selfishly" or "situationally" motivated behaviors as less moral, or indeed premoral, is seen in the writings of cognitively oriented developmental psychologists. Consider, for example, Kohlberg's (1958, 1969b) stages of moral maturity (levels of moral reasoning). Such stage conceptions of moral maturation suggest that in the lowest maturity levels behavior (or its evaluation) is governed by immediate consequences to the self such as fear of retaliation, punishment, or detection. At intermediate levels the conduct and assessment of behavior are said to depend on conformity to external rules and expected benefits to the self versus disapproval from others and from conventional authorities. At the higher levels of maturity, however, behavior is said to become governed by less selfish, less concrete, more abstract considerations. For Kohlberg (1969b), the highest stages of moral development involve a contractual legalistic orientation (Stage 5) and a conscience or principles orientation (Stage 6) "involving appeal to logical universality [and to] conscience as a directing agent and to mutual respect and trust" (p. 376).

But from the present perspective, even the noblest altruism supported by the "highest" levels of moral reasoning still depends on expected consequences, although the consequences are often temporally distant, are not in the immediate external environment, are not easily identified, and reside in the actor himself rather than in social agents. The young child's behavior may be governed primarily by expected immediate concrete consequences for himself, but with greater maturity the evaluation and reinforcement of behavior become increasingly autonomous of external rewards and punishments and include more temporally distant and abstract considerations and self-reaction on the part of the actor. But such autonomy does not imply that the behavior no longer depends on expected consequences; it does suggest that these consequences increasingly hinge on self-evaluations and self-administered outcomes contingent upon one's achieving or violating one's own standards and on more abstract, temporally distant response consequences (as the foregoing section on self-regulation indicated). An individual who says, for example, that a particular action is wrong because it "violates universal standards of justice" or "goes against my conscience" is still considering the consequences of the act, but is evaluating them in more abstract terms, which go beyond immediate, concrete, externally administered outcomes for himself and which encompass a long time span (see Rachlin, 1973).

The Organization of Moral Conduct and Self-Regulation

Traditional personality-oriented approaches to the study of prosocial and self-regulatory behaviors have searched for generalized dimensions on which individual differences in stable, consistent cross-situationally attributes could be discovered. For this purpose, measures of individual differences on dimensions of impulsivity, self-control, moral thought, and conduct were constructed and their networks of correlates elaborated by empirical studies. The

basic intention of this traditional approach was to discover consistent cross-situational individual differences in generalized dispositions to behave in prosocial ways. Proponents of this approach asked such questions as, "Is the individual whose moral attitudes seem immature also likely to show consistently less self-control, greater impulsivity, less altruism, less resistance to temptation?" In accord with common sense, they assumed the answer would be clearly affirmative and sought empirical support for their intuitions. The search for consistent individual differences in moral character structure became a major effort of both trait and psychodynamic approaches to morality for many decades. In this section we will examine briefly the results and implications of these efforts as they bear on the organization of self-control, moral conduct, and moral judgment within individuals.

THE SEARCH FOR CONSISTENCIES

Correlational work on "ego strength" in general, and delay of gratification in particular, as a dimension of individual differences is illustrative of both the strategies and the findings of the dispositional approach to the organization of self-regulation and morality.

On the basis of extensive correlational research including cross-cultural studies, two contrasting patterns of delay versus impulsivity have been conceptualized as extreme poles (e.g., Mischel, 1966, 1974). The person who predominantly chooses larger delayed rewards or goals for which he must either wait or work represents one pole on this dimension. This individual is more likely to be oriented toward the future (Klineberg, 1968) and to plan carefully for distant goals. He is also likely to be brighter and more mature; to have a high level of aspiration, high scores on ego-control measures, high achievement motivation; to be more trusting and socially responsible; and to show less uncontrolled impulsivity and delinquency (e.g., Mischel,

1962, 1966, 1971, 1974; Mischel & Gilligan, 1964). This extreme pattern resembles what has been labeled the "Puritan character structure." This pattern tends to be found most often in middle and upper (in contrast to lower) socioeconomic classes, and in highly achievement-oriented ("Protestant ethic") cultures. This pattern of high ego strength is also related to a relatively high level of competence marked by higher intelligence, more mature cognitive development, and a greater capacity for sustained attention (Grim, Kohlberg, & White, 1968).

At the opposite pole is the individual who predominantly prefers immediate gratification and rejects the option of waiting or working for larger delayed goals and future satisfactions at the cost of immediate pleasures. Correlated with this orientation is a greater concern with the immediate present than with the future, and greater impulsivity. Socioculturally, this pattern is correlated with membership in the lower socioeconomic classes, with membership in cultures in which achievement orientation is low, and with indices of lesser social and cognitive competence. Clinically, persons diagnosed as "delinquents" and "psychopaths" are often characterized by an immediate reward choice pattern.

A dimension of gratification patterns such as this one also has some obvious similarity to a continuum that ranges from ego overcontrol to ego undercontrol which has been emerging from independent work by other investigators, especially the research of Jack Block and Jeanne Block (e.g., 1972; Block & Martin, 1955). While such dimensions are of descriptive value, it is important to recognize that self-control patterns tend to be highly discriminative and idiosyncratically organized within individuals (Mischel, 1973, 1974).

The extensive patterns of correlations obtained with measures of self-control have provided evidence not only for convergent validity but also for discriminant validity, which is equally important in the present theoretical view. To illustrate, Trinidadian lower-class blacks often preferred immediately available, albeit smaller, gratifications in choices offered by a white promise-maker (Mischel, 1958, 1961c). In their past experiences promises of future rewards from whites had often been broken, and they had participated in a culture in which immediate gratification was modeled and rewarded extensively (Mischel, 1961a, 1961b). The same people nevertheless saved money, planned elaborately, and were willing to give up competing immediate gratifications in order to plan ahead for many future outcomes (such as annual feasts, religious events, and carnival celebrations) whose preparation and realization were under their own control, making it plain that any generalizations about their cross-situational "impulsivity" are not justified.

It was also found that responses to questionnaires dealing with attitudes and hypothetical matters may correlate with answers on other questionnaires, but are less likely to predict nonquestionnaire behavior (Mischel, 1962). Children in one study were asked about whether they would postpone immediate smaller rewards for the sake of larger delayed outcomes in hypothetical situations (e.g., "If your father gave you a choice between a cheap new bicycle now or a fancy racing bike next month, which would you take?"). Their answers were related to their verbal responses on other questionnaires dealing with trust and a variety of verbally expressed attitudes. But what they said was not related to what they did in real delay-of-reward choices that went beyond questionnaires—for example, actual choices between things like cheap toys now or more attractive objects later (Mischel, 1962). Preferences for delayed rewards in choice situations also are unrelated to the standards children set for evaluating and rewarding their own behavior (Mischel & Masters, 1966), and to their choice of immediate, as opposed to delayed, unavoidable punishments of different magnitudes (Mischel & Grusec, 1967).

Similarly, measures eliciting direct nonverbal behavior may relate strongly to other behavioral indices in the same domain, but not strongly to questionnaires. Thus real behavioral choices between smaller but immediately available gratifications, as opposed to larger but delayed rewards, correlated significantly with such behavioral indices as resistance to temptation, but not with self-reports on questionnaires (Mischel, 1962, 1966, 1968). These findings further underline the "specificity," or discriminativeness, of behavior and the fact that close links between attitudinal and hypothetical measures, on the one hand, and behavioral ones, on the other, cannot be assumed and in fact generally are tenuous (Abelson, 1972; Mischel, 1968, 1973, 1974).

The relatively great discriminativeness and specificity that characterized research findings on self-regulation in much of the delay-of-gratification data are congruent with results from many studies of prosocial conduct found in other lines of research. Traditional trait approaches to prosocial behavior and moral conduct also have hypothesized global personality dispositions, such as "honesty" and "empathy," as generalized determinants of the individual's prosocial behaviors across diverse situations. In the last few decades empirical research on self-control and moral behavior has tended to concentrate on three areas: moral judgment and verbal standards of right and wrong (Kohlberg, 1963a); resistance to temptation in the absence of external constraint (e.g., Aronfreed & Reber, 1965; Grinder, 1962; Mackinnon, 1938; Mischel & Gilligan, 1964); and posttransgression indices of remorse and guilt (Allinsmith, 1960; Aronfreed, 1964; Sears, Maccoby, & Levin, 1957; J. W. M. Whiting, 1959). Empirical research shows these three areas of moral behavior to be either completely independent or at best only minimally interrelated (Becker, 1964; M. L. Hoffman, 1963a; Kohlberg, 1963a).

Specificity within each area also tends

to be the rule. For example, an extensive survey of all types of reactions to transgression revealed no predictable relationship among specific types of reaction (Aronfreed, 1961). In the same vein, Sears and his co-workers (1965) did not find consistent associations among various reactions to transgression. As a third example, in a study with teen-age boys, Allinsmith (1960) inferred moral feelings from the youngsters' projective story completions of descriptions of various immoral actions. The findings led Allinsmith to conclude that a person with a truly generalized conscience is a statistical rarity. Similarly, R. C. Johnson (1962) found that moral judgments across situations tend to be highly specific and even discrepant in many cases, as MacRae (1954) had noted earlier. Given these data on the discriminativeness of prosocial behavior, it is understandable that a comprehensive review indicates the "search for general [personality] correlates of prosocial behavior is . . . shortsighted" (Gergen, Gergen, & Meter, 1972, p. 105). Instead of broad links between global dispositions and diverse prosocial behaviors, the relations involve highly complex and specific interactions which cannot be adequately understood without carefully delineating the particular situation as well as the particular person variable (e.g., Staub, 1974).[4]

The discriminativeness of morality suggested by correlational findings is paralleled by results from experimental studies. For example, there is no reason to expect the changes produced by specific modeling influences to generalize widely across many contexts unless situational supports are provided to facilitate such generalization. This point is evident in a study by Prentice (1972) which demonstrated that the modeling of intentionality both by live and symbolic modeling cues was highly effective in increasing subjects' sensitivity to intentions, but had no effect on another dimension of moral judgment ("moral relativism") and no effect on antisocial behavior (postexperimental delinquent offenses). The lack of generalization from modeling of intentionality to either moral relativism or moral conduct is not surprising in view of probable differences in the specific variables influencing both of these behaviors.

Similarly, a series of studies reported by Bryan and Walbek (1970b) has indicated the discriminativeness of modeling effects on prosocial behavior. Verbal modeling of generosity (that is, statements endorsing generosity) increased children's verbal advocacy of generosity, but had no effect on their subsequent generous behavior. Conversely, modeled demonstrations of actual sharing had no effect on children's verbal endorsements of either selfishness or generosity. The children's verbal advocacy of generosity was found to be virtually unrelated to their behavioral generosity.

RELATIONS BETWEEN MORAL REASONING AND BEHAVIOR

Kohlberg (1969b), alert to the issue of the discriminativeness of prosocial behavior, provided some evidence for a relationship between level of moral reasoning and moral conduct. A close analysis of the magnitude of these associations, however, shows that they do not justify claims for a strong link. The previously noted high degree of heterogeneity in type of moral reasoning within any given subject raises questions about the internal consistency of moral reasoning across situations and hence about the upper limits of external validity for Kohlberg's measure. In fact, the predictive validity from moral reasoning to moral behavior does not appear to be better than the modest, albeit often statistically significant, personality coefficients (averaging .30) typically found in correlational personality research linking measures across diverse response modes (Mischel, 1968).

A representative example is the study by Schwartz, Feldman, Brown and Heingartner (1969) cited by Kohlberg (1971a)

as evidence for the moral reasoning–moral behavior link. These investigators correlated level of moral thought with two measures of moral behavior: helpfulness and cheating. The relationship with helpfulness was not significant for the sample as a whole. On the cheating measure, of eighteen subjects classified high in moral thought, 17 percent cheated, whereas 53 percent of those low on this dimension cheated. This relationship between cheating and moral level reached statistical significance at the .05 level of probability by means of a one-tailed chi square test. In the same study, an almost equally strong relationship was found between the subject's need for achievement and cheating, and a higher association was found between the need for affiliation and helpfulness ($p < .01$).

The moral reasoning measure seems to predict incorrectly the moral behavior of about half the subjects at the lower stages of moral maturity. Consequently, it is hard to justify the claim of a strong link between moral judgment and action. Correlations of the type obtained so far suggest that, overall, knowledge of individuals' moral reasoning would permit one to predict no more than about 10 percent of the variance in their moral behavior. This degree of predictive accuracy is not better than that found in efforts to predict moral behavior from other individual difference variables (Mischel & Gilligan, 1964), and hence does not support the unique or incremental value of moral reasoning for the prediction of moral behavior. It seems likely that predictive accuracy from moral reasoning to moral behavior would be better for selected subsamples such as the relatively small number of individuals identified as reaching the highest levels of moral maturity, and this does seem to be the case (Staub, 1974), although the sample sizes tend to be too small to permit firm conclusions. On the other hand, the value of moral reasoning for predicting moral behavior undoubtedly would be even less if one partialed out the role of intelligence, socioeconomic level, and age—all of which affect both moral reasoning and moral behavior (Kohlberg, 1969b). To adequately assess the discriminative value of moral reasoning in predicting moral behavior, one would want to compare predictions from moral maturity scores with those achieved from measures of IQ, socioeconomic level, and age in the same sample. One must recall that Hartshorne and May (1928) found IQ to be correlated .344 with honesty—a correlation approximately as large as the average consistency of honest behavior itself.

Kohlberg (1958) did one of the rare studies in this domain which tried to partial out the role of IQ and age. In his study of boys aged 10 to 16 he found a correlation of .46 between maturity of moral judgment and teachers' ratings of the boys' consciences. Since both moral maturity scores and conscience ratings were correlated with both IQ and age, a partial correlation was computed to control for mental age. The resulting coefficient was .31—a figure not discriminable from the average "personality coefficient" found throughout the domain of personality research.[5] This result is even more modest when one considers that in the study of morality, just as in other content areas, correlations tend to be spuriously high when based on trait ratings (as in Kohlberg, 1958) rather than on behavioral tests. Correlations from such trait ratings tend to be inflated by the variety of biases and distorting stereotypes discussed previously (D'Andrade, 1970; Mischel, 1968).

Recognition of the limits of moral-reasoning measures for the prediction of moral conduct should not detract from the interest in the development of moral judgments. How people reason about the solution of moral dilemmas is a fascinating phenomenon, and age-related changes in this activity are especially informative. But it should be apparent that an understanding of moral reasoning does not obviate the need to understand the many other aspects

and determinants of moral (and immoral) behavior. Alston (1971) a philosopher, commenting on Kohlberg's position, puts it this way:

there is no reason to think that [Kohlberg's moral stages (1971a)] will do the whole job. In fact, there is every reason to think that it will not. So long as there is any significant discrepancy between the moral judgment a person makes about a situation (or would make if the question arose) and what he actually does, there will be a need, in describing persons, for an account of what they are likely to do as well as what they are likely to think. And Kohlberg has given us no reason to suppose that there is no such significant discrepancy (p. 283).

In most content domains, different measures of ideology, beliefs, and attitudes tend to be more closely related to each other than to noncognitive indices of behavior in the same content area (Mischel, 1968, 1969). This also seems to hold in the domain of morality, in which indices of moral ideology tend to relate well to other measures of social and political beliefs. For example, it is reassuring (but not particularly surprising) to find that a student responding to Kohlberg's moral dilemmas test with reasons involving principles of equality, the universality of all moral formulations, and concern with the issue of justice (thereby earning a Stage 6 score) would be unlikely to agree with a sexist slogan such as one that denigrates the political role of women on the conservatism scale of an ideology measure (Fishkin, Kenniston, & Mackinnon, 1973). Similarly unsurprising, the same study found that individuals who dominantly justify their moral decisions in terms of law and order are less likely to endorse such slogans as *Kill the pigs, Property is theft,* and *Turn on, tune in, and drop out.* Such internal consistencies in belief statements were demonstrated by high correlations between moral reasoning emphasizing law and order and a conservative opposition to radical violence on an ideology scale. These data provide further support for the well-established conclusion that there is substantial consistency in answers to measures of political and social ideology (e.g., the classical F-scale research on political and social conservatism in beliefs and attitudes). But while cognitive measures of beliefs and values may be both internally consistent and temporally enduring (E.L. Kelly, 1955), the link between attitudes and behavior may be tenuous (Abelson, 1972; Festinger, 1964).

IMPLICATIONS

In sum, data on the discriminativeness of self-control and moral behavior provide little support for belief in a unitary intrapsychic moral agency like the superego or for a unitary trait entity of conscience or honesty (Mischel, 1968, 1971). Rather than acquiring a homogeneous conscience which determines uniformly all aspects of their self-control, people develop subtler discriminations which depend on many moderating variables, involve complex interactions, and encompass diverse components (Mischel, 1973, 1974). These components include moral judgments, voluntary delay of reward, resistance to temptation, self-reactions following transgression, and self-evaluative and self-reinforcing patterns, each of which includes rather discrete subprocesses which tend to be only modestly and complexly interrelated, and which may be idiosyncratically organized within each individual (Mischel, 1974). In light of the multiplicity and complexity of the determinants of the diverse components of choice behavior in general, and of "ego strength" and prosocial behaviors more specifically, it becomes understandable that gross, overall, appraisals of a person's status on any single dimension of individual differences tend to have limited utility. For example, to predict an individual's altruistic behavior accurately one may have to know his age, his sex, the experimenter's sex, the expected consequences of altruism in that situation,

the models to whom the subject has been exposed recently, and the subject's immediately prior experience—to list only a few of the many variables which may be relevant.

This does not mean that predictions cannot be made with some accuracy from subject variables to relevant self-control and prosocial behaviors, but it does imply stringent limits on the range and level of relationships that can reasonably be expected. A representative example comes from a recent attempt to relate individual differences in young children's expectancies about "locus of control" to their behavior in theoretically relevant situations (Mischel, Zeiss, & Zeiss, 1974). To investigate these interactions, the Stanford Preschool Internal–External Scale (SPIES) was developed as a measure of expectancies about whether events occur as a consequence of the child's own action ("internal control") or as a consequence of external forces ("external control"). Expectancies about locus of control were measured separately for positive and negative events so that scores would reflect expectancies for degree of internal control of positive events $(I+)$, of negative events $(I-)$, and a sum of these two (total I). Individual differences in $I+$, $I-$, and total I were then correlated with the children's ability to delay gratification under diverse working and waiting conditions.

The results provided highly specific but theoretically meaningful patterns of relationships. To illustrate, relationships between total I and overall delay behavior were negligible, and $I+$ was unrelated to $I-$. As expected, $I+$ (but not $I-$) was found to be related to persistence in three separate situations where instrumental activity would result in a *positive* outcome; $I-$ (but not $I+$) was related to persistence when instrumental activity could prevent the occurrence of a *negative* outcome. The total findings showed that individual differences in children's beliefs about their ability to control outcomes are partial determinants of their goal-directed behavior; but the relationships depend on extremely specific moderating conditions, with regard to both the type of behavior and the type of belief. If such moderating conditions had not been taken into account, and if all indices of "delay behavior" had been combined regardless of their positive or negative valence, the actual role of the relevant individual differences would have been totally obscured.

Given such results (reviewed in Mischel, 1968), the present orientation to self-regulation emphasizes the relative specificity of the components of self-control behavior and hence the importance of the specific cognitive and situational variables that influence them and interact with person variables (Mischel, 1973, 1974). Consequently it is necessary to be increasingly sensitive to the role of situational variables, and to the need to study experimentally the specific mechanisms that influence self-regulation and prosocial conduct (see Rosenhan, Moore, & Underwood, Chap. 13, and Staub, 1974).

The significance of the psychological situation for prosocial behavior has been vividly demonstrated in a simulated prison study (Haney, Banks, & Zimbardo, 1973). College student volunteers were carefully selected, on the basis of extensive interviewing and diagnostic testing, to have exemplary backgrounds and no antisocial tendencies. Nevertheless, less than one week after being exposed to what the authors refer to as the inherently pathological characteristics of the realistically simulated prison situation itself, all subjects assigned the role of guards were exhibiting extreme antisocial behavior. The authors concluded that few of the "guards'" reactions could be attributed to individual differences on generalized dimensions (such as, empathy, rigid adherence to conventional values, Machiavellianism) existing before the subjects begin to play their assigned roles. The potency of the situation undoubtedly left some lasting effects, particularly in the realm of beliefs as evidenced by the subjects'

postexperimental statements—for example, "I learned that people can easily forget that others are human" (Haney, Banks, & Zimbardo, 1973, p. 88). But it is also most likely that once the prison experiment was over, the "guards" gave up their new affrontive and harassing behavior and all subjects soon started to respond in terms of the current context of their lives.

THE INTERPRETATION OF CONSISTENCY AND DISCRIMINATIVENESS

Affect, attitude, cognition, and behavior are not inevitably linked in any specific or uniform manner. Whether or not they will be correlated depends on whether or not they lead to common or differential consequences. Thus the correlation between the expression of aggressive attitudes or beliefs and hurtful actions will be low when one is allowed but the other is firmly prohibited (Bandura, 1973). Similarly, if moral judgments, prosocial beliefs, and prosocial actions are each influenced by different contingencies in particular situations, they should not be expected to covary. If the same public official is rewarded privately for his special attention to corporate interests, but receives enthusiastic praise and votes for his public utterances on behalf of the consumer, conditions are ripe for discrepant behavior. Indeed, so-called moral dilemmas may be viewed as the result of discrepancies in behavior-outcome contingencies across response modes or situations. People may often be indignant about what they view as a moral outrage, condemn it in principle, experience sincere emotional upset about it, and nevertheless remain uninfluenced in their own conduct.

Since most social behaviors lead to positive consequences in some situations but not in others, highly discriminative specific expectancies tend to be developed and the relatively low correlations typically found among a person's response pattern across situations become understandable (Mischel, 1968). Expectancies also will not become generalized across response modes when the consequences for similar content expressed in different response modes are sharply different, as they are in most life circumstances. Therefore, expectancies tend to become relatively specific, rather than broadly generalized. Although a person's expectancies (and hence performances) tend to be highly discriminative, there certainly is some generalization, but their patterning in the individual tends to be idiosyncratically organized.

From the viewpoint of the traditional personality paradigm, the "specificity" and "inconsistency" found in behavior are construed as a problem that is usually blamed on methodological flaws and inadequate tests. In that light, the specificity of the relations between social behavior and conditions traditionally has been interpreted as reflecting the inadequacies of the measures, poor sampling, and the limitations of the particular clinical judges or raters. These and many other similar methodological problems undoubtedly are sources of error and seriously limit the degree of consistency which can be observed (J. Block, 1968; Emmerich, 1969). But from the present perspective, the specificity so often obtained in studies of noncognitive personality dimensions accurately reflect man's impressive discriminative facility and the inadequacy of the assumption of global dispositions—not merely distortions of measurement (Mischel, 1968). Indeed, as previously noted (Mischel, 1973), the term "discriminative facility" seems to fit the data better than "specificity" and avoids the unfortunate negative semantic connotations of "specificity" when applied to persons (e.g., the implications of inconsistency, insincerity, fickleness, unreliability; see also Gergen, 1968).

An emphasis on the discriminativeness of behavior and its close links to the conditions in which it occurs also leads to a different interpretation of data on the age-related sequence of moral judgment.

Moral judgments which do not fit clearly into a fixed, progressive developmental sequence have been interpreted as representing regressive behavior (Kohlberg & Kramer, 1969) or the disequilibrium of stage transitions (Turiel, 1973). For example, a longitudinal study of moral judgments by Kohlberg and Kramer (1969) reported that a small percentage of subjects who had been assessed primarily at Stage 4 during late high school showed a good deal of Stage 2 thinking during their college years. These same subjects reached Stage 5 by the time they were in their early twenties. Kohlberg and Kramer interpret this interruption in stage progression as a temporary regression caused by the pressures of college life. Turiel (1973), on the other hand, suggests that responses reflecting the conflict and disequilibrium of transition may be incorrectly categorized as regressive because they resemble earlier stages in content. He argues that transitional reasoning has the structure of later stages, thus invoking the phenotypic–genotypic distinction often called in to explain discrepant or anomalous behaviors (Mischel, 1969). But a finding like the one that college students give moral reasons scorable at a lower stage than those they gave in high school can also be seen as reflecting not a regression from an invariant sequence, but a discriminative responsivity to changing models, reference groups, values, and personal contingencies in the individual's changing life-style. The college students in this case may be seen as responding to the relativism encouraged and modeled in a liberal academic atmosphere, rather than either as regressing or as experiencing disequilibrium in their progress through a series of predetermined stages.

ENCODING STRATEGIES AND THE CONSTRUCTION OF CONSISTENCY

Like the psychologist, the layman also groups events into categories and organizes them actively into meaningful units. He encodes and categorizes events rather than describing his experience with operational definitions. Observers readily tend to group information about persons in dispositional categories, such as *honest, intolerant, freaky, do-gooder* (Jeffery & Mischel, 1972). Recognition of the existence of sharp discriminativeness in behavior must be coupled with the realization that people easily construct consistent impressions about their own and others' generalized characteristics. People invoke traits and other dispositions as ways of describing and explaining their experience and themselves, just as professional psychologists do, and tend to go easily beyond the analysis of specific behaviors to the attribution of generalized dispositions. Hopefully the investigations of personal construct systems (e.g., Argyle & Little, 1972), of implicit personality theories (e.g., Hamilton, 1971; Schneider, 1973), and of self-concepts (e.g., Gergen, 1968) will clarify an important set of still inadequately understood person variables.

In the process of grouping personality information about the self and others the subject tends to jump quickly from the observation of discrete acts to the inference of global internalized dispositions (Heider, 1958). While behavior may often be highly situation-specific, it also seems true that in daily life people tend to construe each other as if each were highly consistent, and they construct consistent personalities for each other even on the basis of relatively inconsistent behavioral fragments. Thus perceived unity often exists in the face of behavioral discriminativeness. It is remarkable how each of us usually manages to reconcile his seemingly diverse behaviors into one subjectively consistent whole. The same individual who cheats on one occasion but not on another, who lies in one context but is truthful in another, who steals at one time but helps a friend generously and unselfishly at another, may still readily construe himself as basically honest and moral. People show impressive ingenuity in their ability to transform their seemingly discrepant behaviors into unified wholes (Mischel, 1969).

How can we understand the discriminativeness of behavior in light of the equally compelling impression of basic consistency in ourselves and in the people we know? Many complex factors are probably involved (Jones & Nisbett, 1971; Kahneman & Tversky, 1973; Mischel, 1968, 1969); but part of the answer to this question may be that people tend to reduce cognitive inconsistencies (Festinger, 1957) and, in general, to simplify information so that they can deal with it.

Cognitive consistency also tends to be enhanced by selective attention and coding processes which filter new information in a manner that permits it to be integrated with existing cognitive structures (Norman, 1969). Cognitive processes that facilitate the construction and maintenance of perceived consistency have been elaborated elsewhere (D'Andrade, 1970; Hayden & Mischel, 1972; Mischel, 1968, 1969). After information has been integrated with existing cognitive structures and becomes part of long-term memory, it remains enduringly available and exerts further stabilizing effects. For example, the individual's subjective conception of his own identity and continuity presumably rests heavily on his ability to remember (construct) subjectively similar behaviors on his part over long periods and across many situations. That is, the person can abstract the common elements of his behavior over time and across settings, thereby focusing on his more stable attributes.

In the construction and attribution of dispositional consistencies, observers tend to be self-enhancing. Consider, for example, the attribution of the causes for behavior to internal causes (the person's dispositions) versus external causes (situations). Two studies investigated the attribution of internality (locus of internal–external control) for positive and negative events by children of various ages and by college students (Mischel, Mailer, & Zeiss, 1973). Subjects were asked to make internal versus external attributions for the same positive and negative events occurring to the self, to a liked other, and to a disliked other. Attributions tended to be consistently self-enhancing, with more credit given to the self for positive events and less for negative events (compared especially to a disliked other).

JUSTIFICATION PROCESSES AND HAZARDS

The discriminativeness of prosocial behavior, and its idiosyncratic organization within each person, has important social implications. It should alert us to the fact that the same individual who espouses high moral principles may engage in harmful aggressive actions against others who violate his conceptions of justice. Pascal's comment that "Evil is never done so thoroughly or so well as when it is done with a good conscience" is supported by the many historical and contemporary incidents in which the individuals who committed evil deeds seemed more deficient in compassion and empathy than in moral reasoning (Keniston, 1970).

History is replete with atrocities that were justified by invoking the highest principles and that were perpetrated upon victims who were equally convinced of their own moral principles. In the name of justice, of the common welfare, of universal ethics, and of God, millions of people have been killed and whole cultures destroyed. In recent history, concepts of universal right, equality, freedom, and social equity have been used to justify every variety of murder including genocide. Presidential assassinations, airplane hijackings, and massacres of Olympic athletes have been committed for allegedly selfless motives of highest morality and principle. The supreme moral self-sacrifices of the Japanese suicide pilots in World War II were perceived as moral outrages by others who did not share their perspective.

People tend to be facile about justifying their own diverse actions and commitments—no matter how reprehensible these acts may seem to others. A wide variety of self-deceptive mechanisms may be used to facilitate and excuse the most horrendous acts. Invocation of higher principles, dehumanization of victims, diffusion and displacement of responsibility, blame attribution, and the adoption of inhumane codes for self-reinforcement all may serve to maintain extraordinarily cruel aggressions (Bandura, 1973).

The extremely complex relations among diverse aspects of prosocial behavior within the same person, and the specific interactions between human conduct and the psychological conditions in which it occurs, prevent global generalizations about the overall nature and causes of moral—and immoral—actions. It is tempting but misleading to categorize people into the cross-situationally moral versus the broadly immoral. A world of good guys versus bad guys—as in the Western films in which the cowboys' white or black hats permit easy identification of the virtuous and the villainous—is seductive. More sophisticated social science versions of stratification systems which categorize people in terms of their overall level of morality, unless carefully moderated, can lead to an elitism that is empirically unjustified as well as socially hazardous. While it may be useful for some purposes to label and assess people's status on our dimensions of character and moral value, perhaps the greatest challenge to social science will be to discover the optimal conditions that can help each person realize himself in the ways he construes as best within the great range of capacities open to him.

Chapter 5.   A Cognitive Social-Learning Approach to Morality and Self-Regulation

[1] Preparation of this paper was facilitated by National Institute of Mental Health grant M-6830 and National Science Foundation grant GS-32582 to Walter Mischel.

[2] In the present view, just because a particular cognitive or behavioral tendency occurs later in development does not necessarily mean that it is superior to its predecessors. As Alston (1971, p. 275) has noted, the concept of arbitrary exceptions to rules logically depends on the concept of rules, but it enjoys no moral superiority on those grounds. An example in the realm of moral reasoning is Kohlberg's "Stage 3" conception of the value of human life based on social sharing, community, and love, which may depend logically on the instrumental and hedonistic value of life more characteristic of "Stage 2." This sequence does not necessarily mean, however, that moral thinking involving the former is superior to moral thinking involving the latter.

[3] One also wonders about the degree to which age-related changes in moral reasoning are unique to moral development or are merely one aspect of age-related changes in the cognitive and verbal styles used to explain and justify choices. For example, would similar changes (in terms of use of increasingly general, "universal," abstract rules) be found if one studied age-related changes in the reasons given for esthetic preferences, vocational choices, peer preferences, and so on? Moreover, the links between moral maturity, IQ, and mental age also suggest the need for a scale of verbal intellectual sophistication as a control instrument. On such a scale answers might be scored in terms of their increasing use of higher-order abstractions and generalizations (i.e., references to universals) versus less intellectually sophisticated (i.e., more concrete) self-references and personal preferences and feelings.

[4] Staub (1974) found significant correlations between several indices of prosocial orientation, including moral reasoning and helping behavior; but these associations depend on the specific conditions, the particular measures used, and the exact nature of the help needed.

[5] Noting the grossness of standard IQ tests, Aronfreed (1968c) perceptively questions "whether any significant variation in principles of conscience would be apparent among children who, regardless of their age, had been identified as comparable in general cognitive capacity by techniques which were more sensitive to the specific operations of their thought processes" (p. 266).

The Biology of Morality

H. J. Eysenck

Introduction

The study of morality must begin by asking the right question. The usual problem posed, that of evil, is not the real problem at all. It is pointless to ask why people behave in a selfish, aggressive, immoral manner; such behavior is clearly reinforcing in that it gives the person or organism acting in such a fashion immediate satisfaction. Furthermore, such behavior is demonstrated by animals and young children without any need of teaching; it is "natural" in a real and obvious sense. The proper question is rather the opposite one: How does it come about that people (and animals) do not always act in an immoral, antisocial manner? How can we account for "good" behavior, that is, behavior which at first sight at least goes counter to the interests of the person concerned?

The answer often given is that socialized behavior is enforced on us by the existence of laws, and the sanction of police and prison. But this answer is clearly not sufficient, even though it contains some elements of truth. The force of law

is necessary, but not sufficient, to account for socialized behavior. Many actions are outside the scope of legal sanction, and yet are performed in a socialized manner. Even when we look at criminal activities, law enforcement comes into contact with only a small fraction of these. The majority of crimes are never brought to the attention of the police. Of those which are, only a minority are ever brought home to the perpetrator, and even then he often gets away with a caution. The chances of "getting away with it" are probably between 90 and 99 in 100; in other words, the odds are overwhelmingly in favor of the criminal. On a rational calculus, crime probably does pay; yet most of us do not indulge in serious crime. If this were not so, civilized society would be impossible to maintain; we would need more policemen than private citizens to maintain law and order—and who would maintain law and order among all the policemen? Even among thieves, we are told, there must be honor; how does this come about? Clearly the appeal to the force of the law accounts for only a portion of socialized conduct; for the major part we must look for another explanatory principle. Religion gives us the word *conscience* to explain such conduct; an "inner light" guides our behavior in the direction of morality. But religion fails to tell us just how this miracle is accomplished, and even if the answer were revealed, divine guidance would not be a scientific explanation.

Psychologists often talk about the "internalization" of external (usually parental) rules and precepts. This may serve as a verbal explanation of "conscience," but unless we can independently and experimentally examine this process of internalization, it cannot tell us much about the phenomenon in question. What precisely goes on when rules and precepts are internalized? What are the mechanisms used? Why does this process work in some children and not in others, even when to all appearances circumstances are very similar?

A Conditioning Theory of Conscience

My own explanation links the acquisition of a "conscience" with the conditioning of anxiety. In terms of this hypothesis, *conscience is a conditioned reflex.* Consider the young child's behavior; he will frequently do things that his parents, teachers, and peers regard as *bad, naughty,* or *wicked.* Swift punishment usually follows such actions: a slap, being sent to his room, going without supper, writing five hundred lines, being laughed at, or some other unpleasant consequence. Now here we have a perfect conditioning paradigm. The naughty action is the conditioned stimulus, like Pavlov's bell to which the dog became conditioned. The "punishment" is the unconditioned stimulus, like the food Pavlov presented to his dog after the bell sounded. And the unconditioned response is the pain experienced as a consequence of the punishment, just as in Pavlov's experiment salivation was the unconditioned response. We would expect

that anxiety (conditioned fear) would gradually become the conditioned response to carrying out or even contemplating the naughty action, and that this immediate negatively reinforcing consequence would discourage both contemplation and execution of the action in question. This conditioned anxiety is experienced by the child as "conscience." The acquisition of this "conscience" is, of course, facilitated by labeling, as is its generalization over different types of actions. By calling a variety of actions bad, evil, or naughty, we encourage the child to identify them all in one category, and to react in the future with anxiety to everything thus labeled. This, very briefly and not altogether adequately, is my account of the growth of "conscience." The supporting evidence is discussed in detail in my book *Crime and Personality* (H. J. Eysenck, 1964/1970a).

The advantages of this account of conscience are twofold. In the first place, it makes use of well-established principles based on detailed laboratory experiments; it does not invoke divine guidance or ad hoc concepts. In the second place, it leads to testable deductions. We shall be concerned next with these deductions. Let us here note merely one implication of the scheme set out above. If good conduct results from proper conditioning, then bad behavior and immorality can result from two separate causes (both of which could be acting simultaneously). The first set of causes might be identified as *social factors.* Conditioning of the kind required for socialization will not take place if parents, teachers, and peers fail to provide the requisite unconditioned stimuli; and it will not take place if they provide unconditioned stimuli in response to the wrong conditioned stimuli. Perhaps the very multiplicity of social agents will ensure that some conditioning does take place. A child's parents may be found wanting, but his teachers may play their role, or else the child's peers may set upon him if he is found to steal, lie, or otherwise misbehave. But the lack of adequate social conditioning is clearly an important consideration in the formation of bad behavior, and the laissez-faire doctrines introduced by Freudian fears of repression are likely to have lessened the impact of proper conditioning procedures.

The second set of causes of immoral behavior might be identified as *biological factors*. Pavlov showed that there are enormous differences in conditionability among dogs. Some would need only two or three trials, while others would barely condition after two hundred or three hundred. Similar differences can be found in humans. Some people are very difficult to condition, while others condition with great ease. These individual differences are very important, and they form the basis of my account of moral behavior. In dealing with these biological factors I shall, for the sake of exposition, disregard the social factors mentioned above. I am doing this not because social factors are unimportant, but because little research has been done on them, and also because other authors in this book will be dealing with them. In reading my account, readers should always bear in mind the usual scientific caution of *ceteris paribus*.

Conditioning and Personality

The concept of conditionability provides us with a link between criminality, psychopathy, and general immorality, on the one hand, and personality, on the other. To make clear the nature of this connection, we must first state briefly, and again rather dogmatically, the conception of personality employed here. Descriptively, there is much agreement that two major dimensions of personality account for a good deal of the individual differences which are observed among people. These two major dimensions (or types) are given various names by different authors, but will be referred to here as *extraversion–introversion* (E) and *neuroticism–stability* (N) (H. J. Eysenck & Eysenck, 1969).

Extraverts are typically sociable, impulsive, talkative, carefree, and dominant, while introverts are the opposite. Not everyone is totally an extravert or an introvert, of course; these traits are distributed in the rough shape of the normal probability curve, with most people somewhere in the middle (ambivert) zone. High neuroticism is evidenced by anxiety, worries, sleeplessness, touchiness, restlessness, and other emotional disturbances; with stability being characterized by the opposite qualities. These two dimensions are independent of each other, as shown in Figure 6.1; they are also independent of intelligence. There is strong evidence that heredity plays a powerful part in determining a person's position in this two-dimensional framework (H. J. Eysenck, 1967), and this genetic predisposition interacts with environmental pressure to produce the phenotype, that is, the observable personality.

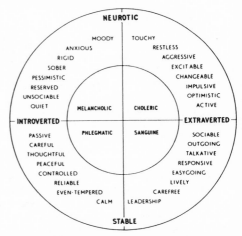

Figure 6.1 Two-dimensional factor pattern showing main dimensions of personality.

This two-dimensional account of personality does not embrace everything that is known about personality, or everything that remains to be known. It is relevant to our discussion for the simple reason that criminals and others whose conduct is "immoral" are found in the high E–high N quadrant, that is, are found to share high neuroticism and high extraversion. (Neurotics were predicted, and have been found, to fall into the high N–low E quadrant, that is, to share high neuroticism and high introversion). These findings have been documented elsewhere (H. J. Eysenck, 1970a) in considerable detail; we will return to them later. Here let me just quote one example of the work that has been done to substantiate the theory. Burt (1965) studied 763 children and followed them over a thirty-year period. These children had been rated by their teachers with respect to E and N; 15 percent and 18 percent, respectively, later became habitual offenders or neurotics. Of those who became offenders, 63 percent had been rated as high on N, and 54 percent had been rated high on E; only 3 percent had been rated high on introversion. Of those who became neurotics, 59 percent had been rated high on N, and 44 percent high on introversion; only 1 percent had been rated high on E. The relationship is far from perfect, but when we consider the many chance factors that confuse lawful connections, and the unreliability attending teachers' ratings, then we may appreciate that there is indeed a link between personality, crime, and neurosis very much as predicted.

What led to the prediction? The writer has put forward a theory of personality, and supported it with much evidence from laboratory research, which may be used to forge the link between these various concepts. Put very briefly, this theory says that behaviors associated with E and N are mediated by certain physiological-anatomical structures, as shown in Figure 6.2. Differences in N are mediated by the autonomic nervous system, which is known to subserve emotional expression and whose functioning is governed and coordinated by the visceral brain (VB). If this system is overactive—reacting too quickly and too strongly to emotional stimuli, and failing to cease acting upon withdrawal of the

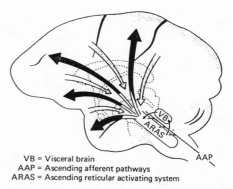

VB = Visceral brain
AAP = Ascending afferent pathways
ARAS = Ascending reticular activating system

Figure 6.2   Diagrammatic representation of physiological basis for two main dimensions of personality.

stimuli in question—then we are dealing with a person predisposed to high degrees of neuroticism or emotionality. Low N subjects, on the other hand, react slowly and weakly, with cessation of reaction immediately after the stimulus is withdrawn. This, then, is the biological basis of N. The biological basis of E is centered on the arousal system, and in particular on the ascending reticular activating system (ARAS). This system maintains tonus in the cortex, alerting it to deal with incoming stimuli. These stimuli activate the reticular system through collateral neurons, and the reticular system in turn activates the cortex to enable it to deal with the incoming information. High degrees of arousal are posited to be associated with introversion, low degrees of arousal with extraversion. In other words, introverts are characterized by a strongly dominant cortex, extraverts by a much less dominant cortex.

It is important to grasp very clearly the implications of this theory, as at first sight the relation may seem to be the wrong way round. The behavior of the extravert is uninhibited, but his cortex is in a state of *disarousal*, or inhibition. Conversely, the cortex of the introvert is in a state of *disinhibition*, or arousal, but his conduct is inhibited. This is so because the main function of the cortex is to inhibit the activities of lower centers; thus a highly aroused cortex inhibits behavior. Alcohol furnishes a good example. It inhibits the cortex, and thus disinhibits behavior, making people more extraverted. So much for the general theory; details and experimental support are given elsewhere (H. J. Eysenck, 1967).

How do we connect these inherited differences in the physiological-anatomical structures of the brain, and the various types of behavior which cause us to label a person extravert or introvert, neurotic or stable? In the case of N there is no difficulty. It is the direct experience of high degrees of excitation of the autonomic system which the individual labels fear or anxiety or worry. But in the case of cortical arousal and extraversion, the connection is less direct. We can indeed introspect and feel degrees of arousal or drowsiness, but only if these states are extreme. The usual run of differences encountered during the course of the day is probably not introspectible at all, or at best only with great difficulty. In any case, these experiences are not themselves motivating, as experiences of autonomic excitation are. Strong sympathetic stimulation—with its attendant quick and strong heartbeat, cessation of digestion, drying up of the mouth, and many other unpleasant consequences—is itself negatively reinforcing, and thus provides motivation for action.

How, then, is cortical arousal linked with behavior? One direct line is through conditioning. Pavlov showed that conditioning is directly dependent on cortical arousal, and experiments with human subjects have since verified this point abundantly. If introverts do indeed live in a general state of higher cortical arousal than do extraverts, then we would expect introverts to condition more quickly; this was the burden of an earlier version of my theory (H. J. Eysenck, 1957). We could go on from there to argue that the failure of extraverts to condition is instrumental

in their tending toward criminality, just as the ease with which introverts form conditioned anxiety responses is responsible for their liability to neurotic disorders. In both cases N would be conceived as a drive that multiplies with the particular habits (criminal or neurotic) that are being established, making these habits much stronger than would be the case in low N subjects. There is evidence that N fulfills precisely this function (H. J. Eysenck, 1970a). The link is clear and direct, but is the theory true?

There are by now almost one hundred studies of the hypothetical relation between E and conditioning, using various types of conditioned response (for example, eye blink to puff of air, galvanic skin response to shock). These experiments do not always support the hypothesis. The reason for the failure is quite simple. The theory I put forward indicates clearly that the predicted relation is dependent on certain parameters, and that improper choice of parameter values will lead to zero correlations, or even to a reversal of the expected relationships. Among the parameters explicitly mentioned were strength of the unconditioned response (weak responses being favorable to introverts), conditioned stimulus–unconditioned stimulus interval (short intervals being favorable to introverts), and partial versus complete reinforcement (partial reinforcement being favorable to introverts). Most of the studies unfavorable to the theory used wrong parameter values, and hence are irrelevant. H. J. Eysenck and Levey (1967) have reported an experiment on eyelid conditioning in which they systematically varied all three parameters; Figures 6.3 and 6.4 report the results. It will be seen that under conditions which the theory predicts as favorable to introverts, introverts condition very much better, while under the reverse conditions extraverts condition somewhat better.[1]

Other criticisms made of the notion of "conditionability" are that (1) it implies that different types of conditioning should

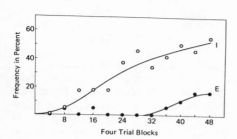

Figure 6.3 Eye-blink conditioning of introverted and extraverted subjects under unfavorable conditions.

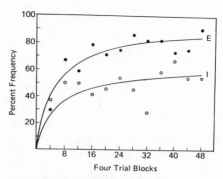

Figure 6.4 Eye-blink conditioning of introverted and extraverted subjects under favorable conditions.

intercorrelate, which on the whole they do not; and (2) aversive conditioning has usually been sampled, and appetitive conditioning might not follow the same laws. The reason for the failure of different types of conditioning to intercorrelate is, as noted, the disregard of experimenters for the proper choice of parameter values; unless these are properly chosen, no correlations can be expected. There is now in existence a study that refutes both of the above criticisms by demonstrating a healthy correlation between an appetitive and an aversive form of conditioning (Barr & McConaghy, 1972). While this whole field is still very much in a state of ferment, the available evidence supports the general theory, with respect to both the personality-conditioning correlation and the importance of parameter values.[2]

Sensation Seeking

The conditioning link is not the only one that connects arousal patterns in the cortex with certain types of conduct; there are many others (H. J. Eysenck, 1967). In religious terms, immoral conduct is mediated through two concepts. *Conscience* warns us against such conduct, and may succeed in preventing us from indulging in it; but we would never have

occasion to contemplate the desirability of behaving in such a fashion were it not for *temptation*. Lack of cortical arousal can generate its own kinds of temptation. Moralists have often pointed out that the devil finds work for idle hands. A state of boredom, which motivates the individual to seek sensations of various kinds, is closely allied to a state of cortical disarousal. I have posited an optimal level of cortical disarousal to which each individual aspires. When there is too little arousal, the individual is bored, and seeks to increase arousal; when there is too much, the individual is overextended, and seeks to decrease arousal (H. J. Eysenck, 1963). This notion of sensation seeking has been taken up and extended by Zuckerman, Kolin, Price, and Zorb (1964), who have constructed a special "sensation-seeking scale" to measure this hypothetical quality. Farley and Farley (1967, 1970) have demonstrated that this scale correlates quite well with extraversion—particularly with impulsivity rather than sociability— and there is also evidence that criminals score more highly on this scale (Zuckerman, 1972). Along this line of argument, we might account for the greater sexual delinquency of extraverts, their liking for constant change (work, sexual partners, homes, etc.), and also their preference for strong sensory input ("bright lights and loud music"). The well-documented greater susceptibility of extraverts to drugs (they drink more, smoke more, and take more soft and hard drugs than do introverts) might also be a consequence of low cortical arousal.

Thus extraverts have a greater built-in susceptibility to temptation, because of their low level of cortical arousal. Their needs are greater than those of introverts; and the pursuit of these needs is likely to bring extraverts into conflict with society —although not necessarily with the law. Many of the sexual practices of the extravert, as compared with those of the introvert, are considered "perverted" but not criminal (H. J. Eysenck, 1971); and although their attitudes in this field are asocial or antisocial, they do not fall foul of the law. However, a liking for wine, women, and song, though at first innocent, may easily lead to other less innocent activities, just as drug taking may often lead to more serious crimes, through a need to obtain money for drugs. There is clearly a continuum here. Whether the extravert will go so far along this continuum that he comes into conflict with the law depends on many factors in his environment, his luck, and so on. What seems to be clear is that sensation-seeking tendencies in the extravert expose him to temptations the introvert does not encounter—or at least not to anything like the same extent. The very dangers inherent in antisocial conduct may act as an incentive to the low-arousal extravert!

We now have a model linking extraversion, through failure to condition and through sensation seeking, with antisocial and asocial conduct. This model has received much support from studies linking extraversion with criminality. The observed correlations are not nearly as strong as one might wish (Passingham, 1972), and it might be useful to look at the reasons for this comparative failure. In the first place, criminals are far from being a homogeneous group. Murderers are notoriously different from thieves, and in fact have been found to be introverted rather than extraverted (S. B. G. Eysenck & Eysenck, 1970). Sex criminals differ from other types of criminal; the violent differ from the inadequate; and so on. It is clearly foolhardy to try to generalize about such a heterogeneous group, and it is surprising that positive results are possible at all.

In the second place, the theory states that it is in the high N–high E quadrant that an undue proportion of criminals should be located. This hypothesis cannot be adequately tested by using one dimension at a time, as has usually been done. Burgess (1972) has shown that even with data where there are no significant differences on E between criminals and controls, highly significant differences can be found in the proportions which fall into the quadrant in question.[3] A third possible reason for the lower than expected correlation between extraversion and criminality is that extraversion is a concept which rests essentially on the intercorrelations among a number of more restricted traits such as sociability, impulsivity, and optimism. The possibility exists that the correlation between E and criminality depends more on some of these traits than on others. It has been shown several times, for example, that impulsivity is far more important than sociability in this context (H. J. Eysenck & Eysenck, 1970; S. B. G. Eysenck & Eysenck, 1971). The finding that sociability is less important might be due to inherent difficulties in the questionnaire study of incarcerated prisoners, difficulties which arise particularly strongly in relation to sociability. Questions relating to partygoing or social intercourse may be rather meaningless to prisoners cooped up in isolation. It is unlikely, however, that this possibility would account fully for the greater significance of impulsivity in the correlation between E and criminality. Levey (1972) has shown that the correlation between E and eye-blink conditioning similarly depends far more on impulsivity than on sociability. Isolating the critical components of extraversion is an important task for future study. (Levey has also shown that the differences in conditioning between introverts and extroverts are much larger with high N subjects than with low N subjects; this clearly links up with the previously cited Burgess quadrant studies, 1972.) When all these cautions are borne in mind, the relation between theory and fact becomes reasonably close.

Psychopathy and Cortical Arousal

In spite of this relatively good correspondence between theory and data, there are sound reasons for looking for alternative ways of testing the theory. The main reason is the very gross fashion in which *criminality* measures *immorality*. Clearly a large measure of error is involved here. Some activities are criminal today but may not be tomorrow. Homosexuality was a crime in England a few years ago, but is not a crime now. Moreover, the criminals we test are not a random sample of all criminals, but only of those who got caught, and there may be marked differences between those who are and those who are not caught. Even among the criminals we study, there are great variations in immorality. Large numbers are criminal to their fingertips—evil, immoral beasts who prey on society and use almost all their talents and strength to harm others. Large numbers are also dull and inadequate—people who have no wish to harm anyone, but who simply cannot get by in our complex society and become criminals *faute de mieux*, as it were. Such men will throw a brick through a shop window on a cold winter's night, and then wait for the police to run them in; this is their only way of securing a warm bed and some food. Clearly our theory does not apply to such prisoners, who are often introverted and solitary, and lack basic social skills. Prisoners are too heterogeneous a conglomerate to make a really satisfactory experimental group—even if the so-called control group could be guaranteed to consist of "good"

men. But, of course, the latter situation is far from likely. Quite a high proportion of any random control group is made up of former or future prisoners, or at least of criminals who may never be found out.

Are alternative groups of subjects better suited to a proper testing of our theory? The answer is probably yes. A better comparison group would be *psychopaths* or *sociopaths*, defined in the *Diagnostic and Statistical Manual of Mental Disorders* of the American Psychiatric Association (1968) as "chronically antisocial individuals who are always in trouble, profiting neither from experience nor punishment, and maintaining no real loyalties to any person, group, or code. They are frequently callous and hedonistic, showing marked emotional immaturity, with lack of responsibility, lack of judgment, and an ability to rationalize their behavior so that it appears warranted, reasonable, and justified." In addition, a detailed and widely accepted description of such individuals has been given by Cleckley (1964), who lists characteristics such as superficial charm; unreliability; untruthfulness and insincerity; lack of remorse or shame; antisocial behavior without good cause; poor judgment and failure to learn from experience; pathological egocentricity and incapacity for love; unresponsiveness in general personal relations; impersonal, trivial, and poorly integrated sex life; and lack of any real life plan. Individuals of this kind may or may not be criminals, and criminals may or may not be psychopaths. There is much overlap, but nothing like identity. Psychopaths are probably much closer to our target group, and our theory in principle applies with much more force to psychopaths than it does to a random assortment of criminals. The difficulty with using psychopaths as the target group, of course, lies in the inevitable subjectivity of diagnosis, and the marked differences in judgment among psychiatrists who perform the diagnosis. Although the imprisonment of men judged criminal may reflect police or court error, diagnostic difficulties with prisoners could be said to be less than with psychopaths. Under the circumstances, we may perhaps say that both prisoners and psychopaths have advantages and disadvantages as target groups for experimental studies, and both may be used with advantage provided that we keep in mind the necessary qualifications when interpreting the results.

Frequently the psychopath as described above is called *primary* in contradistinction to another type of person labeled *neurotic*, or *secondary psychopath*. As Karpman (1961) points out, many antisocial and aggressive acts are committed by people who suffer from severe emotional disturbances, unbearable frustrations, and inner conflicts. Their aggressive or antisocial behavior is believed to be the consequence of these more basic emotional problems. R. D. Hare (1970) has reviewed several studies which give support to the primary–secondary distinction.

We may now restate our hypothesis in a form that permits it to be tested in relation to psychopaths. We would predict that psychopaths will show extraverted personality traits, will be characterized by low cortical arousal, and will perform on laboratory experiments relevant to arousal in such a way as to conform to the pattern of low arousal; for example, they will condition poorly. On such tests, in other words, psychopaths as compared with controls will perform very much as extraverts compared with introverts. All these predictions are eminently testable, and many experiments have been performed in this context. I shall review a representative number; for a full account, R. D. Hare's book (1970) should be consulted.

Direct evidence of low cortical arousal in psychopaths must depend on EEG studies of brain-wave formation. Several such studies agree that psychopaths usually have abnormal brain waves, with an undue preponderance of slow-wave activity. One possible interpretation is that this finding is indicative of lower cortical arousal, although our understanding of the

electrical activity of the brain is not such that we can consider this conclusion certain. There is some similarity here between psychopaths and extraverts, in that the latter are characterized by low alpha frequency and high alpha amplitude (Gale, Coles, & Blaydon, 1969; Savage, 1964).

Fox and Lippert (1963), R. D. Hare (1970), and Lippert and Sentner (1966) have shown that psychopaths have less spontaneous electrodermal activity than controls; this is in agreement with the hypothesis of less cortical arousal. Crider and Lunn (1970) have similarly shown that extraverts show less spontaneous activity in the galvanic skin response (G. S. R.). Rose (1964) found two-flash thresholds to be higher for psychopaths than for controls; this is an indication of lower arousal among psychopaths. Extraverts quite generally have higher sensory thresholds (H. J. Eysenck, 1967); this seems closely related to Rose's finding, if not an exact replicate. Psychopaths, too, have higher sensory thresholds (R. D. Hare, 1968; Schoenherr, 1964).

Vigilance is a direct consequence of arousal, and extraverts and psychopaths should perform more poorly on tasks requiring vigilance than introverts and controls. The evidence regarding extraverts has been reviewed by Stroh (1971), and seems to be in accord with this prediction. Orris (1967) found that psychopaths performed less well than control criminals. Along a different line, preference for novel and complex stimulation should theoretically be higher in psychopaths (Skrzypek, 1969) and extraverts (H. J. Eysenck & Levey, 1965); results seem to bear this out.

We have already discussed the poor conditioning of extraverts. With respect to psychopaths, there is also evidence to suggest poor conditioning on eye-blink (J. G. Miller, 1964) and eye-blink discriminant conditioning (Warren & Grant, 1955), as well as on GSR conditioning (R. D. Hare, 1965a; Lykken, 1955). The results from psychopaths might have been more impressive had experimenters paid more attention to suitable choice of parameter values. As they stand, the data are more suggestive than definitive.

In line with these studies, some rather complex avoidance-learning experiments found psychopaths to be inferior in acquiring conditioned fear responses (Lykken, 1955; Schachter & Latané, 1964; Schoenherr, 1964; Schmauk, 1968). In these experiments the subjects had to learn to thread a path through a maze by manipulating certain levers, and also had to learn to avoid shock associated with some of the levers. Psychopaths learned the maze as well as controls, but they failed to learn to avoid punishment by shock. R. D. Hare (1965c) has argued from results of this type that psychopaths should be characterized by "short-range hedonism," and performed an interesting experiment in which numbers from 1 to 12 were exhibited in turn, with shock accompanying number 8. Electrodermal responses anticipating shock were taken, and these responses were found not only to be weaker in psychopaths but also to be less anticipated. It is interesting to note that Broadbent (1958) has similarly argued that extraverts have less "time-spanning" ability than introverts. Lippert and Sentner (1966) and Schalling and Levander (1964) have reported results similar to Hare's.

R. D. Hare (1970) reports a number of studies on psychopaths in which verbal conditioning was used with inconclusive results. Much the same is true of work with extraverts; some investigators find differences in the expected direction, others do not. The reason lies quite probably in the neglect of an important parameter, namely, *awareness*. An unpublished study from our laboratory found that subjects who are unaware of the contingencies involved in verbal conditioning (for example, that the experimenter says "Good" in order to reinforce a given response) show the expected superiority of introverts over extraverts. When subjects are aware of the contingencies, however, extraverts show better performance. This pattern is very much as expected. Under conditions of awareness, extraverts are more eager to please; this is part of their sociability. Under conditions of nonawareness, however, such social factors are eliminated and conditioning depends much more on cortical arousal. It is suggested, therefore, that in future work on verbal conditioning with psychopaths, the parameter of awareness be strictly controlled. Without such control it is unlikely that worthwhile results can be obtained.

We may with advantage summarize the outcome of our discussions so far. I have suggested that basic to antisocial conduct is a failure to form conditioned responses, which are the building material for a proper "conscience." This failure in turn is attributed to a genetically low level of cortical arousal. Both low arousal and poor conditioning are suggested to be causally related to a whole gamut of personality traits, correlating together and usually referred to as extraversion. Antisocial conduct becomes aggravated when extraversion is coupled with neuroticism. *N* acts as a drive to amplify whatever habits have been formed in the individual's past; and in the case of extraverts these habits are hedonistic, asocial, and selfish.

There is a large literature to support, with varying degrees of strength, deductions from these hypotheses. For the most part, target populations have been chosen to represent individuals characterized as antisocial; the two most widely used groups are prisoners and psychopaths (diagnosed psychiatrically and/or in terms of questionnaire responses). Experimental difficulties are associated with both target groups, but the theory would not be worth retaining if positive results could not be obtained with groups so clearly deviant as these. In the majority of cases, results have been favorable to some such theory as that put forward, although there are still many anomalies, and the differentiation achieved between deviants and controls is far from perfect. It seems likely that many of the difficulties experienced have resulted from the imperfections of the experimental groups, rather than from a failure of the theory. Whether this likelihood is fact or bias, however, can be ascertained only by future experiment.

Psychopathy and Social Factors

The theory as outlined is based on the premise that the differences between criminal-psychopathic groups and control groups are largely due to biological and genetic factors. This view is opposed by many psychiatrists and psychologists who look for social causes. It seems clear to me that both types of cause are implicated, but a discussion of some of the evidence adduced by environmentalists may be useful in ascertaining whether our conclusion requires a reconsideration.

Most of the environmental evidence is related to factors in the upbringing of the child. Thus Gregory (1958) and Greer (1964) reported a high incidence of parental loss in psychopathic individuals; and Craft, Stephenson, and Granger (1964) showed that the more severe the disorder, the more likely is the presence of parental deprivation. It is important to note, however, that such differences seem to be due to parental loss by separation. Moreover, separation from the father seems much more important than separation from the mother (Oltman & Friedman, 1967). The child might have inherited the genes largely responsible for his father's psychopathic conduct and grown up like him not for the environmental reasons given, but because of the action of heredity pure and simple (or possibly in combination with environmental factors). The evidence is clearly not sufficient to enable us to make a decision, but we may note that (1) many children of separated parents grow up into perfectly normal individuals; (2) many psychopaths come from perfectly normal homes; thus Cleckley (1964) comments that "during all my years of experience

with hundreds of psychopaths . . . no type of parent or of parental influence, overt or subtle, has been regularly demonstrable." What is actually responsible for this difference in reaction to similar circumstances?

Bell (1968) has advocated another hypothesis, namely, that the behavior of the parents may be a reaction to the psychopathy of the child. Thus the finding that excessive use of punishment is related to psychopathic tendencies might be interpreted not as punishment causing psychopathy, but as psychopathic behavior inviting excessive punishment. Similarly, as Wiggins (1968) has noted, the frequent finding that inconsistency of parental behavior is related to psychopathy may be simply a result of parental puzzlement, rather than a causal factor of pathology. What all this amounts to, of course, is very simply that this type of data, although interesting, is correlational and hence not capable of throwing much light on causal connections. All or some or none of the theories canvassed might be true, and it certainly would not be admissible to use them either in support of or against a genetic interpretation of psychopathic behavior and its origins.

Primary and Secondary Psychopathy

Before beginning a more detailed discussion of the distinction between primary and secondary psychopathy, we must consider an extension of the general theory presented so far. We have made use of two major personality variables, E and N, in our attempts to account for psychopathic behavior, but this account has certain weaknesses. In the first place, while the theory may explain the type of psychopathy often referred to as *secondary*, which is explicitly linked with neurotic predisposition or even manifest disorder, it does not seem to account for *primary* psychopathy, which by definition is free of neurotic contamination. In the second place, the theory does not properly account for some of the behavior patterns of the primary psychopath, such as the violent, aggressive, and destructive tendencies that make him such a compelling contrast to the secondary psychopath.

Even though we may continue to regard high extraversion (particularly the traits of impulsivity and sensation seeking) as essential in all psychopathy, clearly an alternative additive to N must be found to account for primary psychopathy. It has been suggested (H. J. Eysenck, 1970a) that the missing additive is psychoticism (P), a third major dimension of personality first suggested and empirically researched by H. J. Eysenck (1952a, 1952b) and H. J. Eysenck, Granger, and Brenglemann (1957). This factor bears the same relation to psychosis as neuroticism does to neurosis. In other words, it is conceived as a widely distributed personality trait predisposing a person to a particular kind of mental breakdown under suitable stress. The precise nature of this factor in normal populations, as well as in psychotics and criminals, has been studied in a series of papers (H. J. Eysenck & Eysenck, 1968; S. B. G. Eysenck & Eysenck, 1968, 1969a, 1969b, 1972a; Verma & Eysenck, 1973), and evidence regarding its genetic determination has been offered (H. J. Eysenck, 1972a).

Questionnaire items with high loadings on psychoticism suggest that persons with high scores on this variable are somewhat odd—unsociable, hostile, unemotional, unfeeling, and cruel. It is suggested that whereas $E \times N$ identifies the secondary psychopath, $E \times P$ identifies the primary psychopath—although one qualification must be added to this statement. As pointed out before, we do not conceive of these diagnostic categories as qualitatively different "diseases," but consider them as points in a dimensional framework (H. J. Eysenck, 1970b). Thus psychopaths are not conceived of as *either* primary *or*

secondary, but as located somewhere in the octant high E–high N–high P of the three-dimensional E, P, N, structure. Typical primary psychopaths would be high on E and P, with average N, while typical secondary psychopaths would be high on E and N, with average P. However, not all, or even the majority, of psychopaths would be typical in this sense. In view of the independence of these dimensions, a person might be high on E, P, and N, or high on E and middling on P and N; indeed, all possible combinations might be found. This seems to be a much more realistic picture of what we encounter when we study "immoral" people; the categorical, diagnostic approach is arid and rigid to an extent that falsifies reality. Most psychiatrists have realized the drawback of diagnosis and have tended in recent years to play it down more and more. The well-known lack of reliability in most diagnostic systems is further indication that they do not fit reality very well (H. J. Eysenck, 1968).

The question must now be faced of why we postulate a connection between psychoticism and the performance of antisocial acts. The evidence is twofold. In the first place, there is direct evidence that prisoners score exceptionally high on questionnaire measures of P (H. J. Eysenck & Eysenck, 1971; S. B. G. Eysenck & Eysenck, 1970, 1971). Indeed, the sores on P of prisoners are no lower than those of psychotics (H. J. Eysenck, 1970a). These data support our hypothesis, but they do not explain why the hypothesis was put forward. The second set of evidence does. It has frequently been observed that psychotics (mainly schizophrenics) have an undue number of children who are psychotic, and also an equal or greater number of criminals, psychopaths, or generally antisocial offspring whose behavior closely resembles that described above as typical of high P scorers. In other words, there seems to exist a genetic connection between psychotic disorders, on the one hand, and criminal and psychopathic behavior, on the other.

I will here list only a few of the studies relevant to my point. Ödegard (1963) reported that relatives of psychotic probands were classified as psychopaths, criminals, and alcoholics in 10 percent of all cases. As Planansky (1966b) points out, "The psychopathic personalities are the most persistently reported group among close relatives of schizophrenics, and certain forms of these vaguely defined disorders appear to be not only structurally but also developmentally connected with schizophrenic psychosis." Planansky (1966a) also traces the history of this association from Kahlbaum (1890) through Kraepelin (1913) to Schafer (1951) and Delay, Deniker, and Green (1957), and summarizes the empirical literature by saying "that there is an abundance of reports concerning incidence of schizoid psychopathic personality in families of schizophrenic probands."

These studies have generally started with the psychotic proband (Essen-Möller, 1946; Planansky, 1966c), but of equal interest are studies starting at the other end, using psychopathic probands (Meggendorfer, 1921; Riedel, 1937; but see also Stumpfl, 1936). These investigations have dealt with so-called schizoid-psychopathic personalities. However, there is also a considerable agglomeration of nonschizoid-psychopathic personalities in relatives of schizophrenics (Medow, 1914; Rüdin, 1916). The most important research in this field is Heston's study (1966) of children of schizophrenic mothers. These children had been removed immediately after birth and raised by foster parents. Out of the 47 children, 9 were later diagnosed as sociopathic personalities with antisocial behavior of an impulsive kind, and had long police records. Of the total sample 4 children developed schizophrenia and 20 developed other behavioral abnormalities. These findings demonstrate that the incidence of psychotic and nonpsychotic abnormalities is high in the progeny of schizophrenics, under conditions in which direct environmental determination has been ruled out. The data, then, are very much in accord with our two hypotheses of the close relation of a general factor of psychoticism with inherited predisposition to psychopathic or criminal behavior.

The evidence adduced so far is, of course, not conclusive. Complex theories which try to account for even more complex human behavior patterns have to be tested in many different ways before we can feel any great confidence in their adequacy. The theory here discussed rather briefly has not been in existence long enough to generate the vast amount of supporting evidence required. There is, however, supporting evidence besides that already mentioned. In an unpublished factorial study of personality dimensions and various different types of criminal behavior, it was found that P loaded on the same factor as crimes of violence and sex crimes, while N loaded on crimes of "breaking and entering." Clearly a very important task for future research will be the detailed investigation of specific types of criminal or psychopathic activity, with particular reference to personality factors. The stress hitherto accorded overall gross comparisons between criminal and noncriminal, or psychopathic and nonpsychopathic, behavior is not likely to add much more to our knowledge. Of much interest, too, are follow-up studies. One such unpublished study of Borstal boys (juvenile offenders in special open prisons) over a period of three years found that recidivism correlated with E, P, and N. Within-prison conduct, too, may be of interest; misbehavior in prison, for example, correlates with E.

Many possibilities, therefore, exist for extending our knowledge of the relationship between personality and antisocial behavior. Predictions derived from the theory I have outlined can be made and tested. Until many such tests have been carried out and proved successful, however, the theory can claim only limited acceptance.

Drug Effects on Antisocial Behavior

One area, however, provides us with a strictly experimental test of some of our hypotheses, particularly those linking cortical arousal with moral behavior. While arousal levels are probably largely genetically determined, it is possible to change them chemically. Drugs have been used since time immemorial to produce precisely such changes. In particular, drugs such as alcohol and the barbiturates *depress* the level of cortical arousal and thus have an extraverting effect. Stimulant drugs such as amphetamine or caffeine *increase* the level of cortical arousal, and thus have an introverting effect (H. J. Eysenck, 1963). One would expect that the administration of stimulant drugs would produce noticeable changes in the direction of more socialized behavior in criminals and psychopaths, although these changes would presumably disappear once the drug was withdrawn. The literature on the extraverting and introverting effects, respectively, of depressant and stimulant drugs has been reviewed elsewhere (H. J. Eysenck, 1967), and the results strongly support the theory. Of particular interest are the differences produced by these drugs in conditioning: Stimulant drugs increase conditioning, depressant drugs reduce it.

Do the direct effects of drug administration on behavior (Wender, 1971) also agree with the theory's prediction? Several experiments have been conducted, largely with behavior-disordered children and juvenile delinquents. Treatment consisted of medication with one of the stimulant drugs, usually amphetamine. Observations were made of the behavior of the subjects over a period of weeks. There were no particular attempts to alter their moral behavior and no attempts at psychotherapy. There was an astonishing, almost immediate, improvement in the behavior of the patients. They became much more amenable to discipline and much more socialized in their pattern of activities and often

ceased to show behavior problems. Usually the improvement ceased when the drug treatment was stopped, but sometimes the improvement continued well beyond this point and seemed to become an enduring characteristic of the individual's behavior.

One typical study was carried out by two American psychiatrists, Cutts and Jasper (1949), who investigated 12 behavior-problem children. When given benzedrine, a stimulant, half of these children showed marked improvements in behavior. When the children were given phenobarbital, a depressant, their behavior became definitely worse in 9 out of 12 cases. A similar study has been described by Lindsley and Henry (1942), who studied 13 behavior-problem children of average intelligence with a mean age of 10½ years. The behavior of the children was rated in the ward, the playground, and the schoolroom, with particular focus on the problem behavior for which they had been referred. After a base line was established during an initial control period when no drugs were given, the children were administered benzedrine over a week, and were again rated during this time. During the following week, each subject received phenobarbital, a depressant drug expected to exacerbate their symptoms. Finally, after an interval of two weeks, the children were again rated under conditions of no drugs, this constituting the terminal control. The authors report that "Phenobarbital resulted in an exacerbation of the symptoms. . . . Under benzedrine medication all subjects show better than 10 per cent improvement in their behavior scores over those of the initial control periods; 9 subjects show better than 50 per cent improvement." The results are shown in Figure 6.5 (below). In view of the short periods of medication, they seem remarkable.

In another study, Bradley and Bowen (1941) investigated the effects of amphetamine on 100 behavior-problem children. Of these, they found that 54 became more "subdued." As an example,

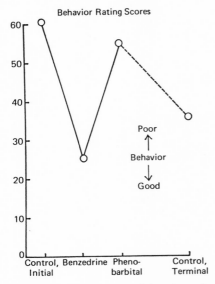

Figure 6.5   Effects of administration of a stimulant drug (benzedrine) and a depressant drug (phenobarbital) on the behavior of 13 behavior-problem children. (Redrawn from Lindsley & Henry, 1942.)

they cite the case of John, a 10-year-old boy who was admitted to the hospital because of hyperactivity, destructive behavior, poor school progress, and failure to mingle satisfactorily with older children. He teased his companions incessantly, quarreled with them, pushed them, and took their toys. His overactivity had been noted since early childhood, but the social problems which it caused worsened when he entered school. Although he was under psychotherapeutic treatment for fifteen months, he was overactive, irritable, noisy and disturbing in the ward, the playground, and the classroom, where he made little progress. He demanded a great deal of attention in school, and worked acceptably only when the teacher left the room. He was restless and distractible in all activities. At mealtimes, he stuffed food in his mouth, laughed and talked noisily, and constantly teased the other children. He gave no evidence of profiting from suggestion or

training. When amphetamine was started, however, there was immediately a definite change in his behavior. On the ward he was much quieter, and none of his usual hyperactivity was noted. He was prompt for meals and school, and became pleasant and congenial with children and adults. He cooperated well in all matters of routine; no longer restless, he applied himself to daily tasks. In the classroom he accomplished a great deal every day and showed excellent initiative.[4]

While these effects of administering drugs to antisocial persons are in line with the prediction, not enough work has been done to allow us any certainty about the particular manner in which the drugs operate. It is unlikely that much conditioning is involved, particularly as the effects seem to be noticeable and quite strong almost from the beginning. Perhaps we are on safer ground in assuming that the drugs operate to reduce impulsivity and sensation-seeking behavior. This interpretation would be consistent with the fact that drug treatments do not have very strong lasting effect (Eisenberg et al., 1963). I have suggested that treatment of criminals should combine a proper course of conditioning with the administration of amphetamine (H. J. Eysenck, 1964/1970a), but this suggestion has not to my knowledge been taken up. Such a program could provide a crucial test of my theory.

Some work has been done on the conditioning of socialized responses in criminals and delinquents without the use of drugs. I have given an extended discussion of this elsewhere (Eysenck, 1972b). Most of this work has used principles of operant conditioning, in particular the so-called token economy. In this method, the subject can obtain tokens which are exchangeable for small privileges, such as fifteen minutes of TV-viewing time, or cigarettes or specially liked foods. The principle on which these tokens are doled out is obedience to a specified set of items of "good" socialized behavior (Ayllon & Azrin, 1968). This procedure was originally introduced into penal treatment by the great innovator Alexander Maconochie almost a hundred years ago. Its revival is too recent, however, to have permitted time for proper follow-up studies, which are vital to ascertaining whether the remarkable short-term effects will endure.

Conclusion

What can we say in conclusion? If we identify "moral" conduct as freely willed and responsible decision-making behavior in accordance with philosophical premises, then the contents of this chapter will hardly seem relevant to a discussion of morality. Indeed, one might say that such a definition of moral conduct would rule out any kind of scientific investigation, and would in addition postulate a meaningless and improbable mentalism that goes counter to all modern biology has to teach us. If we concern ourselves rather with types of behavior to which terms such as *antisocial*, *criminal*, or *immoral* can be applied with a fair degree of consensus, then I think we may say that a number of facts indicate that biological factors play an important part in the genesis of such behavior, and in the causation of individual differences relevant to it.

In particular, there appears to be an important connection between moral behavior and strong cortical arousal. Introverts are found to show such arousal more frequently and more strongly than extraverts, and are also more likely to behave in socially approved ways. Furthermore, there is genetic evidence to show that introverts are more likely to be affected by environmental factors, presumably through conditioning (Jinks & Fulker, 1970). The lesser conditionability of extraverts, especially when associated with some degree of mental abnormality, is likely to lead them into paths of immorality. When E is associated prominently with N, we have the picture of the secondary psychopath. When E is associated prominently with P,

we have the picture of the primary psychopath. These clinical diagnoses are, of course, Platonic ideas closely approached only by a small number of typical cases, but they draw attention to combinations of personality traits which can be measured, and on which research can be undertaken with advantage.

I have suggested that there are two main lines along which the genetically determined cortical arousal level may be linked with the prosocial or antisocial behavior of the individual. My argument is that moral behavior is mediated through the individual's "conscience" and that this conscience is acquired through a process of conditioning. Conditioning in turn is dependent upon the level of cortical arousal. I have also maintained that impulsive, sensation-seeking, behavior is motivated at least in part by low levels of cortical arousal. The combination of these two factors, sensation seeking and poor conditioning, provides the biological background for psychopathic and criminal behavior.

This chapter has pointed out several times that these genotypic factors must interact in complex ways with environmental influences in order to produce the phenotype that is the subject of our empirical investigations; an extended treatment of these environmental factors has perforce been excluded. Similarly, there are many additional factors which for reasons of space have been treated very briefly; clearly our discussion is only an outline of a theory. Nevertheless, this theory does generate a large number of testable predictions; and, insofar as these have been tested, they have been verified in a satisfactory number of instances. It should also be noted that the theory provides suggestions for the rehabilitation of criminals, and quite generally for the improvement of the socialization process in children and adolescents as well as in adults. Future work along these lines should provide the evidence on which to base a more definite decision about the adequacy of this theory.

Chapter 6.   The Biology of Morality

[1] We may ask whether the need to specify parameter conditions for optimal conditioning of extraverts and introverts does not make it unlikely that such a laboratory-based scheme could have any great relevance to ordinary life, where such parameter conditions are extremely unlikely to be encountered. The answer seems to be linked with the fact that conditions must be optimal for conditioning to occur in extraverts, whereas introverts condition almost as well in conditions which are far from optimal. (An optimal situation is here defined as one in which an unselected sample of subjects produces the largest number of conditioned responses over a given number of pairings). In other words, everyday situations are not likely to be optimal, and consequently extraverts are not likely to produce many conditioned responses; introverts, not requiring optimal situations, will condition quite readily under variable circumstances.

[2] Walter (1964, 1966, 1967) has shown several times that individuals described as recidivist delinquents with psychopathic personality have shown only very meager evidence of CNVs. (CNVs are slow, surface-negative shifts in the EEG baseline that typically depend on the contingency of two successive stimuli). CNVs have much in common with conditioned responses, but are of course, quite involuntary; indeed, hardly any subjects would know of CNVs' existence. CNVs are almost certainly linked with the state of arousal of the cortex, and their failure to show up in the groups studied by Walter is therefore in good agreement with the theory under discussion.

[3] Persons who are accident-prone also tend to congregate in this quadrant (Shaw & Sichel, 1971). The reason appears to be that such people are more likely to indulge in the sensation-seeking behavior, and less likely to perform socialized safe-driving behavior. We have here a type of antisocial behavior which is often subcriminal, although occasionally it may actually become punishable by law.

[4] Some children became stimulated by the drug rather than showing more subdued behavior: "Such children became more alert, accomplished their daily tasks with more initiative and dispatch, became more aggressive in competitive activity, and showed an increased interest

in what was going on about them. As a result of these changes, they gave the impression of being more self-sufficient and mature. They also appeared happier and more contented." This paradoxical effect appeared mostly in children who were pathologically shy, withdrawn, and underactive. Too little is known about these withdrawn children and the particular effects observed to make it possible to state to what extent their reactions to the drugs contradict the general theory we have formulated above.

chapter 1

INTRODUCTION
AND RÉSUMÉ

We describe in this monograph an evolution in students' interpretation of their lives evident in their accounts of their experience during four years in a liberal arts college. The evolution consists of a progression in certain forms in which the students construe their experience as they recount it in voluntary interviews at the end of each year. These "forms" characterize the structures which the students explicitly or implicitly impute to the world, especially those structures in which they construe the nature and origins of knowledge, of value, and of responsibility.

"Form" and "structure," even when used at concrete visual levels, refer to concepts notoriously difficult to define. What we mean by "forms in which the students construe their experience" will become clear as the reader proceeds. However, both the abstract level of the "forms" and their relation to concrete "experience" may be suggested here by an illustration in which I shall assume the risk of caricature in the service of brevity:

Let us suppose that a lecturer announces that today he will consider three theories explanatory of——(whatever his topic may be). Student A has always taken it for granted that knowledge consists of correct answers, that there is one right answer per problem, and that teachers explain these answers for students to learn. He therefore listens for the lecturer to state which theory he is to learn.

Student B makes the same general assumptions but with an elaboration to the effect that teachers sometimes present problems and procedures, rather than answers, "so that we can learn to find the right answer on our own." He therefore perceives the lecture as a kind of guessing game in which he is to "figure out" which theory is correct,

1

a game that is fair enough if the lecturer does not carry it so far as to hide things too obscurely.

Student C assumes that an answer can be called "right" only in the light of its context, and that contexts or "frames of reference" differ. He assumes that several interpretations of a poem, explanations of a historical development, or even theories of a class of events in physics may be legitimate "depending on how you look at it." Though he feels a little uneasy in such a kaleidoscopic world, he nonetheless supposes that the lecturer may be about to present three legitimate theories which can be examined for their internal coherence, their scope, their fit with various data, their predictive power, etc.

Whatever the lecturer then proceeds to do (in terms of his own assumptions and intent) these three students will make meaning of the experience in different ways which will involve different assessments of their own choices and responsibilities.

If, for the purposes at hand, this hypothetical lecture is allowed to represent a variety of human experiences, and if students A, B, and C are allowed to represent one and the same person at three stages of his life, the illustration will suggest what we mean by a "progression of forms in which a person construes his experience." Furthermore, such words as "progression," "evolution," or "development" (as distinct from the more generic "difference" or "change") would then refer to the fact that, as I have arranged them in the illustration, the three sets of assumptions are in the order of increasing scope. That is:

B's assumptions are of a form which includes the form of A's; and C's assumptions include, in a different and broader form, the forms of both A's and B's. This is evident in the different predicament of each student in the event that what the lecturer proceeds to do conforms to the expectations of one of the other students. For instance, student C, faced with the lecture expected by either A or B, would have little difficulty in interpreting the experience accurately without revising his basic assumptions about the nature of knowledge. His assumptions logically extend to the possibility that a given lecturer might "have the point of view that" there was but one correct answer. Student A, however, faced with the kind of lecture expected by B or by C, must either revise his basic assumptions or interpret the experience in some such way as, "The lecturer is talking all over the place" or "This just doesn't have anything to do with the course."

A person moving from the assumptions of student A to those of B to those of C may therefore be said to be involved in a development, not simply because his assumptions become "better" or more "true"— which is another question—but because the forms of his later assumptions subtend those of his earlier assumptions in a coherent manner, as cannot be said in reverse.

Of course a person will use a variety of forms in construing different areas of his experience at any given time. However, we made the assumption in this study that within this variety it is possible to identify a dominant form (or central tendency among the forms) in which the person is currently interpreting his experience. The outcome of the experiments which we included in the study support the validity of this assumption, especially in regard to those forms in which a person addresses knowing, valuing, and responsibility.

Since the sequence of these forms in our students' reports appears to us to manifest a logical order—an order in which one form leads to another through differentiations and reorganizations required for the meaningful interpretation of increasingly complex experience—our description itself takes its own second-order form as a pattern or scheme of development. In its full range the scheme begins with those simplistic forms in which a person construes his world in unqualified polar terms of absolute right-wrong, good-bad; it ends with those complex forms through which he undertakes to affirm his own commitments in a world of contingent knowledge and relative values. The intervening forms and transitions in the scheme outline the major steps through which the person, as evidenced in our students' reports, appears to extend his power to make meaning in successive confrontations with diversity.

The young person's discovery of diversity in other people's points of view is of course part of the folklore of adolescence and of "growing up" in the college years. It would seem, too, to be occurring earlier and earlier in life. The impact of this discovery has been directly and indirectly considered in many of the studies we cite in this report or list in its bibliography. The present study focuses on the vicissitudes of the experience over time, and finds in the shapes and sequences of these vicissitudes a major theme of personal growth.

Although we are necessarily limited to the college setting in both our data and the validation of our findings—and to the setting of a single college at that—we proffer our scheme of development for its more general implications. We presume its relevance to the understanding of the intellectual and ethical development of late adolescence in a pluralistic culture.

ORIGIN OF THE STUDY

In 1953 the staff of the Bureau of Study Counsel at Harvard College undertook to document the experience of undergraduates in Harvard and Radcliffe over their four years of college. In our daily counseling with students whose presenting concerns centered on their academic work, we had been impressed with the variety of the ways in which the students responded to the relativism which permeates the intellectual and social atmosphere of a pluralistic university. Among the students who consulted us, a few seemed to find the notion of multiple frames of reference wholly unintelligible.[1] Others responded with violent shock to their confrontation in dormitory bull sessions, or in their academic work, or both. Others experienced a joyful sense of liberation. There were also students, apparently increasing in number in the years following World War II, who seemed to come to college already habituated to a notion of man's knowledge as relative and who seemed to be in full exploration of the modes of thinking and of valuing consequent on this outlook.

This variety in the way students first experienced their pluralistic environment seemed to us to be followed by an equally wide variety in the ways in which students went on to assimilate that experience. Although an occasional student would retreat, defeated, and some would detach themselves through a cynical exploitation of intellectual gamesmanship and moral opportunism, most seemed to go on to develop a personal style of commitment in both their thinking and their care.

We could hardly suppose that these issues were peculiar to the experience of students who came to consult us. Nor indeed did we suppose that these were parochial phenomena limited to the environs of Harvard University. We did suppose that the pervasiveness and inescapability of the impact of relativism on college students might well be a development of the twentieth century, and we have since documented the supposition. Our documentation is limited to Harvard College, but the implications for other colleges with a diverse student body and a pluralistic intellectual outlook seem obvious.

The change in the outlook of the faculty is evident in the character of the intellectual tasks set for students on final examinations. The graph shown in Figure 1 is based on the final examinations for courses in History, Government, English Literature, and Foreign Literatures enrolling the largest number of freshmen in Harvard College at intervals from 1900 to 1960. The assumption made is that the kind of operation called for by an examination question expresses the examiner's conception of knowledge of his subject. Analysis was performed by sorting questions into categories, with appropriate tests of reliability. The graph presents the percentage of weight on each examination given to questions requiring considerations in more than one frame of reference, that is, relativism.

---

[1] For example, in response to such an assignment as "Compare the concepts of the tragic heroine exemplified by Antigone and Cordelia," these students would fail to perceive the direct object of the verb "compare" and would write comparisons of Antigone and Cordelia, as persons, against the background of a single, implicit frame of reference. We came to feel that persistent misperception of the form of such intellectual tasks, even after repeated explanations of them, could not be ascribed to intellective factors alone.

Figure 1 documents a revolution in the very definition of knowledge confronted by freshmen in a college of liberal arts in this century. The new relativism of knowledge has inevitably been accompanied by a relative address to values. In Henry Adams's words: "The movement from unity to multiplicity, between 1200 and 1900, was unbroken in sequence and

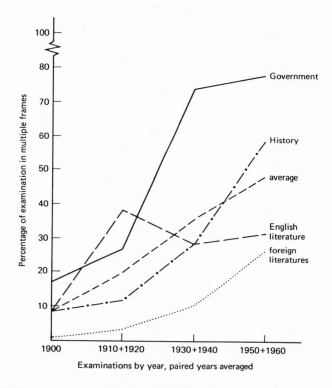

FIGURE 1 Weight of examination requiring consideration of two or more frames of reference. Courses enrolling most freshmen in Government, History, English Literature, and Foreign Literatures 1900–1960.*

rapid in acceleration. Prolonged one generation longer, it would require a new social mind" (Adams, 1931). The rate of acceleration has been greater than perhaps even Adams foresaw, and not one but two generations have passed.

* Since these categories of courses deliberately ignore major changes in curriculum, especially the introduction of the program in General Education in the mid-forties, the graph portrays the minimum of the range of the change. With the large courses in General Education included, the average of relativistic questions confronting freshmen in 1950–60 is estimated at 75 to 80 per cent.

For the college student, the confrontation with pluralism of values has become inescapable, not only in his courses but in his daily life with his peers. Cultural diversity in the student body has become a deliberate policy of selection in nonsectarian colleges of liberal arts. In the instance of Harvard College, the freshman class in 1900 consisted of 537 students drawn from 175 schools. In 1960 the freshman class of 1082 was drawn from 499 schools. In 1900, 45 per cent of entering students came from outside Massachusetts; in 1960, 72 per cent. It could hardly be said any longer, as Adams had said of his classmates in the 1850s, that the students had nothing to give each other because they had been "brought up together under like conditions" (Adams, 1931). The same movement toward diversity is evident in most institutions of higher learning in the country, and extends to socioeconomic as well as geographical criteria.

Such diversity, as faced by a student in a college of liberal arts, would seem to be unique in Western society today only in its concentration and intensity. The increased mobility of the population at large, together with the new mass media, make the impact of pluralism part of experience in the society as a whole. The growing person's response to pluralism in thought and values, and indeed his capacity to generate pluralism himself, are therefore critical to the destiny of a democracy. Whether he responds productively rather than destructively may be up to him in the end, but society may surely nourish the prospect of a productive outcome through an understanding of the learning and the courage the development entails.

This understanding must derive from systematic descriptions of the experience through time—descriptions of its characteristic stages and its major points of choice between fragmentation and integration, alienation and involvement. Several such descriptions will be required, because no one system can encompass the complexities. The several extant systems of conceptualizing child development have shed light on the early years, and even on adolescence. The extension of inquiry into the transition from youth to maturity has only recently begun. However much personal development in the later years may depend on the vicissitudes of earlier experience, it may still be examined in its own right for its normative characteristics. The college years provide an advantageous setting for the initial sweeps of such exploration.

It was in the light of these considerations regarding present-day liberal education and personal development that we set out to learn about the experience of students other than those who came to us for counsel. Our initial intention was purely descriptive, and not even systematically so. We planned simply to collect accounts of the experience of 20 or 30 students as they might tell us about it in open interviews at the end of each of their four years in college. We hoped to be able to reduce these documents to brief, readable portraits expressive of the variety we saw in students' educational experience. We thought that such documents might be interesting in their own right and also suggestive of issues relevant for more systematic research.

PROCEDURE

We started out, then, to illustrate the variety in students' response to the impact of intellectual and moral relativism. Wishing to secure this variety in a small sample of students, we felt it best to obtain the largest possible range between those freshmen bringing with them a strong preference for dualistic, right-wrong thinking and those bringing with them a strong affinity for more qualified, relativistic and contingent thinking. We considered such differences as a manifestation of differences in "personality" (in keeping with much psychological thinking of the time). It had not yet occurred to us that it might be more fruitful, at least for our purpose, to consider such differences primarily as expressions of stages in the very developments we were setting out to explore.

Starting, then, from the research on the authoritarian personality (Adorno et al., 1950) and G. G. Stern's work at Chicago using the *Inventory of Beliefs* (Stern, 1953), we devised a measure called *A Checklist of Educational Views* (CLEV). In preliminary trials in 1953 to 1954, the measure promised to identify students along the dimension we desired.

We administered CLEV to a random sample of 313 freshmen in the fall of 1954 and to the same students in the spring of 1955. On the basis of their scores on the measure, we then sent invitations to 55 students, 31 of whom volunteered to tell us in interview about their college experience. Among these freshmen were some who had scored at the extreme of dualistic thinking, some at the extreme of contingent thinking, some from the mean, and some who had changed their scores markedly from fall to spring.

Our interviews with these students in late May and June of each of their college years resulted in 98 tape-recorded interviews, including 17 complete four-year records. We conducted the interviews themselves in as open-ended a way as possible so as to avoid dictating the structure of a student's thought by the structure of our questions. That is, we asked only for what seemed salient in the student's own experience, beginning interviews with an invitation of the form: "Would you like to say what has stood out for you during the year?" After the student's general statements, we then asked: "As you speak of that, do any particular instances come to mind?" (See pp. 18 ff.)

Perhaps as a consequence of these procedures, the variety in the form and content of the students' reports appeared at first to exceed our expectations and to exclude any possibility of orderly comparison. However, *we gradually came to feel that we could detect behind the individuality of the reports a common sequence of challenges to which each student addressed himself in his own particular way.* For most of the students, their address to these challenges as they experienced them in their academic work, in the social life of the college, and in their extracurricular activities or employment, seemed to represent a coherent development in the forms in which they functioned intellectually, in the forms in which they experienced values, and in the forms in which they construed their world. The reports of those few students who did not evidence this development seemed meaningful as descriptions of deflection from some challenge in the sequence. In this sequence, tendencies toward dualistic thinking and tendencies toward contingent thinking now appeared less as the personal styles we had originally conceived them to be and more saliently as characteristics of stages in the developmental process itself.[2]

At this point we radically extended the purpose of our study and committed ourselves to experimental as well as descriptive procedures. We undertook (1) to obtain a larger sample of students' reports of their experience over their four years of college, (2) to spell out the sequence we had detected in the students' reports to form an articulated developmental scheme, and finally (3) to submit this scheme to tests of validity.

To obtain a second and enlarged sample, we sent invitations to 50 freshmen from the Class of '62 and 104 freshmen from the Class of '63. These freshmen were drawn from a random third of their classmates who had filled out a revised form of the *Checklist of Educational Views* in fall and spring. In this instance, however, we ignored their scores on this instrument and selected those we would invite through a random procedure. A total of 109 students responded, resulting later, in June of 1963, in 366 interviews, including 67 complete four-year reports.

As we were assembling this second set of volunteers, we undertook to describe more precisely the evolving sequence of challenges which we had discerned as the common theme in the accounts of our first informants. We first spelled out the development in first-person phenomenological terms—that is, in the words that might be used by an imaginary "modal" student moving along the center line of that generalized sequence of challenges and resolutions which we thought we saw behind all the variegated reports of our individual volunteers (see description, Chapter 3). We then described in abstract terms, from the outside, the structure of each of the major stages (i.e., the more enduring or stable forms in which the students construed the world). At the same time, we attempted to

---

[2] The developmental aspect of these tendencies was observed by other researchers of the period (Loevinger, 1959), (Sanford, 1956, 1962), (Harvey, Hunt, & Schroder, 1961).

explicate those transitional steps (i.e., the more conflicted and unstable forms) which articulate the development from stage to stage, transforming one structure to the next. With the main theme roughed out, we then traced around it the major variations which our data suggested to us, or which our scheme suggested through its own logic. Among these variations were included those deflections and regressions which we had interpreted as "opting out," or alienation from the course of maturation presumed in the scheme.

This full description of the scheme appears in Chapter 5, illustrated by excerpts from the students' reports. The following brief outline suggests its nature.

MAIN LINE OF DEVELOPMENT

Position 1:   The student sees the world in polar terms of we-right-good vs. other-wrong-bad. Right Answers for everything exist in the Absolute, known to Authority[3] whose role is to mediate (teach) them. Knowledge and goodness are perceived as quantitative accretions of discrete rightnesses to be collected by hard work and obedience (paradigm: a spelling test).

Position 2:   The student perceives diversity of opinion, and uncertainty, and accounts for them as unwarranted confusion in poorly qualified Authorities or as mere exercises set by Authority "so we can learn to find The Answer for ourselves."

Position 3:   The student accepts diversity and uncertainty as legitimate but still *temporary* in areas where Authority "hasn't found The Answer yet." He supposes Authority grades him in these areas on "good expression" but remains puzzled as to standards.

Position 4:   (*a*) The student perceives legitimate uncertainty (and therefore diversity of opinion) to be extensive and raises it to the status of an unstructured epistemological realm of its own in which "anyone has a right to his own opinion," a realm which he sets over against Authority's realm where right–wrong still prevails, or (*b*) the student discovers qualitative contextual relativistic reasoning as a special case of "what They want" within Authority's realm.

Position 5:   The student perceives all knowledge and values (including authority's) as contextual and relativistic and subordi-

---

[3] The implication of upper-case initials is probably clear enough in context here. Their particular denotations throughout this monograph, especially when paired against lower-case initials (e.g., Authority vis-à-vis authority), are defined in the Glossary next to the foldout Chart of Development at the end of this monograph.

nates dualistic right–wrong functions to the status of a special case, in context.

Position 6:   The student apprehends the necessity of orienting himself in a relativistic world through some form of personal Commitment (as distinct from unquestioned or unconsidered commitment to simple belief in certainty).

Position 7:   The student makes an initial Commitment in some area.

Position 8:   The student experiences the implications of Commitment, and explores the subjective and stylistic issues of responsibility.

Position 9:   The student experiences the affirmation of identity among multiple responsibilities and realizes Commitment as an ongoing, unfolding activity through which he expresses his life style.

CONDITIONS OF DELAY, DEFLECTION, AND REGRESSION

Temporizing: The student delays in some Position for a year, exploring its implications or explicitly hesitating to take the next step.

Escape: The student exploits the opportunity for detachment offered by the structures of Positions 4 and 5 to deny responsibility through passive or opportunistic alienation.

Retreat: The student entrenches in the dualistic, absolutistic structures of Positions 2 or 3.

Although such a brief outline cannot express the articulation or coherence of the development traced by the scheme, it does suggest the level of generality of those forms in which we thought we saw a coherent evolution in the students' reports. In their free interviews the students had of course rarely spoken explicitly at such an abstract level. The distance was necessarily considerable between such general philosophical forms and the variegated, concrete details of the students' talk (e.g., a student's account of a conversation with his adviser or another's description of his experience in an extracurricular activity). We could bridge this distance, in respect to most of our data, only by inference. Any such inferential construct as our scheme, drawn from such varied data, faces the question of being no more than the observer's way of seeing an order where it does not exist. We therefore endeavored to reduce our scheme from its broadly discursive expression into a representation sufficiently condensed, rigorous and denotative to be susceptible to a test of reliable use by independent observers. The result of these efforts were (*a*) a glossary of twenty words to which we assigned specific meanings, and (*b*) a two-dimensional map or chart delineating and coding sequential forms of the developmental scheme itself. (This Glossary and Chart of Development appear in a foldout at the end of this monograph.)

We were then ready to present independent observers with random samples of students' reports and to ask them to identify that point on the developmental scheme which they felt best represented the dominating or modal form among the structurings of the world evident in each report. The extent to which the several observers' placements or "ratings" might agree with one another, beyond the level of chance, would then be the measure of the validity or "existence" of our scheme in the students' accounts of their experience.

Such a test would at best certify the relevance of our scheme in respect to the accounts of students from which we had derived it. However, the investment required to carry out this limited assessment promised to involve our full resources, and we postponed any testing of our conviction that the relevance of the scheme of development extended into the experience of people in this general age group in wide areas of the society.

The study up to this point of actual test constitutes the subject of this monograph: Chapter 2 will summarize our sampling procedures and describe in full the kind of interview in which the students gave their reports; Chapter 3 will describe the experience of the development through an informal essay; Chapter 4 will describe our solutions to the problems involved in conceptualizing the development as a scheme; Chapter 5 will present and illustrate the scheme itself; and Chapter 6 will consider its significance for issues in education. As for the subsequent tests, a summary of their nature and outcome appears directly below. These tests were supported by Cooperative Research Contract SAE–8973, Project No. 5–0825. Their full details and the statistical procedures used in their analysis are reported in the Final Report for that Project.[4]

---

[4] W. G. Perry, Jr., *Patterns of Development in Thought and Values of Students in a Liberal Arts College: A Validation of a Scheme* (U.S. Dept. of Health, Education, and Welfare, Office of Education, Bureau of Research, Final Report, Project No. 5–0825, Contract No. SAE–8973, April 1968). The Report includes also a detailed analysis of the student samples and a study of the *Checklist of Educational Views*.

The issue at hand, we think our records show, is responsibility. If all I have been taught up to now is open to question, especially to *my* question, then my sense of who is responsible shifts radically from outside to me. But I see too that my questions and my answers are likewise open to question. Yet if I am not to spend my life in questions about questions and am to act, choose, decide and live, on what basis am I to do it? I even see now that I have but one life to live.

This then is the issue of individual personal commitment in a relative world, the next step beyond the questions of the "sophomore." Its central burden, and joy, is responsibility. If one quails before it, there are many well trodden paths to postponement, escape, or even retreat. We shall mention these as they appear in our records later. They can be seen most clearly against the experience of those who take up the challenge.

The commitment we are talking about is of a special form. We have called it personal commitment in a relative world. By this we mean to distinguish it from commitments which have been taken for granted to the extent that they have never been questioned, never compared to alternatives which could be "thinkable" to the self. All of us operate on many habitual never-questioned commitments. For some they constitute the entirety of life—that is, the unexamined life. Socrates said such a life was not worth living. Surely this statement is extreme and reveals the snobbery of consciousness. People with unexamined lives have been known to fight for their lives very well indeed. Of course they could not tell you why and remain people with unexamined lives.

Unexamined commitments can exist in all areas of life. One of our students, diligently "committed" to his goal of medicine ever since he could remember, never asked himself whether he really wanted to be a doctor until he was admitted to medical school. At this point the question hit him like an earthquake. When he had weathered the crisis and decided to go on, his commitment was of the form to which we particularly refer.

In religious life the distinction has long been familiar as the difference between simple belief and faith. Belief may come from one's culture, one's parents, one's habit; faith is an affirmation by the person. Faith can exist only after the realization of the possibility of doubt. We shall have more to say about the relation of religion to the intellectual and emotional growth of our students. We are concerned now with their experience of commitment as we have defined it.

Our students experience all such commitments as affirmations of themselves. Many of our students use the terms of existential philosophy in describing them, though most do so apologetically, knowing the ease with which the jargon can take over. The feeling they describe is one of some decision, some choice among actions, values or meaning which comes from themselves and defines them as individuals. Not that they feel self-created, as if they could choose all their values without reference to their past. On the contrary their commitments seem always to be made in acceptance of their past. Even when a student is breaking with the tradition of his upbringing, he seems first to have to accept the fact of it, that this happened to him, that he lived in it, and that now he must take a stand over against it, knowing that a part of himself must pay the cost.

More usually commitments follow lines similar to those laid down in the unexamined past, but the act of affirmation brings a new and different feel to it. The student who finally "decided" to become a doctor was not unmindful that his long efforts carried weight and momentum into his choice. Yet he did not feel trapped or resigned or passive. He knew he might be fooling himself, but had to take this chance also. He had to decide for himself even about the degree to which he could feel that he had really "decided."

What is required is a capacity for detachment. One must be able to stand back from oneself, have a look, and *then* go back in with a new sense of responsibility.

The act of standing back is forced in a liberal arts college by the impact of pluralism of values and points of view. The shock may be intentional on the part of individual professors, as it is most frequently, though not always, in courses in General Education, or it may be simply the by-product of the clash of different professors, each one of whom is sure he teaches "the" truth. Only in the smallest and most carefully guarded faculties can this diversity be avoided.

We gather from what our students have told us that the educational impact of diversity can be at its best when it is deliberate. When a teacher asks his students to read conflicting authorities and then asks them to assess the nature and meaning of the conflict, he is in a strong position to assist them to go beyond simple diversity into the disciplines of relativity of thought through which specific instances of diversity can be productively exploited. He can teach the relation, the relativism, of one system of thought to another. In short, he can teach disciplined independence of mind.

This is the commonplace of good teaching of the liberal arts in colleges and in good schools of today. And the idea is older than Socrates. In more recent times Henry Adams said that if he were ever to do college lecturing again it would be in the company of an assistant professor whose sole duty would be to present to the students an opposite point of view.

We think we are describing, however, a new thing under the sun. Deliberate teaching of this sort seems to be no longer the exception but the rule—so much the rule that it becomes the very heart of liberal education as revealed in these records. We wonder if this event is not the product of a great educational revolution of the past fifty years.

Some evidence is at hand. [Here the Manual describes the evidence from examination questions presented on pp. 4 and 5 of this report and then continues as follows.] On this evidence, the faculty at Harvard appears to have revised its conception of the educated man in the past fifty years. The Harvard faculty may not, of course, be representative of institutions of higher learning in this country. But even in the face of notable instances of leadership by other colleges, we doubt that Harvard has ever been more than ten or fifteen years behind the times in its definition of knowledge in its students.

The faculty's emphasis on independence of thought in examinations coincides, then, with the students' concerns in these records. There is hardly any doubt that the faculty's deliberate effort is a good thing. One would have to be quite anti-rational to maintain that education consciously and thoughtfully considered is less to be desired than that which happens accidentally. But it is not without its pitfalls. Education for independence of mind is a tricky business, as these records show. Unlike the haphazard clash of dogmatic professors, it can double back on itself and undo its own good works.

The problem is not simply that a teacher's bias can sneak back into his efforts to be impartial and subvert his offer of freedom. It often does, but the students soon discover how to deal with it, even when it appears in forms subtle and unlovely. The problem, as these records occasionally document, is that, where independence of mind is demanded by authority, its forms can be mastered and "handed in" while the spirit remains obediently conformist. As a student said of his performance on an examination, "Well, I decided to be in favor of that book they asked about, but I did not forget to be balanced."

The "pros and cons," the glib presentation of "several points of view," the summary which judiciously selects one position to be in favor of, "all things considered"—these become the stock armamentarium of the gamesman who has "caught on" to "what they want" and is giving it to them in exchange for grades and a diploma.

From what our students have revealed to us in their candor we find it impossible to imagine an educational system that would be proof against a wish on their part to defeat its ends. They would always find ways of imitating, of holding before the tired eyes of the professor the image of his fondest hope, all done up in his favorite words and his pet references and treasured qualifications. While their souls . . .

Students' souls, we have learned from both these researches and our daily counseling, are safe even against being saved. We find this encouraging. Certainly we prefer to see gamesmanship played cynically, if it is to be played at all, rather than automatically and unconsciously. The cynic, at least, maintains a claim to independence.

Modern pluralistic education, with all its pros and cons on every subject, is criticized for not teaching commitment, indeed for leading students away from it. What we have been saying from our understanding of our records is that: (1) without a clear view of pluralism, commitment as we define it is impossible; and (2) commitment can be provided for and given recognition, but it can never be brought about or forced.

There are too many ways out. As in *Pilgrim's Progress* there are stopping places, Sloughs of Despond, paths that lead aside or back. The first crucial trial is in the student's initial confrontation with multiplicity—with pluralism, ambiguity and contingency. One or two of our students would have none of it at all. Presumably, for them to have answers black and white, clear, known, available was so important emotionally that any other world was intolerable. These students either left college or retreated into a deep reaction. Another student stated in effect that this "many-points-of-view business" was O.K. for other people but not for him! A few others accepted the fact of multiplicity, in the loose sense that "everybody has a right to his own opinion," and struggled against the college's demand that they think further.

Perhaps the most critical point in most of the records comes at the moment where the student has indeed discovered how to think further, how to think relatively and contingently, and how to think about thinking. For here it is up to him in what crucial spirit he is to employ this discovery.

He appears to have a number of options. He may allow this form of thought to be simply "what they want" and assume no responsibility himself. He may put his mind in the service of this opportunism and become a cynical gamesman. He may isolate his discovery in the world of academics alone and never allow it to raise questions about his own life and purposes. Or he may see clearly enough what is now encumbent upon him and yet not feel up to it. He can feel not quite old enough or strong enough to make his commitments, and simply procrastinate.

Or he may go on. If he does so, his first commitment may well be to his major, his field of concentration. He has had enough of too much "breadth." He sees now the breadth of his ignorance; it is time to take the plunge, to know some one thing well. And so as a junior he works at his peak and looks forward to his thesis.

Not infrequently, he discovers later, the old hope for certainty has just gone underground, and in his senior year he has the whole job to do over again. "Knowing one thing well" turns out to have meant "Knowing something for sure," and when his thesis, that looked so narrow and specialized, opens out on him into the uncertainties of the whole universe again, he is taken aback.

We think this is the most crucial moment in higher education. Here the student *has* his tools; he has learned how to compare "models" of thought, how to relate data and frames of reference and points of observation. But now differences of opinion among experts in his field appear even more irreconcilable than ever. No one can *ever* be sure. "It's all up to the individual in the end."

Well, indeed it is. But the tone of this statement too often implies "So why bother. If it's all a matter of opinion in the end, why not in the beginning? Why bother with all the intellectual effort?" This is a retreat to simple multiplicity, to "everyone has a right to his own opinion." It says that unexamined opinion is as good as examined opinion. It is the moral defeat of the "educated" man.

It was our wonder and delight, therefore, to hear most of our students survive this crisis also. Many would laugh when they came to the realization that a commitment must be made and remade in time and at deeper levels. They would see also that many areas remained where they had not yet begun to take their stands. But they would go on.

Perhaps the reader will find his reading of a few records more meaningful if we spell out briefly here what we think we have learned from the whole series of records about the anatomy of commitments and the way they go together to make a style of life.

Students seemed to think of their commitments in two ways which we will call *area* and *style*. Area refers primarily to social content: decisions regarding major field, career, religion, tastes, morality, politics, finances, social concerns, friendships, and marriage.

The *stylistic* aspects of commitments concern balances both external and subjective. The external balances concern decisions of emphasis between studies and extra-curricular activities, number and intensity of friendships, amounts of altruistic social service, degree of specialization vs. breadth and so on. Issues among these external stylistic balances are closely interwoven with commitments in given areas, often determining them or affected by them.

A student's subjective style in regard to his commitments also appears to be both an important part of them and influenced by them. This subjective style involves certain inner commitments or affirmations or acceptances. In these records the students speak often of such inner balances as those between action and contemplation ("I've come to learn when to say to myself 'well, now, enough of this mulling and doubting, let's do something'"); permanence and flexibility ("Sometimes you have to go into something with the feeling you'll be in it forever even when you know you probably won't be" or "I used to think I had to finish anything I started or I'd be a quitter; now I see it's a nice point when to stop something that may be unprofitable and put the effort in more hopeful directions"); control vs. openness ("Well, you have to let experience teach you; it's good to have a plan, but if you insist on following it without a change ever—"); intensity vs. perspective ("That's the trick, I guess, you have to have detachment, or you get lost, you can't see yourself and your relation to what you're doing, and yet if you stay detached you never learn from total involvement, you never live; you just have to do it by waves, I guess").

It is the particular equilibrium that a student finds for himself among such subjective polarities that define him in his feeling of who he is as much as the concrete commitments he makes in different areas of his life. There are others too—a sense of continuity of self through mood and time in the face of the need to take one's immediate feelings seriously; and most particularly the realization that however much one wants to feel one has "found oneself" one wants more to keep growing all one's life ("I sometimes wonder how many times I'll be confronted").

With some moving, flowing equilibrium, some kind of style, among all these issues, the senior in our records tends to look more outward. His competence assured, he tends to be less preoccupied with the ingredients of self-hood, to accept himself as he is and grows, and to hanker for action. In a curious way he may startlingly resemble himself as a freshman. Here is the promising freshman-scientist who has established his competence, is accepted at graduate school and knows just where he's headed. Here is the once freshman-who-would-be-doctor and who next year will be called Doctor "on rounds." They look ahead and outward. They may find little to say in interviews except to allow in a quiet aside that they are getting married next week. Ironically enough these seniors have some of them forced us to consider what the difference may be between their kind of outwardness and that of the most hard-shelled anti-intellectual. The difference defines a liberal education—not as an ideal, but as an actuality in real people.

The difference is surely not simply the "content" of so many courses in Chemistry or History. Anti-intellectuals have been known to master mountains of data and technology. The anti-intellectual cannot be passed off as one who refuses to think. Many think dangerously well. Similarly the liberally educated man cannot be caricatured as one who sees so many sides of a subject that he cannot act. Our records belie such stereotypes.

We have come to believe from all these hours of listening that the anti-intellectual, be he in or out of college, is definable not as "against thinking," but against thinking about one particular thing: thought. Most particularly his *own* thought.

In contrast, the liberally educated man, be he a graduate of college or not, is one who has learned to think about even his own thoughts, to examine the way he orders his data and the assumptions he is making, and to compare these with other thoughts that other men might have.

If he has gone the whole way, as most of our students have done, he has realized that he thinks this way not because his teachers ask him to but because this is how the world "really is," this is man's present relation to the universe. From this position he can take responsibility for his own stand and negotiate—with respect—with other men.

ACKNOWLEDGMENTS

Kohlberg, Lawrence. "Stage and Sequence: The Cognitive-Developmental Approach to Socialization." In David A. Goslin, ed., *Handbook of Socialization Theory and Research* (Chicago, IL: Rand McNally, 1969): 347–480. Reprinted with the permission of David Goslin. Courtesy of Yale University Cross Campus Library.

Bandura, Albert and Frederick J. McDonald. "Influence of Social Reinforcement and the Behavior of Models in Shaping Children's Moral Judgments." *Journal of Abnormal and Social Psychology* 67 (1963): 274–81. Copyright 1963 by the American Psychological Association. Reprinted by permission. Courtesy of Yale University Sterling Memorial Library.

Aronfreed, Justin. "The Socialization of Altruistic and Sympathetic Behavior: Some Theoretical and Experimental Analyses." In J. Macaulay and L. Berkowitz, eds., *Altruism and Helping Behavior: Social Psychological Studies of Some Antecedents and Consequences* (New York: Academic Press, 1970): 103–26. Reprinted with the permission of Academic Press, Inc. Courtesy of Yale University Cross Campus Library.

Aronfreed, Justin. "Moral Development from the Standpoint of a General Psychological Theory." In Thomas Lickona, ed., *Moral Development and Behavior: Theory, Research, and Social Issues* (New York: Holt, Rinehart and Winston, 1976): 54–69. Reprinted with the permission of Thomas Lickona, copyright holder. Courtesy of Yale University Cross Campus Library.

Mischel, Walter and Harriet N. Mischel. "A Cognitive Social-Learning Approach to Morality and Self-Regulation." In Thomas Lickona, ed., *Moral Development and Behavior: Theory, Research, and Social Issues* (New York: Holt, Rinehart and Winston, 1976): 84–107. Reprinted with the permission of Thomas Lickona, copyright holder. Courtesy of Yale University Cross Campus Library.

Eysenck, H.J. "The Biology of Morality." In Thomas Lickona, ed., *Moral Development and Behavior: Theory, Research, and So-*

cial Issues (New York: Holt, Rinehart and Winston, 1976): 108–23. Reprinted with the permission of Thomas Lickona, copyright holder. Courtesy of Yale University Cross Campus Library.

Perry, William G. Jr., Excerpts from *Forms of Intellectual and Ethical Development in the College Years: A Scheme.* (New York: Holt, Rinehart and Winston, 1968, 1970): 1–12, 34–40. Reprinted with the permission of Holt, Rinehart and Winston. Courtesy of Yale University Divinity Library.